Microsoft® Office for Mac 2011

ILLUSTRATED

Fundamentals

Microsoft® Office for Mac 2011

ILLUSTRATED

Kelley P. Shaffer

COURSE TECHNOLOGY
CENGAGE Learning™

Australia • Brazil • Japan • Korea • Mexico • Singapore • Spain • United Kingdom • United States

Microsoft® Office for Mac 2011—Illustrated Fundamentals
Kelley P. Shaffer

Vice President, Publisher: Nicole Jones Pinard

Executive Editor: Marjorie Hunt

Associate Acquisitions Editor: Amanda Lyons

Senior Product Manager: Christina Kling Garrett

Associate Product Manager: Kim Klasner

Editorial Assistant: Brandelynn Perry

Director of Marketing: Elisa Roberts

Senior Marketing Manager: Ryan DeGrote

Contributing Authors: Marjorie Hunt, Barbara M.
    Waxer, Carol Cram

Developmental Editor: Karen Stevens

Content Project Manager: Lisa Weidenfeld

Copy Editor: Mary Kemper

Proofreader: Karen Annett

Indexer: Rich Carlson

QA Manuscript Reviewers: Jeff Schwartz, Ashlee Welz
    Smith, Susan Whalen

Print Buyer: Fola Orekoya

Cover Designer: GEX Publishing Services

Cover Artist: Mark Hunt

Composition: GEX Publishing Services

For product information and technology assistance, contact us at
Cengage Learning Customer & Sales Support, 1-800-354-9706

For permission to use material from this text or product, submit all requests online at **www.cengage.com/permissions**
Further permissions questions can be emailed to
permissionrequest@cengage.com

Trademarks:

Some of the product names and company names used in this book have been used for identification purposes only and may be trademarks or registered trademarks of their respective manufacturers and sellers.

Library of Congress Control Number: 2011929446

ISBN-13: 978-1-111-82431-0

ISBN-10: 1-111-82431-2

Course Technology
20 Channel Center Street
Boston, MA 02210
USA

Cengage Learning is a leading provider of customized learning solutions with office locations around the globe, including Singapore, the United Kingdom, Australia, Mexico, Brazil, and Japan. Locate your local office at:
www.cengage.com/global

Cengage Learning products are represented in Canada by Nelson Education, Ltd.

To learn more about Course Technology, visit **www.cengage.com/coursetechnology**

To learn more about Cengage Learning, visit **www.cengage.com.**

Purchase any of our products at your local college store or at our preferred online store **www.cengagebrain.com**

Printed in the United States of America
2 3 4 5 6 7 8 9 18 17 16 15 14 13 12

Brief Contents

Contents

Internet

PowerPoint 2011

Preface

Welcome to *Microsoft Office for Mac 2011—Illustrated Fundamentals*. If this is your first experience with the Illustrated series, you'll see that this book has a unique design: each skill is presented on two facing pages, with steps on the left and screens on the right. The layout makes it easy to learn a skill without having to read a lot of text and flip pages to see an illustration.

This book is an ideal learning tool for a wide range of learners—the "rookies" will find the clean design easy to follow and focused with only essential information presented, and the "hotshots" will appreciate being able to move quickly through the lessons to find the information they need without reading a lot of text. The design also makes this a great reference after the course is over!

About This Edition

- **Coverage.** This book covers essential skills for using Microsoft Office for Mac 2011, along with introductions to computer concepts, Snow Leopard OSX, and the Safari browser.

- **Streamlined Approach.** This book covers concepts and skills at a high level, so that you can cover a lot of ground in a short amount of time. (If you need additional projects to supplement this book for a longer course, *Microsoft Office for Mac 2011 Projects Binder 1133427051* is a good option.)

- **What's New.** All units are updated to reflect the changes in Microsoft Office 2011 for Mac. Content enhancements include new lessons on using absolute cell references in Excel and formatting a research paper in Word. New Appendix provides information on using Microsoft Office Web Apps.

Each two-page spread focuses on a single skill.

Introduction briefly explains why the lesson skill is important.

A case scenario motivates the the steps and puts learning in context.

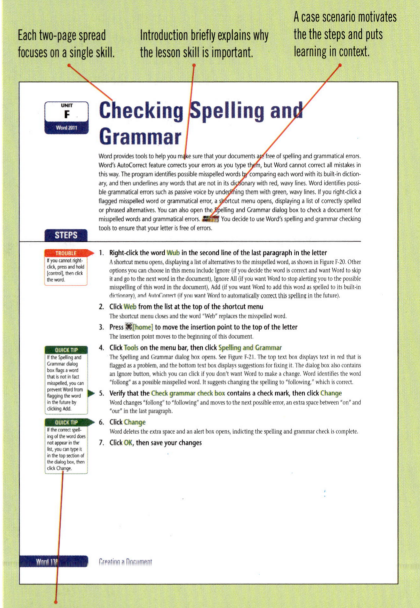

Tips and troubleshooting advice, right where you need it–next to the step itself.

- **Teach both Mac and PC skills.** This text was designed to make teaching easier in a dual-platform lab easier. Office units correspond to similar units in *Microsoft Office 2010—Illustrated Fundamentals* (0-538-74944-X)

Assignments

The lessons feature Outdoor Designs, a fictional company that produces outdoor recreational products, as the case study. The assignments on the light yellow pages at the end of each unit provide a wide range of reinforcement exercises featuring different fictional companies and scenarios. Assignments include:

- **Concepts Review** consist of multiple choice, matching, and screen identification questions.

- **Skills Reviews** are guided, step-by-step exercises that review the skills covered in each lesson in the unit.

- **Independent Challenges** are case projects requiring critical thinking and application of the unit skills. The Independent Challenges increase in difficulty, with the first one in each unit being the easiest. Independent Challenges 2 and 3 become increasingly open-ended, requiring more independent problem solving.

- **Real Life Independent Challenges** are practical exercises in which students create documents to help them with their every day lives.

- **Advanced Challenge Exercises** set within the Independent Challenges provide optional steps for more advanced students.

- **Visual Workshops** are capstone exercises that require students to look at a picture of a completed project, and then create that project using skills covered in the unit.

Large screen shots keep students on track as they complete steps.

Brightly colored tabs indicate which section of the book you are in.

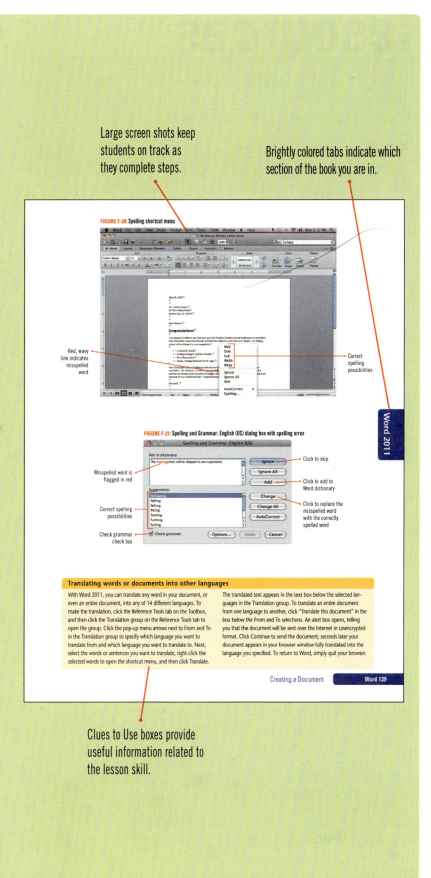

Red, wavy line indicates misspelled word

Correct spelling possibilities

FIGURE F-20: Spelling shortcut menu

FIGURE F-21: Spelling and Grammar: English (US) dialog box with spelling error

Misspelled word is flagged in red

Click to skip

Click to add to Word dictionary

Correct spelling possibilities

Click to replace the misspelled word with the correctly spelled word

Check grammar check box

Translating words or documents into other languages

Clues to Use boxes provide useful information related to the lesson skill.

Creating a Document   Word 139

Instructor Resources

The Instructor Resources CD is Course Technology's way of putting the resources and information needed to teach and learn effectively into your hands. With an integrated array of teaching and learning tools that offer you and your students a broad range of technology-based instructional options, we believe this CD represents the highest quality and most cutting edge resources available to instructors today. The resources available with this book are:

- **Instructor's Manual**—Available as an electronic file, the Instructor's Manual includes detailed lecture topics with teaching tips for each unit.

- **Sample Syllabus**—Prepare and customize your course easily using this sample course outline.

- **PowerPoint Presentations**—Each unit has a corresponding PowerPoint presentation that you can use in lecture, distribute to your students, or customize to suit your course.

- **Figure Files**—The figures in the text are provided on the Instructor Resources CD to help you illustrate key topics or concepts. You can create traditional overhead transparencies by printing the figure files. Or you can create electronic slide shows by using the figures in a presentation program such as PowerPoint.

- **Solutions to Exercises**—Solutions to Exercises contains every file students are asked to create or modify in the lessons and end-of-unit material. Also provided in this section, there is a document outlining the solutions for the end-of-unit Concepts Review, Skills Review, and Independent Challenges. An Annotated Solution File and Grading Rubric accompany each file and can be used together for quick and easy grading.

- **Data Files for Students**—To complete most of the units in this book, your students will need Data Files. You can post the Data Files on a file server for students to copy. The Data Files are available on the Instructor Resources CD-ROM, the Review Pack, and can also be downloaded from cengagebrain.com. For more information on how to download the Data Files, see the inside back cover.

Instruct students to use the Data Files List included on the Review Pack and the Instructor Resources CD. This list gives instructions on copying and organizing files.

- **ExamView**—ExamView is a powerful testing software package that allows you to create and administer printed, computer (LAN-based), and Internet exams. ExamView includes hundreds of questions that correspond to the topics covered in this text, enabling students to generate detailed study guides that include page references for further review. The computer-based and Internet testing components allow students to take exams at their computers, and also saves you time by grading each exam automatically.

Content for Online Learning.

Course Technology has partnered with the leading distance learning solution providers and class-management platforms today. To access this material, visit www.cengage.com/webtutor and search for your title. Instructor resources include the following: additional case projects, sample syllabi, PowerPoint presentations, and more. For additional information, please contact your sales representative. For students to access this material, they must have purchased a WebTutor PIN-code specific to this title and your campus platform. The resources for students might include (based on instructor preferences): topic reviews, review questions, practice tests, and more.

Acknowledgements

Author Acknowledgements

Kelley P. Shaffer   I'd like to thank my wonderful family for all their love and support while writing this book. Without them, this book wouldn't be possible. I'd also like to thank my editors and production team for their patience and great input.

Credits

UNIT A

A-1	Courtesy of Apple
A-2	Courtesy of Apple
A-3	Courtesy of Apple
A-4	© vario images GmbH & Co.KG / Alamy
A-5	Kayros Studio "Be Happy!"/Shutterstock.com
A-6	Courtesy of Intel
A-10	studio_chki/Shutterstock.com
A-11a	Courtesy of Apple
A-11b	Ximagination/Shutterstock.com
A-12a	Courtesy of Apple
A-12b	Andrew Buckin/Shutterstock.com
A-13	Courtesy of Apple
A-14	Courtesy of Apple
A-15	Courtesy of Apple
A-16a	kavione/Shutterstock.com
A-16b	jocic/Shutterstock.com
A-17a	Courtesy of Apple
A-17b	Courtesy of Apple
A-18	broukoid/Shutterstock.com
A-19a	300dpi/Shutterstock.com
A-19b	Vladru/Shutterstock.com
A-19c	kavione/Shutterstock.com
A-19d	Eugene Shapovalov/Shutterstock.com
A-20	300dpi/Shutterstock.com
A-25a	Courtesy of Apple
A-25b	Courtesy of Apple
A-25c	Courtesy of Apple
A-25d	Courtesy of Apple

UNIT B

B-3a	© Lana Sundman / Alamy
B-3b	Hannu Liivaar/Shutterstock.com
B-3c	Graham Taylor Photography/ Shutterstock.com
B-3d	Handout/MCT/Newscom

UNIT M

Afgan Rug video courtesy of Barbara M. Waxer

Music supplied by Getty Images

U.S. Fish and Wildlife Service

Figures M-9, M-10, M-11, M-19 and M-29 are used under the terms of licenses from MorgueFile (www.morguefile.com)

Read This Before You Begin

Frequently Asked Questions

What are Data Files?

A Data File is a partially completed Word document, Excel workbook, PowerPoint presentation, or another type of file that you use to complete the steps in the units and exercises to create the final document that you submit to your instructor. Each unit opener page lists the Data Files that you need for that unit.

Where are the Data Files?

Your instructor will provide the Data Files to you or direct you to a location on a network drive from which you can download them. For information on how to download the Data Files from cengagebrain.com, see the inside back cover.

What software was used to write and test this book?

This book was written and tested using a typical installation of Microsoft Office 2011 for Mac Home & Business on a computer with a typical installation of Mac OS X 10.6 (Snow Leopard).

The browser used for any Web-dependent steps is Safari 5.

Do I need to be connected to the Internet to complete the steps and exercises in this book?

Some of the exercises in this book require that your computer be connected to the Internet. If you are not connected to the Internet, see your instructor for information on how to complete the exercises.

What do I do if my screen is different from the figures shown in this book?

This book was written and tested on computers with monitors set at a resolution of 1024 × 768. If your screen shows more or less information than the figures in the book, your monitor is probably set at a higher or lower resolution. If you don't see something on your screen, you might have to scroll down or up to see the object identified in the figures.

The Ribbon in Microsoft Office for Mac 2011 adapts to different resolutions. If your monitor is set at a lower resolution than 1024 × 768, you might not see all of the buttons shown in the figures. The groups of buttons will always appear, but the entire group might be condensed into a single button that you need to click to access the buttons described in the instructions.

Please Note: Because students could be using Macs that include a mouse or a trackpad, steps use the generic terminology "press the button" and "release the button", instead of specifying the mouse button or trackpad button.

COURSECASTS Learning on the Go. Always Available...Always Relevant.

Our fast-paced world is driven by technology. You know because you are an active participant—always on the go, always keeping up with technological trends, and always learning new ways to embrace technology to power your life. Let CourseCasts, hosted by Ken Baldauf of Florida State University, be your guide into weekly updates in this ever-changing space. These timely, relevant podcasts are produced weekly and are available for download at http://coursecasts.course.com or directly from iTunes (search by CourseCasts). CourseCasts are a perfect solution to getting students (and even instructors) to learn on the go!

Understanding Essential Computer Concepts

Computers are essential tools in almost all kinds of activity in virtually every type of business. In this unit, you will learn about computers and their components. You will learn about input and output, how a computer processes data and stores information, how information is transmitted, and ways to secure that information.  Quest Specialty Travel is expanding its North American offices and just purchased Sheehan Tours, an established travel agency in Boston, Massachusetts. Sheehan Tours has been in business for over 40 years and has a large customer base. Unfortunately, its computer system is outdated. Its office contains a hodge-podge of computer equipment, most of which was purchased used, and only one computer is connected to the Internet. Kevin O'Brien, the manager of the New York office, has been sent to the new Boston office to help them switch to Quest's business practices. He has already ordered and installed new computer equipment. His next task is to teach the staff how to use the new equipment.

OBJECTIVES

Investigate types of computers

Examine computer systems

Investigate data representation

Understand memory

Understand storage media

Examine input devices

Examine output devices

Explore data communications

Learn about networks

Learn about security threats

Understand system software

Understand application software

Investigating Types of Computers

A **computer** is an electronic device that accepts information and instructions from a user, manipulates the information according to the instructions, displays the information in some way, and stores the information for retrieval later. Computers are classified by their size, speed, and capabilities.  Most of the staff at Sheehan Tours does not know anything about computers except for the ones that sit on their desks, so Kevin decides to start with a basic explanation of the types of computers available.

The following list describes various types of computers:

- **Personal computers (PCs)** are computers typically used by a single user, for use in the home or office. Personal computers are used for general computing tasks such as word processing, manipulating numbers, working with photographs or graphics, exchanging e-mail, and accessing the Internet. In common usage, the term "PC" refers to personal computers that use Microsoft Windows. Personal computers that are sold only by Apple Inc. are referred to as Macs (short for Macintosh).

- The following are types of personal computers:

  - **Desktop computers** are designed to sit compactly on a desk.
  - **Notebook computers** (also referred to as **laptop computers**), similar to the MacBook shown in Figure A-1, are small, lightweight, and designed for portability.
  - **Tablet PCs** are notebook computers that have a screen on which the user can write with a stylus.
  - **Subnotebook computers**, sometimes called **ultraportable computers** or **mini notebooks**, are notebook computers that are smaller and lighter than ordinary notebooks. **Netbooks**, a type of subnotebook computer, are notebooks that are primarily designed to allow users to access the Internet and check e-mail.
  - **Slate computers**, like the iPad shown in Figure A-2, are thin computers that do not have an external keyboard or a mouse. Users touch the screen or use a stylus to accomplish tasks. Slate computers are primarily used to read electronic books, view video, and access the Internet, although additional applications are added daily.

- **Handheld computers** are small computers that fit in the palm of your hand. Handheld computers have more limited capabilities than personal computers.

  - **Smartphones**, like the iPhone shown in Figure A-3, are used to make and receive phone calls; maintain an address book, electronic appointment book, calculator, and notepad; send e-mail; connect to the Internet; play music; take photos or video; and even perform some of the same functions as a PC, such as word processing.
  - **MP3 players** are handheld computers that are primarily used to store and play music, although some models can also be used to play digital movies or television shows.

- **Mainframe computers** are used by larger businesses and government agencies to provide centralized storage, processing, and management for large amounts of data. The price of a mainframe computer varies widely, from several hundred thousand dollars to close to one million dollars.

- The largest and fastest computers, called **supercomputers**, are used by large corporations and government agencies when the tremendous volume of data would seriously delay processing on a mainframe computer. A supercomputer, like the one shown in Figure A-4, can cost millions of dollars.

Converging technologies

Every year, the lines between the types of computers are growing more and more blurry. Handheld devices like smartphones are more powerful than the first notebook computers were, and today's desktop PCs are far more powerful than the mainframe computers of a few decades ago. As new technologies are developed, consumers will need fewer and fewer devices to accomplish their tasks.

FIGURE A-1: Apple MacBook

FIGURE A-2: Apple iPad

FIGURE A-3: Apple iPhone

FIGURE A-4: Supercomputer

Examining Computer Systems

A **computer system** includes computer hardware and software. **Hardware** refers to the physical components of a computer. **Software** refers to the intangible components of a computer system, particularly the **programs**, or lists of instructions, that the computer needs to perform a specific task. The **operating system** is special software that controls basic input and output, allocates system resources, manages storage space, maintains security, and detects equipment failure.  Kevin explains how computers work and points out the main components of a computer system.

DETAILS

The following list provides an overview of computer system components and how they work:

- The design and construction of a computer is referred to as its **architecture** or **configuration**. The technical details about each hardware component are called **specifications**. For example, a computer system might be configured to include a printer; a specification for that printer might be a print speed of eight pages per minute or the capacity to print in color.

- The hardware and the software of a computer system work together to process data. **Data** refers to the words, numbers, figures, sounds, and graphics that describe people, events, things, and ideas. Modifying data is referred to as **processing**.

- In a computer, processing tasks occur on the **motherboard**, which is located inside the computer and is the main electronic component of the computer. See Figure A-5. The motherboard is a **circuit board**, which is a rigid piece of insulating material with **circuits**—electrical paths—on it that control specific functions. The motherboard contains the following processing hardware:

  - The **microprocessor**, also called the **processor** or the **central processing unit (CPU)**, consists of transistors and electronic circuits on a silicon chip (an integrated circuit embedded in semiconductor material). See Figure A-6. The processor is mounted on the motherboard and is responsible for executing instructions to process information.

  - **Cards** are removable circuit boards that are inserted into slots in the motherboard to expand the capabilities of the motherboard. For example, a sound card translates the digital audio information from the computer into analog sounds that the human ear can hear.

- The data or instructions you type into the computer are called **input**. The result of the computer processing input is referred to as **output**. The computer itself takes care of the processing functions, but it needs additional components, called **peripheral devices**, to accomplish the input, output, and storage functions.

  - You use an **input device**, such as a keyboard or a mouse, to enter data and issue commands. **Commands** are input instructions that tell the computer how to process data. For example, you might want to center the title and double-space the text of a report. You use the appropriate commands in the word-processing program that instruct the computer to modify the data you have input so the report text is double-spaced and the report title is centered.

  - Output can be in many different forms, including reports, documents, graphs, sounds, and pictures. Computers produce output using **output devices**, such as a monitor or printer.

  - The output you create using a computer can be stored either inside the computer itself or on an external storage device, such as a DVD. You will learn more about storage devices later in this unit.

FIGURE A-5: Motherboard

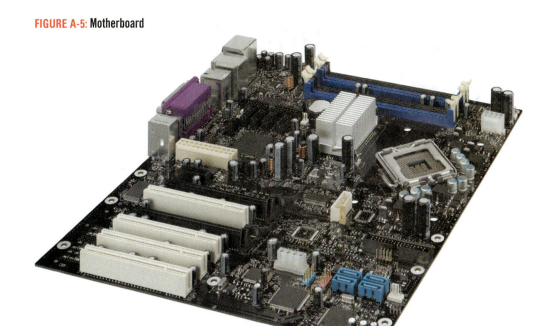

FIGURE A-6: Intel microprocessor (CPU)

Comparing microprocessor speeds

How fast a computer can process instructions depends partially on the speed of the microprocessor. Among other factors, the speed of the microprocessor is determined by its clock speed, word size, and whether it is single or dual core. **Clock speed** is measured in **megahertz (MHz)**, millions of cycles per second, or in **gigahertz (GHz)**, billions of cycles per second. **Word size** refers to the number of bits—the smallest unit of information in a computer—that are processed at one time; for example, a 32-bit processor processes 32 bits at a time. A computer with a large word size can process faster than a computer with a small word size. PCs come with 32-bit or 64-bit processors. Finally, a **dual-core processor**, one that has two processors on a single chip, can process information up to twice as fast as a **single-core processor**, one with one processor on the chip. Likewise, a **quad-core processor**, with four processors on a chip, processes information up to four times as fast as a single-core processor.

Investigating Data Representation

To understand how data is processed in a computer, you first need to learn how the computer represents and stores data. To a computer, the characters used in human language, such as the characters in a word-processed document, are meaningless because it is an electronic device.  Kevin gives a basic description of how information is represented inside a computer.

The following information will help you understand data processing:

- Like a lightbulb, the computer must interpret every signal as either "on" or "off." To do this, a computer represents data as distinct or separate numbers. Specifically, it represents "on" with a 1 and "off" with a 0. These numbers are referred to as **binary digits**, or **bits**.

- A series of 8 bits is called a **byte**. As Figure A-7 shows, the byte that represents the integer value 0 is 00000000, with all 8 bits "off" or set to 0. The byte that represents the integer value 1 is 00000001, and the byte that represents 255 is 11111111.

- A **kilobyte (KB** or simply **K)** is 1,024 bytes, or approximately one thousand bytes. A **megabyte (MB)** is 1,048,576 bytes, or about one million bytes. A **gigabyte (GB)** is 1,073,741,824 bytes, or about one billion bytes. A **terabyte (TB)** is 1,024 GB, or approximately one trillion bytes. See Table A-1.

- Personal computers commonly use the ASCII system to represent character data. **ASCII** (pronounced "ASK-ee") stands for **American Standard Code for Information Interchange**. Each ASCII number represents an English character. Computers translate ASCII into binary data so that they can process it.

  - The original ASCII system used 7 bits to represent the numbers 0 (0000000) through 127 (1111111) to stand for 128 common characters and nonprinting control characters. Because bits are usually arranged in bytes, the eighth bit is reserved for error checking.

  - Extended ASCII uses 8 bits and includes the numbers 128 (10000000) through 255 (11111111) to represent additional characters and symbols. Extended ASCII was developed to add codes for punctuation marks, symbols, such as $ and ©, and additional characters, such as é and ü, that were not included in the original 128 codes.

  - Most computers use the original ASCII definitions, but not all computers use the same definitions for Extended ASCII.

FIGURE A-7: Binary representation of numbers

Number	Binary representation
0	00000000
1	00000001
2	00000010
3	00000011
4	00000100
5	00000101
6	00000110
7	00000111
8	00001000

TABLE A-1: Data measurements

bits (used for measuring data transfer rates)	
term	**description**
Bit	Single Binary Digit (1 or 0)
Kilobit (Kb)	1,000 bits
Megabit (Mb)	1,000,000 bits
Gigabit (Gb)	1,000,000,000 bits

bytes (used for measuring data storage)	
term	**description**
Byte	8 bits
Kilobyte (KB)	1,024 Bytes
Megabyte (MG)	1,048,576 Bytes
Gigabyte (GB)	1,043,741,824 Bytes
Terabyte (TB)	1,099,511,627,776 Bytes
Petabyte (PB)	1,125,899,906,842,624 Bytes
Exabyte (EB)	1,152,921,504,606,846,976 Bytes

Understanding Memory

In addition to the microprocessor, another important component of personal computer hardware is the **memory**, which stores instructions and data. Your computer has five types of memory: random access memory, cache memory, virtual memory, read-only memory, and complementary metal-oxide semiconductor memory. Kevin realizes that most of the Sheehan Tours staff don't understand the difference between memory types, so he explains the different types of memory.

Types of memory include the following:

QUICK TIP

When the computer is off, RAM is empty.

- **Random access memory (RAM)** temporarily holds programs and data while the computer is on and allows the computer to access that information randomly; in other words, RAM doesn't need to access data in the same sequence in which it was stored. For example, if you are writing a report, the microprocessor temporarily copies the word processing program you are using into RAM so the microprocessor can quickly access the instructions that you will need as you type and format your report. The characters you type are also stored in RAM, along with the character formats, graphics, and other objects that you might use. RAM consists of chips on cards that plug into the motherboard.

  - Most personal computers use **synchronous dynamic random access memory (SDRAM)**, which is synchronized with the processor to allow faster access to its contents.
  - RAM is sometimes referred to as **volatile memory** or **temporary memory** because it is constantly changing as long as the computer is on and is cleared when the computer is turned off.
  - **Memory capacity**, sometimes referred to as **storage capacity**, is the amount of data that the computer can handle at any given time and is measured in megabytes or gigabytes. For example, a computer that has 2 GB of RAM has the capacity to temporarily store more than two billion bytes of data at one time.

- **Cache memory**, sometimes called **RAM cache** or **CPU cache**, is a special, high-speed memory chip on the motherboard or CPU itself that stores frequently accessed and recently accessed data and commands instead of in RAM.

QUICK TIP

You can often add more RAM to a computer by installing additional memory cards on the motherboard. You cannot add ROM; it is permanently installed on the motherboard.

- **Virtual memory** is space on the computer's storage devices that simulates additional RAM. It enables programs to run as if your computer had more RAM by moving data and commands from RAM to the computer's permanent storage device and swapping in the new data and commands. See Figure A-8. Virtual memory, however, is much slower than RAM.

- **Read-only memory (ROM)** is a chip on the motherboard that has been prerecorded with data. ROM permanently stores the set of instructions that the computer uses to check the computer system's components to make sure they are working and to activate the essential software that controls the processing function when you turn the computer on.

QUICK TIP

The act of turning on the computer is sometimes called **booting up**.

  - ROM contains a set of instructions called the **BIOS (basic input/output system)**, which tells the computer to initialize the motherboard, how to recognize devices connected to the computer, and to start the boot process. The **boot process** is the set of events that occurs between the moment you turn on the computer and the moment you can begin to use the computer. The set of instructions for executing the boot process is stored in ROM.
  - ROM never changes and it remains intact when the computer is turned off; therefore, it is called **nonvolatile memory** or **permanent memory**.

- **Complementary metal-oxide semiconductor (CMOS**, pronounced "SEE-moss") **memory** is a chip installed on the motherboard that is activated during the boot process and identifies where essential software is stored.

  - A small rechargeable battery powers CMOS so its contents are saved when the computer is turned off. CMOS changes every time you add or remove hardware on your computer system.
  - CMOS, often referred to as **semipermanent memory**, changes when hardware is added or removed, but doesn't empty when the computer is shut off.
  - Because CMOS retains its contents when the computer is turned off, the date and time are stored there.

FIGURE A-8: How virtual memory works

1. Your computer is running a word processing program that takes up most of the program area in RAM, but you want to run a spreadsheet program at the same time.

2. The operating system moves the least used segment of the word processing program into virtual memory on the computer's permanent storage device (hard disk drive).

3. The spreadsheet program can now be loaded into the RAM vacated by the least used segment of the word processing program.

4. If the least used segment of the word processing program is later needed, it is copied from virtual memory back into RAM. To make room, some other infrequently used segment of a program will need to be transferred into virtual memory.

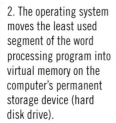

Upgrading RAM

One of the easiest ways to make your computer run faster is to add more RAM. The more RAM a computer has, the more instructions and data can be stored there. You can often add more RAM to a computer by installing additional memory cards on the motherboard. Currently, you can buy from 512 MB to 16 GB RAM cards, and, usually, you can add more than one card. Check your computer's specifications to see what size RAM cards the slots on your motherboard will accept. Note that if your computer has a 32-bit processor, it can't use more than 4 GB of RAM, even if the computer has places to plug in more cards.

Understanding Storage Media

RAM retains data only while the power is on, so your computer must have a more permanent storage option. As Figure A-9 shows, a storage device receives data from RAM and stores it on a storage medium, some of which are described below. Later, the data can be read and sent back to RAM to use again. All data and programs are stored as files. A computer **file** is a named collection of stored data. An **executable file** contains the instructions that tell a computer how to perform a specific task; for instance, the files that are used while the computer starts are executable. A **data file** is created by a user, usually with software. For instance, a report that you write with a word processing program is data, and must be saved as a data file if you want to access it later. Kevin explains the types of storage media available.

The types of storage media are discussed below:

- **Magnetic storage media** store data as magnetized particles on a surface. A **hard disk**, also called a hard disk drive, is the most common type of magnetic storage media. It contains several magnetic oxide-covered metal platters that are usually sealed in a case inside the computer. You can also purchase external hard drives for extra or backup storage.

> **QUICK TIP**
> Optical storage devices, such as CDs and DVDs, are much more durable than magnetic storage media.

- **Optical storage devices** are polycarbonate discs coated with a reflective metal on which data is stored using laser technology as a trail of tiny pits or dark spots in the surface of the disc. The data that these pits or spots represent can then be "read" with a beam of laser light.

    - The first standard optical storage device available for personal computers was the **CD (compact disc)**. One CD can store 700 MB of data.
    - A **DVD**, though the same size as a CD, can store between 4.7 GB and 15.9 GB of data, depending on whether data is stored on one or two sides of the disc and how many layers of data each side contains. The term *DVD* is no longer an acronym, although it was originally an acronym for *digital video disc* and later was sometimes updated to *digital versatile disc*.
    - **Blu-ray** discs store 25 GB of data per layer. They are used for storing high-definition video.

- **Flash memory** (also called **solid state storage**) is similar to ROM except that it can be written to more than once. **Flash memory cards** are small, portable cards encased in hard plastic to which data can be written and rewritten. They are used in digital cameras, handheld computers, video game controllers, and other devices.

- A popular type of flash memory is a **USB flash storage device**, also called a **USB drive** or a **flash drive**. See Figure A-10.

    - USB drives for personal computers are available in a wide range of sizes from 1 GB to 128 GB of data. They are becoming more popular for use as a secondary or backup storage device for data typically stored on a hard disk drive.

> **QUICK TIP**
> There is only one way to insert a flash drive, so if you're having problems inserting the drive into the slot, turn the drive over and try again.

    - USB drives plug directly into the USB port of a personal computer; the computer recognizes the device as another disk drive. The location of USB ports varies with the brand and model of computer you are using, but the physical port may be on the front, back, or side of a computer.
    - USB flash storage devices are about the size of a pack of gum and often have a ring that you can attach to a key chain.

FIGURE A-9: Storage devices and RAM

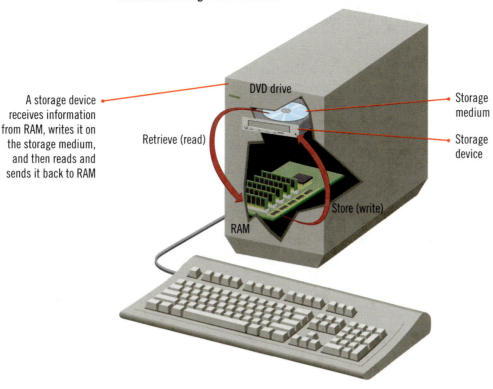

A storage device receives information from RAM, writes it on the storage medium, and then reads and sends it back to RAM

DVD drive

Retrieve (read)

Storage medium

Storage device

Store (write)

RAM

FIGURE A-10: USB flash storage device

Rewriting on optical storage

To store data on a CD, you need to record it on a **CD-R (compact disc recordable)** or **CD-RW (compact disc rewritable)** drive and a CD-R or CD-RW disc. CDs that you buy with software or music already on them are CD-ROMs (compact disc read-only memory)—you can read from them, but you cannot record additional data onto them. On a CD-R, after the data is recorded, you cannot erase or modify it, but you can add new data to the disc, as long as the disc has not been finalized. In contrast, you can rerecord a CD-RW. Recordable DVD drives are also available. As with CDs, you can buy a DVD to which you can record only once, or a rewritable DVD to which you can record and then rerecord data. Recordable DVDs come in two formats, **DVD-R** and **DVD+R**, and likewise rerecordable DVDs come in two formats, **DVD-RW** and **DVD+RW**. DVD drives on new computers are capable of reading from and writing to both -RW and +RW DVDs and CDs, as well as DVDs with two layers. **BD-R** are Blu-ray discs that you can record to once, and **BD-RE** are Blu-ray discs that you can record to multiple times. You need a Blu-ray drive to use Blu-ray discs.

Examining Input Devices

Before a computer can produce useful information, people must get data into the computer. This is accomplished by using input devices. In a typical personal computer system, you input data and commands by using an **input device** such as a keyboard or a mouse. Computers can also receive input from a storage device. You will learn about storage devices later in this unit.  As Kevin explains peripheral devices to the Sheehan Tours staff, they ask several questions about input devices. For example, one person doesn't understand the difference between a mouse and a trackball. Kevin continues his explanation with a discussion of various input devices.

DETAILS

There are many types of input devices, as described below:

QUICK TIP
Another way to avoid repetitive-motion injuries is to take frequent breaks when working at a computer and stretch your hands and wrists.

- One of the most frequently used input devices is a **keyboard**. The top keyboard in Figure A-11 is a standard Mac keyboard. The bottom keyboard in Figure A-11 is **ergonomic**, which means that it has been designed to fit the natural placement of your hands and should reduce the risk of repetitive-motion injuries.

- Another common input device is a **pointing device**, which controls the **pointer**, a small arrow or other symbol on the screen. Pointing devices are used to select commands and manipulate text or graphics on the screen.

  - The most popular pointing device for a desktop computer is a **mouse**, such as the one shown on the left side in Figure A-12. An ordinary mouse has a rolling ball on its underside, and an optical mouse has a tiny camera on its underside that takes pictures as the mouse is moved. You control the pointer by moving the entire mouse. A mouse usually has two or more buttons for clicking commands. A mouse might also have a **scroll wheel** that you roll to scroll the page on the screen and that may function as one of the buttons.

  - The **trackball**, such as the one shown on the right side in Figure A-12, is similar to a mouse except that the rolling ball is on the top side and you control the movement of the pointer by moving only the ball.

  - MacBooks (notebook computers) are usually equipped with multitouch technology, such as a Multi-Touch trackpad. Macintosh computers come equipped with a trackpad or Magic Mouse. The **trackpad** is a touch-sensitive device that you drag your finger over to control the pointer. See Figure A-13. It does not contain any buttons. The trackpad itself is the button.

- A **touchscreen** is a display that while showing you the output, allows you to touch it with your finger or a stylus to input commands. Touchscreens are found on some ATMs, smartphones, and MP3 players. Tablet PCs and slate computers also use touchscreen technology.

- A **scanner** is a device that transfers the content on a piece of paper into memory. To do this, you place a piece of paper on the glass, a beam of light moves across the glass similar to a photocopier, and the scanner stores the image or words on the paper as digital information. You can scan a document or a photo and save it as an image file, or you can scan a document and have the text "read" by the scanner and saved in a document file for editing later.

- Microphones are another type of input device. You can use them to record sound for certain types of files, or, if you have voice-recognition software, you can use them to input data and commands.

- Input devices can be connected to the computer with cables or wirelessly. Wireless input devices connect to the computer using infrared or radio-frequency technology, similar to a remote control for a television.

Understanding assistive devices

People with physical impairments or disabilities can use computers because of advances in making computers accessible to everyone. For example, people who cannot use their arms or hands instead can use foot, head, or eye movements to control the pointer. People with poor vision can use keyboards with large keys for input, screen enlargers to enlarge the type and images on the monitor, or screen readers to read the content of the screen aloud. Computers have even been developed that can be controlled by a person's thoughts, that is, the brain's electromagnetic waves.

FIGURE A-11: Keyboards

FIGURE A-12: Personal computer pointing devices

 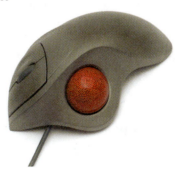

FIGURE A-13: Multi-Touch trackpad

Examining Output Devices

As stated earlier, output is the result of processing data; **output devices** show you those results. The most commonly used output devices are monitors and printers.  Kevin continues his discussion of peripheral devices with an explanation of output devices.

DETAILS

Output devices are described below:

- The **monitor** displays the output from a computer.

  - The monitor shown in Figure A-14 is a **flat panel monitor**, a lightweight monitor that takes up very little room on the desktop. Most flat panel monitors use **LCD (liquid crystal display)** technology, which creates the image you see on the screen by manipulating light within a layer of liquid crystal. LCD monitors require a backlight. Flat panel monitors labeled as **LED (light-emitting diode)** monitors use LEDs to provide the backlight. LED backlighting is more energy efficient than ordinary backlighting. The Apple iMac combines the LED monitor and the internal components of the computer into one unit, as shown in Figure A-15.
  - Monitor **screen size** is the diagonal measurement from one corner of the screen to the other. In general, monitors on desktop computers range in size from 15" to 30", whereas monitors on notebook computers range in size from 11" to 20".
  - Most monitors have a **graphics display**, which divides the screen into a matrix of small dots called **pixels**. **Resolution** is the number of pixels the monitor displays. Standard resolutions range from 640×480 to 2560×1440. If your screen is small, a 1600×1200 resolution will make the objects on the screen too small to see clearly. **Dot pitch (dp)** measures the distance between pixels, so a smaller dot pitch means a sharper image. A .28 or .26 dot pitch is typical for today's monitors.
  - To display graphics, a computer must have a **graphics card**, also called a **video display adapter** or **video card**, or a built-in **graphics processor** (sometimes called a **built-in graphics card**). The graphics card or processor controls the signals the computer sends to the monitor.

- A **printer** produces a paper copy, often called **hard copy**, of the text or graphics processed by the computer. There are three popular categories of printers: laser printers, inkjet printers, and dot matrix printers.

  - **Laser printers**, like the one shown on the left in Figure A-16, are popular for business use because they produce high-quality output quickly and efficiently. In a laser printer, a temporary laser image is transferred onto paper with a powdery substance called **toner**.
  - **Inkjet printers**, such as the one shown on the right in Figure A-16, are popular printers for home use. These printers spray ink onto paper and produce output whose quality is comparable to that of a laser printer.
  - **Dot matrix printers** transfer ink to the paper by striking a ribbon with pins. A 24-pin dot matrix printer produces better quality print than a 9-pin dot matrix printer. Dot matrix printers are most often used when a large number of pages need to be printed fairly quickly or when a business needs to print multipage continuous forms.

- Speakers allow you to hear sounds from the computer. Speakers can be separate peripheral devices attached to the computer, or they can be built in to the monitor. For speakers to work, a sound card must be installed on the motherboard. The sound card converts sounds so that they can be broadcast through speakers.

FIGURE A-14: LED monitor

FIGURE A-15: iMac

FIGURE A-16: Printers

Laser printer

Inkjet printer

Exploring Data Communications

Data communications is the transmission of data from one computer to another or to a peripheral device. The computer that originates the message is the **sender**. The message is sent over some type of **channel**, such as a telephone or coaxial cable. The computer or device at the message's destination is the **receiver**. The rules that establish an orderly transfer of data between the sender and the receiver are called **protocols**. The transmission protocol between a computer and its peripheral devices is handled by a **device driver**, or simply **driver**, which is a computer program that can establish communication because it contains information about the characteristics of your computer and of the device.  The Sheehan Tours staff will use their computers to connect to the computers at the Quest headquarters in California as well as to surf the Internet, so Kevin next explains how computers communicate.

The following describes some of the ways that computers communicate:

QUICK TIP

An internal periph-eral device such as a hard disk drive may plug directly into the mother-board, or it may have an attached controller card.

QUICK TIP

USB ports can be on the front, back, or side of a computer.

- The data path between the microprocessor, RAM, and the peripherals along which communication travels is called the **data bus**.

- An external peripheral device must have a corresponding **expansion port** and **cable** that connect it to the computer. Inside the computer, each port connects to a **controller card**, sometimes called an **expansion card** or **interface card**. These cards plug into electrical connectors on the motherboard called **expansion slots** or **slots**. Personal computers can have several types of ports, including parallel, serial, SCSI, USB, MIDI, and Ethernet. Figure A-17 shows the ports on the back of a Mac Pro and an iMac (your port configuration may differ).

- A **USB (Universal Serial Bus) port** is a high-speed serial port that allows multiple connections at the same port. The device you install must have a **USB connector**, a small rectangular plug, as shown in Figure A-18. When you plug the USB connector into the USB port, the computer recognizes the device and allows you to use it immediately. USB flash storage devices plug into USB ports. For most USB devices, power is supplied via the port, so there is no need for extra power cables.

- Another standard for transferring information between digital devices similar to USB is **FireWire**. FireWire was developed by Apple and the Institute of Electrical and Electronics Engineers (IEEE) standardized the technology as the **IEEE 1394 interface**. Data transfers are significantly faster using this type of connection than using a USB connection.

- Monitors are connected to computers through HDMI, DVI, mini-DVI, or VGA ports. **HDMI (High-Definition Multimedia Interface)** transmits video and audio digitally, **DVI (Digital Video Interface)**, and mini-DVI transmit video digitally, and **VGA (video graphics array)** allows analog video transmission.

- Speakers and a microphone connect to a computer via ports on the sound card.

- A keyboard and a mouse connect via **PS/2 ports** or USB ports. A wireless keyboard or mouse connects via a special connector that plugs into a USB port. Printers also connect via a USB port.

- You can connect to another computer, a LAN, a **modem** (a device that connects your computer to a standard telephone jack or to a cable connection), or sometimes directly to the Internet using an **Ethernet port**. Ethernet ports allow data to be transmitted at high speeds.

FIGURE A-17: Computer ports

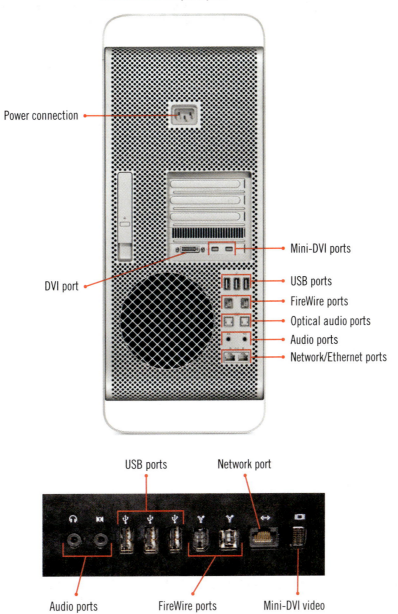

Power connection

Mini-DVI ports

DVI port

USB ports

FireWire ports

Optical audio ports

Audio ports

Network/Ethernet ports

USB ports   Network port

Audio ports   FireWire ports   Mini-DVI video
                                       output port

FIGURE A-18: USB connector

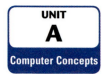

Learning about Networks

A **network** connects one computer to other computers and peripheral devices, enabling you to share data and resources with others. There are a variety of network configurations; however, any type of network has some basic characteristics and requirements that you should know. Kevin continues his discussion of how computers communicate with an explanation of networking.

DETAILS

Components of networks and the types of networks are described below:

- Each computer that is part of the network must have a **network interface card (NIC)** installed. This card creates a communications channel between the computer and the network. A cable is used to connect the NIC port to the network.

- **Network software** is also essential, establishing the communications protocols that will be observed on the network and controlling the "traffic flow" as data travels throughout the network.

- Some networks have one or more computers, called **servers**, that act as the central storage location for programs and provide mass storage for most of the data used on the network. A network with a server and computers dependent on the server is called a **client/server network**. The dependent computers are the **clients**.

- When a network does not have a server, all the computers essentially are equal, and programs and data are distributed among them. This is called a **peer-to-peer network**.

- A personal computer that is not connected to a network is called a **stand-alone computer**. When it is connected to the network, it becomes a **workstation**. Any device connected to the network is called a **node**. A **router** is a device that controls traffic between network components. Figure A-19 illustrates a typical network configuration.

- In a **local area network (LAN)**, computers and peripheral devices are located relatively close to each other, generally in the same building.

QUICK TIP
The **World Wide Web** is subset of the Internet, and is a huge database of information stored on network servers.

- A **wide area network (WAN)** is more than one LAN connected together. The **Internet** is the largest example of a WAN.

- In a **wireless local area network (WLAN)**, computers and peripherals use high-frequency radio waves instead of wires to communicate and connect in a network. **Wi-Fi** (short for **wireless fidelity**) is the term created by the nonprofit Wi-Fi Alliance to describe networks connected using a standard radio frequency established by the Institute of Electrical and Electronics Engineers (IEEE). Wi-Fi is used over short distances to connect computers to a LAN.

- A **personal area network (PAN)** is a network that allows two or more devices located close to each other to communicate or to connect a device to the Internet. In a PAN, devices are connected with cables or are wireless.

  - **Infrared technology** uses infrared light waves to beam data from one device to another. The devices must be compatible, and they must be positioned close to each other with their infrared ports pointed at each other to communicate. This is the technology used in TV remote controls.
  - **Bluetooth** uses short-range radio waves to connect a device wirelessly to another device or to the Internet. The devices must each have a Bluetooth transmitter, but unlike infrared connections, they can communicate around corners or through walls.

- **WiMAX** (short for **Worldwide Interoperability for Microwave Access**), another standard defined by the IEEE, allows computer users to connect over many miles to a LAN. A WiMAX tower sends signals to a WiMAX receiver built or plugged into a computer. WiMAX towers can communicate with each other or with a company that provides connections to the Internet.

FIGURE A-19: Typical network configuration

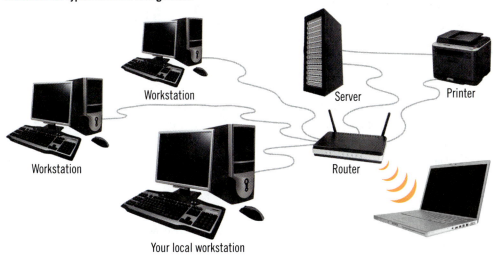

Workstation

Server

Printer

Workstation

Router

Your local workstation

Understanding telecommunications

Telecommunications means communicating over a comparatively long distance using a phone line or some other data conduit. To make this connection, you must use a modem. Modem stands for *m*odulator-*dem*odulator. The modem converts the **digital**, or stop-start, **signals** your computer outputs into **analog**, or continuous wave, **signals** (sound waves) that can traverse ordinary phone lines. Figure A-20 shows the telecommunications process, in which a modem converts digital signals to analog signals at the sending site (modulates) and a second modem converts the analog signals

back into digital signals at the receiving site (demodulates). Most computers today come with a built-in 56K modem and NIC (network interface card). 56K represents the modem's capability to send and receive about 56,000 **bits per second (bps)**. People who want to use a high-speed connection either over phone lines, such as a **DSL (digital subscriber line)**, or over a cable connection, usually need to purchase an external DSL or cable modem separately. High-speed connections are often called **broadband connections**.

FIGURE A-20: Using modems to send and receive data

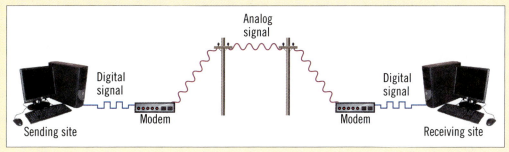

Analog signal

Digital signal

Modem

Modem

Digital signal

Sending site

Receiving site

Learning about Security Threats

Security refers to the steps a computer owner takes to prevent unauthorized use of or damage to the computer. Once a computer is connected to a network, it is essential that the computer be protected against possible threats from people intent on stealing information or causing malicious damage. Kevin explains how important it is to be vigilant about keeping the office computers secure and reviews ways to do this.

Several types of security threats are discussed below:

- **Malware** is a broad term that describes any program that is intended to cause harm or convey information to others without the owner's permission.

  - Unscrupulous programmers deliberately construct harmful programs, called **viruses**, which instruct your computer to perform destructive activities, such as erasing a disk drive. Some viruses are more annoying than destructive, but some can be harmful, erasing data or causing your hard disk to require reformatting. **Antivirus software**, sometimes referred to as **virus protection software**, searches executable files for the sequences of characters that may cause harm and disinfects the files by erasing or disabling those commands. Figure A-21 shows the dialog box that appears when the Norton antivirus program is scanning a computer for potential threats.

  - Some software programs contain other programs called **spyware** that track a computer user's Internet usage and send this data back to the company or person who created it. Most often, this is done without the computer user's permission or knowledge. **Antispyware software** can detect these programs and delete them.

- A **firewall** is like a locked door on your computer. It prevents other computers on the Internet from accessing your computer and prevents programs on it from accessing the Internet without your permission. A firewall can be either hardware or software.

  - A hardware firewall provides strong protection against incoming threats. A router usually has a built-in firewall.

  - Software firewalls track all incoming and outgoing traffic. If a program that never accessed the Internet before attempts to do so, the user is notified and can choose to forbid access. There are several free software firewall packages available.

- Criminals are getting more aggressive as they try to figure out new ways to access computer users' personal information and passwords.

  - A Web site set up to look exactly like another Web site, such as a bank's Web site, but which does not actually belong to the organization portrayed in the site, is a **spoofed** site. The site developer creates a **URL** (address on the Web) that looks similar to a URL from the legitimate site. Usually, spoofed sites are set up to try to convince customers of the real site to enter personal information, such as credit card numbers, Social Security numbers, and passwords, so that the thief collecting the information can use it to steal the customer's money or identity.

  - **Phishing** refers to the practice of sending e-mails to customers or potential customers of a legitimate Web site asking them to click a link in the e-mail. If the customer clicks the link, his or her **browser** (the software used to access Web sites) displays the spoofed site where the customer is then asked to verify or enter personal information.

  - Sometimes a criminal can break into a **DNS server** (a computer responsible for directing Internet traffic) and redirect any attempts to access a particular Web site to the criminal's spoofed site. This is called **pharming**.

FIGURE A-21: Antivirus scan in progress

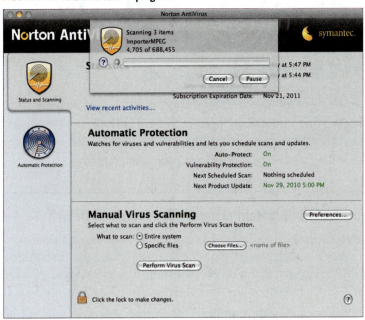

Protecting information with passwords

You can protect data on your computer by using passwords. You can set up accounts on your computer for multiple users and require that users sign in with a user name and password before they can use the computer. This is known as **logging in** or **logging on**. You can also protect individual files on your computer so that people who try to open or alter a file need to type the password before they are allowed access to the file. Many Web sites require a user name and password to access the information stored on it. To prevent anyone from guessing your passwords, you should always create and use strong passwords. A **strong password** consists of at least eight characters of upper- and lowercase letters and numbers. Avoid using common personal information, such as birthdays and addresses, in your password.

Understanding System Software

Sometimes the term software refers to a single program, but often the term refers to a collection of programs and data that are packaged together. **System software** helps the computer carry out its basic operating tasks.  Before Kevin describes the various types of software that people use to accomplish things like writing memos, he needs to describe system software.

The components of system software are described below:

- System software manages the fundamental operations of your computer, such as loading programs and data into memory, executing programs, saving data to disks, displaying information on the monitor, and transmitting data through a port to a peripheral device. There are four types of system software: operating systems, utilities, device drivers, and programming languages.

- Recall that an **operating system** allocates system resources, manages storage space, maintains security, detects equipment failure, and controls basic input and output. **Input and output**, or **I/O**, is the flow of data from the microprocessor to memory to peripherals and back again.

  - The operating system allocates system resources so programs run properly. A **system resource** is any part of the computer system, including memory, storage devices, and the microprocessor, that can be used by a computer program.
  - The operating system is also responsible for managing the files on your storage devices. Not only does it open and save files, but it also keeps track of every part of every file for you and lets you know if any part is missing.
  - While you are working on the computer, the operating system is constantly guarding against equipment failure. Each electronic circuit is checked periodically, and the moment a problem is detected, the user is notified with a warning message on the screen.
  - Microsoft Windows, used on many personal computers, and the MAC OS, used exclusively on Macintosh computers, are referred to as **operating environments** because they provide a **graphical user interface** (**GUI**, pronounced "goo-ey") that acts as a liaison between the user and all of the computer's hardware and software. Figure A-22 shows the starting screen on a computer using Snow Leopard.

- **Utilities** are another category of system software that augment the operating system by taking over some of its responsibility for allocating hardware resources.

- As you learned earlier in the discussion of ports, device drivers handle the transmission protocol between a computer and its peripherals. When you add a device to an existing computer, part of its installation includes adding its device driver to the computer's configuration.

- Computer **programming languages**, which a programmer uses to write computer instructions, are also part of the system software. The instructions are translated into electrical signals that the computer can manipulate and process.

FIGURE A-22: Mac OS X (Snow Leopard) starting screen

Menu bar

Desktop

Dock

Icon (you
might see
additional
icons on your
screen)

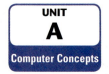
Understanding Application Software

Application software enables you to perform specific computer tasks. Many programs allow users to use data created in one application in a document created by another application. **Object linking and embedding (OLE)** refers to the ability to use data from another file, called the **source**. **Embedding** occurs when you copy and paste the source data in the new file. **Linking** allows you to create a connection between the source data and the copy in the new file. The link updates the copy every time a change is made to the source data. The seamless nature of OLE among some applications is referred to as **integration**. Now that the Sheehan Tours staff understands system software, Kevin describes some common application software.

DETAILS

Typical application software includes the following:

QUICK TIP
Most document production software allows you to perform **copy-and-paste** and **cut-and-paste operations**, to duplicate or move words around.

- **Document production software** includes word processing software, desktop publishing software, e-mail editors, and Web authoring software. All of these production tools have a variety of features that assist you in writing and formatting documents, including changing the **font** (the style of type) or adding color and design elements. Most offer **spell checking** to help you avoid typographical and spelling errors, as shown in Figure A-23.

- **Spreadsheet software** is a numerical analysis tool. Spreadsheet software creates a **worksheet**, composed of a grid of columns and rows. You can type data into the cells, and then enter mathematical formulas into other cells that reference the data. Figure A-24 shows a typical worksheet that includes a simple calculation and the data in the spreadsheet represented as a simple graph.

- **Database management software** lets you collect and manage data. A **database** is a collection of information stored on one or more computers organized in a uniform format of records and fields. A **record** is a collection of data items in a database. A **field** is one piece of information in the record. An example of a database is the online catalog of books at a library; the catalog contains one record for each book in the library, and each record contains fields that identify the title, the author, and the subjects under which the book can be classified.

- **Graphics** and **presentation software** allow you to create illustrations, diagrams, graphs, and charts that can be projected before a group, printed out for quick reference, or transmitted to remote computers. You can also use **clip art**, simple drawings that are included as collections with many software packages.

- **Photo-editing software** allows you to manipulate digital photos. You can make the images brighter, add special effects, add other images, or crop the photo to include only relevant parts of the image. Examples of photo-editing software are Adobe Photoshop and Picasa. **Video-editing software**, such as QuickTime or Final Cut Express, allows you to edit video by clipping it, adding captions and a sound track, or rearranging clips.

- **Multimedia authoring software** allows you to record digital sound files, video files, and animations that can be included in presentations and other documents.

QUICK TIP
Some information management software allows you to synchronize information between a PDA and a desktop or notebook computer.

- **Information management software** keeps track of schedules, appointments, contacts, and "to-do" lists. Most e-mail software allows users to add all the information about contacts to the list of e-mail addresses. In addition, some software, such as Microsoft Outlook, combines a contact list with information management components, such as a calendar and to-do list.

- **Web site creation and management software** allows you to create and manage Web sites. They allow you to see what the Web pages will look like as you create them.

FIGURE A-23: Checking the spelling in a document

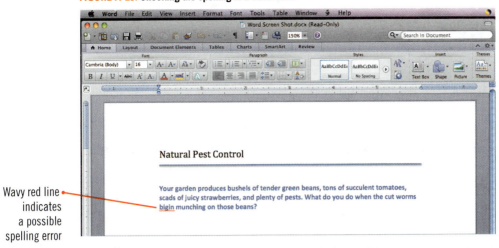

Wavy red line
indicates
a possible
spelling error

FIGURE A-24: Typical worksheet with numerical data and a chart

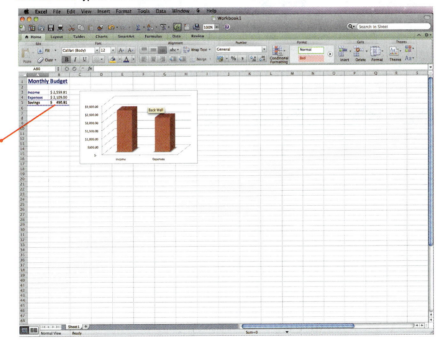

Cell B5 contains the
result of a calculation
performed by the
spreadsheet software

Computing in the cloud

Cloud computing means that data, applications, and even resources are stored on servers accessed over the Internet rather than on users' computers, and you access only what you need when you need it. Many individuals and companies are moving toward "the cloud" for at least some of their needs. For example, some companies provide space and computing power to developers for a fee. Individuals might subscribe to a backup service such as Carbonite or Mozy so that their data is automatically backed up on a computer at the physical location of those companies. Google Docs and Microsoft Web Apps provide both free and paid versions of various applications that you access by logging in to their Web sites. For now, these applications are not as robust as the applications you install on your own machine, but that is likely to change in the future.

Practice

Concepts Review

Match the statements with the elements labeled in the screen shown in Figure A-25.

FIGURE A-25

1. Which component is used to enter text?
2. Which component do you use to point to items on the screen?
3. Which component processes data?
4. Which component displays output?

Match each term with the statement that best describes it.

5. netbook
6. commands
7. byte
8. RAM
9. hard disk
10. expansion slot
11. server
12. spyware
13. operating system
14. database

a. Temporarily holds data and programs while the computer is on

b. A type of subnotebook computer that is primarily designed to allow users to access the Internet and check e-mail

c. Magnetic storage media that is usually sealed in a case inside the computer

d. A collection of information stored on one or more computers organized in a uniform format of records and fields

e. A series of 8 bits

f. A computer on a network that acts as the central storage location for programs and data used on the network

g. Software that allocates resources, manages storage space, maintains security, and controls I/O

h. A program that tracks a user's Internet usage without the user's permission

i. A slot on the motherboard into which a controller card for a peripheral device is inserted

j. Input instructions that tell the computer how to process data

Select the best answer from the list of choices.

15. Which one of the following would not be considered a personal computer?
   a. Desktop
   b. Mainframe
   c. Notebook
   d. Tablet PC

16. The intangible components of a computer system, including the programs, are called:
   a. Peripherals.
   b. Hardware.
   c. Software.
   d. Price.

17. What part of the computer is responsible for executing instructions to process information?
   a. Peripheral device
   b. Card
   c. Motherboard
   d. Processor

18. What are the technical details about each hardware component called?
   a. Configuration
   b. Specifications
   c. Circuits
   d. Cards

19. Keyboards, monitors, and printers are all examples of which of the following?
   a. Peripheral devices
   b. Input devices
   c. Output devices
   d. Software

20. Which of the following is a pointing device that allows you to control the pointer by moving the entire device around on a desk?
   a. Mouse
   b. Trackball
   c. Trackpad
   d. Pointing stick

21. To display graphics, a computer needs a monitor and a(n):
   a. Expansion port.
   b. Graphics card or processor.
   c. Network card (NIC).
   d. Sound card.

22. What do you call each 1 or 0 used in the representation of computer data?
   a. An ASCII
   b. A pixel
   c. A bit
   d. A byte

23. **What is a megabyte?**
    a. 10 kilobytes
    b. About a million bytes
    c. One-half a gigabyte
    d. About a million bits

24. **Which of the following permanently stores the set of instructions that the computer uses to activate the software that controls the processing function when you turn the computer on?**
    a. RAM
    b. ROM
    c. The hard disk
    d. CPU cache

25. **Which of the following is space on the computer's storage devices that simulates additional RAM?**
    a. Read-only memory
    b. Cache memory
    c. Volatile memory
    d. Virtual memory

26. **Which of the following temporarily stores data and programs while you are using them?**
    a. RAM
    b. ROM
    c. The hard disk
    d. CPU cache

27. **Which of the following is not a permanent storage medium?**
    a. Hard disk
    b. Optical disk
    c. DVD
    d. RAM

28. **The transmission protocol between a computer and its peripheral devices is handled by a:**
    a. Driver.
    b. Controller card.
    c. Channel.
    d. Data bus.

29. **Which of the following is the data path between the microprocessor, RAM, and the peripherals?**
    a. Cable
    b. Data bus
    c. Data channel
    d. Data port

30. **The computer that originates a message to send to another computer is called the:**
    a. Channel.
    b. Sender.
    c. Receiver.
    d. Driver.

31. **A personal computer that is connected to a network is called a:**
    a. Netbook.
    b. Desktop.
    c. Workstation.
    d. Channel.

32. **Which of the following acts as a locked door on a computer?**
    a. DNS server
    b. Antivirus software
    c. Spyware
    d. Firewall

33. **A _____ consists of connected computers and peripheral devices that are located relatively close to each other.**
    a. PAN
    b. LAN
    c. WAN
    d. WLAN

34. **When data, applications, and resources are stored on servers rather than on users' computers, it is referred to as _____.**
    a. Sky computing
    b. Cloud computing
    c. Shared computing
    d. Leased computing

35. **A Web site set up to look exactly like another Web site, such as a bank's Web site, but which does not actually belong to the organization portrayed in the site is a _____ site.**
    a. Phished
    b. Spoofed
    c. Served
    d. Malware

Independent Challenge 1

This Independent Challenge requires an Internet connection.

To run the newest software, many people need to upgrade their existing computer system or buy a brand-new one. What do you do with your old computer when you purchase a new one? Most municipalities have enacted laws regulating the disposal of electronics. Research these laws in your city and state and write a brief report describing them.

a. Start your browser, go to your favorite search engine, and then search for information about laws regarding the disposal of electronics in your city and state. Try finding your city's Web site and searching it for the information, or use **electronics disposal laws** followed by your city name as a search term and then repeat that search with your state's name in place of your city's name.

b. Open each Web site that you find in a separate tab or browser window.

c. Read the information on each Web site. Can some components be thrown away? Are there laws that apply only to monitors? Are there different laws for individuals and businesses? Does the size of the business matter? Are manufacturers or resellers required to accept used components that they manufactured or sold?

Advanced Challenge Exercise

- Search for organizations to which you can donate your computer.
- How do these organizations promise to protect your privacy?
- Can you take a deduction on your federal income tax for your donation?

d. Write a short report describing your findings. Include the URLs for all relevant Web sites. (*Hint*: If you are using a word processor to write your report, you can copy the URLs from your browser and paste them into the document. Drag to select the entire URL in the Address or Location bar in your browser. Right-click the selected text, then click Copy on the shortcut menu. Position the insertion point in the document where you want the URL to appear, then press [command][V].)

Independent Challenge 2

This Independent Challenge requires an Internet connection.

New viruses are discovered on an almost-daily basis. If you surf the Internet or exchange e-mail, it is important to use updated antivirus software. Research the most current virus threats and create a table listing the threats and details about them.

a. Start your browser, go to Trend Micro's Web site at **www.trendmicro.com**, and then click the Learn more at ThreatTrends link under the ThreatTrends meters. On the TrendWatch page, click the Current Threat Activity link, click the Malware & Vulnerability Information link, and then click the View the Malware Map link. (If you don't see that link, type **Malware Map** in the Search box on the page, then click the link to Malware Map in the list of search results.)

b. Click links to the top five threats, and then read the description of each threat. The pages describing the threats might open in a new tab.

c. Open a new word processing document and create a table listing each virus threat, a description of what each virus does, how widely each virus is distributed based on the number of infected computers, and how damaging each virus is (the Risk level).

d. In your browser, go to the Security Advisor on CA's Web site at **www3.ca.com/securityadvisor**, and then click the Virus link in the Newly Discovered Threats area. If any of the top five virus threats are different from the ones on the Trend Micro site, add them to your table. (*Hint*: After you click a virus name, check the "Also known as" list.)

e. For any viruses that are already in your table because they were on the Trend Micro site, read the CA description to see if there is any additional information describing how the virus could damage your system. Add this information to your table.

Independent Challenge 3

This Independent Challenge requires an Internet connection.

One of the keyboards shown in this unit is an ergonomic keyboard. Ergonomics is the study of the design of a workspace so that the worker can work efficiently and avoid injury. The U.S. Occupational Safety and Health Administration (OSHA) has developed guidelines that describe a healthy computer work environment. Research these guidelines and evaluate your workspace.

    a. Start your browser, and then go to **www.osha.gov/SLTC/etools/computerworkstations**.

    b. Read the information on the main page. Follow links to descriptions of the best arrangement for equipment you use when working on a computer. (*Hint*: Look for the Workstation Components link, and point to it to open a submenu of links.)

    c. Locate and print the checklist for evaluating your workspace. (*Hint*: Click the Checklists link, then click the View/Print the Evaluation Checklist PDF link.)

    d. Using the checklist, evaluate each of the conditions listed. If a condition does not apply to you, write N/A (not applicable) in the Yes column.

Advanced Challenge Exercise

- Use the OSHA Web site or a search engine to research repetitive-motion injuries to which computer users are susceptible.
- Evaluate your risk for at least three common injuries.
- On the OSHA checklist, note what injury or injuries each applicable item or behavior will help prevent.

Real Life Independent Challenge

This Independent Challenge requires an Internet connection.

You are buying a new Mac for home use, but you're having trouble deciding between a desktop and a notebook. You know that the computer you buy will need to run Snow Leopard and Microsoft Office for Mac 2011 and have enough hard disk space for all your files, and you want to make sure you are protected against security threats. You'll also need a printer and external speakers.

a. To help you make a decision and organize the information to make it easy to compare, create the table shown in Figure A-26.

FIGURE A-26

Name:	**Your Name**				
	Your Requirements	**Notebook**		**Desktop**	
		Technical Specs.	**Price**	**Technical Specs.**	**Price**
Model (and starting price):		MacBook		iMac	
Hardware:	Processor (brand and speed)				
	RAM (amount)				
	Video RAM (amount)				
	Hard disk (size)				
	Printer (type and speed)				
	Screen Size				
	Resolution				
Maintenance Plan:	Apple Care				
Software:	Snow Leopard (Mac OS X – v.10.6.4 or higher)				
	Office 2011				
	Antivirus Software				
	Additional Software (your choice)				
Total Price:					

Information Source(s):

_____
_____
_____
_____

b. You'll need to determine which edition of Office for Mac 2011 you should get (Home & Student or Home & Business). Use the Internet to research which edition will best suit your needs. Enter the cost for the edition in the appropriate cells in the table.

c. Research the hardware requirements for running Microsoft Office for Mac 2011. Enter the technical specifications required in the appropriate cells in the table.

d. Research the cost of a new iMac that has Mac OS X Snow Leopard as its operating system and that meets the system requirements needed to run Office 2011. Next, research the cost of a new MacBook or MacBook Pro with the same or similar configuration. To begin, go to **www.apple.com** to review the technical information to ensure that you are comparing models with similar hardware characteristics. Enter the starting costs for each model in the appropriate cells in the table. (*Hint*: The Apple store at www.apple.com can help you configure your computer and provide you with the cost of the AppleCare Protection Plan.)

e. Search the Web to find an inexpensive inkjet printer that will work with your Mac. Enter the cost in the appropriate cells in the table.

f. Search the Web to find external speakers that will work with your Mac. Enter the cost in the appropriate cells in the table.

g. Search the Web to find antivirus software for your Mac. Enter the cost in the appropriate cells in the table.

h. Review the items to make sure you have entered information in all the rows. Total the costs you entered in the table for the various items.

i. Based on the information you found, determine whether the better purchase would be the notebook (MacBook or MacBook Pro) or the iMac. Write a brief summary justifying your decision.

j. Submit the completed table and your summary to your instructor.

Getting Started with Mac OS X Snow Leopard

Files You Will Need:

No files needed

Mac OS X v10.6, or **Snow Leopard**, is an **operating system** (OS), which is software that manages the operation of your computer and keeps all the hardware and software working together properly. When you start your Mac, the operating system starts automatically; it activates **Finder**, which provides access to files and programs on your computer; and it displays the **desktop**—a graphical user interface (GUI) that you use to interact with the operating system and the other software on your computer. Finder helps you organize **files** (collections of stored electronic data, such as text, pictures, video, music, and programs) in **folders** (containers for files) so that you can easily find them later. When you open a file or program, Snow Leopard displays the file or program in a rectangular-shaped work area known as a **window**. As a new tour manager for Quest Specialty Travel (QST), you need to develop basic skills on your company's Mac computer to keep track of all the tour bookings.

OBJECTIVES

Start Mac OS X Snow Leopard

Use a pointing device

Start a program

Move and resize windows

Use menus

Use dialog boxes

Get Mac Help

End a Snow Leopard session

Starting Mac OS X Snow Leopard

When you start your Mac, Snow Leopard steps through a process called **booting** to get the computer up and running. During this time, you might need to enter your user name and password, which identifies you to the operating system as an authorized user of the computer. As part of the boot process, Snow Leopard activates Finder and displays the Mac desktop. The desktop is a way for you to interact with your Mac and to access its tools. The desktop appears with preset, or **default**, settings; however, you can change these settings to suit your needs. When your computer starts, the desktop displays the Finder menu bar, an icon for the Macintosh HD (hard drive), and the Dock. Your supervisor and Quest's tour developer, Evelyn Swazey, asks you to become familiar with the Mac and its features before your upcoming tour.

STEPS

1. **If your computer and monitor are turned off, press the Power button**

   Depending on the Mac model you have, the power button may be located in the middle of your tower, on the back of your iMac or Mac mini, or near the monitor of your laptop. After your computer starts, you might be prompted to enter a user name and password (if your Mac is part of a network or if it is set up for multiple users), or you'll see the desktop. If you're prompted for a user name and password, continue with Step 2 and compare your computer screen to Figure B-1. If not, skip to Step 4.

   QUICK TIP

   User names and passwords are case sensitive. If you don't know your user name or password, ask your instructor or technical support person.

2. **In the Name box, type your user name**

3. **In the Password box, type your password, then press [return] or click Log In**

   After Leopard verifies your user name and password, you see the desktop.

4. **Compare your computer screen to Figure B-2**

   Your desktop may look slightly different and contain different items. The standard Mac desktop contains the following items:

   - The **menu bar** is located at the top of your computer screen and contains the drop down menus available for the active program. If no program is open, the Finder menu is active by default. The name of the current program appears next to the Apple menu. The right end of the menu bar contains icons that represent additional menu items, such as computer status menus like Time Machine, Bluetooth, AirPort/Networks, speaker volume, system date and time, and Spotlight.

   - The **Macintosh HD icon** is typically located in the upper right corner of your computer screen. This icon gives you quick access to the contents of your hard disk.

   - The **Dock** is a glossy ribbon at the bottom of your screen that contains icons for frequently used programs, folders and files, and the Trash.

   - The **Trash** is an icon on the Dock that represents a storage area on your computer's hard disk for deleted files and folders.

QUICK TIP

You may have additional icons on your desktop. For example, the computer in Figure B-2 contains the Boot Camp icon, because it has been set up as dual boot. A dual boot Mac can run both Mac and Windows operating systems.

FIGURE B-1: Mac Log In screen

Type user name here

Type password here

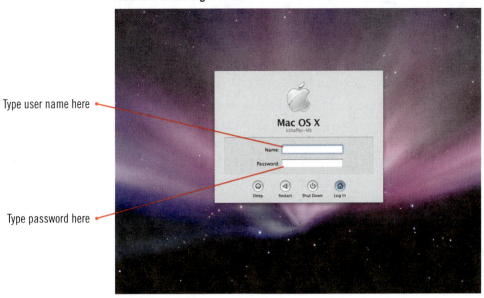

FIGURE B-2: Mac OS X Snow Leopard desktop

Menu bar

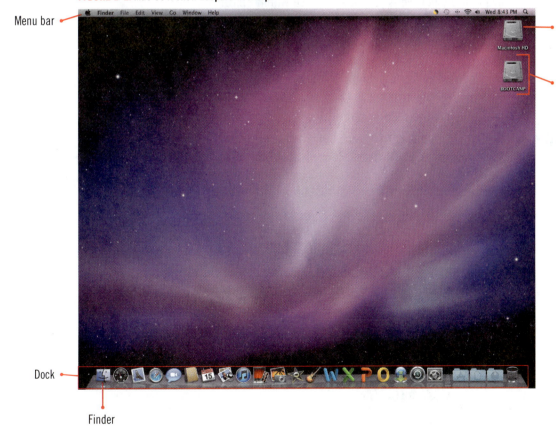

Macintosh HD icon

You may have additional hard disk icons on your desktop for network drives or external hard disks; the Boot Camp icon appears when you are using a dual boot Mac

Dock

Finder

Using a Pointing Device

The most common way to interact with your Mac and the software you are using is with a **pointing device**, such as a mouse or a trackpad, as shown in Figure B-3. As you move your mouse on your desk or swipe your fingers on your trackpad, a small arrow (or other symbol) called a **pointer** moves on the screen in the same direction. Table B-1 illustrates common pointer shapes and their functions. You press a button on the pointing device to select and move objects (such as icons and desktop windows); to open programs, windows, folders, and files; and to select options for performing specific tasks, such as saving your work. Table B-2 lists the basic ways in which you can use a pointing device. Pointing devices work through a cable (for a wired mouse) or through a wireless connection that transmits data using radio waves. You decide to practice using your pointing device so you can work more efficiently.

STEPS

QUICK TIP

If your pointing device is a trackpad, move your finger across the trackpad to control the pointer.

1. **Locate the pointer on the desktop, then move your pointing device**

   The pointer moves across the desktop in the same direction as you move your pointing device.

2. **Move the pointer so the tip is directly over the Finder icon 🖥 on the Dock**

   Positioning the pointer over an item and hovering is called **pointing**. As you point to an item, a **Help Tag** appears with a brief description of the item.

QUICK TIP

To single-click with a Magic Mouse or a Mighty Mouse, press the left side of its touch-sensitive button; with a trackpad that has a separate button, click the button; with a Magic trackpad, press down on the trackpad with one finger.

3. **Move the pointer so the tip is directly over the Macintosh HD icon 🖴 on the desktop, then press and release the left button on your pointing device**

   Pressing and releasing the left button, called **clicking** or **single-clicking**, selects an icon on the desktop or in a window, and selects options and objects within a program.

4. **With 🖴 still selected, press and hold down the left button on your pointing device, move your pointing device to another location on the desktop, then release the left button**

   A dimmed icon of the Macintosh HD icon moves with the pointer. When you release the left button on your pointing device, the Macintosh HD icon is placed on the desktop at a different location. You use this technique, called **dragging**, to move icons and windows.

5. **Drag 🖴 back to its original desktop location**

QUICK TIP

To right-click with a Magic Mouse or a Mighty Mouse, press the right side of its touch-sensitive button; with a trackpad with a separate button or a single button mouse, press and hold [control] while pressing the button; with a Magic trackpad, press down on the trackpad with two fingers.

6. **Position the pointer over 🖴, then press and release the right button on your pointing device**

   This action, called **right-clicking**, opens a shortcut menu, as shown in Figure B-4. A **shortcut menu** lists common commands for the object that is right-clicked. A **command** is an instruction to perform a task, such as renaming an object. If a command is dimmed, it is not currently available.

7. **Click the desktop background**

   The shortcut menu closes and the Macintosh HD icon remains selected.

8. **Point to 🖴, then quickly press the left button twice on your pointing device and release it**

   Quickly clicking the left button twice is called **double-clicking**, which opens a window or a program. In this case, the Finder window opens to display the contents of the Macintosh hard drive.

9. **Click the Close button 🔴 in the upper-left corner of the Finder window**

   The Finder window closes. Every window has a Close button; clicking it is the fastest way to close a window.

TABLE B-1: Common pointer shapes

shape	name	description
▶	Arrow pointer	Points to an object and selects a command
🌈 or ✳	Progress indicator	Indicates that the operating system or another program is busy and you must wait before continuing
I	I-beam	Identifies where you can type, select, insert, or edit text
👆	Link pointer	Identifies a link you can click to jump to another location, such as a Help topic or a Web site

FIGURE B-3: Common Mac pointing devices

Magic Mouse

Wireless Mighty Mouse

Trackpad with separate button

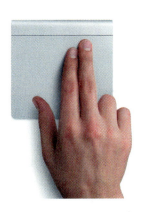

Magic Trackpad

FIGURE B-4: Shortcut menu

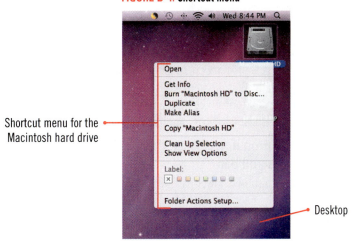

Shortcut menu for the
Macintosh hard drive

Desktop

TABLE B-2: Basic pointing device techniques

technique	function	operation
Pointing	Points to an item; sometimes displays a Help Tag about the item	Move the pointing device to position the tip of the on-screen pointer over an object, then hover
Clicking	Selects an item, such as a file or folder, or opens an item that resides on the Dock	Point to an object, then quickly press and release the left button area once
Double-clicking	Opens an item or resource, such as a file, folder, or software program (not residing on the Dock)	Point to an object, then press the left button area twice in quick succession
Right-clicking	Opens a shortcut menu	Point to an object, then quickly press and release the right button area once
[control]-clicking	Opens a shortcut menu; functions as a right-click for a single-button pointing device	Point to an object, press and hold [control], then press the button once
Drag	Moves an object to a new location	Point to an object, press and hold the left button, move the object to a new location, then release the left button

Starting a Program

In addition to Finder, Snow Leopard includes a variety of programs, such as Dashboard, Mail, Safari, iChat, Address Book, iCal, Preview, iTunes, Photo Booth, iPhoto, iMovie, and GarageBand, which by default are all available on the Dock. The Dock is a glossy ribbon at the bottom of your screen that contains **icons**, or small images that represent programs, folders and files, and the Trash. The purpose of the Dock is to give you quick, easy access to the most frequently used items on your computer. By default, the Dock is open and located at the bottom of your computer screen, but it can be moved or hidden. The Dock is divided into two areas by the separator line (a vertical dashed line); programs appear on the left side of the dashed line, and folders, files, and the Trash appear on the right. To open a program, simply click the program's icon on the Dock. Once you open a program, you can adjust your view of the program window using the scroll track located on the right side and/or bottom of the window. Because you need to schedule events for your upcoming tour, you want to try working with the iCal program, a calendar program. Once you open the program, you scroll through the program window to get a look at the workspace.

STEPS

TROUBLE

If the icon for iCal does not appear on the Dock, double-click the hard drive icon on the desktop, click Applications, then double-click the iCal icon.

1. **Locate the Dock on your computer screen**

   If the Dock is not visible, move the on-screen pointer to the bottom of your screen and the Dock will slide into view. Snow Leopard offers options for customizing your experience of the Dock. To hide or show the Dock, click the Apple icon on the menu bar, point to Dock, then click Turn Hiding On or Off. To show a larger icon as you point to an item on the Dock, click Turn Magnification On after pointing to Dock.

2. **Point to the iCal icon 🗓 on the Dock**

   As shown in Figure B-5, the word "iCal" appears as a Help Tag above the icon on the Dock.

TROUBLE

Your iCal window might differ from Figure B-6. If it does not contain a left pane, click View on the menu bar, then click Show Calendar List to display the left pane.

3. **Click 🗓 on the Dock**

   As shown in Figure B-6, the iCal program opens in a window on the desktop. Programs that are currently running have a blue light beneath their program icons on the Dock. The blue light identifies an open program. Because Finder controls the desktop, a blue light always appears beneath its icon on the Dock. On the right side of the iCal window, a vertical scroll bar appears that you can use to adjust your view.

4. **Click the Week View button if necessary, then click the down scroll arrow ▼ at the bottom of the vertical scroll bar**

   The window scrolls down to show a lower part of the calendar and the upper part of the calendar has now disappeared from view.

5. **Drag the vertical scroller slowly down the window to the bottom of the vertical scroll track**

   The window view changes in larger increments, and the bottom part of the calendar is visible at the bottom of the window.

6. **Click in the vertical scroll track just above the vertical scroller**

   The view moves up approximately the height of one window.

FIGURE B-5: The Dock

iCal icon

Program icons

Dashed line divides the Dock

Files and folders

Trash

FIGURE B-6: iCal program open on desktop

iCal menu bar

iCal window

Blue lights identify open programs

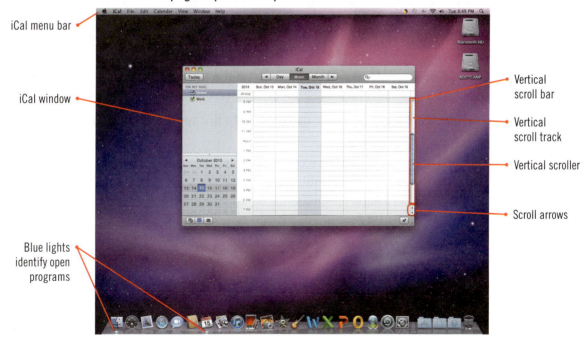

Vertical scroll bar

Vertical scroll track

Vertical scroller

Scroll arrows

Starting a program not found on the Dock

If you'd like to use a program that is installed on your computer but is not on the Dock, click the Finder icon ![Finder icon] on the Dock to open the Finder window. Click Applications in the sidebar (the left side of the Finder window), locate the program you'd like to use on the right side of the Finder window, and then double-click the program to open it. To save time in the future, you can add the program to the Dock by dragging the program icon from the Finder window to the location on the Dock where you'd like the icon to appear. Icons already on the Dock will move to make room for the new icon. To open an icon on the Dock, single-click it.

Getting Started with Mac OS X Snow Leopard

Mac OS X 39

Mac OS X

Moving and Resizing Windows

Each program you start opens in its own window. If you open more than one program at once, you are **multitasking**—performing several tasks at the same time—and each program appears in a different window. As you multitask, you will invariably need to move and resize windows so that you can see more of one window or view two or more windows at the same time. To minimize a window to the Dock or to increase a window to full size, you use the **window control buttons**—Minimize and Zoom—in the upper-left corner of the window. To adjust a window's height or width (or both), you drag the size control located on the lower-right corner of the window. To move a window, you drag its **title bar**—the area across the top of the window that displays the window name or program name. The **active window** is the window you are currently using. An **inactive window** is an open window that you are not currently using. As you work on the schedule for your upcoming tour, you need to move and resize the iCal window.

STEPS

1. **Click the Zoom button ⬤ in the upper-left corner of the iCal window**
   The iCal window expands to full size, filling the screen, as shown in Figure B-7. If the window is already the fullest size available, clicking the Zoom button decreases the window size.

2. **Click ⬤ again**
   The iCal window is restored to the size it was when you first opened it.

3. **Click the Minimize button ⬤ in the upper-left corner of the iCal window**
   The iCal window is still open, just not visible. A **minimized window** collapses to an icon on the right side of the Dock, as shown in Figure B-8. You can use this feature to hide a window that you are not currently using, but may use later.

4. **Click the minimized iCal window icon ▦ on the Dock**
   The iCal window returns to its original size and position on the desktop.

5. **Drag the iCal title bar to move the window to the upper-left corner of the desktop**
   The iCal window is repositioned on the desktop.

6. **Position the pointer on the size control ◪ on the lower-right corner of the iCal window, then drag down and to the right**
   Both the height and width of the window change, as shown in Figure B-9.

7. **Click the Apple icon on the menu bar, then click System Preferences**
   This opens System Preferences on top of the iCal window.

TROUBLE
If your keyboard does not contain a ▦ key, press [F9] or press [fn] and [F9] to activate Exposé.

8. **Press the Exposé key ▦ on your keyboard to activate Exposé**
   Exposé is a feature that allows you to easily manage open windows by displaying thumbnail images of all open windows, as shown in Figure B-10. **Thumbnails** are miniature images of the resources they represent.

9. **Click the System Preferences window, then click the Close button ⬤ to close System Preferences**

FIGURE B-7: iCal window expanded to full size

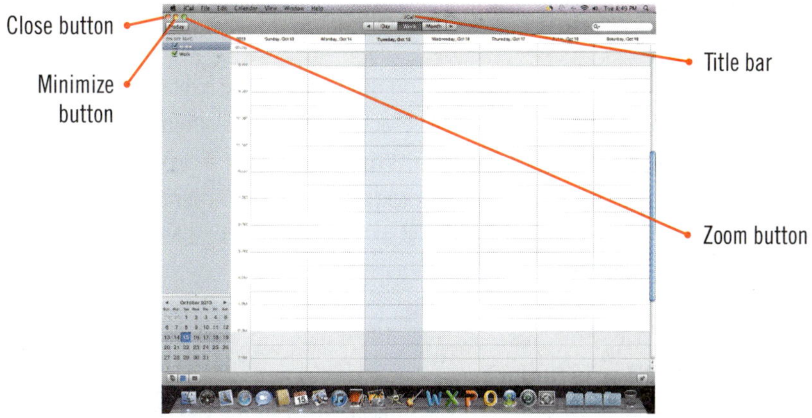

Close button

Minimize
button

Title bar

Zoom button

FIGURE B-8: Minimized iCal window

iCal window minimized to
the Dock

FIGURE B-9: Resized iCal window

Apple icon

Size control

FIGURE B-10: Exposé displaying all open windows

Using Menus

A **menu** displays a list of commands that you use to accomplish a task. The menu bar is displayed at the top of your screen and contains menus for the active program. When no programs are open, the menu bar contains options for working with Finder. When you open a new program, the menu bar changes to accommodate the menu options for that program. Clicking a menu name on the menu bar opens a menu of available options. Table B-3 contains a list of items on a typical Mac menu. 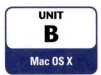 You decide to explore the menu bar options for iCal.

STEPS

1. **Click iCal on the menu bar**

   The iCal menu opens, as shown in Figure B-11. You can use the commands on this menu to find out more information about iCal, change the iCal's default preference settings, access iCal services, hide iCal or other programs, and quit iCal.

2. **Point to View on the menu bar**

   The View menu opens. This menu contains commands for changing the view shown in the iCal window.

3. **Click By Month**

   The calendar in the iCal window changes to display the entire month.

4. **Click View on the menu bar**

   As shown in Figure B-12, the By Month command is checked on the menu, indicating that the current view shown in iCal is monthly.

5. **Click By Week**

   The iCal window shows the current calendar week.

6. **Click the Close button ⦿ in the upper-left corner of the iCal window**

   The iCal window closes. However, because the Close button affects the iCal window only and not the iCal program, the iCal program is still open and running, as indicated by the iCal menu bar at the top of the screen and by the blue light beneath the iCal icon on the Dock.

TABLE B-3: Typical menu items

item	description
Bold command	Command or operation that can be executed
Dimmed command	Command or operation that is not currently available
Ellipsis (...)	Indicates that the command opens a dialog box containing additional options
Disclosure triangle	Indicates that a submenu is available containing an additional list of commands
Keyboard shortcut	Displays the combination of keys that, when pressed, executes the command listed next to the keyboard shortcut
Check mark	Indicates the command is currently selected or active

FIGURE B-11: iCal menu

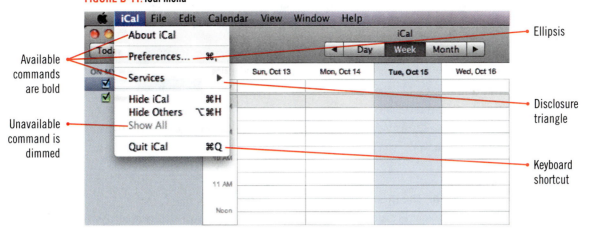

Available commands are bold

Ellipsis

Unavailable command is dimmed

Disclosure triangle

Keyboard shortcut

FIGURE B-12: iCal View menu

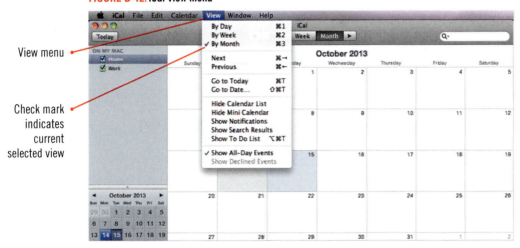

View menu

Check mark indicates current selected view

TABLE B-4: Shortcut key symbols

shortcut key symbol	modifier key name
⌘	Command
⌥	Option
⌫	Delete
⇧	Shift
⏎ or ↵	Return
⏏	Eject
⌃	Control

Using keyboard shortcuts

You can execute a command without opening a menu by using a **keyboard shortcut**, which is a combination of keyboard keys that you press to perform a command. Available keyboard shortcut keys are listed to the right of a menu item. The **modifier key(s)** is pressed and held while you press the other key(s). Table B-4 lists the common shortcut key symbols and names.

Using Dialog Boxes

If a program needs more information to complete an operation, it may open a **dialog box**, which enables you to select options or provide the information needed to complete the operation. Dialog boxes look similar to windows, but they do not contain the window control buttons and usually cannot be resized. Table B-5 lists typical elements found in a dialog box, and Figure B-13 shows many of these elements in a Print dialog box. You want to review the iCal default settings to determine whether they meet your needs while you work.

STEPS

1. **Click iCal on the menu bar, then click Preferences**

   The iCal Preferences dialog box opens, with the General preferences displayed, as shown in Figure B-14. The iCal Preferences dialog box provides access to the default iCal settings, such as days per calendar week, what day starts each week, and at what time each day's calendar starts. The first six settings in the dialog box are **pop-up menus** that you click to open a menu that displays one or more options. **Check boxes** at the bottom of the dialog box turn an option on when checked and off when unchecked.

2. **Click the Day starts at pop-up arrows, then review the available options on the pop-up menu**

   The pop-up menu enables you to select the time of day that each day will start in iCal, as shown in Figure B-15.

3. **Press [esc]**

   The pop-up menu closes without any change to the selected day.

4. **Click the Close button in the dialog box**

   The iCal Preferences dialog box closes.

5. **Click iCal on the menu bar, then click Quit iCal**

   The iCal program closes. The menu bar changes to show the Finder menu options and the blue light no longer appears under iCal on the Dock.

TABLE B-5: Typical elements found in a dialog box

item	description
Check box	A box that turns an option on when checked and off when unchecked
Collapse/Expand button	A button that shrinks or expands a portion of a dialog box to hide or unhide some settings
Command button	A button that completes or cancels an operation
Pop-up menu	A button that, when clicked, displays a menu of options from which you can choose
Option button	A small circle you click to select only one of two or more related options
Spin box	A text box with up and down arrows; you can type a value in the text box or click the arrows to increase or decrease the value
Text box	A box in which you type text (such as a password)
Tab	A clickable item at the top of a dialog box that switches to a different set of dialog box options; tabs are not available in all dialog boxes

FIGURE B-13: Print dialog box

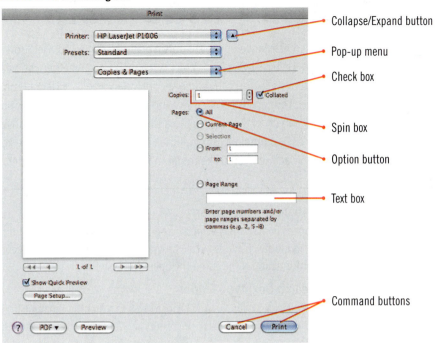

Collapse/Expand button

Pop-up menu

Check box

Spin box

Option button

Text box

Command buttons

FIGURE B-14: iCal Preferences dialog box

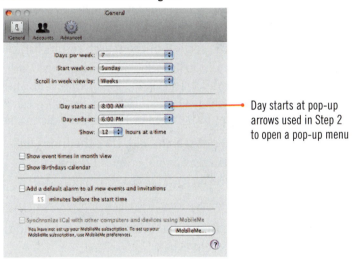

Day starts at pop-up arrows used in Step 2 to open a pop-up menu

FIGURE B-15: Day starts at pop-up menu

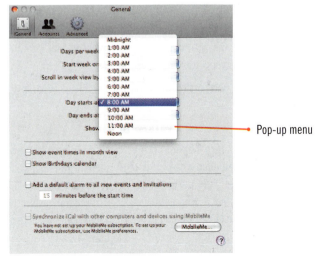

Pop-up menu

Getting Mac Help

When you need assistance or more information about how to use Snow Leopard, help is available right at your fingertips. Help is always an option on the menu bar, whether you need help with a program or with the operating system itself. You can search the interactive built-in Help files for Snow Leopard or your currently active program. You can also go to www.apple.com and search Apple's Support section. To search the built-in Help files, you can open the Help menu and type one or more descriptive words called **keywords**, such as "organizing files," to obtain a list of all the Help topics that include the keyword or phrase. Because you are a new Mac user, you'd like to get more information about Finder. You decide to use Help.

STEPS

1. **Click Help on the menu bar**

   A menu opens containing a Search box and Mac Help as a menu option. The Help menu provides access to Help files about the currently active program. When no program is open, the Help menu provides Mac Help, which is information about using the operating system.

2. **In the Search box, type Finder**

   As soon as you start typing, Snow Leopard begins searching the built-in Help files to narrow down the search results. As shown in Figure B-16, the results are divided into two sections: Menu Items and Help Topics.

3. **Point to About Finder at the top of the search results**

   When you point to an item in the Menu Items section of the search results, the menu containing that command opens and an arrow indicates the selected command. In this case, the Finder menu opens and a large blue arrow points to the About Finder command on the menu, as shown in Figure B-17.

4. **In the Help Topics section of the search results list, click Your computer's desktop**

   When you select a topic in the Help Topics section of the search results list, the Mac Help window opens and displays the selected Help topic, as shown in Figure B-18. After you've reviewed the topic shown, you can enter a keyword in the Spotlight search field in the upper-right corner of the window to find help on a different topic. You can also access the Mac Help index by clicking the Index link below the Spotlight search field.

5. **Under the Spotlight search field, click the Index link**

   The Mac Help index opens, listing keywords alphabetically. See Figure B-19.

6. **Click the letter F, scroll down to locate Finder, then click Finder**

   A list of Mac Help topics related to Finder is displayed in the window.

7. **Click one of the topics that interests you, then read the information presented**

   The chosen topic appears in the Mac Help window.

8. **Click the Home link**

   The Mac Help home page opens in the Mac Help window. From here, you can select a topic to get more information, click the More topics link to find other topics of interest, click Index to access the Mac Help index again, or click the www.apple.com link under Other resources to open the Safari browser and go to the Apple Web site. You can find additional help about Mac products by clicking the Support link on the home page of the Apple Web site.

9. **Click the Close button to close the Mac Help window**

Opening Help for programs

Your Mac has extensive Help features available. Help is always an option on your menu bar, regardless of what program is open and running. When you click Help on the menu bar with a program such as iCal or Microsoft Word open, you can then click a Help command option (such as "iCal Help" or "Word Help") to open Help that is specific to the currently active program. You'll also find additional access to Help features within programs themselves. For example, each Microsoft Office for Mac 2011 program has a Help button on the Standard toolbar. Clicking the Help button opens Help for that program, which provides thorough information on the program and includes a link to go to the Microsoft for Mac Web site for additional assistance.

FIGURE B-16: Help search results

Help menu

Menu Items
section

Help Topics
section

Search field

Search
results list

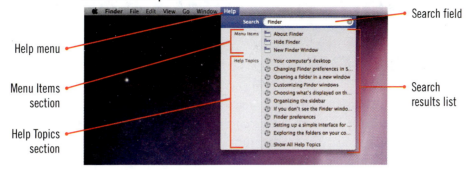

FIGURE B-17: Menu item containing keyword

Help opens the
menu and points to
the command

Click Your
computer's desktop
in Step 4

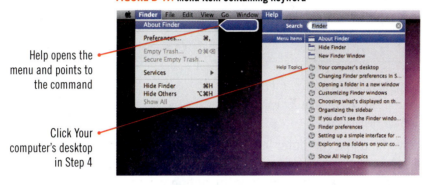

FIGURE B-18: Mac Help window

Help topic

Spotlight search field

Link to an index of
Mac Help topics

FIGURE B-19: Mac Help index

Close button

Link to Mac Help
home page

Click F in Step 6

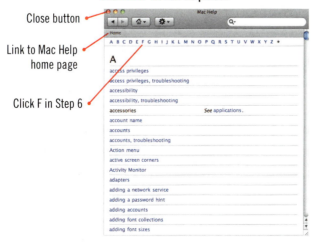

Ending a Snow Leopard Session

When you finish working on your Mac, you should save and close any open files, close any open programs, close any open windows, and shut down the operating system. As shown in Table B-6, there are four options for ending your Snow Leopard session. Whichever option you choose, it's important to shut down your computer in an orderly manner. If you turn off the computer while Snow Leopard is running, you could lose data or damage the operating system and your computer. If you are working in a computer lab, follow your instructor's directions and your lab's policies and guidelines for ending your Snow Leopard session. 🎨 You have examined the basic ways in which you can use the Mac, so you are ready to end your Snow Leopard session.

STEPS

1. **Click the Apple icon on the menu bar**

   The Apple menu has four options for ending a Snow Leopard session—Sleep, Restart, Shut Down, and Log Out, as shown in Figure B-20.

2. **If you are working in a computer lab, follow the instructions provided by your instructor or technical support person for ending your Snow Leopard session; if you are working on your own computer, click Shut Down or the option you prefer for ending your Snow Leopard session**

   After you shut down your computer, you might also need to turn off your monitor and other hardware devices, such as a printer, to conserve energy.

FIGURE B-20: Snow Leopard shutdown options

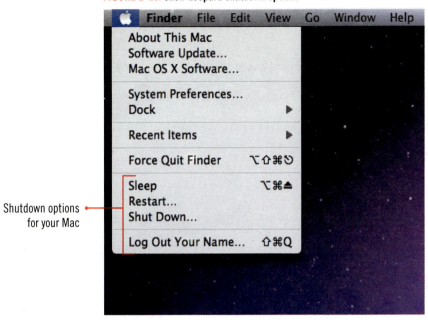

Shutdown options for your Mac

TABLE B-6: Options for ending a Snow Leopard session

option	description
Sleep	Puts your Mac in a low power state to conserve energy while not in use. All drives are disengaged to protect your drives and data. You press any key on the keyboard to "wake up" your Mac and resume using it.
Restart	All open files and programs are closed. All drives are disengaged and memory is cleared. Your Mac safely shuts down, and then it restarts automatically.
Shut Down	All open files and programs are closed. All drives are disengaged and memory is cleared. Your Mac then safely shuts down and turns off.
Log Out	All open files and programs are closed. All drives are disengaged and memory is cleared. Your Mac then logs out the current user, but continues running so the next user can log in and begin using the computer immediately, without waiting for the computer to boot up. This option also prevents others from accessing your files once you've logged out.

Practice

Concepts Review

Identify each of the items labeled in Figure B-21.

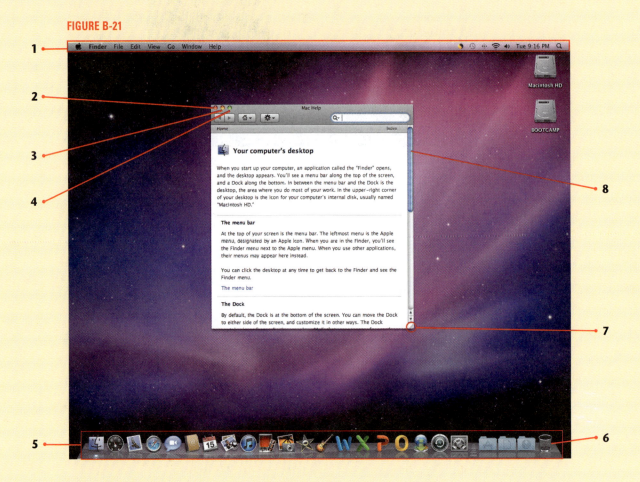

Match each statement with the term it describes.

9. The part of the operating system that is always active on the Snow Leopard desktop and Dock
10. A glossy ribbon at the bottom of your computer screen that contains icons
11. A silver bar across the top of the desktop that gives you easy access to operational commands
12. Small images that represent programs, folders and files, and the Trash
13. A type of window that opens after you select a menu command so you can specify settings for completing the operation

a. Dialog box
b. Menu bar
c. Dock
d. Icons
e. Finder

Select the best answer from the list of choices.

14. **Snow Leopard is an operating system that:**
    a. Interferes with your use of a computer.
    b. Manages the operation of a computer.
    c. Performs a single task, such as connecting to the Internet.
    d. Creates documents, such as a résumé.

15. **When you right-click with a pointing device such as a mouse, the operating system:**
    a. Opens a program.
    b. Moves an object, such as a desktop icon.
    c. Opens a shortcut menu.
    d. Deletes the object.

16. **Default settings are:**
    a. Preset settings that cannot be changed.
    b. Preset settings that can be changed.
    c. Viewable on the Dock.
    d. Permanent settings for the menu bar.

17. **To open a menu:**
    a. Click the title or word on the menu bar.
    b. Click the item on the Dock.
    c. Click a folder on the Dock.
    d. Click the Trash.

18. **Which operation opens an item on the Dock?**
    a. Point
    b. Click
    c. Double-click
    d. Right-click

19. **When you set your Mac to Sleep to end a Snow Leopard session, the operating system:**
    a. Completely shuts down the computer.
    b. Provides an option for switching users.
    c. Restarts your computer.
    d. Puts your Mac in a low power state so you can later resume use quickly.

20. **Which of the following options for ending your Snow Leopard session safely turns your Mac off?**
    a. Sleep
    b. Restart
    c. Shut Down
    d. Log Out

Skills Review

1. Start Mac OS X Snow Leopard.

   a. Turn on your computer, then enter your user name and password (if necessary).

   b. Identify the Finder menu bar, the Dock, and the Macintosh HD icon on the desktop without referring to the lessons.

   c. Compare your results to Figure B-2 to make sure that you have identified all the desktop items correctly.

2. Use a pointing device.

   a. Point to the Trash icon to display its Help Tag.

   b. Drag the Macintosh HD icon to a new location on the desktop.

   c. Double-click the Macintosh HD icon to open a Finder window.

   d. Close the Finder window.

   e. Drag the Macintosh HD icon back to its original location.

3. Start a program.

   a. By pointing and looking at the Help Tags, locate the Microsoft Excel icon on the Dock, then click it.

   b. When the Excel Workbook Gallery window opens, click the Choose button to open a blank workbook.

   c. In the Microsoft Excel window, click the down scroll arrow at the bottom of the scroll bar.

   d. Drag the vertical scroller slowly down the window to the bottom of the vertical scroll track.

   e. Click above the vertical scroller in the vertical scroll track to move the view of the window up.

4. Move and resize windows.

   a. Click the Zoom button to expand the Microsoft Excel window to full size. (*Hint*: The size of the window might not change dramatically.)

   b. Click the Minimize button to collapse the Microsoft Excel window to an icon on the Dock.

   c. Click the minimized Excel window on the Dock to restore it to the desktop.

   d. Drag the Excel window to the right on the desktop.

   e. Drag the Excel window back to its original position.

   f. Click and drag the size control in the lower-right corner to change the window width and height.

   g. Close the Excel window, but don't quit the program.

5. Use menus.

   a. Click Excel on the menu bar, then click Quit Excel.

   b. Click Finder on the menu bar, then click About Finder.

   c. Click Window on the menu bar, then view the options on the menu.

   d. Click away from the Window menu to close it.

   e. Close the About Finder window.

6. Use dialog boxes.

   a. Click the Apple icon on the menu bar, then click System Preferences.

   b. In the System Preferences window, click the Speech icon under the System category.

   c. Click the Text to Speech tab at the top of the Speech dialog box, if it is not already selected.

   d. Click the arrows next to System Voice, click the male or female voice of your choice, then click Play to hear the voice play. (*Hint*: You might need to press [F12] or use the volume option on the right side of the menu bar to turn up the speaker volume.)

   e. Click the Announce when alerts are displayed check box.

   f. Click Set Alert Options.

   g. Click Play to hear the announcement.

   h. Click OK.

   i. Click the Announce when alerts are displayed check box to deselect it.

   j. Close the Speech dialog box.

Skills Review (continued)

7. **Get Mac Help.**

   a. Click Help on the menu bar.

   b. In the Search box, type **dock**.

   c. In the list next to Help Topics, click **If you can't see the Dock**.

   d. In the Mac Help window, read the instructions in the box titled "To make the Dock reappear."

   e. Go to the Mac Help index.

   f. Click the letter D in the Mac Help index, scroll down, then click Dock.

   g. Read the Help topic about the Dock.

   h. Close the Mac Help window.

8. **End a Snow Leopard session.**

   a. If you are working in a computer lab, follow the instructions provided by your instructor for using the Apple menu to put the computer to sleep, restart the computer, shut down the computer completely, or log out of the computer. If you are working on your own Mac, use the Apple menu to choose the shutdown option you prefer.

Independent Challenge 1

You work as a teacher for ABC Computer Mentors. You need to prepare a set of handouts that provides an overview of some of the desktop features in Snow Leopard for individuals enrolled in an upcoming class on Mac Survival Skills.

   a. Click Help on the menu bar.

   b. Type **menu bar** in the Search box, then click The menu bar.

   c. Use the vertical scroll track to read the information presented, click one of the links under Related Topics at the end, then read that information as well.

   d. Prepare a handwritten list of five features that you learned about using menus and the menu bar. Use the following title for your list: **Interesting Information about Using Menus**.

   e. Close the Mac Help window, write your name on your list, and submit it to your instructor.

Independent Challenge 2

A friend of yours has just purchased an iMac to use at home. She recently read an article about the Preview program that comes with all new Macs and would like your help to find out more about this program.

   a. Click Help on the menu bar, then type **Preview** in the Search box.

   b. From the list of search results, open the About Preview topic and read the information presented.

   c. After reading the information in the About Preview topic, click the link to open the Preview program.

   d. On the Preview menu bar, click Help, then click Preview Help.

   e. Find out about Preview by clicking the links in the Preview Help window. Read the information provided.

   f. Prepare two or three handwritten paragraphs summarizing some of the information you found about this topic. Use the title **What is Preview?**.

   g. Close the Preview Help window, write your name on your summary, and submit it to your instructor.

Independent Challenge 3

The Dashboard is a feature of Mac OS X that displays information such as the weather, time, and date. As a marketing analyst for Expert AI Systems in Philadelphia, Pennsylvania, you contact and collaborate with employees at an Australian branch of the company. Because your colleagues live in a different time zone, you want to add another clock to the Dashboard and customize it to show the time in Sydney, Australia. This way, you can quickly determine when to reach these employees at a convenient time during their workday hours.

a. Use the Help menu to search for information on **Dashboard and widgets**.

b. Navigate Mac Help to learn how to change the city on the World Clock widget (use your city or the closest big city in your time zone).

c. Add a second World Clock to the Dashboard and set the time for Sydney, Australia.

Advanced Challenge Exercise

- Add a Unit Converter to the Dashboard.
- In the Unit Converter, change the Convert option to Temperature.
- Type **70** in the Fahrenheit box.

d. Search for a Help topic about removing Dashboard widgets, then remove all widgets that you added to the Dashboard in this exercise.

e. Close the Dashboard by clicking the Dashboard icon on the Dock or click away from a widget.

f. Close the Help window.

g. Prepare a handwritten summary titled **Using Widgets** that describes how you might use them in your daily life, write your name on your summary, then submit it to your instructor.

Real Life Independent Challenge

As a New Year's resolution, you have decided to automate more of your life and depend less on paper files. You've investigated the features of the Mac and found that your Mac has an Address Book program where you can store the contact information for family, friends, and business associates. This is a great step toward meeting your resolution, so you decide to use this program.

a. Using Help Tags, locate the Address Book icon on the Dock, then open it.

b. Click All Contacts on the left side of the Address Book window to select the All Contacts group.

c. Below the Name column in the Address Book window, click the Create a new card button. (*Hint*: The button has a plus sign on it.)

d. In the right pane, add your first and last name in the spaces provided and complete the Company, work Phone, and work Email entries with fictional information.

e. When you're finished entering information, click the Edit button at the bottom of the right pane to add your information to the Address Book.

f. Add fictitious contact information for four additional people.

Advanced Challenge Exercise

- Click the All Contacts group to select it.
- Click File on the menu bar, then click Print.
- In the Print dialog box, click the Expand button to the right of the Printer arrows to expand the dialog box, if necessary.
- Click the Style arrows, then click Lists.
- Click Print.
- Circle your name on the printed list and submit it to your instructor.

g. Close the Address Book window.

h. Click Address Book on the menu bar, then click Quit Address Book.

Visual Workshop

Now that you've been introduced to the Mac, you'd like to learn how to use the Grab program to take a picture of your screen. Use the skills you learned in this unit to print a screen shot like that shown in Figure B-22.

- Search Mac Help for information about Grab, then open the Help topic shown in Figure B-22.
- Click the Open Grab link within the Help topic to open the Grab program on the desktop (as shown in Figure B-22, the Grab menu bar appears but a Grab window does not).
- Following the instructions in the Help topic, click Capture on the Grab menu bar, then click Screen to capture a picture of the computer screen. Follow the instructions in the dialog box that opens. The screen shot will appear in a new window.
- Close the Mac Help window, click File on the Grab menu bar, click Print to open the Print dialog box, then click Print to print the screen shot. Write your name on the printed screen shot, and submit it to your instructor.
- Close the screen shot window, then quit Grab.

FIGURE B-22

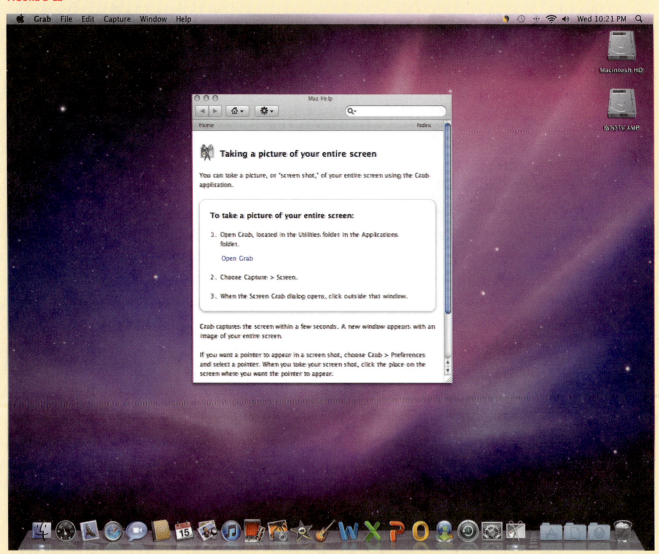

Getting Started with Mac OS X Snow Leopard

Understanding File Management

Files You Will Need:

No files needed

Finder is a program, which is part of the Snow Leopard operating system, that you use to access the folders and files in your various storage devices. Each **storage device**, or **drive**, is a physical location for storing files. Most people store their files on the computer's hard disk and keep duplicate copies on other storage devices, such as a USB flash drive or a CD. The **hard disk** is a built-in, high-capacity, high-speed storage device for all the software, folders, and files on a computer. When you work with a program, you save the results in a **file**, which consists of stored electronic data such as text, a picture, a video, or music. Files are stored in **folders**, which are containers that allow you to group files into categories such as reports, correspondence, or e-mail contacts.  Your supervisor and the manager of the Boston office of Quest Specialty Travel (QST), Evelyn Swazey, has asked you to become acquainted with Finder so you can manage the files you need for proposing, planning, organizing, and documenting QST tours.

OBJECTIVES

Understand file management

Open the Finder window

Change views

Create and save documents

Open, edit, and print files

Copy, rename, and move files

Search for files

Delete and restore files

Understanding File Management

Most of the work you do on a computer involves using programs to create files, which you then store in folders. Over time, you create many folders and files and save them on different storage devices. The process of finding your folders and files can become a challenge. **File management** is a strategy for organizing your files and folders so you can find your data quickly and easily. Finder is the primary tool you'll use for file management. ▨ As a QST tour manager for destinations in the South Pacific, you work with many types of files. You want to review how Finder can help you organize your files so you can find them when you need them.

DETAILS

You can use Finder to:

- **Create folders for storing and organizing files**

  Folders provide a location for your files and a way to organize them into groups of related files so that you can easily locate them later. Snow Leopard by default has a **home folder** for each user. This folder contains several subfolders in which you can save your files on the hard disk. The name of the user's home folder is the user's name. When you save or open files, most programs automatically open and use the **Documents folder**, a subfolder of your home folder. You can also create additional folders or subfolders. You give each folder you create a unique, descriptive **folder name** that identifies the files you intend to place in the folder. A folder can also contain other folders, called **subfolders**, to organize files into smaller groups. This structure for organizing folders and files is called a **file hierarchy** because it describes the logic and layout of the folder structure on a disk. Figure C-1 illustrates how you might organize your tour folders and files within the Documents folder. In addition to the Documents folder, the operating system also provides folders in your home folder that are dedicated to specific types of files, such as the Pictures folder for image files, the Music folder for music or sound files, and the Downloads folder for content that you download from the Internet. Figure C-2 shows the standard folders that Snow Leopard creates for each user in his or her home folder.

- **Rename, copy, and move folders and files**

  If you want to change the name of a folder or file, you can rename it. For example, you might change the name of the "Niue Tour Proposal" file to "Niue Tour" after your supervisor approves the tour. If you need a duplicate of a file, you can copy it. You can also move a folder or file to another folder or device.

- **Delete and restore folders and files**

  Deleting folders and files you no longer need frees up storage space on your devices and helps keep your files organized. Folders and files you delete are moved to the Trash. If you accidentally delete an important folder or file, or if you change your mind and want to restore a deleted folder or file, you can retrieve it from the Trash. If you're sure your Trash has nothing in it you might want to restore, you can empty it, which permanently removes the files or folders.

- **Locate folders and files quickly**

  Finder's search options help you quickly locate a folder or file if you forget where you stored it. For example, if you know the date you last used the file or the type of the file, use the Search For group in the sidebar in the Finder window to find the file. Or, if you can provide part of the folder or filename, or some text that appears in the file, use the Search field in the Finder window to easily locate it.

- **Use aliases to access frequently used files and folders**

  As your file structure becomes more complex, a file or folder might end up several levels down the file hierarchy and require multiple steps to open. To save time, you can create aliases on your desktop to the files and folders you use frequently. An **alias** is a link that gives you quick access to an item, whether it's a folder, file, or program. Each icon on the Dock is an alias for a program, folder, or file stored elsewhere on your computer.

FIGURE C-1: Sample folder and file hierarchy

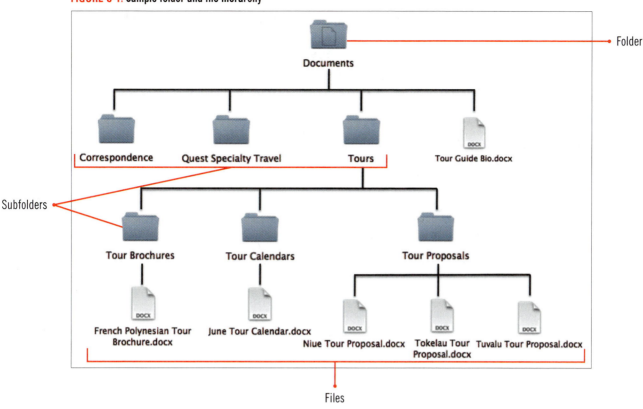

Folder

Subfolders

Files

FIGURE C-2: Default user folders

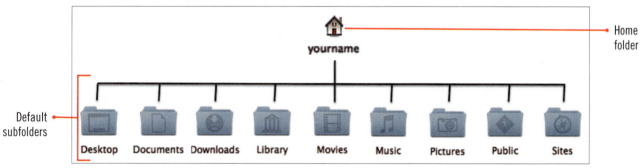

Home folder

Default subfolders

Organizing your folders and files efficiently

Good planning is essential for effective file management. First, identify the types of files you work with, such as images, music, reports, and so on, and then determine a logical system for organizing your files. The Pictures and Music folders are good places to store images and music. The Documents folder is the most common place to store all of your other files. Within each folder, use subfolders to organize the files into smaller groups. For example, use subfolders in the Pictures folder to separate family photos from vacation photos, or to group them by year. In the Documents folder, you might group personal files in one subfolder and business files in another subfolder, and then create additional subfolders to further distinguish sets of files. For example, your personal files might include subfolders for résumés, letters, and income tax returns, to name a few. Your business or school files might include subfolders for clients, projects, and invoices. You should periodically reevaluate your folder structure to ensure that it continues to meet your needs.

Opening the Finder Window

Finder is unique to the Mac and is the main tool you'll use to interact with your computer. Finder starts automatically when you start your computer. The Finder window is an interactive window that provides access to your storage devices, files, search options, and file management tools. The Finder window is accessible from the default menu bar at the top of the screen or from the Finder icon on the Dock.  You decide to become acquainted with the Finder window so you can quickly and easily locate the files you'll need for QST tours.

STEPS

1. **Click the Finder icon 🖥 on the Dock**

   The Finder window opens with the home folder selected and the home folder's contents displayed in the right pane. Refer to Figure C-3 to identify the following elements of the Finder window:

   - The **title bar** contains the name of the resource, such as a folder or a device, whose contents are displayed in the right pane of the Finder window.
   - The **toolbar** appears directly below the title bar and contains tools that aid with navigation, views, and file management. Table C-1 describes the tools on the Finder toolbar.
   - The light blue area that makes up the left pane of the Finder window is called the **sidebar**. The sidebar is a navigation tool that provides quick access to many frequently used resources on your Mac. When an item is selected in the sidebar, the item's contents are displayed in the right pane of the Finder window. The sidebar is divided into three or four groups:
     - The **Devices** group provides quick access to all of the storage devices available to your Mac, such as the hard disk and any external drives.
     - The **Shared** group is shown only if your Mac is connected to a network or to other computers. It lists all shared computers and servers to which the user has access.
     - The **Places** group provides quick access to the Desktop folder, your home folder, the Applications folder, and your Documents folder.
     - The **Search For** group helps you find a file quickly by viewing files you've used recently or by viewing only a certain type of file.
   - The **toolbar control** in the upper-right corner of the window hides the toolbar and sidebar when clicked. Once the toolbar and sidebar are hidden, click the toolbar control again to show them.
   - The **size control** at the lower-right corner of the window enables you to resize the Finder window.
   - The **status bar** lists the number of items in the selected folder or storage device. It also lists the available space on the selected storage device.

> **QUICK TIP**
>
> You can close or open a group in the sidebar by clicking the disclosure triangle next to it. When the triangle points to the right, the contents of the group are hidden; when the triangle points down, the contents appear below the group name.

TABLE C-1: Tools on the Finder toolbar

tool	used to
Back and Forward buttons	Display the previous or next location in the window
View buttons	Change the arrangement and view of the files and folders in the window
Quick Look button	Display the contents of a selected file as a large preview without opening the file
Action button	Perform file management commands such as creating a new folder, opening a file, or copying a file or folder
Search field	Search for files by filename or file content

FIGURE C-3: Finder window

View buttons

Back and Forward buttons

Home folder

Disclosure triangle

Title bar

Action button

Toolbar control

Search field

Quick Look button

Contents of the home folder appear in the right pane (your view of the contents might be different)

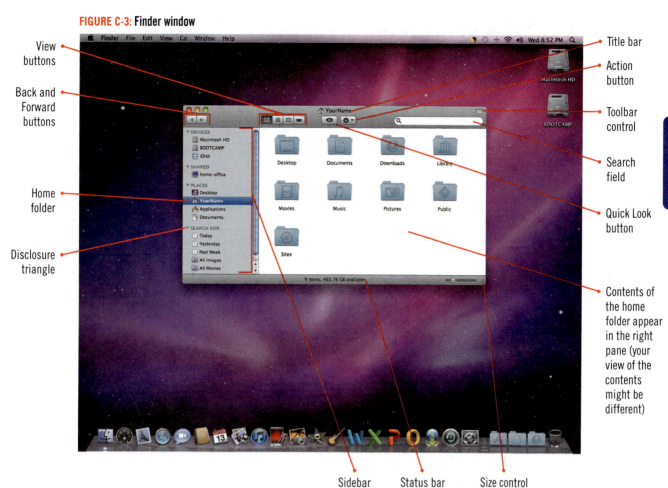

Sidebar   Status bar   Size control

Understanding the home folder and its contents

The user's home folder is the location designated by the operating system to store all of the files created by the user. By default, each time you click the Finder icon on the Dock, the Finder window opens with the home folder selected. Inside the home folder are the Documents folder and eight additional folders, each for different kinds of files. The Desktop folder contains all items on the user's desktop, except for external storage devices such as USB flash drives. The Downloads folder is the default location for all files downloaded from the Internet. The Library folder is the designated location for preferences files and user data and is maintained by Snow Leopard.

The Movies, Music, and Pictures folders are the designated locations for all movies, music, and picture files, respectively. These folders open by default when you perform actions involving movies, music, and pictures, such as when you import a video from a digital camera, download music from iTunes, or import digital photo files. The Public folder is the designated folder to place any files you'd like to share with other users of your Mac. The Sites folder is the location for your active Web pages. With the exception of the Public and Sites folder, all folders in the home folder are private and available only to the user.

Changing Views

Snow Leopard provides several ways of displaying your files and folders in the Finder window. Each display, or **view**, presents the items shown in the main area of the Finder window in a different way. The four main views, **icon view**, **list view**, **columns view**, and **Cover Flow**, can be selected using the View buttons in the Finder window or using the View option on the Finder menu bar. The fifth view, **Quick Look**, is accessible only from the Finder window. When you open the Finder window, the current view is the view that was selected when Finder was last used. You decide to look at the different views in Finder to determine the view that you would most like to use as you work.

STEPS

1. **In the Finder window, click the Icon View button ⊞ on the toolbar if necessary**

   The right pane displays the contents of your home folder as icons, as shown in Figure C-4.

2. **Click the List View button ☰ on the toolbar to switch to list view**

   As shown in Figure C-5, the right pane displays the contents of your home folder in an alphabetical list with additional details about each file and folder provided, such as Name, Date Modified, Size, and Kind. The Size column shows the sizes of files but does not list sizes for folders. The Kind column lists the file type or the program that created the file.

3. **Click the Columns View button ▥ on the toolbar to switch to columns view**

   The right pane displays the contents of your home folder in a multicolumn format.

4. **In the right pane of the Finder window, click the Pictures folder in the first column**

   The contents of the Pictures folder are displayed in the column to the right.

> **TROUBLE**
>
> If you don't have an iChat icons sub-folder in your Pictures folder, click the Library folder in the first column of the right pane, then scroll down in the second column and click the Safari sub-folder. In Steps 6 and 7, use the Safari subfolder and the History.plist file in place of the Planets subfolder and Jupiter.gif file.

5. **In the second column, click the iChat icons subfolder, then click the Planets subfolder in the third column**

   The Planets subfolder contains the planet figure files available for use as icons in the iChat program that comes with Snow Leopard. Compare your computer screen to Figure C-6.

6. **With the Planets subfolder selected, click the Cover Flow button ▭ on the toolbar**

   The right pane of the Finder window is divided in two. In the top section of the pane, a preview of the first file in the Planets subfolder appears with a horizontal scroll track beneath it. The bottom section of the right pane displays the selected subfolder's contents as a detailed list. Compare your screen with Figure C-7.

> **TROUBLE**
>
> If the Quick Look button is not displayed, press [control] and click the toolbar, then click Customize Toolbar. Drag the Quick Look icon 👁 to the toolbar, then click Done.

7. **Scroll down if necessary and click the Jupiter.gif file in the bottom section of the right pane, then click the Quick Look button 👁 on the toolbar**

   When you initially click the file in the bottom section of the pane, a preview of the file appears in the top section of the pane. When you click the Quick Look button, a larger preview of the file is displayed in front of the Finder window, as shown in Figure C-8. Quick Look is a feature of the Snow Leopard operating system that allows you to preview the contents of a file without actually opening it. You can click the Full Screen button at the bottom of the Quick Look window to enlarge the Quick Look preview to full-screen size.

> **QUICK TIP**
>
> You can also activate Quick Look by selecting a file, then pressing [spacebar], or by clicking File on the menu bar, then clicking Quick Look "[filename]".

8. **Close Quick Look, then click ▥ on the toolbar**

   The Finder window changes to columns view again. A preview of the selected Jupiter.gif file appears in the furthest right column.

9. **Close the Finder window**

FIGURE C-4: Icon view

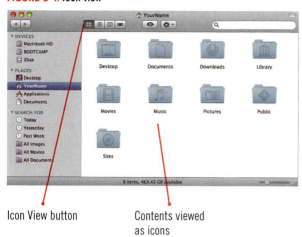

Icon View button

Contents viewed
as icons

FIGURE C-5: List view

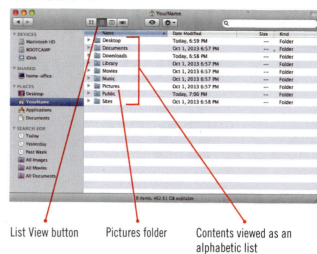

List View button

Pictures folder

Contents viewed as an
alphabetic list

FIGURE C-6: Planets subfolder selected in columns view

Columns View
button

iChat icons
subfolder

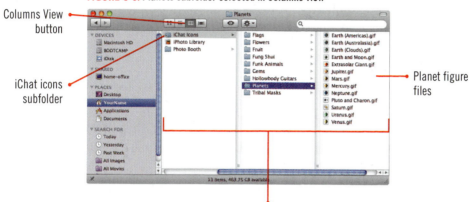

Planet figure
files

Contents viewed in a multicolumn format

FIGURE C-7: Cover Flow

Cover Flow
button

Detailed list of
contents

Preview

FIGURE C-8: Quick Look

Close Quick
Look button

Full Screen
button

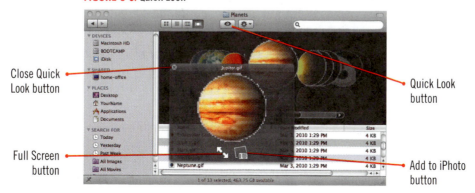

Quick Look
button

Add to iPhoto
button

Understanding File Management

Creating and Saving Documents

Any file you create with a program is temporarily stored in **RAM (random access memory)**, your computer's main memory. Anything stored in RAM is lost when you turn off your computer or if the power fails unexpectedly. Therefore, before you close a file or exit a program, you must create a permanent copy of the file by saving it on a disk or device. You can save files in the Documents folder in your home folder, on your hard disk, or on a removable storage device such as a USB flash drive. When you save a file, choose a **filename** that clearly identifies the file contents. Filenames can be no more than 255 characters, including spaces, and can include letters, numbers, and certain symbols.  You want to use Microsoft Word to create a document for your next tour, and you plan to save the file to the Documents folder.

STEPS

TROUBLE
If Word Document is not an option in the Word Document Gallery, click All in the navigation pane.

1. **Click the Microsoft Word icon**  **on the Dock**

   Microsoft Word 2011 opens with the Word Document Gallery window and Word Document selected, as shown in Figure C-9.

2. **Click Choose**

   A new, blank document window appears on the desktop. In the document window, a blinking cursor identifies the insertion point, which is where any text you type will appear.

QUICK TIP
If you make a typing mistake, press [delete] on the keyboard to delete the character to the left of the insertion point.

3. **Type Meeting Notes, October 11 on the first line, then press [return] twice**

   Each time you press [return], Word inserts a new blank line and places the insertion point at the beginning of the line.

4. **Type The 2013 tour will visit:, press [return], type Australia, press [return], type Micronesia, press [return], type New Zealand, press [return] twice, then type your name; see Figure C-10**

5. **Click File on the menu bar, then click Save As**

   The Save As dialog box opens with the Documents folder selected as the Where location in which to save the file, as shown in Figure C-11. By default, Word 2011 creates a temporary filename of Meeting Notes in the Save As text box, with the phrase Meeting Notes highlighted in blue. You'll need to type a more descriptive filename.

6. **In the Save As text box, replace Meetings Notes with Oceania Meeting, then click the Expand button to the right of the Save As text box if necessary**

   The Save As dialog box expands to show the contents of the Documents folder, as shown in Figure C-12.

TROUBLE
If a Confirm Save As dialog box asks if you want to replace a file with the same name, click Yes.

7. **Click Save in the Save As dialog box**

   Word saves the document in a file named "Oceania Meeting" in the Documents folder and closes the Save As dialog box. The title bar of the Word window now displays "Oceania Meeting.docx"—the filename you entered, followed by the file extension .docx. A **file extension** identifies the type of file. Each program assigns a file extension to files you create, so you only need to enter a name for the file. Depending on how Snow Leopard is set up on your computer, you might not see the file extensions.

8. **Click Word on the menu bar, then click Quit Word**

   The Word file and program close.

FIGURE C-9: Word Document Gallery

Word icon on Dock

FIGURE C-10: Word 2011 document

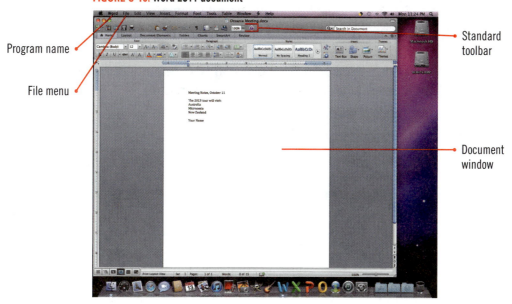

Program name

File menu

Standard toolbar

Document window

FIGURE C-11: Save As dialog box

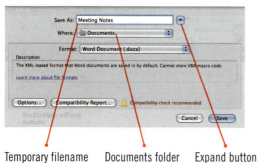

Temporary filename   Documents folder   Expand button

FIGURE C-12: Expanded Save As dialog box

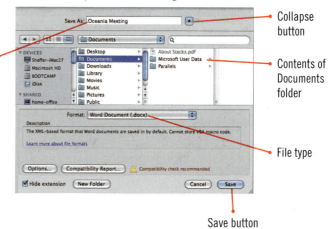

New filename

Collapse button

Contents of Documents folder

File type

Save button

Understanding File Management

Opening, Editing, and Printing Files

You create many new files as you work, but often you want to change a file that you or someone else already created. After you open an existing file stored on a disk, you can **edit**, or make changes, to it. For example, you might want to add or delete text, or change the **formatting** (the appearance) of the text. After you finish editing, you usually save the file with the same filename, which replaces the file with the copy that contains your changes. If you want to keep the original file, you can save the edited file with a different filename; this keeps the original file without the edits and creates a new file with the most recent changes. When you want a **hard copy**, or paper copy, of the file, you need to print it. You need to add two items to your Oceania Meeting document, so you want to open and edit it, and then print it.

STEPS

1. **Click the Finder icon 🖼 on the Dock**

   The Finder window opens with the contents of the home folder displayed in columns view.

2. **Click the Documents folder in the first column of the right pane of the Finder window**

   A second column in the right pane displays the contents of the Documents folder, as shown in Figure C-13.

QUICK TIP
You can also open the file by selecting the file, clicking File on the menu bar, then clicking Open; by right-clicking the file and then clicking Open; or by dragging the file on top of the icon on the Dock for the program that was used to create it, then releasing the button.

3. **Double-click Oceania Meeting in the second column**

   The program that created the file, Word, loads and opens the selected file, Oceania Meeting, in the Word window.

4. **Click at the beginning of the line following New Zealand in the document, then type Evelyn Swazey closed the meeting!, then press [return]**

   The edited document includes the text you just typed. See Figure C-14.

5. **Click the Save button 💾 on the Standard toolbar**

   The original Oceania Meeting.docx file is replaced by the edited Oceania Meeting.docx file in the Documents folder.

6. **Click the Print button 🖨 on the Standard toolbar, then retrieve your printed copy from the printer**

   Using the **Print button** on the Standard toolbar is a quick, easy way to print your entire document.

FIGURE C-13: Documents folder in Finder window

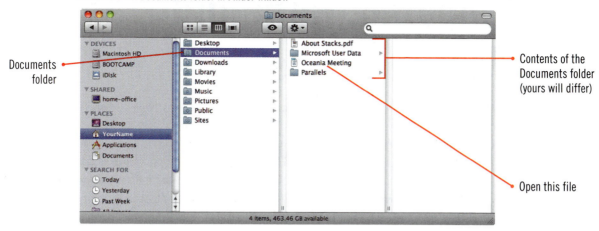

Documents folder

Contents of the Documents folder (yours will differ)

Open this file

FIGURE C-14: Edited Oceania Meeting file

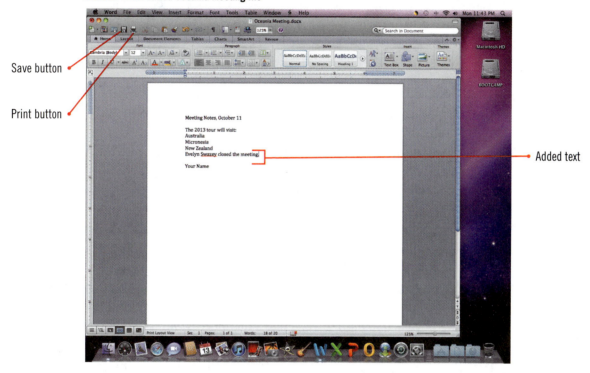

Save button

Print button

Added text

Previewing a document

To save ink and paper, it's a good idea to preview a document before printing. This will help you catch errors in form and content before printing. Word 2011 no longer offers a Print Preview option, but allows you to see a Quick Preview, or small version of the document, from the Print dialog box. To open the Print dialog box, click File on the menu bar, then click Print. The Print dialog box is shown in Figure C-15. To see a larger version of the document as a preview, click the Preview button. This button opens the Preview application and allows you to see what the entire document will look like before printing. To return to Word, click Preview on the menu bar, then click Quit Preview.

FIGURE C-15: Print dialog box

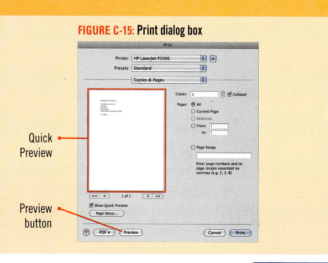

Quick Preview

Preview button

Copying, Renaming, and Moving Files

Periodically, you might need to copy, rename, or move a file to keep your files organized and easy to find. You can copy or move a file, a group of files, or a folder from one storage device to another or from one folder to another. When you **copy** a file, the original file stays in its current location and a duplicate of the file is created in another location. This feature lets you make a backup of your important files. A **backup** is a copy of a file that is stored in another location. If you lose the original file, you can make a new working copy from your backup. When you **move** a file, the original file is stored in a different location and no longer remains in the original location. One of the fastest ways to move a file is with **drag and drop**, in which you use your pointing device to drag a file or folder to a new location. You might also need to rename a file, giving it a name that more clearly describes the file's contents and how you intend to use the file. 🎨 So that you can work with your Oceania Meeting.docx file when you travel, you want to copy the file to a new folder on your USB flash drive and then rename it. You also want to move the original file to the desktop so you can easily access it to update the list for your next tour.

STEPS

1. **Attach your USB flash drive to your computer and wait for its icon to appear on the desktop**

   When the icon for your USB flash drive appears on the desktop and is listed under Devices in the Finder window, it is ready to use.

2. **In the Finder window, click the USB flash drive under Devices, click the Action button ⚙▾ on the toolbar, then click New Folder**

   A new folder, temporarily named "untitled folder", is added to your USB flash drive, as shown in Figure C-16. The folder name is highlighted so you can type a more descriptive name.

3. **Type Meeting Notes as the name of the new folder, then press [return]**

   The name of the folder changes and the folder is selected in the Finder window. Because the folder is empty, there are no contents to display in the next column.

4. **Click Documents in the sidebar, click and drag the Oceania Meeting.docx file from the Documents folder on top of the USB flash drive until a rounded rectangle appears around the name of your USB flash drive, a plus sign appears with the pointer, and the contents of the drive appear in the right pane of the Finder window (do not release the button)**

5. **Drag the file on top of the Meeting Notes folder in the right pane of the Finder window until the folder is highlighted blue, then release the button**

   As shown in Figure C-17, the Oceania Meeting.docx file has been copied to the Meeting Notes folder on your USB flash drive. This method of copying files is called drag and drop. The **spring-loaded folders** feature of Snow Leopard, in which dragging the file on top of a folder causes the folder to "spring" open and display its contents in the Finder window, enables you to drag and drop files without having to open additional Finder windows. There are now two copies of the Oceania Meeting.docx file stored in two different locations.

6. **Click the Oceania Meeting.docx file in the second column, then press [return]**

   If your computer is set up to show file extensions, the first part of the filename is highlighted and can be edited. If not, the entire filename will be highlighted.

7. **Type Tour Preparation, then press [return]**

   The name of the file on your USB drive changes to Tour Preparation.docx.

8. **Click Documents in the sidebar, then click and drag the original Oceania Meeting.docx file to the desktop**

   The file moves from the Documents folder to the desktop, as shown in Figure C-18.

FIGURE C-16: Creating a new folder

New folder

USB flash drive

Action button

FIGURE C-17: File copied with drag and drop

Copied file

Drag Oceania
Meeting file
here in Step 4

Drag Oceania
Meeting file
here in Step 5

FIGURE C-18: File moved with drag and drop

Original file moved
to desktop from
Documents folder

Using drag and drop to copy and move files

If you drag and drop a file to a folder on the same storage device, the file is moved into that folder. However, if you drag and drop a file to a folder on another device, the file is copied instead. If you want to move a file to another device, press and hold down ⌘ while you drag and drop. If you want to copy a file to another folder on the same drive, press and hold down [option] while you drag and drop.

Understanding File Management

Searching for Files

After creating, saving, and renaming folders and files, you might forget where you stored a particular folder or file, forget its name, or both. Your Mac has several tools that can aid you in your search for a file. The sidebar in the Finder window contains the Search For group, which gives you quick access to predefined subsets of files on your computer organized by date saved or by file type. In addition, the **Search field** of your Finder window can help you find a file by name or content. Table C-2 lists the available search options that come with the Snow Leopard operating system. You want to quickly locate the copy of the Oceania Meeting for your next tour.

STEPS

TROUBLE
Your search results might appear as a different view in the Finder window.

1. **In the Search field in the upper-right corner of the Finder window, type Oceania**

   As soon as you start typing, the operating system goes to work. Searches are not case sensitive, so you can use uppercase or lowercase letters when you type search criteria. When you finish typing your entry, the search results are listed in the right pane of the Finder window, as shown in Figure C-19. Your search results will differ; however, all of the search results will have the characters "Oceania" somewhere either in the name of the item or in the file's contents. By default, the results are listed in order of the date each file was Last Opened, but can easily be sorted by Name or Kind by clicking the appropriate column heading in list view.

2. **In the right pane, double-click Oceania Meeting.docx**

   The Oceania Meeting.docx file opens in Microsoft Word.

3. **Click Word on the menu bar, then click Quit Word**

4. **Under Search For in the sidebar, click Today**

   Using any option in the Search For group narrows the search based on predefined criteria. Today lists all files and programs opened or saved today. Yesterday lists all files and programs opened or saved yesterday. Past Week lists all files and programs opened or saved within the last week. All Images lists only image files; All Movies lists only video and movie files; All Documents lists all other file types on your computer.

TABLE C-2: Search options available with Snow Leopard

search option	location	description
Search For group	Finder sidebar	Performs searches with predefined criteria
Search field	Finder toolbar	Performs searches based on filename and content
Spotlight search field	Accessible by clicking the magnifying glass icon on right side of the menu (available in all programs)	Performs searches on your entire computer and displays the results in several categories such as Top Hit, Definition, Documents, and Folders bar
Find command	Finder File menu	Performs the same search operation as Finder's Search field

FIGURE C-19: Search results

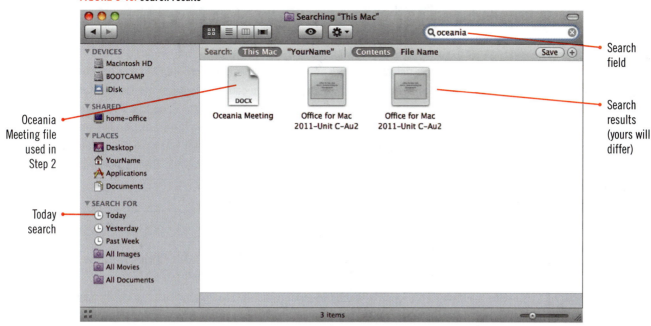

Search field

Search results (yours will differ)

Oceania Meeting file used in Step 2

Today search

Mac OS X

Working with stacks

By default, the Documents, Downloads, and Applications folders appear both in the Finder window and on the Dock (to the right of the dashed line and next to the Trash). When you click a folder on the Dock, it doesn't open in a separate window; instead, the folder springs open in an arc or grid to reveal its contents, as shown in Figure C-20. This method of displaying the contents of the folder is called a **stack**. Once a stack is open, you can click an item in the stack, such as a file or folder, to open it.

FIGURE C-20: Documents folder displayed as a stack

Deleting and Restoring Files

If you no longer need a folder or file, you can delete (or remove) it from your computer. If you delete a folder, its contents are also deleted. The operating system places folders and files you delete in the Trash. If you later discover that you need a deleted file or folder, you can drag it out of the Trash as long as you have not yet emptied the Trash. Emptying the Trash removes the deleted folders and files from your computer. By deleting files and folders you no longer need and periodically emptying the Trash, you free up valuable storage space on your devices and keep your computer uncluttered. ▨▩ You have the updated copy of the Tour Preparation.docx file stored on your USB flash drive, so you want to delete the Oceania Meeting.docx from the desktop.

STEPS

1. **Click Desktop in the sidebar in the Finder window**

QUICK TIP
You can also right-click a file or folder, then click Move to Trash to delete the file or folder.

2. **Drag the Oceania Meeting file from the Desktop folder in the Finder window to the Trash icon on the Dock**

   The Oceania Meeting file is deleted from the desktop and the Desktop folder, as shown in Figure C-21. If your Trash icon on the Dock appeared empty before this step, it will now appear to contain crumpled paper. This indicates that it contains deleted files or folders.

3. **Click the Trash icon on the Dock**

   A new Finder window opens displaying the contents of the Trash, as shown in Figure C-22. Your Trash's contents might differ.

QUICK TIP
You can also delete a folder by moving it to the Trash. Keep in mind that all files in the folder are also moved to the Trash.

4. **Click and drag the Oceania Meeting file from the right pane to Documents in the sidebar until a rounded rectangle appears around Documents, then release the button**

   When you release the button, the file is **restored**, or moved from the Trash to a new location on your computer (in this case, the Documents folder).

5. **Click Documents in the sidebar if necessary, then drag the Oceania Meeting file from the Documents folder to the Trash icon on the Dock**

QUICK TIP
You can also empty the trash by clicking the Empty button in the upper-right area of the Trash Finder window, or by right-clicking the Trash icon, then clicking Empty Trash.

6. **Click Finder on the menu bar, click Empty Trash, then click Empty Trash in the dialog box that appears**

   The trash is emptied, and the Trash icon on the Dock no longer has crumpled paper in it.

7. **Close all open Finder windows**

FIGURE C-21: Empty Desktop folder

Desktop folder is empty

Icon is removed from the desktop

Trash icon contains crumpled paper

FIGURE C-22: Trash contents in Finder window

Empty button

Contents of the Trash (yours might differ)

Emptying the Trash

When you empty the Trash, the operating system marks the physical location of the files and folders in the Trash for reuse. Disk reading utilities can recover these files until the space has been reused. If you want to delete files that contain sensitive information and prevent them from being recovered, click Finder on the menu bar, then click Secure Empty Trash. Secure Empty Trash overwrites the space previously occupied by the deleted files and folders.

Practice

Concepts Review

Label each of the elements of the Finder window shown in Figure C-23.

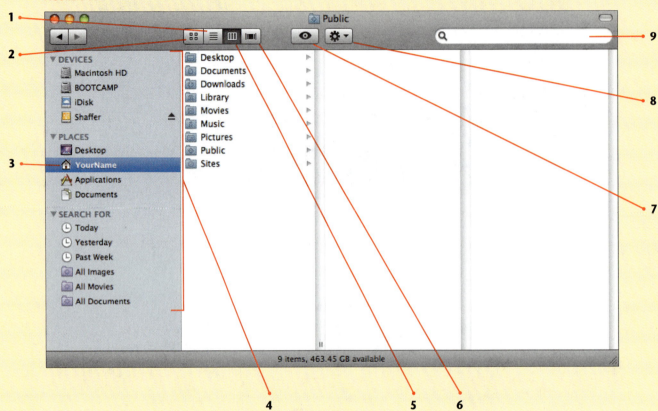

Match each statement with the term it best describes.

10. file management
11. filename
12. folder
13. storage device
14. alias

a. A container for related files
b. A link that provides quick access to a folder, file, or program
c. A physical location for storing files and folders
d. Organizing and managing folders and files
e. The name that you assign to a file to identify its contents

Select the best answer from the list of choices.

15. The _____ is a built-in, high-capacity, high-speed storage medium for all the software, folders, and files on a computer.
    a. Hard disk
    b. Home folder
    c. Sidebar
    d. USB flash drive

16. A _____ is a unit of stored, electronic data.
    a. Device
    b. File
    c. Folder
    d. Search

17. _____ is a strategy for organizing your files and folders.
    a. The desktop
    b. The hard disk
    c. File hierarchy
    d. File management

18. _____ view displays the contents of the current folder as an alphabetical list with additional details about each file and folder provided.
    a. Icon
    b. List
    c. Columns
    d. Cover Flow

19. _____ view allows you to preview the contents of files within a folder and to see the folder's contents as a list.
    a. Icon
    b. List
    c. Columns
    d. Cover Flow

20. After you copy a file, you have:
    a. Only one copy of the file.
    b. A duplicate copy of the file in a different location.
    c. Moved the original file to a new location.
    d. Deleted the file.

21. When you delete a file from your hard disk, the operating system:
    a. Puts the deleted file in the Trash.
    b. Permanently deletes the file from the hard disk drive.
    c. Stores a duplicate copy of the file in the Trash.
    d. Moves the file to a removable disk.

Skills Review

1. **Understand file management.**
   a. Assume you manage a small travel agency. How would you organize your business files using a hierarchical file structure?
   b. What aliases would you place on your desktop for easier access to your business files?

2. **Open the Finder window.**
   a. List and describe the functions of as many components of the Finder window as you can without referring to the lessons.
   b. Compare your results with Figure C-3 to make sure that you have identified all the elements.

3. **Change views.**
   a. Double-click the Macintosh HD icon on the desktop to open its contents in a Finder window.
   b. If necessary, change the view to icon view.
   c. Change the view to list view.
   d. Change the view to columns view.
   e. Click the Applications folder in the first column of the right pane to view its contents in the next column.
   f. Scroll down, locate the Utilities folder, then click the Utilities folder to view its contents in the next column.
   g. Change the view of the Utilities folder to Cover Flow to preview the icon images that represent the utilities.
   h. Scroll through the bottom section of the right pane until you find Disk Utility, click Disk Utility, then view Disk Utility in the Quick Look window.
   i. Close the Quick Look window.
   j. Change the view to columns view.

Skills Review (continued)

4. Create and save documents.

  a. Open Microsoft Word using the icon on the Dock.

  b. Open a blank document.

  c. Type **Oceania Tours** on the first line of the document, followed by one blank line.

  d. Type your name, followed by two blank lines.

  e. Use Word to create the following list of current Oceania tours. (*Hint*: After you type the first numbered line, the rest of the lines will be automatically numbered.)

    Current Tours:

    1. French Polynesia

    2. Fiji Islands

    3. Pitcairn Islands

    4. Tonga

    5. Niue

    6. Tokelau

  f. Save the Word file with the filename **Oceania Tours** in the Documents folder. (If you are prompted, "Oceania Tours already exists. Do you want to replace it?", click Replace.)

  g. View the filename in the Word title bar, click Word, and then click Quit Word.

5. Open, edit, and print files.

  a. Use the Finder window to open the file named Oceania Tours from the Documents folder.

  b. Click at the end of the line containing the last current tour (Tokelau), press [return], then add the names of two more tours on two separate lines: **7. Palau** and **8. Tuvalu**.

  c. Click File on the menu bar, then click Save to save the edited Word file.

  d. Click File, then click Print to display the Print dialog box and a Quick Preview of the document.

  e. Print the Oceania Tours document, then quit Word.

6. Copy, rename, and move files.

  a. Attach your USB flash drive to your computer.

  b. When your USB flash drive has been recognized by your Mac, open the drive and create a folder on it with the name **Oceania Tours**.

  c. Copy the Oceania Tours file from your Documents folder to the Oceania Tours folder on your USB flash drive.

  d. Rename the Oceania Tours file on your USB drive to be **Current Oceania Tours**.

  e. Move the original Oceania Tours.docx file from your Documents folder to the Desktop folder.

7. Search for files.

  a. In the Finder window Search field, type **Oceania**.

  b. Examine the search results, then open the original Oceania Tours file.

  c. Quit Word.

  d. Using the Search For group on the sidebar, click Past Week to list all the programs and files open and saved within the last week.

8. Delete and restore files.

  a. Click and drag the original Word file with the name Oceania Tours from the desktop (or the Desktop folder in the Finder window) to the Trash.

  b. Open the Trash to view its contents.

  c. Drag the file named Oceania Tours to the Documents folder.

  d. Select the Oceania Tours file in the Documents folder, move it to the Trash again, then close all open Finder windows.

  e. Empty the Trash.

  f. Submit the printed copy of your revised Word document and your answers to Step 1 to your instructor.

Independent Challenge 1

To meet the needs of pet owners in your town, you have opened a pet-sitting business named PetCare. Customers hire you to care for their pets in their own homes when the pet owners go on vacation. To promote your new business, you want to develop a newspaper ad and a flyer.

a. Connect your USB flash drive to your computer, if necessary.

b. Create a new folder named **PetCare** on your USB flash drive.

c. In the PetCare folder, create two subfolders named **Advertising** and **Flyers**.

d. Use Word to create a short ad for your local newspaper that describes your business:

- Use the name of the business as the title for your document.
- Write a short paragraph about the business. Include a fictitious location, street address, and phone number.
- After the paragraph, type your name.

e. Save the Word document with the filename **Newspaper Ad** in the Advertising folder.

f. Use Quick Preview in the Print dialog box to preview your document, print your Word document, submit the document to your instructor, then quit Word.

Independent Challenge 2

As a freelance editor for several national publishers, you depend on your computer to meet critical deadlines. Whenever you encounter a computer problem, you contact a computer consultant who helps you resolve the problem. This consultant asked you to document, or keep records of, your computer's current settings.

a. Connect your USB flash drive to your computer, if necessary.

b. Open a Finder window so that you can view information on your drives and other installed hardware.

c. View the Finder window in the different views, then choose the one you prefer.

d. Open Word and create a document with the title **My Hardware Documentation** and your name on separate lines.

e. List the names of the devices connected to your computer.

f. List the folders and files in your Documents folder (if there are more than five, list only the first five).

g. List the folders and files on your desktop (if there are more than five, list only the first five).

Advanced Challenge Exercise

- Navigate your computer's file hierarchy, and determine its various levels.
- On paper, draw a diagram showing your file hierarchy, starting with your home folder at the top, and going down at least two levels if available.

h. Save the Word document with the filename **My Hardware Documentation** on your USB flash drive.

i. Preview your document, submit the document to your instructor, then quit Word.

Independent Challenge 3

You are an attorney at Lopez, Rickland, and Willgor, a large law firm. You participate in your firm's community outreach program by speaking at career days at area high schools. You teach students about career opportunities available in the field of law. You want to create a folder structure on your USB flash drive to store the files for each session.

a. Connect your USB flash drive to your computer, then open the drive in Finder.

b. Create a folder named **Career Days**.

c. In the Career Days folder, create a subfolder named **Mather High**.

Advanced Challenge Exercise

- In the Mather High folder, create subfolders named **Class Outline** and **Visual Aids**.
- Rename the Visual Aids folder to **Class Handouts**.
- Create a new folder named **Interactive Presentations** in the Class Handouts subfolder.

d. Close the Finder window.

e. Use Word to create a document with the title **Career Areas** and your name on separate lines, and the following list of items:

Career Opportunities:

Attorney

Corrections Officer

Forensic Scientist

Paralegal

Judge

f. Save the Word document with the filename **Careers Listing** in the Mather High folder. (*Hint*: After you switch to your USB flash drive in the Save As dialog box, open the Career Days folder, then select the Mather High folder before saving the file.)

g. Quit Word.

h. Using pencil and paper, draw a diagram of your new folder structure.

i. Open a Finder window and type **car** in the Search field. Locate the Careers Listing document in the list, and open the file.

j. Add **Court Reporter** to the bottom of the list, then save the file, submit the document to your instructor, then quit Word.

Real Life Independent Challenge

Think of a hobby or volunteer activity that you do now, or one that you would like to do. You will use your Mac to help you manage your plans or ideas for this activity.

a. Using paper and a pencil, sketch a folder structure using at least two subfolders that you could create on your USB flash drive to contain your documents for this activity.

b. Connect your USB flash drive to your computer, then open your USB flash drive.

c. Create the folder structure for your activity, using your sketch as a reference.

d. Think of at least three tasks that you can do to further your work in your chosen activity.

e. Open Word and create a document with the title **Next Steps** at the top of the page and your name on the next line.

f. List the three tasks, then save the file in one of the folders you created on your USB flash drive, using the filename **To Do**.

g. Quit Word, then open a Finder window and locate the folder where you stored the document.

h. Create a copy of the file, give the copy a new name, then place a copy of the document in the Documents folder.

i. Delete the copy from the Documents folder.

j. Open the Trash, and drag the document to the Documents folder.

k. Submit the document to your instructor.

Visual Workshop

You are a technical support specialist at Emergency Services. The company supplies medical staff members to hospital emergency rooms in Los Angeles. You need to respond to your company's employee questions quickly and thoroughly. You decide that it is time to evaluate and reorganize the folder structure on your Mac. That way, you'll be able to respond more quickly to staff requests. Create the folder structure shown in Figure C-24 on your USB flash drive. As you work, use Word to prepare a simple outline of the steps you followed to create the folder structure. Add your name to the document and store it in an appropriate location.

FIGURE C-24

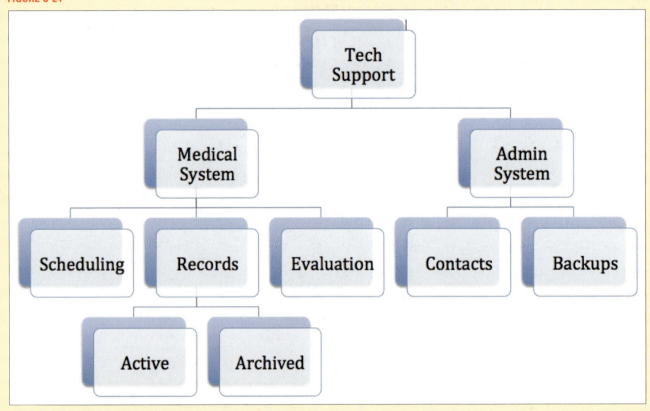

Understanding File Management

Getting Started with Safari

Files You Will Need:

No files needed

In this unit, you learn how to use the Safari browser to find information on the World Wide Web (WWW or the Web). You learn how to navigate from one Web page to another and how to search for information on the Web. You also learn how to print Web pages and how to get helpful information about using Safari. You need to connect to the Internet to complete this unit. At Quest Specialty Travel (QST), the tour managers use the Internet extensively to research information for future tours. Your supervisor, Evelyn Swazey, has asked you to become familiar with the Safari browser to be able to search the Internet more confidently with your Mac.

OBJECTIVES

Understand Web browsers

Start and explore Safari

View and navigate Web pages

Use tabbed browsing

Bookmark Web pages

Print a Web page

Search for information

Get Help and quit Safari

Understanding Web Browsers

The **World Wide Web** (also called the **Web** or **WWW**) is the part of the Internet that contains linked Web pages. **Web pages** are documents that can contain text, graphics, sound, and video. **Web browsers** (also called **browsers**) are software programs used to access and display Web pages. You must have a computing device, an Internet connection, and a browser to view Web pages. Browsers such as Safari, Microsoft Internet Explorer, Opera, and Firefox make navigating the Web easy. When you view Web pages with a browser, you click words, phrases, or graphics called **hyperlinks**, or simply **links**, to connect to and view other Web pages. Links can also open graphics files or play sound or video files. This unit features **Safari**, a popular browser from Apple. Figure D-1 shows how the Safari browser displays a Web page from the U.S. government's White House Web site.  Your supervisor has asked you to familiarize yourself with the capabilities of the Safari browser window.

Using Safari, you can:

*   **Display Web pages**

    You can access Web sites from all over the world with a Web browser. A **Web site** is a group of Web pages focused on a particular subject. Web sites exist for individuals, businesses, museums, governments, charitable organizations, and educational institutions. There are Web sites for the arts, music, politics, education, sports, and commerce—for any topic, interest, or endeavor in the world. The QST tour managers use the Web to research information for future tours.

*   **Use links to move from one Web page to another**

    You can click the hyperlinks on a Web page to get more information about a business, city, or organization. For example, if you'd like to tour a museum, you can visit the museum's Web site and click links to Web pages that describe current exhibits, visiting hours, or special tours.

*   **Play audio and video clips**

    A Web browser can play audio and video clips if it has been configured to do so and if your computer has the appropriate hardware, such as speakers. In their research, tour managers might find Web pages that include video clips of historic buildings, shopping trips, local stories and customs, or other information about a region.

*   **Search the Web for information**

    A **search engine** is a special Web site that quickly searches the Internet for Web sites based on keywords or phrases that you enter. Tour managers can take advantage of search engines to look for Web sites that focus on a country, government, or region of travel or on a specific topic of interest.

*   **Bookmark Web pages**

    You can bookmark Web pages that you might need to visit again, such as a page for a specific museum, city, or map. Safari makes it easy to bookmark your favorite Web sites so they are easily accessible when you want to view them later. Tour managers can save pages for historic sites or museums for each city when planning a tour.

*   **Print or save the text and graphics on Web pages**

    If you want to keep a hard copy of the information or images you find on the Web, you can simply print the Web page, including any graphics. You can also save the text or graphics on a Web page or copy the information temporarily to the operating system **Clipboard**, where it is available for pasting into other programs. Tour managers can print maps or informational paragraphs from the Web as they plan each tour.

*   **E-mail Web pages**

    If you want to share a Web page with a colleague, you can e-mail a link to the page or e-mail the page itself directly from the browser window. The person receives the page or the link as part of an e-mail message.

FIGURE D-1: A sample Web page

Understanding the Internet, computer networks, and intranets

A **computer network** is the hardware and software that makes it possible for two or more computers to share information and resources. An **intranet** is a private computer network with restricted access, such as computers in a company's office. Users can connect to intranets from remote locations to share company information and resources. The **Internet** is a network of connected computers and computer networks located around the world. The Internet is an international community; Web pages exist from nearly every country in the world. There are over a billion users worldwide currently connected to the Internet through telephone lines, cables, satellites, and other telecommunications media. Through the Internet, users can share many types of information, including text, graphics, sound, video, and computer programs. Anyone who has access to a computer and a connection to the Internet through a computer network or modem can use this rich information source.

The Internet has its roots in the U.S. Department of Defense Advanced Research Projects Agency Network (ARPANET), which

began in 1969. In 1986, the National Science Foundation formed NSFNET, which replaced ARPANET. NSFNET expanded the foundation of the U.S. portion of the Internet with high-speed, long-distance lines. In 1992, the U.S. Congress further expanded the Internet's capacity and speed, and they opened it to commercial use. The World Wide Web was created in Switzerland in 1991 to allow links between documents on the Internet. The first graphical Web browser, Mosaic, was introduced at the University of Illinois in 1993, leading to the development of browsers such as Netscape Navigator and Internet Explorer. With the boom in the personal computer industry and the expanding availability of inexpensive desktop machines and powerful, network-ready servers, many companies were able to join the Internet for the first time in the early 1990s. The Web is now an integral component of corporate culture, educational institutions, and individuals' personal lives. The Web is used daily for commerce, education, and entertainment by billions of people around the world.

Starting and Exploring Safari

To use the Internet, you need a computing device, an Internet connection, and a Web browser. Safari, the Web browser from Apple, reads and displays Web pages, enabling you to view, print, and search for information on the Web. Typically, after Safari is installed, its icon appears on the Dock. Before you can use the Internet for research, it's a good idea to explore the Safari browser window.

STEPS

QUICK TIP

If the Safari icon is not on your Dock, click the Finder icon 🟦 on the Dock, then click Applications in the sidebar. In the right pane, scroll down until you locate Safari, then double-click Safari.

1. **Locate the Safari icon 🔵 on the Dock, as shown in Figure D-2, then click**

   Safari opens and displays your home page. A **home page** is the first Web page that opens every time you start a browser. The term "home page" also applies to the main page of a Web site. Figure D-3 shows the Apple home page. The home page for your browser may be different. Look at the home page on your screen and compare the elements described, using Figure D-3 as a guide.

DETAILS

The elements of the Safari window include the following:

- The **menu bar** provides access to most of the browser's features through a series of menus.
- The **toolbar** contains the following tools to help you browse Web pages with Safari:
  - **Back and Forward buttons** allow you to access the Web pages that you have viewed since opening the browser.
  - The **Add a bookmark button** opens a dialog box that you use to name a bookmark and add it to the bookmarks bar or the Bookmarks menu.
  - The **address field** displays the address of the Web page that's open in the active tab. The Web page's address, called the **Uniform Resource Locator (URL)**, appears in the address field after you open (or load) the page. A button for reloading the current page appears on the right side of the address field.
  - The **Search field** uses the Google search engine to help you search the Internet for Web sites about a particular topic. You can enter a keyword or words in the Search field, and then press [return] to produce a Google Web page displaying relevant search results. To view your recent searches, you can click the magnifying glass button on the left side of the Search field.
- The **bookmarks bar** contains buttons you can use to go directly to Web pages you have bookmarked, to the Bookmarks menu, to a page showing your Top Sites, and to several popular Web sites whose bookmarks are added to the bookmarks bar by default.
- The **browser window** is the area where the current Web page appears.
- The **status bar** displays information about the page that is loading. It also displays the Web address of a link when you hold your pointer over one.
- The **vertical scroll bar** appears along the right side of a page if the page is longer than the window's viewable area. The **horizontal scroll bar** appears along the bottom of a page if the page is wider than the window's viewable area. The **scroller** within each scroll bar indicates your relative position within the Web page.

QUICK TIP

By default, the status bar is hidden. To display it, click View on the menu bar, then click Show Status Bar.

FIGURE D-2: Starting Safari

Safari icon

FIGURE D-3: Elements of the Safari window

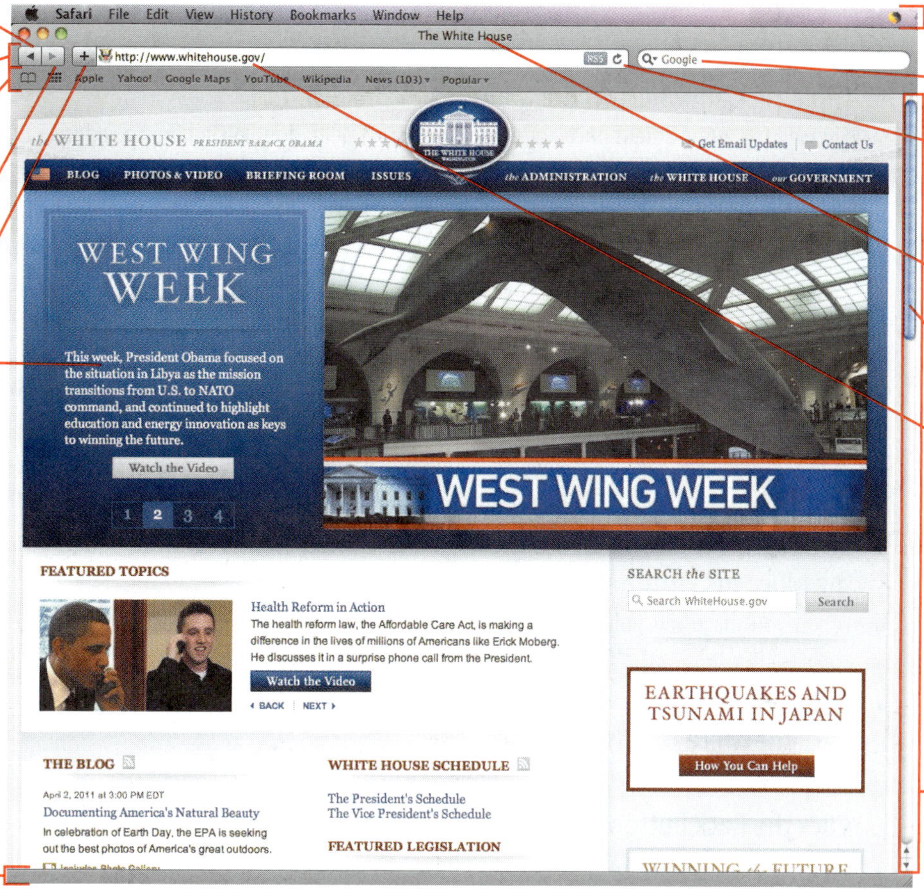

Back button
Toolbar
Bookmarks bar
Forward button
Add a bookmark button
Browser window
Status bar

Menu bar
Search field
Reload the current page button
Title bar
Vertical scroller
Address field
Vertical scroll bar

Internet

Understanding URLs

Every Web page has a unique address on the Web, also known as the URL (Uniform Resource Locator) for the page. Browser software locates a Web page based on its address. All Web page addresses begin with "http," which stands for Hypertext Transfer Protocol, the set of rules for exchanging files on the Web. This is followed by a colon and two forward slashes. Most pages begin with "www" (which indicates that the page is on the World Wide Web), followed by a dot, or period, and then the Web site's name, known as the **domain name**. Following the domain name is another dot and the **top-level domain**, which tells you the type of site you are visiting. Examples of top-level domains are com (for commercial sites), edu (for educational institutions), and org (for organizations). After the top-level domain, another slash and one or more folder names and a filename might appear.

Viewing and Navigating Web Pages

Moving among Web pages is simple with hyperlinks. When you click a hyperlink, you navigate to, or open, another location on the same Web page or jump to an entirely different Web page. You can follow a link to obtain more information about a topic by clicking a linked word or phrase. In addition to links on Web pages themselves, you can use the navigation tools in Safari to move around the Web. You can navigate from page to page using the Forward and Back buttons, and you can use the History menu to return to your home page or to view a list of previously viewed Web pages. You look at the Library of Congress Web site for information for a potential tour traveling to Washington, D.C.

STEPS

1. **Triple-click anywhere in the address field**

   Clicking the address field once activates the address field; double-clicking the address field highlights a word or part of the Web site address; and triple-clicking the address field highlights the entire Web site address. Any text you type when the entire address is highlighted replaces the address.

   QUICK TIP
   If you previously entered an address in the address field beginning with the same set of letters, the AutoFill feature suggests the remaining characters of the Web site address. Press [return] if you want to accept the address Safari suggests in the address field.

2. **Type www.loc.gov, then press [return]**

   After you press [return], Safari automatically adds the "http://" (Hypertext Transfer Protocol) to the beginning of the address you type. As the page loads, the status bar displays the current status of the Web site; when the page is completely loaded, the status bar is blank. After a moment, the home page for the Library of Congress opens in the browser window, as shown in Figure D-4. The name of the Web page appears on the title bar at the top of the window. A Web page icon matching the Library of Congress logo appears to the left of the Web page name in the address field. Web pages change frequently, so the Web page in your window might look different from that shown in the figure. The page contains both pictures and text, some of which are hyperlinks.

3. **Scroll down until you locate the Visit the Library heading, then place your pointer over the More for Visitors link**

   When you place the pointer over a hyperlink, the pointer changes to 🖑 and the URL for the hyperlink appears after the words "Go to" on the status bar. A Help Tag may also appear, giving you more information about the linked page.

   QUICK TIP
   Click the Reload the current page button ⟳ on the toolbar to update a page that might have changed since it was last loaded in the browser window.

4. **Click the More for Visitors link**

   The Visitors page opens in your Web browser window, as shown in Figure D-5.

5. **Click the Back button ◀ on the toolbar**

   The Web page that you last viewed, the Library of Congress home page, opens in the browser window.

6. **Click the Forward button ▶ on the toolbar**

   The Forward button opens the Visitors page in the browser window again.

7. **Click History on the menu bar, then click Home on the History menu**

   The home page for your installation of Safari appears in the browser window.

8. **Click History on the menu bar, then click Show All History**

   As shown in Figure D-6, the view changes to Cover Flow and the bookmarks library opens in the browser window. The **Bookmarks menu** contains collections of links to sites you have visited or want to visit frequently. In the sidebar, the History collection is selected in the Collections group. The right side of the window shows the contents of your History: The bottom section contains a list of the Web pages you have most recently visited, and the top section provides a preview of the Web page selected in the list.

   QUICK TIP
   You can also return to the Library of Congress home page by double-clicking Library of Congress Home from the list in the bottom section of the window.

9. **In the top section of the window, drag the scroll bar to the left until you see the preview for Library of Congress Home, then click the Library of Congress Home preview**

   The home page of the Library of Congress Web site opens in the browser window.

FIGURE D-4: Home page for the Library of Congress

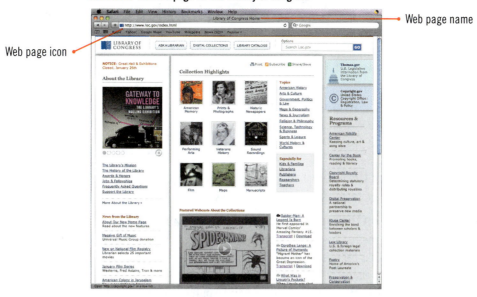

Web page name

Web page icon

FIGURE D-5: Visitors Web page at the Library of Congress Web site

Back button

Forward button

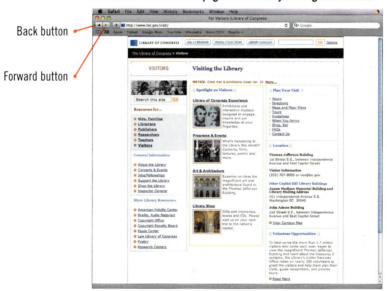

FIGURE D-6: History collection in Bookmarks menu

Collections group

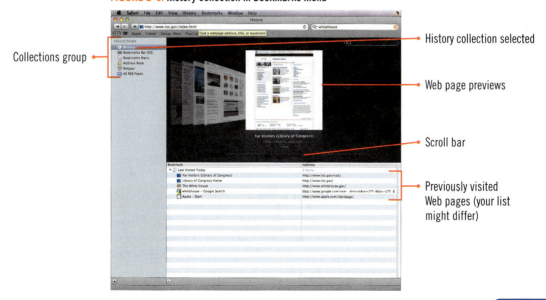

History collection selected

Web page previews

Scroll bar

Previously visited Web pages (your list might differ)

Getting Started with Safari

Using Tabbed Browsing

When you open multiple Web pages on separate tabs within the same browser window, you are using **tabbed browsing**. This method for organizing Web pages while browsing makes navigation between Web pages fast and simple, and minimizes the number of windows you need to open as you browse the Web. You want to learn how tabbed browsing allows you to compare events in a location by viewing multiple Web pages in one browser window.

STEPS

1. **Triple-click the address field, type www.usa.gov, then press [return]**
   The Web page for the U.S. government opens.

QUICK TIP
To open Top Sites in the current tab rather than on a new tab, click the Show Top Sites button ▦ on the bookmarks bar.

2. **Click File on the menu bar, then click New Tab**
   By default, the Top Sites page opens in the new tab of the browser window, and the tab bar is displayed below the bookmarks bar. See Figure D-7. The **tab bar** shows the tabs currently open in the Web browser. The tab that appears on top in the tab bar is the tab currently active in the browser window. You can click the **Create a new tab button** ➕ on the far right side of the tab bar to open a new tab. The **Top Sites** page displays your 12 most frequently visited Web sites as thumbnail images; to go to one of the sites, you simply click its thumbnail.

3. **Click any thumbnail on the Top Sites page**
   The selected Web page opens in the browser window and the tab on the tab bar changes to display the name of the Web page, as shown in Figure D-8. Your Web page might differ.

QUICK TIP
To display the tab bar without opening another tab, click View on the menu bar, then click Show Tab Bar.

4. **Click the Back button ◀ on the toolbar**
   The browser window collapses into a thumbnail image on the Top Sites page.

5. **Point to the Top Sites tab, then click the Close tab button ⊠ on the Top Sites tab in the tab bar**
   The Close tab button is hidden until you point to a tab. When it is clicked, the tab closes. With the Top Sites tab closed, the tab bar is no longer visible, and the USA.gov Web page is now in the browser window.

TROUBLE
To right-click with a single-button mouse, press [control] and click.

6. **Right-click the Site Index link on the USA.gov Web page to open the shortcut menu shown in Figure D-9, click Open Link in New Tab on the shortcut menu, then click the Site Index of USA.gov tab on the tab bar to display the Web page**

7. **Right-click any link on the Site Index of USA.gov Web page, click Open Link in New Tab, then click the new tab on the tab bar**
   Using tabbed browsing, you now have three Web pages open in one browser window.

QUICK TIP
To close all tabs except one, press and hold [option], then click ⊠ on the tab for the Web page you want to keep open. All other tabs will close, the tab bar will be hidden, and the Web page you selected will appear in the browser window.

8. **Position the pointer over each tab to display a Help Tag**
   Each Help Tag tells you the full name of the Web page on the tab.

9. **Click ⊠ on the second and third tabs**
   The Site Index of USA.gov Web page and the Web page for the link you selected on the Site Index page close, and the tab bar is hidden. The USA.gov home page is open in the window.

Quitting Safari when you have multiple tabs open

When you finish looking at Web pages using Safari, you might find that you have several tabs open. When you quit Safari and you have more than one tab open, a dialog box appears noting how many tabs are open and asking you if you're sure you want to quit Safari.

If you're done using the Web and want to quit Safari, click Quit. If you want to keep Safari open and meant only to close a tab, click Cancel, and then click the Close tab button on each Web page tab that you want to close.

FIGURE D-7: Top Sites

Show Top Sites button

Tabs

Create a new tab button

New (active) tab

Top Sites

FIGURE D-8: New page in a second tab

Name of Web page

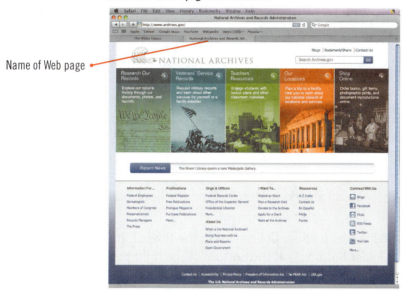

FIGURE D-9: Shortcut menu

Site Index link

Shortcut menu

Getting Started with Safari

Bookmarking Web Pages

When you find a Web page that you know you will want to revisit, you can bookmark it. When you **bookmark** a Web page, it is added to the bookmarks bar or Bookmarks menu, where you can easily access the page in the future without having to enter the URL for the Web page in the address field. The tour managers like the capability to be able to revisit some travel site Web pages without having to type the URLs in the address field each time, so you want to learn to bookmark sites you visit frequently.

STEPS

1. **Triple-click the** address field, **type** www.nps.gov/brca, **then press** [return]

   The home page for Bryce Canyon National Park opens, providing information about the park. You decide to bookmark this page.

2. **Click the** Add a bookmark for the current page button ⊞ **on the toolbar**

   The Add a bookmark dialog box opens, as shown in Figure D-10. The Add a bookmark dialog box contains a text box for the name of the bookmarked page and a pop-up menu for selecting the location for the bookmark. By default, the full name of the Web page appears in the text box and the most recently used location is selected. You decide to shorten the name so it will be completely visible on a small tab on the bookmarks bar.

   > **QUICK TIP**
   >
   > To add a bookmark to the Bookmarks menu, select Bookmarks Menu as the location in the Add a bookmark dialog box.

3. **Type** Bryce Canyon Park **in the text box, click the** location pop-up menu, **click** Bookmarks Bar **if necessary, then click** Add

   A Bryce Canyon Park button is added to the bookmarks bar. You decide that instead of adding it to the bookmarks bar, you'd prefer to create a folder called National Parks that appears on the Bookmarks menu and add the Bryce Canyon Park page as a bookmark in the folder. First, you need to remove the button from the bookmarks bar.

   > **QUICK TIP**
   >
   > If you point to a button on the bookmarks bar, a Help Tag appears with the URL of the Web page.

4. **Click and drag the** Bryce Canyon Park button **off the bookmarks bar and over the browser window, then release the button**

   A small puff of smoke appears on your computer screen where you release the button, and the button is removed from the bookmarks bar.

5. **Click the** Show all bookmarks button 📖 **on the bookmarks bar**

   The bookmarks library is displayed in the browser window.

   > **QUICK TIP**
   >
   > To add a folder to the bookmarks bar, click the Bookmarks Bar collection in the Bookmarks menu, then click the Create a bookmarks folder button below the right pane. To open a bookmarked Web page from a folder on the bookmarks bar, click the folder name on the bookmarks bar, then click a bookmark on the list that opens.

6. **Click** Bookmarks Menu **under Collections in the sidebar, then click the** Create a bookmarks folder button ⊞ **at the bottom of the right pane**

   As shown in Figure D-11, an untitled folder appears in the list of bookmarks in the Bookmarks Menu collection.

7. **Type** National Parks, **then press** [return]

   The untitled folder is renamed National Parks.

8. **Click the** Show all bookmarks button 📖 **to return to the Bryce Canyon National Park Web page, click** ⊞, **click the** location pop-up menu, **click the** National Parks folder **under Bookmarks Menu, then click** Add

9. **Click** History **on the menu bar, click** Home **to return to your home page, click** Bookmarks **on the menu bar, point to** National Parks, **then click** Bryce Canyon National Park (U.S. National Park Service)

   Clicking the Bryce Canyon National Park bookmark on the Bookmarks menu opens the Bryce Canyon National Park Web page.

10. **Click** 📖 **on the bookmarks bar, click** Bookmarks Menu **under Collections if necessary, then compare your screen with Figure D-12**

11. **Right-click the** National Parks folder, **click** Delete, **click** History **on the menu bar, then click** Home

   The National Parks folder and bookmark are deleted. Your browser window returns to your home page.

FIGURE D-10: Add a bookmark dialog box

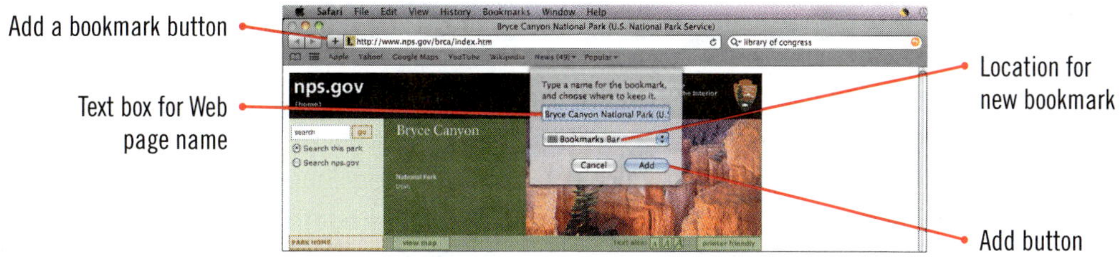

Add a bookmark button

Text box for Web page name

Location for new bookmark

Add button

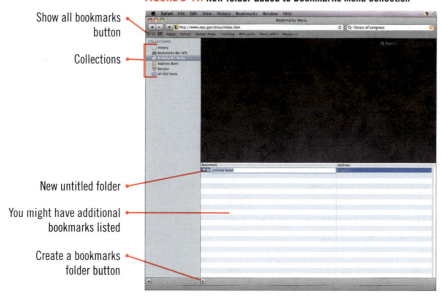

FIGURE D-11: New folder added to Bookmarks Menu collection

Show all bookmarks button

Collections

New untitled folder

You might have additional bookmarks listed

Create a bookmarks folder button

FIGURE D-12: Bookmark added to National Parks folder in Bookmarks Menu collection

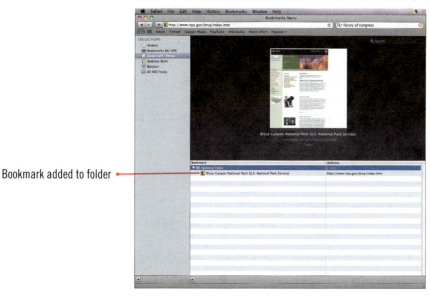

Bookmark added to folder

Creating and organizing bookmarks

Once you bookmark a Web page, returning to that page is much easier. To keep your bookmarks manageable, add only pages that you expect to visit frequently. You can organize bookmarks by placing them into folders by category. For example, you might want to create bookmark folders according to your interests, such as sports, cooking, and travel. You might want to create folders in which each member of a household can place his or her own favorites. Bookmarks can be listed individually or placed in folders on the bookmarks bar or on the Bookmarks menu.

Printing a Web Page

When you print a Web page, its text and any graphics appear on the printed page. You can use the Print dialog box to change the number of copies, number of pages, paper size, and orientation of the Web page before printing. In addition, a preview of the printed Web page appears in the Print dialog box; this is helpful because some Web pages are lengthy and you might want to print only the pages that have the information relevant to your task. Table D-1 explains the Print dialog box options in more detail. You explore how to print a copy of a Web page so you can provide the information as handouts to the tour guides.

STEPS

1. **Triple-click the address field on the toolbar, type www.nps.gov, press [return], then click the Discover History link**

   The Discover History page for the National Park Service opens.

QUICK TIP

If your Print dialog box contains more options than those shown in Figure D-13, click the Collapse button ▲ to collapse the dialog box.

2. **Click File on the menu bar, then click Print**

   The Print dialog box opens, as shown in Figure D-13. From this dialog box, you can select a printer, print the Web page, save the Web page as a Portable Document File (PDF) document, or view the Web page as a PDF in the Preview program. More print options are available when the Print dialog box is expanded.

QUICK TIP

To print a Web page without previewing it or changing any settings, click the Print button in the Print dialog box when it first opens.

3. **Click the Expand button ▼ to the right of the Printer pop-up menu**

   The Print dialog box expands, as shown in Figure D-14. On the left side of the dialog box, the Preview box shows what the first page of the printed Web page will look like. By default, a header will be printed at the top of each page containing the name of the Web page on the left and the current date and time on the right, and a footer will be printed at the bottom of each page containing the URL on the left and page number on the right.

4. **Click the Landscape button ▢ in the Orientation section**

   The Preview box shows the Web page in landscape orientation.

QUICK TIP

To print a range of pages other than the first page, click the From option button, enter the starting page number in the range in the first text box, then enter the ending page number in the second text box. To print a Web page no matter how many pages, click the All option button.

5. **Click the Next page button ▶ below the Preview box**

   The contents of page 2 of the printed document appear in the Preview box.

6. **Click the Previous page button ◀ below the Preview box, then click the Portrait button ▢ in the Orientation section**

   You prefer portrait orientation for the handout, and you'd like to print the first page only of the two-page Web page.

7. **Click the From option button in the Pages section**

   With the range of pages to be printed set to From 1 to 1, only the first page of the Web page will be printed.

TROUBLE

If your computer is not connected to a printer or if an error message appears, ask your technical support person for assistance.

8. **Make sure 1 appears in the Copies text box, then click Print**

   The Print dialog box closes, and one copy of the first page of the current Web page prints.

FIGURE D-13: Safari Print dialog box

Expand button

Print button

FIGURE D-14: Expanded Safari Print dialog box

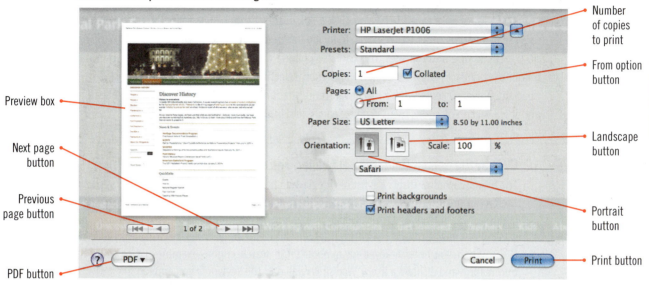

Number of copies to print

From option button

Landscape button

Portrait button

Print button

Preview box

Next page button

Previous page button

PDF button

TABLE D-1: Print dialog box options

option	use to
Printer	Select the printer to use; click the pop-up menu to change or view a list of available printers for your computer
Copies	Indicate the number of copies of each page to print
Pages	Indicate whether all pages or a range of pages should be printed
Paper Size	Select the paper size; click the pop-up menu to change or view a list of available paper sizes for your printer
Orientation	Select portrait or landscape orientation for the printed page
Scale	Increase or decrease the size of the item on the printed page
Print backgrounds check box	Indicate (when checked) that the background colors on a Web page are to be printed
Print headers and footers check box	Indicate (when checked) that the headers and footers on each page are to be printed
PDF button	Preview, save, or mail the Web page as a PDF (Portable Document Format) document

Copying information from a Web page

As you create files, such as flyers, newsletters, or presentations, you might want to include text or pictures from Web pages you visit. You can select text on a Web page and use the Copy and Paste commands to insert the information into a file made with another program, such as Microsoft Word. You can also save a graphic image from a Web page by dragging it to the desktop or by right-clicking the image and clicking Save Image As on the shortcut menu, and then specifying where to save the image; then you can insert it into many different files. To copy an image to the operating system Clipboard so that you can paste the copy in a new location, right-click the image, click the Copy Image command on the shortcut menu, and then paste it in the file or folder you choose. Keep in mind that the same copyright laws that protect printed works generally protect information and graphics published on a Web page. Do not use material from a Web page without citing its source, and check the site carefully for any usage restrictions.

Internet

Searching for Information

A vast and ever-increasing number of Web pages and other information sources are available through the Internet. To find information on the Web on a specific topic, you can use the built-in **Search field** in Safari. When searching for relevant Web sites, you need to identify criteria or **keywords**, which are words related to the topic for which you are searching. To search using the Search field, you enter a keyword or words in the field, and then press [return]. By default, Safari uses the Google search engine to find relevant sites on the Web based on your keywords. After you press [return], Safari opens a Google Web page containing your **search results**, a list of links called **hits**. You click a link in the search results list to go to a Web site. If you prefer to use a search engine other than Google to locate information on the Web, such as Bing, Ask, or Yahoo!, you can go directly to one of these sites. You can also change the default search engine used by Safari by clicking the magnifying glass in the Search field, and then selecting Google, Yahoo!, or Bing. 🎨 Many of Quest Specialty Travel's clients who visit Hawaii request tours of volcanoes. You decide to search for information about Hawaiian volcanoes by using the Search field in the browser.

STEPS

QUICK TIP
Some search results include a Sponsored Links or Ads box at the top of the results list. These sites have usually paid a fee to the search engine to be listed first when certain keywords are used for a search.

1. **Click in the Search field, type Hawaiian volcanoes, then press [return]**

   The browser window displays a list of Google search results for Hawaiian volcanoes, as shown in Figure D-15. Each result provides a link to a Web site, a short description highlighting your keywords, and the URL of the Web site. Search engines such as Google, Bing, and Yahoo! routinely use software programs to methodically catalog, or crawl, through the entire Internet and create huge databases with links to Web pages and their URLs. When you enter a keyword or phrase, the search engine examines its database index for relevant information and displays a list of Web sites related to the keywords you entered.

2. **Click any link to view a Web page**

3. **Click File on the menu bar, then click New Tab to open a new tab**

4. **Click the magnifying glass ▾ on the left side of the Search field**

QUICK TIP
You can also use the Back button ◀ to return to previously viewed Web pages.

   A list of Recent Searches opens, as shown in Figure D-16. Your list might differ. You want to access the search results for Hawaiian volcanoes again.

5. **Under Recent Searches, click Hawaiian volcanoes**

   The search results from Google about Hawaiian volcanoes open on the new tab.

6. **Click a link different than the one clicked in Step 2**

7. **Click the SnapBack button ↻ on the right side of the Search field**

   The most recent Google search results are displayed on the current tab.

8. **Right-click a third Web site link on the Google search results page, click Open Link in New Tab, then click the new tab**

   You now have three Web sites open in the same browser window, each on a different tab, as shown in Figure D-17. An advantage of using tabbed browsing when searching for information is that it allows you to compare information from different Web sites in the same window.

9. **Close all open tabs except the first tab, click History on the menu bar, then click Home**

   Your home page appears in the browser window.

Blocking pop-up windows

Pop-ups are windows that open on your screen as you visit Web sites, generally to advertise products you might or might not want. Most people find them annoying, so Safari blocks pop-ups by default. If you want to enable pop-ups to appear, click Safari on the menu bar, and then click Block Pop-Up Windows to deselect it.

FIGURE D-15: Google search results

Search field

Number of hits

Search results

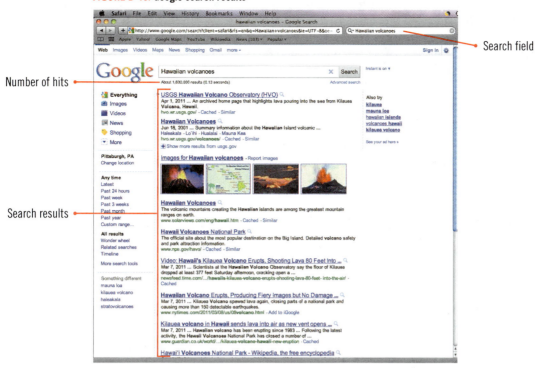

FIGURE D-16: List of recent searches

Click in Step 4

Click in Step 5

FIGURE D-17: Multiple tabs open based on your search

Three open tabs

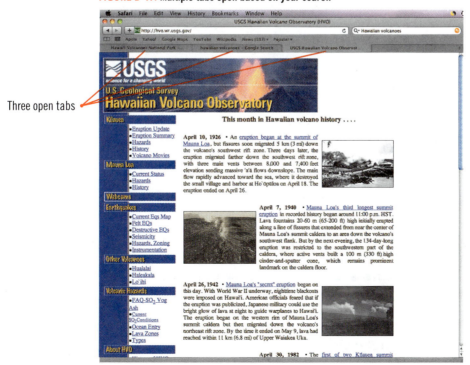

Internet

Getting Help and Quitting Safari

Safari provides a Help system with information and instructions on various features and commands in the browser.  After exploring Safari, a coworker asked you how to protect private information such as Web site passwords on computers that are used by other people. Private browsing is a feature of Safari that protects users' private information. You want to help your coworker by finding out more about private browsing.

STEPS

1. **Click Help on the menu bar, then type private in the Search box**

   As you type, potential matches to your keywords are immediately provided. As shown in Figure D-18, Private Browsing appears under Menu Items, and Browsing privately appears under Help Topics.

2. **Click Browsing privately under Help Topics**

   The Safari Help window opens, displaying information about private browsing and how to turn it on. See Figure D-19.

3. **Read the information presented, then click the Close button to close the window**

   The Help window closes. You are now ready to quit Safari.

> **TROUBLE**
> Clicking the Close button on the Safari window closes only the window. Safari continues to run until you quit Safari.

4. **Click Safari on the menu bar, then click Quit Safari**

5. **If you connected to the Internet by telephone line, follow your normal procedure to close your connection**

Setting the home page

Each time you start Safari and each time you click Home on the History menu, your home page appears in the browser window. If you want to change the home page, open the Web page that you want to be your new home page, click Safari on the menu bar, click Preferences, and then click General (if necessary). The URL of the current home page is highlighted in the Home page text box. Click the Set to Current Page button to change the URL in the Home page text box to the URL for the Web page currently open in the browser. Close the General dialog box.

FIGURE D-18: Safari Help menu search results

Click to view menu item

Click to view Safari Help topic

FIGURE D-19: Topic in Safari Help window

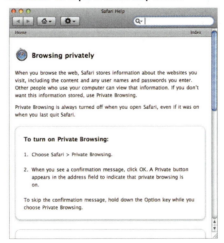

Saving or mailing a Web page

Before quitting Safari, you might want to save a copy of the current Web page or send someone a copy of the page. To save the current Web page, click File on the menu bar, click Save As, and then select a location in which to save the complete Web page, including any graphics, as a Web Archive file. If you want to e-mail the Web page to someone, click File on the menu bar, click Mail Contents of This Page, and then use your e-mail program to address and send the message containing the Web page. If you want to e-mail only a link to the page, not the whole page, click File on the menu bar, click Mail Link to This Page, and then address and send the message containing the link.

Practice

Concepts Review

Label each element of the Safari browser window shown in Figure D-20.

FIGURE D-20

Match each term with the statement that best describes it.

7. **Hyperlink**
8. **Top Sites**
9. **Bookmarks menu**
10. **Address field**
11. **Uniform Resource Locator (URL)**

a. Click to view a new Web page
b. Displays the URL for the currently displayed page
c. Displays your most frequently visited Web pages as thumbnails
d. Displays a list of saved Web pages
e. A Web page's address

Select the best answer from the list of choices.

12. Software programs such as Safari and Firefox are called _____.
    - **a.** Web companions.
    - **b.** Web browsers.
    - **c.** Web documents.
    - **d.** Web windows.

13. A(n) _____ is the hardware and software that makes it possible to share information and resources.
    - **a.** Computer network
    - **b.** Extranet
    - **c.** Internet
    - **d.** Intranet

14. The page that opens every time you start a browser is called the:
    - **a.** First page.
    - **b.** Home page.
    - **c.** Title page.
    - **d.** Web page.

15. _____ browsing allows you to open more than one Web page at a time in a browser window.
    - **a.** Favorites
    - **b.** Linked
    - **c.** Tabbed
    - **d.** Web

16. The letters following the dot after the domain name are called the _____ domain and indicate the type of site you are visiting.
    - **a.** Top-level
    - **b.** Home-level
    - **c.** Dot-com
    - **d.** Main-level

17. Which button on the toolbar should you click if you want to view the previous Web page on your computer?
    - **a.** Home
    - **b.** Last
    - **c.** Back
    - **d.** Link

18. The toolbar that contains bookmarked Web sites is called the:
    - **a.** Top Sites.
    - **b.** Toolbar.
    - **c.** Search field.
    - **d.** Bookmarks bar.

19. Safari's Search field uses the _____ search engine by default.
    - **a.** Ask
    - **b.** Bing
    - **c.** Yahoo!
    - **d.** Google

Skills Review

1. **Start and explore Safari.**
   - **a.** Make sure your computer is connected to the Internet.
   - **b.** Start Safari.
   - **c.** Identify and list as many components of the Safari window as you can without referring to the lessons.
   - **d.** Compare your results with Figure D-3 to ensure that you have identified all the essential components.
   - **e.** Identify the complete URL of your current Web page.

Skills Review (continued)

2. View and navigate Web pages.

a. Open the Web page **www.nasa.gov** using the address field, then compare your screen with Figure D-21. (The NASA Web site might differ from the one shown here.)

FIGURE D-21

b. Click the For Students link on the Web page.

c. Return to the home page for your browser.

d. Click the Back button.

e. Follow another link on the NASA Web site to investigate the content.

f. Click History on the menu bar, click Show All History, then click the NASA - Home preview in the top section of the History collection in the bookmarks library to open the NASA home page in the browser window.

g. Return to the home page for your browser.

3. Use tabbed browsing.

a. Open the Web page **www.nytimes.com** using the address field.

b. Right-click a link on the Web page to open an article in a new tab.

c. Create a third tab in the browser window, then open **www.cnn.com** in the new tab.

d. Create a fourth tab in the browser window, then click the first thumbnail on the Top Sites page. Your browser tab bar should resemble that shown in Figure D-22.

FIGURE D-22

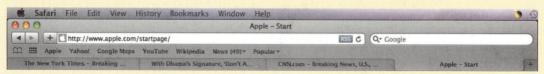

e. Close all tabs except the New York Times home page tab.

Skills Review (continued)

4. Bookmark Web pages.

a. Open the Web page **www.nasa.gov** in the browser window again. (*Hint*: If a pop-up window appears asking for your feedback, click the Close button and make sure that your Safari settings are set to Block Pop-Up Windows.)

b. Open the bookmarks library, then add a folder to the Bookmarks menu called **Science Sites**.

c. Close the bookmarks library, then add the NASA Web page to the Science Sites folder on the Bookmarks menu.

d. Return to the default home page for your browser.

e. Using the Bookmarks menu, return to the NASA home page.

f. Open the Bookmarks menu, delete the Science Sites folder from your Bookmarks menu, then close the bookmarks library. (*Hint*: Right-click the Science Sites folder, then click Delete, or click the Science Sites folder, then press [delete].)

5. Print a Web page.

a. Click any link on the NASA home page that is interesting to you.

b. Open the Print dialog box, then view all of the Web page's printed pages in the Preview box.

c. Change the orientation of the printed page to landscape.

d. Print one copy of the first page of the Web page only.

6. Search for information.

a. Click the Search field on the toolbar. (*Hint*: If the Search field already contains text, triple-click the text in the field to select it so it can be replaced in the next step.)

b. Type any keyword or phrase for which you would like to find information, then execute the search and review the results.

c. Click any link in the search results page and read the Web page.

d. Click a link found on the selected Web page and read the new Web page.

e. Use the SnapBack button to return to your search results.

f. Explore some of the other hyperlinks you found.

7. Get Help and quit Safari.

a. Using the Help menu, type search in the box provided.

b. Click any link for the topic you want to learn more about.

c. Read the results.

d. Close the Safari Help window.

e. Quit Safari.

Independent Challenge 1

This Independent Challenge requires an Internet connection.

You are an aspiring journalist interested in understanding how different journalists approach the same story. You decide to use the Web to find some articles for comparison.

a. Start Safari.

b. Read and compare the coverage of a current international news story using two of the following sites by clicking the World (or World News) link:

- CNN   www.cnn.com
- MSNBC News   www.msnbc.com
- ABC News   www.abcnews.com
- CBS News   www.cbsnews.com

c. Open each news story in its own tab in the browser window.

d. Print one page of the same story from both sites that you chose.

Independent Challenge 1 (continued)

Advanced Challenge Exercise

- You should be able to find English-language versions of many non-U.S. papers. Use the Search field or your favorite search engine to locate an online news media source from a country other than the United States. You can search on keywords such as "**Asian newspapers**" or "**European newspapers**."
- See if you can find the news story you researched in Step b.
- Read the article.
- Print one page of the article from the site that you chose.

e. Close all but one of the tabs, then quit Safari.

f. Write your name on your printed pages and hand them in to your instructor.

Independent Challenge 2

This Independent Challenge requires an Internet connection.

You have been asked by your local community college to teach a short course on classic films from the 1940s and 1950s. The class will meet four times; each class will begin with a screening and will be followed by a discussion. You decide to use the Web to research the material.

a. Start Safari.

b. Using the Search field, find a Web site that contains information about films made in the 1940s.

c. Identify two films from the 1940s that you want to show as part of the course. View information about each film in a separate tab in the browser window.

d. Open a new tab in your browser window and search for two films from the 1950s. View information about each film in a separate tab in the browser window.

e. Using the Bookmarks menu, create a folder on the Bookmarks menu. Name the folder with your name.

f. Bookmark a Web page for each film and put it in your folder on the Bookmarks menu.

g. Use the Bookmarks menu to open each film Web page in the browser window, and print the first page from each Web page.

Advanced Challenge Exercise

- Find one Web page that includes a link for media such as audio or video about a 1940s or 1950s film.
- Click the link and listen to the audio or play the video.
- After listening to or viewing the media file, close the window.
- Bookmark this Web page in your Bookmarks menu folder.

h. Open the bookmarks library, then delete your folder from the Bookmarks menu.

i. Quit Safari, write your name on your printed pages, then submit them to your instructor.

Independent Challenge 3

This Independent Challenge requires an Internet connection.

As a student of American political history, you want to learn about your representatives in the U.S. government. You decide to use the Web to get information about this topic.

a. Start Safari, then open the Web site **www.house.gov**.

b. Explore the site to find information about members of Congress. Print one page from this site.

c. In a new tab, open the Web site **www.senate.gov**.

d. Click the Senators link, then find a link to a Web site for a senator who represents the state that you would most like to visit. Click the link, then print one page from this site.

e. Explore three links on the senator's Web site to learn more about those topics, opening each page in a new tab.

f. Print one page from each of these links.

g. Quit Safari.

h. Write your name on the printed pages and hand them in to your instructor.

Real Life Independent Challenge

This Independent Challenge requires an Internet connection.

You decide to compare several search engines to determine if there are differences in appearance or the number of hits you receive when you use them to search the Web.

a. Start Safari. Using two of the search engines listed below, type **nobel prize winners** in the Search text box, and then search for the topic.

• Yahoo!	www.yahoo.com
• Bing	www.bing.com
• Google	www.google.com
• Ask	www.ask.com

b. Print the first page of the results from each search. Circle the name of the search engine and the number of hits, or results, it produced.

c. Compare and contrast the appearance and number of hits you received from each site. Also indicate which search engine you prefer and why.

Advanced Challenge Exercise

■ In the Bookmarks menu, create a folder in the Bookmarks Bar collection called **Search Results**.

■ Bookmark the home page for your favorite search engine in the Search Results bookmark folder.

■ Return to your home page, then use the Search Results folder on the bookmarks bar to go to the search engine home page.

■ Delete the Search Results bookmark folder from the bookmarks bar. (*Hint*: Drag the bookmark folder off of the bookmarks bar, then click Delete Folder in the dialog box that opens.)

d. Quit Safari, write your name on your printed pages, then submit them to your instructor.

Visual Workshop

This Visual Workshop requires an Internet connection.

Graphics you find as you view pages on the Web can be static photographs or drawings, videos, or animated graphics. Find two Web sites that include a video. You may be given the option to watch the video using a player such as QuickTime. Other viewing options may include other players or the video may play in a viewing window on the Web page. Keep in mind that Windows Media Player files will not play on your Mac unless you have Windows Media Player software installed on your Mac. View at least one video on a news site and one video on a topic-specific Web site such as an organization or tourism site. An example is shown in Figure D-23. Write a brief summary of the videos you watched. Identify the Web sites on which the videos were located, then submit it to your instructor.

FIGURE D-23

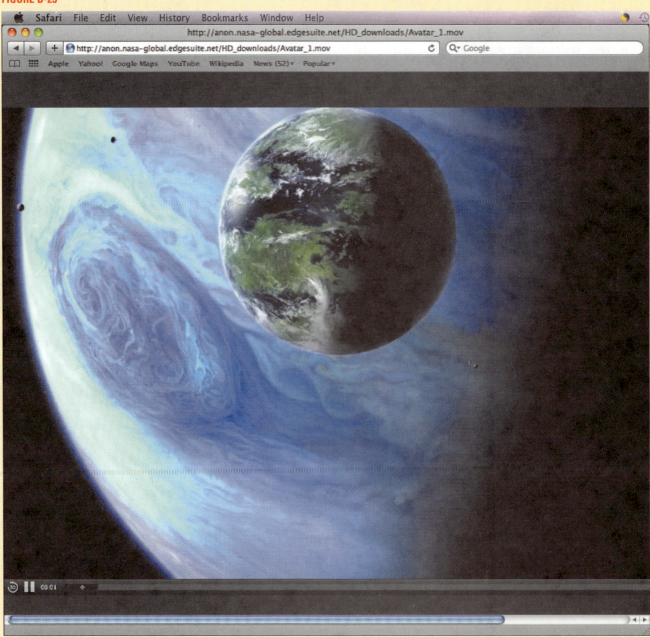

Getting Started with Safari

UNIT E
Office 2011

Getting Started with Microsoft Office for Mac 2011

Microsoft Office for Mac 2011, often referred to as Office, is a collection (or **suite**) of programs that you can use to produce a wide variety of documents, including letters, budgets, mailing lists, presentations, and Web pages. Microsoft Office for Mac Home and Business 2011 includes Word, Excel, PowerPoint, and Outlook. Microsoft Office for Mac Home and Student 2011 includes Word, Excel, and PowerPoint. One of the biggest new benefits of Microsoft Office for Mac 2011 is that it allows you to work collaboratively in real time with others, whether they are in your office or on the other side of the world. You have just joined the marketing team at Outdoor Designs, a company that sells outdoor recreational products. You need to familiarize yourself with Microsoft Office for Mac 2011 and create a simple to-do list for your first week on the job.

OBJECTIVES

Understand Microsoft Office for Mac 2011

Start an Office program

Use menus and the Standard toolbar

Explore the ribbon and View options

Explore the Toolbox and Media Browser

Save and close a file

Create a new file from a template

Get Help and quit an Office program

Understanding Microsoft Office for Mac 2011

Microsoft Office for Mac 2011 comes with a variety of **programs** and tools you can use to create documents, analyze data, and complete almost any business task. In this book, you learn how to use Word, Excel, and PowerPoint. One of the most powerful new benefits of Microsoft Office for Mac 2011 is **Microsoft Office Web Apps**, which is a set of scaled-down versions of Microsoft Office programs that run over the Internet. Using Microsoft Office Web Apps, you and your colleagues can work collaboratively on a single document even if you are in different locations, as long as your computer is connected to the Internet.   Karen Rivera, marketing director at Outdoor Designs, suggests that you familiarize yourself with the programs in Office 2011.

DETAILS

Microsoft Office for Mac 2011 is available in two versions: Home and Student, and Home and Business. Both versions contain the following programs:

- **Microsoft Word** is a **word processing program** you can use to create text documents, such as letters, memos, newsletters, and reports. You can also use Word to add pictures, drawings, tables, and other graphical elements to your documents. At Outdoor Designs, you will use Word to create memos, letters, flyers, and reports to communicate with staff, customers, and distributors. Figure E-1 shows an Outdoor Designs' quarterly report created using Word.
- **Microsoft Excel** is a **spreadsheet program** you can use to manipulate, analyze, and chart quantitative data. Excel is often used to calculate financial information. In your work at Outdoor Designs, you will use Excel to create sales results worksheets, invoices, sales reports, and charts like the one shown in Figure E-2, which presents quarterly sales results.
- **Microsoft PowerPoint** is a **presentation graphics program** you can use to develop materials for presentations, including slide shows, computer-based presentations, speaker's notes, and audience handouts. The staff at Outdoor Designs is preparing for the spring selling season, so you will use PowerPoint to create a presentation for the sales reps that describes the new spring products. Figure E-3 shows one of the slides from this presentation.

In addition to the three programs you learn about in this book, Microsoft Office for Mac Home and Business 2011 also includes the following program:

- **Microsoft Outlook** (not available in Microsoft Office for Mac Home and Student 2011) is an e-mail program and information manager used to send and receive e-mail; schedule appointments; maintain to-do lists; and store names, addresses, and other contact information.

FIGURE E-1: Report created in Microsoft Word

OUTDOOR
DESIGNS

Winter 2013 | Quarterly Report and The Road Ahead

This quarterly report to shareholders presents a summary of
profitability and revenue results for the quarter ending December
31, 2012. This report also summarizes the status and progress of
key business initiatives designed to fuel further growth in products
and services for the next twenty-four months. The road ahead
promises continued growth and profitability.

FIGURE E-2: Worksheet and chart created in Microsoft Excel

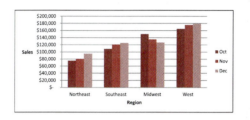

OUTDOOR DESIGNS

Quarterly Sales by Region

	Oct	Nov	Dec	Total
Northeast	$ 75,209	$ 80,967	$ 95,376	$ 251,552
Southeast	$ 108,789	$ 120,987	$ 125,698	$ 355,474
Midwest	$ 150,119	$ 135,333	$ 126,543	$ 411,995
West	$ 164,567	$ 176,009	$ 178,998	$ 519,574
Total	$ 498,684	$ 513,296	$ 526,615	$ 1,538,595

FIGURE E-3: Presentation slide created in Microsoft PowerPoint

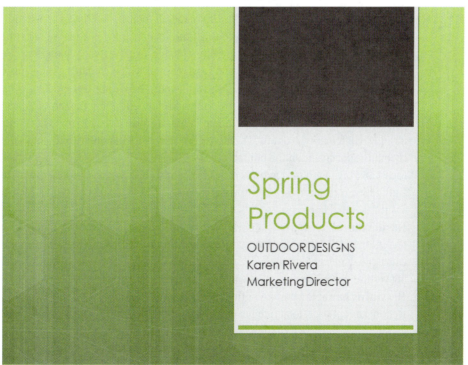

Starting an Office Program

To get started using Microsoft Office, you need to open, or **launch**, the Office program you want to use. When you launch an Office program, your computer reads the program stored on your computer's hard disk and displays it on the screen for you to use. There are several ways you can start an Office program, including the icon on the Dock. 🎨 You decide to familiarize yourself with Office by starting Microsoft Word and getting acquainted with the user interface. A **user interface** is the collection of buttons and tools you use to interact with a software program.

STEPS

QUICK TIP

For any item on the Dock, single-click to open it. If the Word icon is not on your Dock, click the Finder icon 🗂 on the Dock, then click Applications in the sidebar. In the right pane, scroll down until you locate the Microsoft Office 2011 folder, then open it. Locate Microsoft Word, then double-click the icon to launch Word.

1. **Click the Word icon W on the Dock, as shown in Figure E-4**

   Microsoft Word starts and the Word Document Gallery opens, as shown in Figure E-5.

2. **If necessary, click Print Layout View in the left pane, click Blank in the middle pane, then click Choose to open a blank Word document**

   A blank document opens on your computer screen. (Your screen might look a little different, depending on your settings.) Refer to Figure E-6 to identify the elements of the program window described below:

   • The **menu bar** appears at the top of the screen and includes the names of all the Word menus. Menus are lists of commands you can click to perform tasks. Clicking a menu name on the menu bar opens its menu.

   • The **title bar** is at the top of the program window. It contains the name of the document (currently the temporary name Document1). At the left end of the title bar are the Close, Minimize, and Zoom buttons, which you use to close the current document, minimize the document to the Dock, and restore the window to its original size.

   • The **Standard toolbar**, located directly below the title bar, contains buttons that perform the most common tasks in a program, such as creating a new blank document; creating a new document from a template; and opening, saving, and printing a document. Buttons on the Standard toolbar are often easier to remember than their menu counterparts because they display a picture called an **icon** that depicts the function that will be executed.

   • The **ribbon** is the band directly below the Standard toolbar. It contains commands in the form of buttons, lists, galleries, and text boxes. A **command** is an instruction you give to a computer to complete a task, such as printing a document, inserting a picture, or saving your changes.

   • Across the top of the ribbon are several **tabs**, each of which contains a different set of commands for completing a particular type of task. At the moment, the **Home tab** is active, so it appears in front of the other tabs. The Home tab contains commands for performing the most frequently used commands for creating a document. Clicking a different tab displays a different group of commands related to performing a different type of task. For instance, clicking the **Layout tab** displays commands to help you lay out the document on the printed page.

   • Each tab is organized into **groups** of related commands, such as the Font group, the Paragraph group, and the Styles group. You can see these group names at the top of each group. Each group is separated by a vertical dotted line.

   • The **document window** is the work area within the Word program window. This is where you type text into your document and format it to look the way you want. The work area looks different in each Office program based on the type of document you are creating. The **insertion point** is a small flashing vertical line in the document window that indicates where text will be inserted when you type.

   • The **status bar** at the bottom of the screen displays key information, such as the current view, current section, current page, total number of pages, number of words in the document, and spelling and grammar status. At the far left of the status bar are the **View buttons**, which you use to change your view of the document. In Word, you can choose among six view buttons on the status bar and an additional view is available as an option on the View menu. You can use the **Zoom slider**, located at the far right of the status bar, to set the magnification level of your document. If your vision is less than perfect, you can use the Zoom slider to get a close-up view of your document.

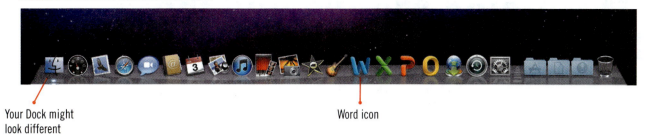

Your Dock might
look different

Word icon

FIGURE E-5: Word Document Gallery

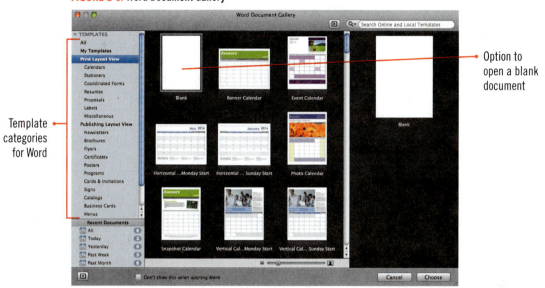

Option to
open a blank
document

Office 2011

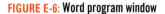
Template
categories
for Word

FIGURE E-6: Word program window

Menu bar
Close button
Minimize
button
Zoom button
Home tab

Insertion point

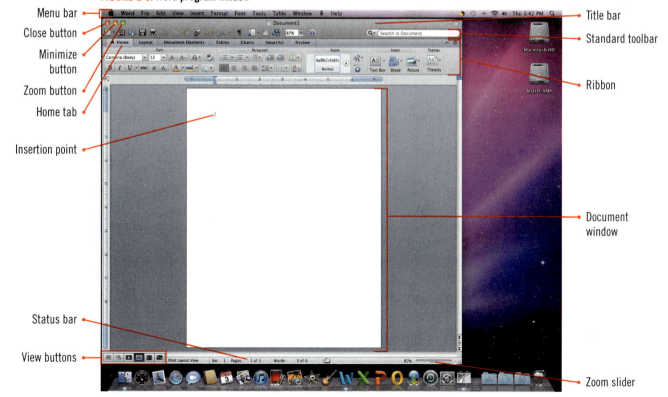

Title bar
Standard toolbar

Ribbon

Document
window

Status bar

View buttons

Zoom slider

Using Menus and the Standard Toolbar

All Office 2011 programs share similar tools that help you complete tasks. Similar menus and toolbars appear in all the Office 2011 programs and contain buttons or commands that you select to perform a task. If Office needs more information in order to carry out a particular command from a menu, it displays a dialog box that presents options you select to complete the task. Once you learn how to use these tools to select commands in Word, you will be able to use them in any Office program. You decide to use Word to create a simple to-do list for yourself.

1. **Click Format on the menu bar**

   The Format menu opens, as shown in Figure E-7. As you click the options on the menu bar, drop-down menus appear, giving you access to all the options available in this program.

2. **Click Font on the Format menu**

   The Font dialog box opens, as shown in Figure E-8. You use this dialog box to change the font and font attributes, such as font style, size, and color.

3. **Click Cancel**

   The Font dialog box closes.

4. **With the insertion point at the top of the Word document window, type To Do List, then press [return] twice**

   The text you typed appears in the first line of the document, and the insertion point moves down two lines.

   <blockquote>
   QUICK TIP

   When you place the pointer over a button, a Help Tag appears in a yellow box that provides a brief description about the function of the button. Help Tag is the term used with a Mac. Windows computers refer to them as ScreenTips.
   </blockquote>

5. **Click the Undo button ⟲ on the Standard toolbar**

   The words you typed, "To Do List", and the blank lines are deleted, and the insertion point moves back up to the top of the page. The Undo button reverses your last action.

6. **Click the Redo button ⟳ on the Standard toolbar**

   The Redo button restores your document to the state it was in before you clicked the Undo button.

7. **Type Order business cards, press [return], type Get photo ID, press [return], then type Sign up for orientation class. Press [return] twice, then type your name**

   Compare your screen with Figure E-9.

FIGURE E-7: Format menu

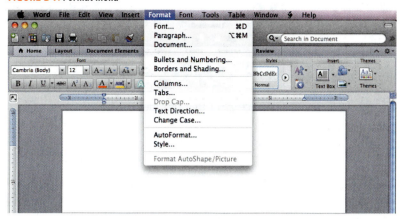

FIGURE E-8: Font dialog box

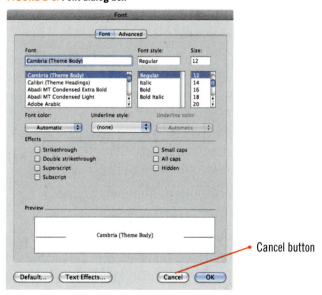

Cancel button

FIGURE E-9: Completed To Do List document

Undo button

Redo button

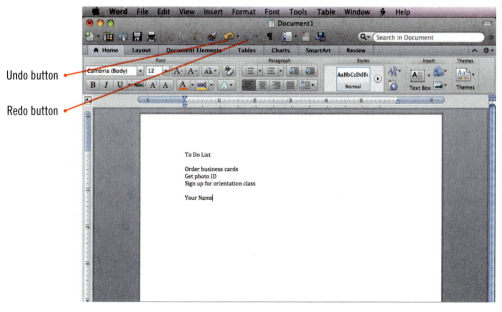

Exploring the Ribbon and View Options

The ribbon is a new feature in Office 2011 that provides quick access to the tools you use as you work with an Office program. Some commands on the ribbon are the same across all Office programs, whereas others vary according to the program. For instance, all Office programs have similar commands on the Home tab for changing font attributes, paragraph formatting options, and adding styles. The View buttons, described in Table E-1, are available at the left end of the status bar and from the View menu. You can use the View buttons to switch to a different predefined view, such as Draft or Outline view. You continue working on your to-do list while exploring the ribbon and different view options.

STEPS

1. **Click the Layout tab on the ribbon**

   The Layout tab becomes active. This tab contains commands for changing the layout of your document on the printed page, as shown in Figure E-10. This tab contains the groups Page Setup, Margins, Text Layout, Page Background, and Grid.

2. **In the Margins group, click the Left margin spin box, then click the down arrow five times**

   As you click, the left margin gets smaller, so your to-do list items move left in the document window. The left margin of the document changes to 1 inch. A margin is the blank space on the top, bottom, left, and right sides of a document.

3. **Click the Right margin spin box, then click the down arrow five times**

   The Right margin of the document changes to 1 inch. Compare your screen with Figure E-11.

4. **Locate the six view buttons on the status bar**

   By default, the Print Layout view is selected.

5. **Click the Full Screen View button**

   Full Screen view is a new feature in Word 2011. Your To Do List document now appears full screen, allowing you to concentrate on the content of your document. Compare your screen with Figure E-12. Changing your view does not change the document itself; you simply see a document differently in order to focus on specific stages of the project, such as entering text, formatting, or reading.

6. **Click Exit on the toolbar at the top of your computer screen**

   Your document returns to the previous view option used. In this example, your To Do List document returns to Print Layout view.

FIGURE E-10: Layout tab on the ribbon

Layout tab

Margins group

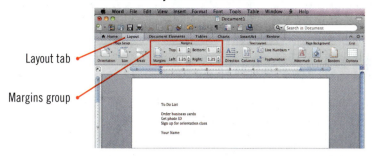

FIGURE E-11: Left and right margins changed to 1 inch

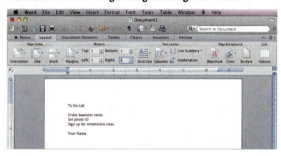

FIGURE E-12: Full Screen view

Toolbar

Exit button

TABLE E-1: View options

view	icon	Office program	description
Draft view	☰	Word	Create and edit text in a simplified layout
Outline view	☷	Word	Create an outline with multiple levels
Publishing Layout view	▣	Word	Create newsletters, brochures, and more, using desktop publishing tools
Print Layout view	▤	Word	Create a document as it will appear on the printed page; the default view in Word
Notebook Layout view	▥	Word	Take notes, flag items, and record audio notes in a specialized notebook document
Full Screen view	▦	Word	Maximize the space while working in a reading or authoring mode
Web Layout		Word	See how your document will appear when uploaded to the Web (available from View menu)
Normal view	▦	Excel	Create and edit worksheet data in a simplified layout; the default view in Excel
Page Layout view	▦	Excel	Create a worksheet with all elements as they will appear on the printed page
Normal view	▣	PowerPoint	Create and edit slides in a presentation with a three-pane layout that includes the slide/outline pane, the slide pane, and the notes pane; the default view in PowerPoint
Slide Sorter view	▦	PowerPoint	View each slide as a thumbnail, making it easy to reorder slides and add effects
Slide Show	�&	PowerPoint	View presentation slides full screen with all effects
Notes Pages view		PowerPoint	Edit speaker's notes with a view of the slide (available from View menu)
Presenter view		PowerPoint	Practice your presentation skills with a timer, speaker notes, and a preview of your next slide (available from View menu)

Exploring the Toolbox and Media Browser

The Toolbox and Media Browser are updated with new features in Office 2011 that provide quick access to tools you'll use in the Office programs. The updated Toolbox contains several tools you activate by clicking the appropriate tab, such as Reference Tools and Compatibility Report. See Table E-2 for a description of the Toolbox tabs. The Media Browser is a new feature that contains the tools needed to insert photos, sound, movies, clip art, symbols, and shapes into your documents. You'd like to enhance your to-do list, so you review the available options in the Toolbox and Media Browser.

STEPS

TROUBLE
The Toolbox and Media Browser might appear in another location on your screen. If so, you can move it by clicking and dragging its title bar.

1. **Click the Toolbox button on the Standard toolbar, then click the Compatibility Report tab**
   The Toolbox opens and displays the Compatibility Report tab, as shown in Figure E-13.

2. **Click the Check compatibility with pop-up menu arrows , then click Word 2010**
   The Compatibility Report is run and no issues were found that would create problems if you open the To Do List document in Word 2010.

3. **Click the Close button to close the Toolbox**

QUICK TIP
You can also close the Toolbox or Media Browser by clicking the Toolbox or Media Browser button on the Standard toolbar to deselect it.

4. **Click after Your Name on your To Do List document, if necessary, then press [return] twice**

5. **Click the Media Browser button to open the Media Browser**
   The Media Browser opens to the right of the document window, as shown in Figure E-14.

6. **Click the Clip Art tab on the Media Browser**
   The available clip art is displayed as miniature images called thumbnails.

7. **Scroll down until you find a piece of clip art that you would like to add to your to-do list, then click and drag it from the Media Browser onto your document below your name**
   The piece of clip art will be added to your document below the text, as shown in Figure E-15.

8. **Click the Close button to close the Media Browser**

TABLE E-2: Toolbox tabs

tab	icon	description
Styles		Word only; enables you to format text and paragraphs using predefined formatting attributes to give your document a professional, cohesive look
Citations		Word only; enables you to insert citations and build a bibliography
Scrapbook		Enables you to copy and paste multiple items to and from documents and among files created with all the Office programs
Reference Tools		Contains dictionary, thesaurus, and translation tools
Compatibility Report		Enables you to check compatibility issues with other versions of Office, including both Mac and Windows versions
Formula Builder	f_x	Excel only; helps you create mathematical calculations
Custom Animation		PowerPoint only; enables you to manage your animation effects effectively

FIGURE E-13: Toolbox

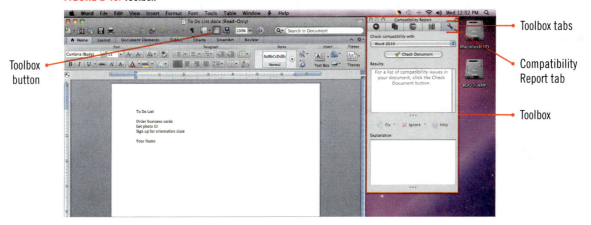

Toolbox button

Toolbox tabs

Compatibility Report tab

Toolbox

FIGURE E-14: Media Browser

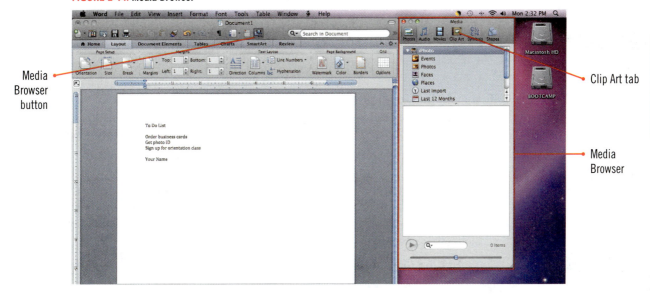

Media Browser button

Clip Art tab

Media Browser

FIGURE E-15: Clip art added to the To Do List document

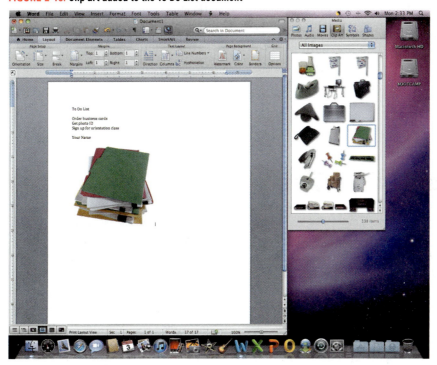

Office 2011

Saving and Closing a File

To keep a document permanently so that you can access it later, you must save it as a **file** (an electronic collection of data). When you save a file, you choose a **filename**, which is a unique name for a file, so that you can identify it later; you also specify a location, such as a folder on your computer's hard drive, on a removable flash drive, or on a drive located on a network or on the Internet. You use the Save As command to save a file for the first time. You access the Save As command from the File option on the menu bar. You have finished your to-do list for now, so you decide to save it.

STEPS

1. **Click File on the menu bar**

   The File menu opens. The menu contains a Save command and a Save As command, as shown in Figure E-16. You use the Save As command when you need to save a file for the first time or to save a file with a different filename or in a different location, and you use the Save command when you want to save any changes made to an existing file since the last time you saved.

2. **Click Save As**

   The Save As dialog box opens, displaying the Documents folder. At the top of the dialog box is the Save As text box, where you enter the name you want for the file.

QUICK TIP

When you save a file for the first time, if you click the Save command on the File menu or the Save button 🖫 on the Standard toolbar, the Save As dialog box opens, so that you can assign the file a name and folder location.

3. **Verify that To Do List appears in the Save As text box**

   By default, the first words in your document, "To Do List", appear highlighted in the Save As text box as a suggested filename. The default location for all files created using the programs in the Office suite is the Documents folder. When you save a file, the program automatically assigns it a **file extension** to identify the program that created it. Documents created in Word 2011 have the file extension .docx; Excel 2011 documents have the file extension .xlsx; and PowerPoint 2011 documents have the file extension .pptx. Your computer might not be set to display the file extensions, in which case you won't see this information in the Save As text box, on the title bar of the document windows, or in Finder windows. This is not a problem; the information is still saved with the file.

QUICK TIP

You may need to click the Expand button ▾ to access the expanded Save As dialog box, as shown in Figure E-17.

4. **Navigate to the drive and folder where you store your Data Files**

   Compare your screen with Figure E-17.

5. **Click Save**

   The Save As dialog box closes and your To Do List document is saved in the drive and folder you specified. Notice that the title bar now displays the new filename.

6. **Click the Close button 🔴 to close the file**

   The To Do List document and the Word window close. Word remains open, but only the menu bar is visible at the top of your screen.

Using the Reference Tools in the Toolbox

As you create documents in Word, spreadsheets in Excel, or presentations in PowerPoint, you occasionally might want to look up words and other information on the Internet. Before you go to a search engine or dictionary Web site, you should know that you have a powerful research tool at your fingertips in Office 2011 called Reference Tools. Reference Tools lets you look up information from several data sources provided by Microsoft. For instance, if you want to look up a word, right-click the word, point to Look Up on the shortcut menu, and then click Definition. Reference Tools opens in the Toolbox on the right side of your screen and provides access to the Thesaurus for meanings and synonyms and the Dictionary for definitions. Other tools available in Reference Tools are the Bilingual Dictionary, Translation, and Web Search (Bing). Some of these options can also be opened using the Tools menu. To open Reference Tools manually, click the Toolbox button 📠 on the Standard toolbar, and then click the Reference Tools tab 📖 on the Toolbox.

FIGURE E-16: Word File menu

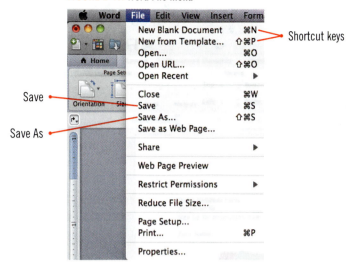

Save

Save As

Shortcut keys

FIGURE E-17: Save As dialog box

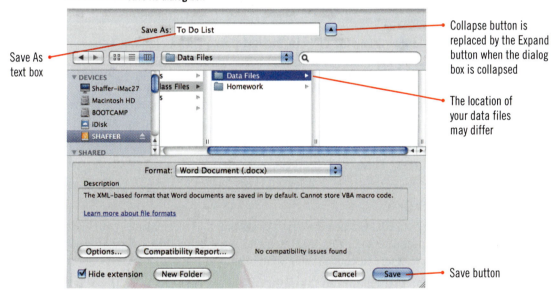

Save As text box

Collapse button is replaced by the Expand button when the dialog box is collapsed

The location of your data files may differ

Save button

Office 2011

Creating a New File from a Template

Though it's easy to create a document from scratch, you can take advantage of templates to quickly create professionally designed documents. A **template** is a special file that contains predesigned formatting, text, and other tools for creating business documents, such as letters, invoices, and business presentations. When you start a new document using a template, a predesigned document opens immediately on your screen, ready for you to customize and save. In all of the Office programs for Mac, you have access to the **Template Gallery**. The Template Gallery stores the templates for each program and opens by default when you open the program. In Word, it is titled the Word Document Gallery and contains the templates for Word; in Excel, it is titled the Excel Workbook Gallery and contains the templates for Excel; in PowerPoint, it is titled the PowerPoint Presentation Gallery and contains the templates for PowerPoint. Because you are new to Outdoor Designs, you decide to create a calendar for the first month to keep your work deadlines organized.

STEPS

QUICK TIP
The Word Document Gallery can also be accessed by clicking the New from Template button on the Standard toolbar, when a document window is open.

1. **Click File on the menu bar, then click New from Template**

   The Word Document Gallery opens with the left pane displaying the categories of templates available in Word, as shown in Figure E-18. The middle pane displays thumbnails of the available templates. The right pane displays a larger image of the selected template and additional options such as colors and fonts when available.

2. **Under Print Layout View in the left pane, click Calendars**

   The templates for Calendars are displayed in the middle pane.

3. **Click the Horizontal Sunday Start template, then click Choose**

   The template opens on your screen with the Select Calendar Dates dialog box open that allows you to select the month and year for the calendar you'd like to create, as shown in Figure E-19.

4. **If necessary, click the Month down arrow ▾, then click January. Next, click the Year down arrow ▾, click 2014, then click OK**

   The Select Calendar Dates dialog box closes and the Word 2011 Calendar dialog box opens.

5. **Click OK**

   The Word 2011 Calendar dialog box closes and a calendar for January 2014 is created with a section below the calendar dates for events. Next to Events you'll notice three columns that contain Latin words. The Office templates for Mac contain Latin words in all areas that need to be replaced with your original content.

6. **In the first column to the right of Events, click Dolor şit amet**

   This text will be highlighted in light blue. Any time text is highlighted in light blue, simply type the text you'd like to replace it with.

7. **Type January 1, click the paragraph of Latin words directly beneath it, then type New Years Day**

   The Latin words Sed egestas... are replaced with the new text.

8. **Press [tab] to move to the second column, then press [delete]**

   The contents of the second column are deleted.

9. **Press [tab] to move to the third column, then press [delete]**

   The contents of the third column are deleted. Compare your screen with Figure E-20.

10. **Save the file with the name January 2014 Calendar in the location where you store your Data Files, then click the Close button ⬤**

    The file is saved and the document window closes, but Word is still open and running.

FIGURE E-18: Word Document Gallery

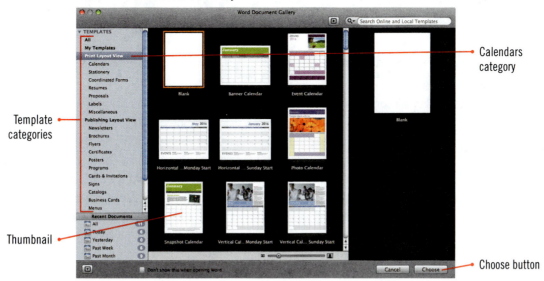

Template categories

Thumbnail

Calendars category

Choose button

FIGURE E-19: Template with dialog box

Down arrows used to make a selection

FIGURE E-20: Completed calendar

Getting Help and Quitting an Office Program

Office 2011 has a context-sensitive Help system designed to help you complete any task or use any feature in an Office program. The Office Help system is seamlessly integrated with the Microsoft Office Online Web site and provides a wide range of content to help answer your questions. Help is **context sensitive** in that it displays topics and instructions geared to the task you're performing. For example, if you point to a button on the Standard toolbar, a Help Tag displays a description of what the button does. Your Mac is unique in that closing a window does not close the program you are using. Once you are finished with a program or application, you need to quit it. You decide to familiarize yourself with the Help system by finding out more about the new features of Word 2011 and practice quitting a program. *Note*: You must be connected to the Internet to perform the steps in this lesson.

STEPS

1. **Click File on the menu bar, point to Open Recent, then click To Do List.docx**

   The To Do List document opens in the window. Using the Open Recent option on the File menu is a fast way to open frequently used files created or accessed with the open program.

2. **Position the pointer over the Line Spacing button ⬛ in the Paragraph group on the Home tab until the Help Tag appears**

   As shown in Figure E-21, the Help Tag displays the command name Line Spacing.

3. **Click the Microsoft Office Help button ⓘ on the Standard toolbar**

   The Word Help window opens and lists Help topics, as shown in Figure E-22. From this window, you can access the built-in Help files that come with the Office suite or you can access the online Microsoft Office for Mac Help files.

4. **Click Printing Documents, click Print a document, then click Print a document**

   The Word Help window displays step-by-step instructions on how to print a document, as shown in Figure E-23.

5. **Read the information in the Word Help window**

6. **Click the Search field of the Word Help window, type keyboard shortcuts, then press [return]**

   Word searches the built-in Help files for the keywords "keyboard shortcuts," then lists Help topics that contain those words. A **keyword** is a searchable word that is contained in the Help database.

7. **Click Common Office keyboard shortcuts in the results list, read the topic, then click the Close button ⬤**

   The Help window closes, but your To Do List document remains open. You're now ready to quit Word.

8. **Click Word on the menu bar, then click Quit Word**

   Both the To Do List document and the Word program close. If you had made changes to the To Do List since you saved it, a dialog box would have opened, prompting you to save the changes before quitting Word. You can save changes to a document at any time by clicking the Save button on the Standard toolbar.

FIGURE E-21: Example of a Help Tag

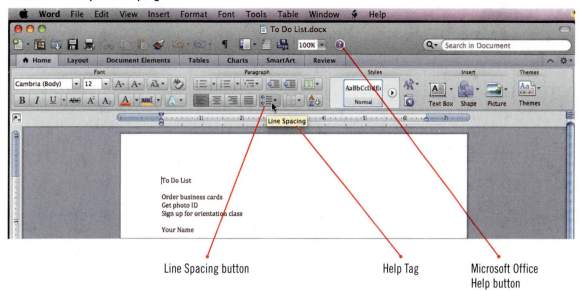

Line Spacing button   Help Tag   Microsoft Office
Help button

FIGURE E-22: Word Help window

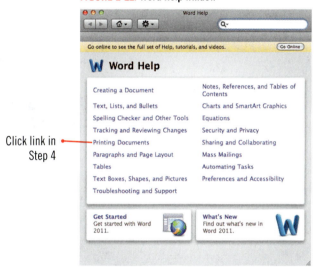

Click link in
Step 4

FIGURE E-23: Print a document Help topic

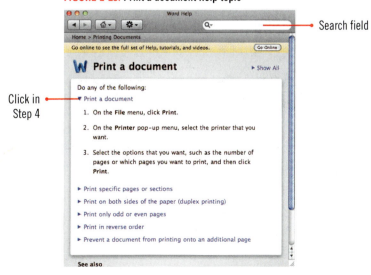

Search field

Click in
Step 4

Practice

Concepts Review

Label each of the elements shown in Figure E-24.

FIGURE E-24

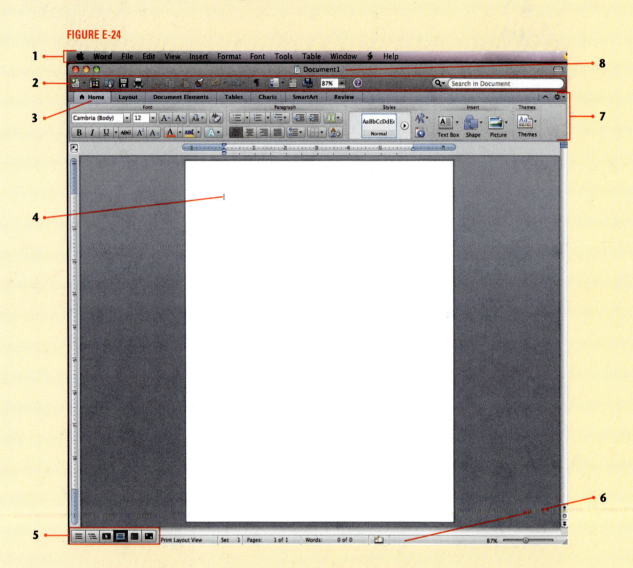

Match each of the following tasks with the most appropriate program for completing it.

 9. Create a report containing graphics
10. Create a budget
11. Store contact information and send e-mail
12. Create slides for a company meeting presentation

a. Microsoft Excel
b. Microsoft Word
c. Microsoft PowerPoint
d. Microsoft Outlook

Creating a Document

Files You Will Need:

F-1.docx
F-2.docx
F-3.docx
F-4.docx
F-5.docx

You can create professional-looking documents using Microsoft Word 2011, the word processing program that comes with Microsoft Office for Mac 2011. In this unit, you learn some basic skills to help you create, edit, and print a document. You also learn how to copy and move text, find and replace text, enhance the appearance of text, and check your spelling and grammar.  Karen Rivera, the marketing director for Outdoor Designs, asks you to finish a letter to the winner of the annual Outdoor Designs birdhouse competition. The letter congratulates the winner and provides information on his prizes and benefits. Karen has already created a document that contains part of the letter. You open Karen's letter; add, edit, and rearrange text in it; proof it for spelling errors; and then print it.

OBJECTIVES

Create a new document from an existing file

Enter text in a document

Select and edit text

Copy text

Move text

Find and replace text

Format text using the ribbon

Check spelling and grammar

Preview and print a document

Creating a New Document from an Existing File

Sometimes it is useful to create a document that uses content from an existing document. For instance, suppose you need to write a memo that will use content from a memo you already wrote. You use the Open dialog box to open the existing memo. Then, before making any changes to the opened memo, you can use the Save As command to save a copy of it with a new name. This keeps the original file intact in case you want to use it again, while saving you the trouble of creating the new memo from scratch. 🎨 You need to complete Karen's letter to the winner of the birdhouse competition. To do this, you decide to open Karen's document and save it with a different name, to use her content but keep her original letter intact.

STEPS

QUICK TIP
If the Word icon is not on the Dock, click the Finder icon on the Dock, click Applications in the Finder window, locate and click Microsoft Office 2011, then double-click Microsoft Word.

1. **Click the Microsoft Word icon 🅦 on the Dock**
   Word starts and displays the Word Document Gallery, as shown in Figure F-1.

2. ▶ **If All is selected under Templates, click Word Document if necessary, then click Choose. If Print Layout View is selected under Templates, click Blank if necessary, then click Choose**
   A blank document opens in the document window.

QUICK TIP
You can also click File on the menu bar, and then click Open to open the Open: Microsoft Word dialog box.

3. ▶ **Click the Open a document button 📖 on the Standard toolbar**
   The Open: Microsoft Word dialog box opens and displays the folders and files in the current folder.

4. **Navigate to the location where you store your Data Files**
   See Figure F-2.

5. **Click F-1.docx, then click Open**
   Karen's partially completed document opens in the document window.

6. **Click File on the menu bar, then click Save As**
   The Save As dialog box opens, as shown in Figure F-3. You use the Save As dialog box to create a copy of the document with a new name. Notice that the name in the Save As text box is also **selected**, or highlighted. Any words you type replace the selected text in the Save As text box.

7. **Type F-Birdhouse Winner Letter**
   The Save As text box now contains the new filename you typed. The filename begins with "F-" so you will be able to identify it as a file you created for Unit F of this book.

8. **Navigate to the location where you store your Data Files if necessary, then click Save**
   Word saves the F-Birdhouse Winner Letter file on the selected storage device in the folder you specified. The title bar changes to reflect the new name, as shown in Figure F-4. The file F-1 closes and remains intact.

FIGURE F-1: Word Document Gallery

If All is selected, click
Word Document

If Print Layout View is
selected, click Blank

Word Document

Choose button

FIGURE F-2: Open: Microsoft Word dialog box

View buttons

Back button

Forward button

Sidebar

Click to select a different
folder or drive

F-1.docx

Click to select file type
to display in dialog box

Open button

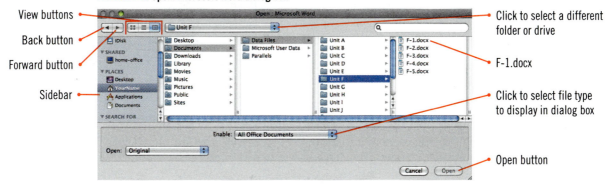

FIGURE F-3: Save As dialog box

Filename

Click to create a
new folder in the
current folder

Click to select format
for saved document

Save button

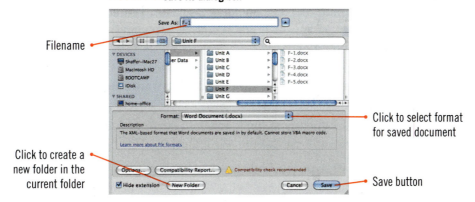

FIGURE F-4: Word program window with F-Birdhouse Winner Letter file open

Title bar shows
new name of file

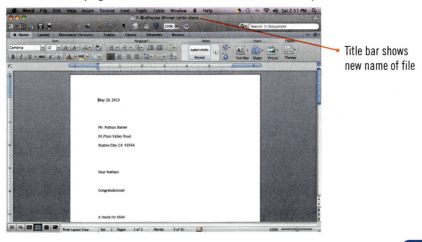

Entering Text in a Document

To add text to a document, you first need to click where you want to insert text, and then start typing. Typing text is also called **entering** text. Before you start typing, you should check that you are viewing the document in a way that's suitable for entering and editing text. **Draft** view is best for entering and editing text because several of the page elements are hidden so that you can focus on writing and editing. It's also a good idea to turn on formatting marks when you enter text in a document so that you can see blank spaces and paragraph marks. Karen's letter contains some text. You need to add a paragraph informing the recipient that he won the contest.

STEPS

1. **Click the Show all nonprinting characters button ¶ on the Standard toolbar**

   Your screen now displays formatting marks. Dots between words represent spaces, and a ¶ (paragraph mark) represents a paragraph return that Word inserts when you press [return]. Showing formatting marks when you write and edit makes it easier to see extra spaces, paragraph returns, and other punctuation errors.

2. **Click the Draft View button ≡ on the left end of the status bar**

   The document now appears in Draft view, which is a better view for focusing on editing text. Notice that you can see more of the document text in Draft view. You can also switch to Draft view by clicking View on the menu bar, and then clicking Draft.

3. **Click to the right of the word Congratulations! in the sixth line of text**

   Clicking in the document window places the **insertion point**, the blinking vertical line on the screen, to indicate where text will be inserted when you type.

4. **Press ↓ (the down arrow key) two times**

   The insertion point is now next to the second paragraph mark below "Congratulations!"

5. **Type the following text, but do *not* press [return] when you reach the right edge of your document: I am pleased to inform you that you won the Outdoor Designs annual birdhouse competition!**

   The insertion point moved to the right as you typed each word. At some point, the words you typed moved down, or **wrapped**, to the next line. This is known as **word wrap**, a feature that automatically pushes text to the next line when the insertion point meets the right margin.

6. **Press [spacebar], then type the following text: Your Chickadee Cottage birdhouse received the highest scores from our judges.**

7. **Press [spacebar], type teh, then press [spacebar]**

   Notice that even though you typed "teh", Word assumed that you meant to type "The" and automatically corrected it. This is called **AutoCorrect**.

8. **Type the following text exactly as shown (including errors): follong prizes will be shipped shipped to you separately:**

   You should see red, wavy lines under the word "follong" and the second instance of "shipped." These red lines indicate that the spelling checker identified these as either misspelled or duplicate words. Green, wavy lines indicate possible grammatical errors.

9. **Press [return], then click the Save button 🖫 on the Standard toolbar**

   Your changes are saved to the file. Compare your screen with Figure F-5. Pressing [return] moved the insertion point down one line at the left margin because of the default style in this document. **Styles** are settings that control how text and paragraphs are formatted. Each document has its own set of styles, which you can easily change. You will work with styles in a future unit.

FIGURE F-5: Letter with new text entered

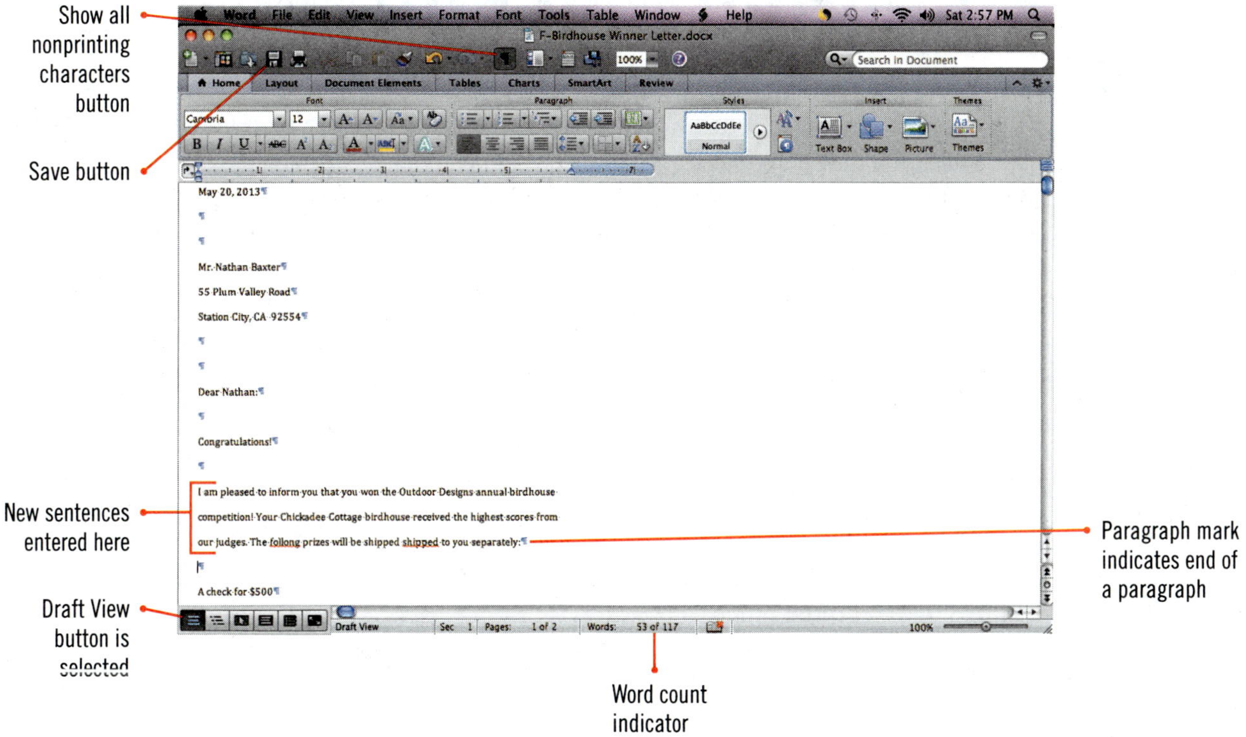

Show all nonprinting characters button

Save button

May 20, 2013

Mr. Nathan Baxter
55 Plum Valley Road
Station City, CA 92554

Dear Nathan:

Congratulations!

New sentences entered here

I am pleased to inform you that you won the Outdoor Designs annual birdhouse competition! Your Chickadee Cottage birdhouse received the highest scores from our judges. The follong prizes will be shipped shipped to you separately:

A check for $500

Paragraph mark indicates end of a paragraph

Draft View button is selected

Draft View   Sec   1   Pages: 1 of 2   Words: 53 of 117   100%

Word count indicator

Using AutoCorrect

Like the spelling checker in Word, AutoCorrect is a feature that proofs your typing, making corrections to certain words as you type. For example, if you type "comapny" instead of "company", Word corrects the misspelling as soon as you press [spacebar]. After Word makes the correction, you can point to the word to make a small blue bar appear under the corrected text. If you place the pointer over this bar, the AutoCorrect Options button appears. Click the AutoCorrect Options button to display a menu of options, as shown in Figure F-6, and then click an option.

You can change AutoCorrect settings in the AutoCorrect dialog box. To open this dialog box, click Control AutoCorrect Options in the AutoCorrect Options menu, or click Word on the menu bar, click Preferences, and then click AutoCorrect in the Authoring and Proofing Tools group in the Word Preferences dialog box.

FIGURE F-6: AutoCorrect Options menu

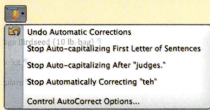

Undo Automatic Corrections
Stop Auto-capitalizing First Letter of Sentences
Stop Auto-capitalizing After "judges."
Stop Automatically Correcting "teh"
Control AutoCorrect Options...

Selecting and Editing Text

You can **edit**, or modify, the text in a Word document in several ways. To delete individual letters, first click to the right of the unwanted letters to place the insertion point, and then press [delete], or click to the left of the letters, and then press [delete ⊠]. To delete several words or paragraphs, you must first select, or highlight, the unwanted text, and then press [delete]. To select text, click, drag the I-beam across the text, then release the button. To edit text, you need to move the insertion point around the document. You can do this by pointing and clicking or by using the keyboard. Table F-1 describes other useful methods for selecting text. Table F-2 describes keys you can use to move the insertion point around the document. (Note that the [home], [end], and [delete ⊠] keys appear on the standard Mac keyboard but do not appear on Mac laptop keyboards.) 🎨 As you read the memo, you decide to make some changes to correct errors and improve the wording.

STEPS

1. **Click to the right of $500 in the line of text below the paragraph you typed**

   The insertion point is just after the second 0 in 500.

2. **Press [delete] three times**

   You deleted "500." Each time you pressed [delete], you deleted a character to the left of the insertion point.

3. **Type 250**

   The amount of the prize money now reads $250, the correct amount.

4. **Double-click the second instance of shipped in the third line of the new paragraph you typed**

   The word "shipped" is now selected. Double-clicking a word selects the entire word.

5. **Press [delete]**

   The second instance of the word "shipped" is removed from the document. You could have deleted either instance of the duplicated word to remove the red wavy line to correct the error. The text after the deleted word wraps back to fill the empty space.

6. **If necessary, scroll to the end of the document, place the pointer to the left of Karen Rivera (the last line of the document) until the pointer changes to ↗, then click**

   See Figure F-7. The entire line of text (Karen Rivera) is selected, including the ¶ at the end of the line. The left margin of the document is the area you can use to select entire lines. When you place the pointer in the left margin, it changes to ↗.

7. **Type your name**

   Your name replaces Karen's name in the letter.

8. **Press ⌘[A] to select the entire document, click ⯆ in the Styles Gallery on the Home tab of the ribbon, then click the No Spacing style**

   The document is now single-spaced. The font and font size has changed to Calibri (Body), 11 point.

9. **Press ⌘[home] to move the insertion point to the top of the document, then click the Save button 💾 on the Standard toolbar**

   Compare your screen with Figure F-8.

FIGURE F-7: Selecting an entire line of text

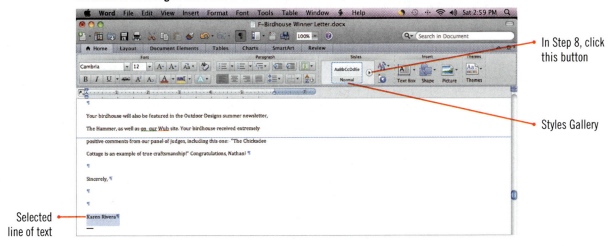

In Step 8, click this button

Styles Gallery

Selected line of text

FIGURE F-8: Edited document

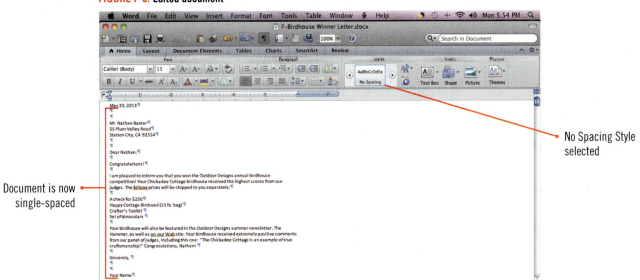

No Spacing Style selected

Document is now single-spaced

TABLE F-1: Methods for selecting text

text to select	selection method
One word	Double-click the word
A paragraph	Triple-click any word in the paragraph
A line of text	Position ⬀ to the left of the line, then click
An entire document	Press ⌘[A]

TABLE F-2: Useful keys for moving the insertion point around a document (using a standard Mac keyboard)

keyboard key	moves insertion point
⬆ or ⬇	Up or down one line
⬅ or ➡	Left or right one character
[option]⬅ or [option]➡	One word to the left or right
[home] or [end]	To the beginning or end of the line
⌘[home] or ⌘[end]	To the beginning or end of the document

Copying Text

When editing a document, you often need to copy text from one place to another. **Copying** leaves the text in its original location, and **pasting** places a duplicate of it to the location you specify. When you copy and paste text, you first need to select the text you want to copy. Next, you use the Copy command to place a copy of the selected text on the operating system's **Clipboard**, a temporary storage area in your computer's memory for copied items. Finally, you use the Paste command to insert the copied text to a new location. If you need to copy multiple items, you can use the **Scrapbook**, which works like the operating system Clipboard but stores an unlimited number of items at a time; it is available only in Office programs. You can also duplicate text using a technique called **drag and drop**, where you select the text you want to copy, press and hold [option], and then use the pointer to drag a copy of it to a new location. Items you drag and drop do not get copied to the Clipboard or the Scrapbook. While checking your memo, you decide to copy text from one location and paste it to another.

STEPS

1. **Click to the left of the first C in Chickadee in the second line of the second paragraph to set the insertion point, press and hold the left button, drag the pointer to the end of the Cottage and the space after it, then release the button**

   The words "Chickadee Cottage" and the space after it are now selected.

QUICK TIP
You can use keyboard shortcuts to copy selected text to the Clipboard by pressing ⌘[C]. To paste text from the Clipboard, press ⌘[V].

2. **Click the Copy button ▭ on the Standard toolbar**

   Though you don't see a change on the screen, the selected text is copied to the operating system Clipboard.

3. **Click to the left of birdhouse in the first line of the last paragraph, then click the Paste button ▭ on the Standard toolbar**

   The copied text is pasted into the document and also remains on the Clipboard, where you can paste it as many more times as you like (until you replace the item on the Clipboard with another copied or cut item). See Figure F-9. The Paste Options smart tag ▭ appears under the pasted text.

4. **Click the Paste Options smart tag ▭**

   The Paste Options menu opens and displays several options for applying formatting to the pasted text. By default, the pasted text maintains its original formatting, which in this situation is fine because it matches the text.

5. **Press [esc] to close the Paste Options menu**

6. **Select Outdoor Designs and the space after it in the first line of the second paragraph**

7. **Press and hold [option], drag the selected text to the left of Crafter's Toolkit three lines below the paragraph, release the button, then release [option]**

   As you drag, the pointer changes to the Copy pointer ▭ and a transparent image of the selection moves with the pointer. As shown in Figure F-10, "Outdoor Designs" is copied to the new location to the left of "Crafter's Toolkit".

8. **Click the Save button ▭ on the Standard toolbar**

FIGURE F-9: Text pasted from the operating system Clipboard

Copy button

Paste button

Copied text

Pasted text

Paste Options
smart tag

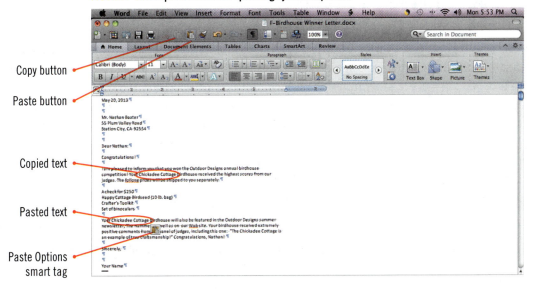

FIGURE F-10: Dragged and copied text

Original text

Dragged and
copied text

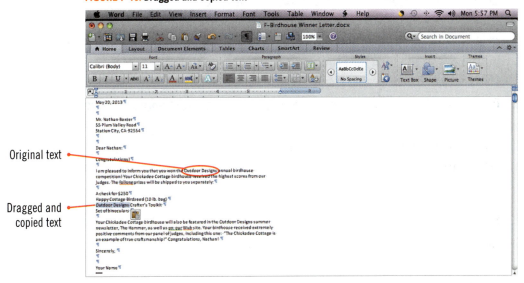

Copying and pasting items with the Scrapbook

If you need to copy multiple items, you can use the Scrapbook located in the Toolbox. To open the Scrapbook, click the Toolbox button ▣ on the Standard toolbar, and then click the Scrapbook tab ▣ at the top of the Toolbox. To add an item to the Scrapbook, select it, and then click the Add button on the Scrapbook. Repeat the process for any additional items you want to add to the Scrapbook. See Figure F-11. An item added to the Scrapbook is called a **clip**. To paste a clip into a document, first place the insertion point where you'd like the item to be pasted, select the clip on the Scrapbook, and then click the Paste button on the Scrapbook. The Scrapbook can store unlimited clips, although only when the Scrapbook is active (open on the Toolbox). If the Scrapbook is not active, you can copy only one item at a time using the operating system Clipboard. Items placed in the Scrapbook remain there until deleted, even after you quit Word, so that you can use them again if needed.

FIGURE F-11: Scrapbook containing multiple clips

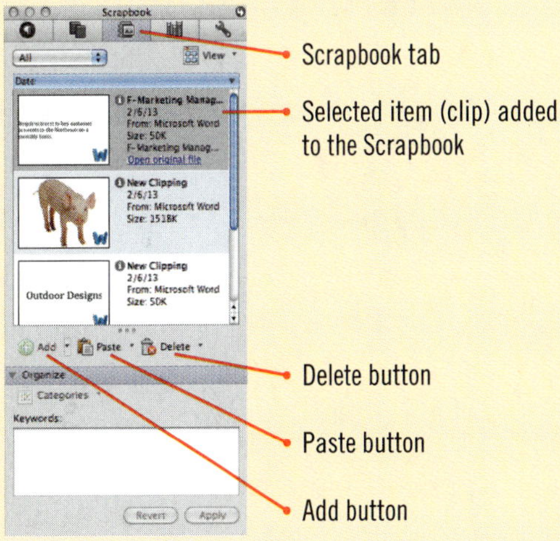

Scrapbook tab

Selected item (clip) added
to the Scrapbook

Delete button

Paste button

Add button

Moving Text

While editing a document, you may decide that certain text works better in a different location. Perhaps you want to switch the order of two paragraphs or of two words in a sentence. Instead of deleting and retyping the text, you can move it. **Moving** text removes it from its original location and places it in a new location that you specify. You can move text to a new location using the Cut and Paste commands. Using the **Cut** command removes selected text from your document and places it on the operating system Clipboard. To place the cut text in another location, you use the Paste command. You can also move text by selecting it and then dragging it to a new location. Items that you move using the drag-and-drop method do not get copied to the Clipboard or to the Scrapbook.  While checking your memo, you decide that you want to rearrange the list of prizes so that they appear in a more logical order.

STEPS

1. **Position the pointer to the left of Outdoor Designs Crafter's Toolkit until it changes to ⬈, then click**

   The entire line, including the paragraph mark, is selected. See Figure F-12.

QUICK TIP

To cut selected text to the Clipboard using the keyboard shortcut, press ⌘[X].

2. **Click the Cut button ✄ on the Standard toolbar**

   The text is removed from the document and placed on the Clipboard.

3. **Click to the left of the H in Happy Cottage Birdseed (10 lb. bag), then click the Paste button 📋 on the Standard toolbar**

   The text is pasted from the Clipboard to the new location, on the line below "A check for $250."

4. **Place the pointer to the left of Set of binoculars until it changes to ⬈, then click to select the entire line**

5. **Move the pointer over the selected text, click and drag it up to the left of Happy, then release the button**

   As you drag, the selection becomes transparent and moves with the pointer. Also, an indicator line shows you where the text will be placed. Now the prizes are listed in a more logical order, with the best prizes listed first, as shown in Figure F-13.

6. **Click the Save button 💾 on the Standard toolbar**

FIGURE F-12: Selecting a line of text

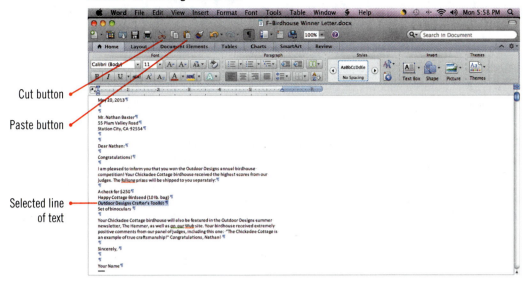

Cut button

Paste button

Selected line of text

FIGURE F-13: Moving text by dragging it

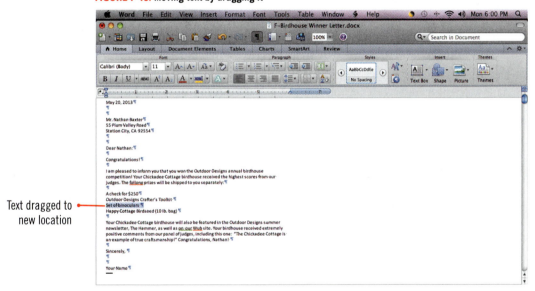

Text dragged to new location

Using the Thumbnails Pane to navigate in your document

You can use the Thumbnails Pane to quickly navigate in a multipage document. To open the Thumbnails Pane, click the Sidebar button [icon] on the Standard toolbar. If necessary, click the Thumbnails Pane tab [icon] to open it. As shown in Figure F-14, a thumbnail of each page of your multipage document is visible on the left side of your screen, with the active page highlighted in blue. To move to another page, simply click the thumbnail of the page you'd like to move to. To close the sidebar, click the Close button [icon].

FIGURE F-14: Thumbnails Pane on the sidebar

Finding and Replacing Text

Once in a while, you might need to locate a specific word or phrase in a long document or you might want to make a global change in a document. For instance, let's say you are writing a novel about two characters named Bob and Gracey. After writing 50 pages, you want to know when Gracey first appears in the novel; you also decide to change the male character's name to George. You could manually search for the first instance of Gracey, and you could edit the document to change each occurrence of Bob to George, but there are easier, automated methods. The **Find**, or **search**, **command** helps you quickly and easily find a word or phrase in a document. The **Replace command** helps you quickly and easily substitute a new word or phrase for one or more occurrences of a particular word or phrase in a document. Choosing the Replace command opens the **sidebar** with the Find and Replace tab selected, where you can specify the text you want to find and the text with which you want to replace it. You can replace every occurrence of the text in one action or you can review each occurrence and choose to replace or keep the text. 🎨🖌️ Karen just told you to make sure that the letter mentions that the winner's birdhouse will be featured in the company newsletter and that the winning birdhouse name in the letter is incorrect. You need to ensure that the newsletter is mentioned in the letter and to replace all instances of the incorrect name with the correct name. You decide to use the Find and Replace commands to make these changes.

STEPS

1. **Press ⌘[home] and locate the Search field, as shown in Figure F-15**

   Pressing ⌘[home] moves the insertion point to the beginning of the document. This ensures that Word starts searching for occurrences of your specified text at the beginning of the document.

2. **Click in the Search field**

   When you click in the Search field, the dimmed words "Search in Document" disappear and the Search field becomes active.

3. **Type newsletter**

   As shown in Figure F-16, the word "newsletter" is highlighted with a dark yellow color. If "newsletter" occurred in this document more than once, the remaining words would be highlighted in a lighter shade of yellow. You would then use the back and forward arrows in the Search field to move to the next occurrence of the word.

4. **Click anywhere in your document and press ⌘[home] to move to the top of your document**

5. **Double-click newsletter in the Search field, type Cottage, click the magnifying glass button 🔍▾ next to the Search field, then click Replace on the pop-up menu**

   The sidebar opens with the Find and Replace tab selected, as shown in Figure F-17. "Cottage" appears in the Search In Document text box and the four matches are listed beneath it.

6. **Type Cabana in the Replace With text box, then click Replace**

   The first instance of Cottage is replaced with Cabana, Word moves to the next match, and the first match is deleted from the Matches list.

7. **Click Find to skip Happy Cottage Birdseed, then click Replace two times**

   Word replaces the two remaining instances of "Cottage" with "Cabana" and only Happy Cottage Birdseed (10 lb. bag) remains on the Matches List.

8. **Click the Close button ⊗ to close the sidebar**

   The sidebar closes and your document once again fills the program window.

9. **Click the Save button 💾 on the Standard toolbar**

   Your changes are saved.

Creating a Document

FIGURE F-15: Search field

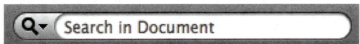

FIGURE F-16: First occurrence of found text

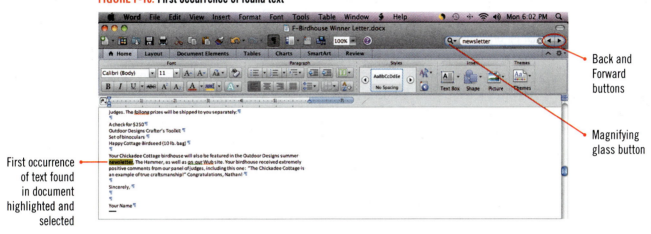

Back and Forward buttons

Magnifying glass button

First occurrence of text found in document highlighted and selected

FIGURE F-17: Sidebar with Find and Replace tab selected

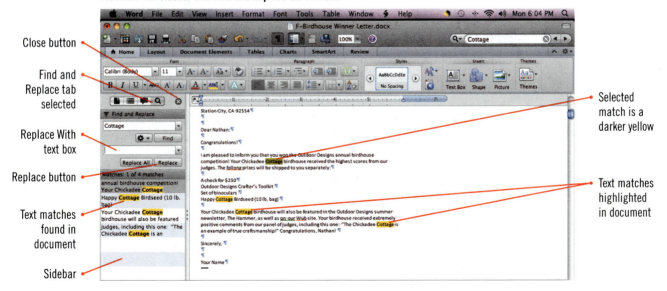

Close button

Find and Replace tab selected

Replace With text box

Replace button

Text matches found in document

Sidebar

Selected match is a darker yellow

Text matches highlighted in document

Creating a Document

Formatting Text Using the Ribbon

As you work in Word 2011, you will discover many tools for **formatting** a document, or enhancing its appearance and readability. Perhaps the simplest of these tools is the Font group on the Home tab of the ribbon. The Font group contains common formatting commands, so it's perfect for making quick changes to text. For instance, you can use the Font group to change the font of selected text. A **font** is the design of a set of characters, such as Arial or Times New Roman. You can also use the Font group to change the **font style** by applying bold, italic, or underline formatting, or to change the **font size** of selected text so that it is larger or smaller. You can also format selected paragraphs as a bulleted list using the Paragraph group on the Home tab of the ribbon.  You decide to enhance the appearance of the letter by formatting the word "Congratulations!" in bold with a larger font size, formatting the list of prizes as a bulleted list, and applying italic font style to the newsletter title.

STEPS

1. **Click the Print Layout View button 🖻 on the status bar**

   Now that you are going to make formatting changes to your document, it's a good idea to change the view to Print Layout so you can see a more accurate picture of how the changes will look on the page.

2. **Position the pointer ⬈ to the left of Congratulations! in the first paragraph, then click**

   The word "Congratulations" and the exclamation point and ¶ that follow it are selected.

3. **Click the Bold button B**

   The selected text "Congratulations!" now appears in a darker and thicker font, to set it apart from the other text in the memo.

4. **Click the Increase Font Size button A⁴ three times**

   The selected text grows in size from 11 to 16, as shown in Figure F-18. The new font size appears in the Font Size text box in the Font group. You measure font size using points. A **point** is $1/72$", so a font size of 12, for example, is $1/6$".

5. **Select the four lines of text containing the prizes, starting with A check for $250 and ending with Happy Cottage Birdseed (10 lb. bag)**

   The four prizes are now selected. You can now apply formatting to the selected text. You decide to make the prizes look more ordered by formatting them as a bulleted list.

6. **Click the Bulleted List button ☰ in the Paragraph group, then click outside the list**

   Each item in the list is indented and preceded by a small round dot or **bullet**. The listed items now stand out much better from the body of the memo text and help create a more organized appearance.

7. **Select the text The Hammer in the second line of the paragraph below the bulleted list, then click the Italic button I in the Font group**

   The title of the Outdoor Designs newsletter, *The Hammer*, now appears in italic. Compare your screen with Figure F-19.

8. **Save your changes**

Creating a Document

FIGURE F-18: Font size of text increased and bold applied

Font group

Bold button

Italic button

Increase Font Size button

Bulleted List button

Bold text with larger font size

Print Layout View button

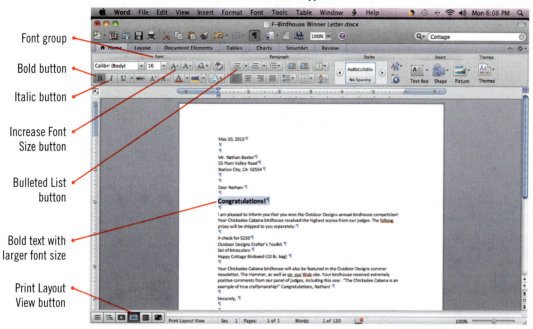

FIGURE F-19: Letter with formatted text and bulleted list

Bulleted list

Title in italic

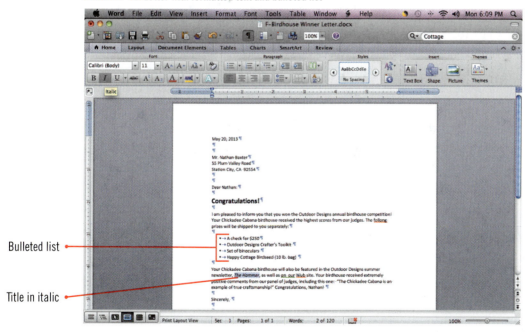

Checking Spelling and Grammar

Word provides tools to help you make sure that your documents are free of spelling and grammatical errors. Word's AutoCorrect feature corrects your errors as you type them, but Word cannot correct all mistakes in this way. The program identifies possible misspelled words by comparing each word with its built-in dictionary, and then underlines any words that are not in its dictionary with red, wavy lines. Word identifies possible grammatical errors such as passive voice by underlining them with green, wavy lines. If you right-click a flagged misspelled word or grammatical error, a shortcut menu opens, displaying a list of correctly spelled or phrased alternatives. You can also open the Spelling and Grammar dialog box to check a document for misspelled words and grammatical errors. You decide to use Word's spelling and grammar checking tools to ensure that your letter is free of errors.

STEPS

TROUBLE
If you cannot right-click, press and hold [control], then click the word.

1. **Right-click the word Wub in the second line of the last paragraph in the letter**

   A shortcut menu opens, displaying a list of alternatives to the misspelled word, as shown in Figure F-20. Other options you can choose in this menu include Ignore (if you decide the word is correct and want Word to skip it and go to the next word in the document), Ignore All (if you want Word to stop alerting you to the possible misspelling of this word in the document), Add (if you want Word to add this word as spelled to its built-in dictionary), and AutoCorrect (if you want Word to automatically correct this spelling in the future).

2. **Click Web from the list at the top of the shortcut menu**

   The shortcut menu closes and the word "Web" replaces the misspelled word.

3. **Press ⌘[home] to move the insertion point to the top of the letter**

   The insertion point moves to the beginning of this document.

QUICK TIP
If the Spelling and Grammar dialog box flags a word that is not in fact misspelled, you can prevent Word from flagging the word in the future by clicking Add.

4. **Click Tools on the menu bar, then click Spelling and Grammar**

   The Spelling and Grammar dialog box opens. See Figure F-21. The top text box displays text in red that is flagged as a problem, and the bottom text box displays suggestions for fixing it. The dialog box also contains an Ignore button, which you can click if you don't want Word to make a change. Word identifies the word "follong" as a possible misspelled word. It suggests changing the spelling to "following," which is correct.

5. **Verify that the Check grammar check box contains a check mark, then click Change**

   Word changes "follong" to "following" and moves to the next possible error, an extra space between "on" and "our" in the last paragraph.

QUICK TIP
If the correct spelling of the word does not appear in the list, you can type it in the top section of the dialog box, then click Change.

6. **Click Change**

   Word deletes the extra space and an alert box opens, indicting the spelling and grammar check is complete.

7. **Click OK, then save your changes**

Creating a Document

FIGURE F-20: Spelling shortcut menu

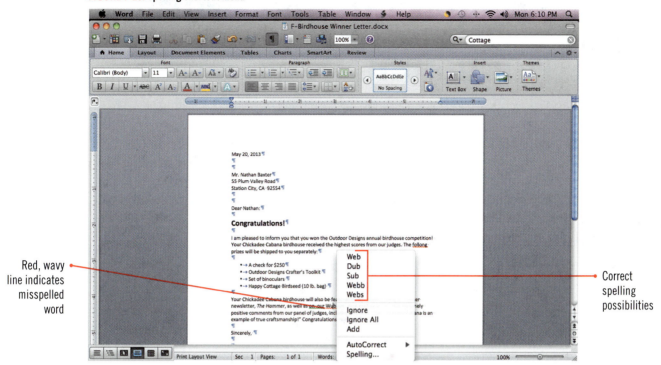

Red, wavy line indicates misspelled word

Correct spelling possibilities

FIGURE F-21: Spelling and Grammar: English (US) dialog box with spelling error

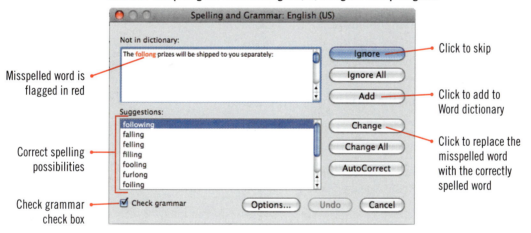

Misspelled word is flagged in red

Correct spelling possibilities

Check grammar check box

Click to skip

Click to add to Word dictionary

Click to replace the misspelled word with the correctly spelled word

Translating words or documents into other languages

With Word 2011, you can translate any word in your document, or even an entire document, into any of 14 different languages. To make the translation, click the Reference Tools tab on the Toolbox, and then click the Translation group on the Reference Tools tab to open the group. Click the pop-up menu arrows next to From and To in the Translation group to specify which language you want to translate from and which language you want to translate to. Next, select the words or sentences you want to translate, right-click the selected words to open the shortcut menu, and then click Translate.

The translated text appears in the text box below the selected languages in the Translation group. To translate an entire document from one language to another, click "Translate this document" in the box below the From and To selections. An alert box opens, telling you that the document will be sent over the Internet in unencrypted format. Click Continue to send the document; seconds later your document appears in your browser window fully translated into the language you specified. To return to Word, simply quit your browser.

Creating a Document

Previewing and Printing a Document

When you finish creating and editing a document, you are ready to print it. The tools in the Print dialog box let you specify various print settings, including the printer you want to use, how many copies to print, and the specific pages of the document you want to print. The Print dialog box also displays a preview of your document so that you can see exactly how it will look when printed. Seeing the preview of the document before printing it is useful and can save paper, ink, and time.  You are ready to preview and print the letter now. (*Note:* Many schools limit printing in order to conserve paper. If your school restricts printing, skip Step 6.)

STEPS

QUICK TIP

Click the Print button on the Standard toolbar to automatically print the document using the default print settings. When you use this option, the Print dialog box does not open.

1. **Click File on the menu bar, then click Print**

   The Print dialog box opens, as shown in Figure F-22. The Quick Preview box on the left shows how the document will look when printed. Notice that the letter starts at the top of the paper. You need to move it down to make room for the company letterhead, which is preprinted on Outdoor Designs company paper. To move the text down, you'll need to close the Print dialog box.

2. **Click Cancel**

   The Print dialog box closes so you can move the letter down on the printed page.

3. **Press ⌘[home] to move to the top of the document, then press [return] seven times**

   You inserted seven blank lines at the top of the document. The text is now positioned further down the page to accommodate the company letterhead.

4. **Click File on the menu bar, then click Print**

   The Print dialog box opens again, and you can see that the document text looks more centered in the Quick Preview box. The options on the Print dialog box let you specify your print settings, such as the printer, number of copies, and range of pages you want to print in case you do not want to print an entire document.

5. **Verify that the correct printer is selected**

6. **If your school allows printing, click Print; otherwise click Cancel**

   The Print dialog box closes. After a few moments, the letter is printed. Compare your letter with Figure F-23.

7. **Save your changes, click Word on the menu bar, then click Quit Word**

   The letter is saved, and the document and Word both close.

FIGURE F-22: Print dialog box

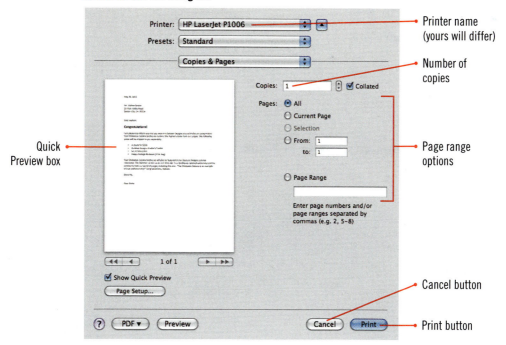

Printer name
(yours will differ)

Number of
copies

Quick
Preview box

Page range
options

Cancel button

Print button

FIGURE F-23: Final printed letter

May 20, 2013

Mr. Nathan Baxter
55 Plum Valley Road
Station City, CA 92554

Dear Nathan:

Congratulations!

I am pleased to inform you that you won the Outdoor Designs annual birdhouse competition!
Your Chickadee Cabana birdhouse received the highest scores from our judges. The following
prizes will be shipped to you separately:

- A check for $250
- Outdoor Designs Crafter's Toolkit
- Set of binoculars
- Happy Cottage Birdseed (10 lb. bag)

Your Chickadee Cabana birdhouse will also be featured in the Outdoor Designs summer
newsletter, *The Hammer*, as well as on our Web site. Your birdhouse received extremely positive
comments from our panel of judges, including this one: "The Chickadee Cabana is an example
of true craftsmanship!" Congratulations, Nathan!

Sincerely,

Your Name

Practice

Concepts Review

Label the Word window elements shown in Figure F-24.

FIGURE F-24

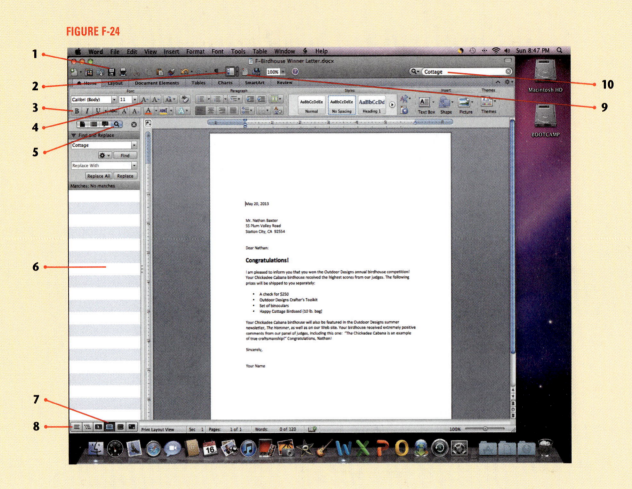

Match each of the buttons with its function.

11.
12.
13.
14.
15.

a. Opens the sidebar
b. Displays current document in Print Layout view
c. Saves a document to disk
d. Prints a document using the default print settings
e. Opens the Toolbox

Select the best answer from the list of choices.

16. **Which of the following statements about the Clipboard is *not* true?**
    a. To activate the Clipboard, click the Clipboard tab on the Toolbox.
    b. The Clipboard stores only one item at a time.
    c. The Clipboard lets you paste only the most recent item that you copied.
    d. To copy and paste text to the Clipboard, you must first select the text.

17. **Which of the following views is best for seeing exactly what your document will look like when printed?**
   - **a.** Print Layout view
   - **b.** Outline view
   - **c.** Draft view
   - **d.** Print Preview

18. **Which of the following keyboard shortcuts moves the insertion point to the beginning of the document?**
   - **a.** ⌘[A]
   - **b.** ⌘[home]
   - **c.** [control][A]
   - **d.** [control][home]

Skills Review

1. **Create a new document from an existing file.**
   - **a.** Start Word, open a blank document, then open the Open dialog box.
   - **b.** Use the Browse button to navigate to the location where you store your Data Files, then open the file F-2.docx.
   - **c.** Save the file as **F-Restaurant Info Sheet** in the location where you store your Data Files.

2. **Enter text in a document.**
   - **a.** Make sure formatting marks are displayed in the document.
   - **b.** Switch to Draft view.
   - **c.** Move the insertion point to the right of -2100 (the end of the fax number at the end of Line 4), then press [return] twice.
   - **d.** Type the following text: **About the Company**, then press [return].
   - **e.** Type the following text: **The company was created to serve working parents who want to feed their families nutritious meals made with the freshest ingredients.**
   - **f.** Move the insertion point to the end of the paragraph below the heading About Our Chef, press [spacebar], then type **Chef Nancy is also the author of the best-selling cookbook Dinner in a Flash.**
   - **g.** Save your changes.

3. **Select and edit text.**
   - **a.** In the paragraph under the heading About Our Kitchen, replace the text 2500 with **3500**.
   - **b.** In the paragraph above the heading About Our Kitchen, delete **New York's** in the second line and replace it with **Boston's**.
   - **c.** Scroll down if necessary so you can see the paragraph under the heading Our Menus, then use the [delete] key to delete the words **Monday through Friday** at the end of that paragraph.
   - **d.** Type **five days a week** so that the last sentence of that paragraph reads "Here are just a few of our best-selling meals, available five days a week:"
   - **e.** Select the entire document, then apply the No Spacing style.
   - **f.** Save your changes.

4. **Copy text.**
   - **a.** Select the text **The Last Minute Chef** in the first line of the document, then copy this text to the operating system Clipboard.
   - **b.** Delete the words **the Company** in the heading About the Company.
   - **c.** Paste the copied text where the deleted text used to be. (*Note*: If a blank line was inserted between the heading and paragraph, delete it before proceeding to Step d.)
   - **d.** Select the text **Last Minute Chef** in the heading About The Last Minute Chef.
   - **e.** Drag a copy of the selected text to the line just below it and to the left of the word "company" while holding [option].
   - **f.** Edit the **c** in company that follows the dragged text so that it is capitalized.
   - **g.** Save your changes.

5. **Move text.**
   - **a.** In the paragraph below the heading Our Hours, select the text **Stop by or call tonight!** and the space following it, then use the Cut command to move this text to the Clipboard.
   - **b.** Paste the text after the sentence **Or go straight home and call us: we deliver!** at the end of the paragraph.

Skills Review (continued)

c. Scroll down if necessary so that the bottom of the document is visible on your screen.

d. Select the heading **Our Hours**, the paragraph below it, and the paragraph mark below the paragraph, then drag to move the entire selection down to the end of the document.

e. Save your changes.

6. Find and replace text.

a. Move the insertion point to the beginning of the document.

b. Use the Search field to find Lemon Chicken.

c. Use the Replace command to replace all instances of the word **Green Beans** with **Asparagus**.

d. Close the sidebar.

e. Save your changes.

7. Format text using the ribbon.

a. Change the view to Print Layout view.

b. Select **The Last Minute Chef** in the first line of the document, then apply bold formatting to this text.

c. With the first line of text still selected, increase the font size of **The Last Minute Chef** to 20.

d. Apply bold formatting to each of the following headings in the document: **About The Last Minute Chef**, **About Our Chef**, **About Our Kitchen**, **Our Menus**, and **Our Hours**.

e. At the end of the paragraph below the heading About Our Chef, apply italic formatting to the book title **Dinner in a Flash**.

f. Scroll down if necessary so that all the text under the heading Our Menus is visible, then select the list of meals starting with **Pot Roast with Garlic Mashed Potatoes and Peas** and ending with **Beef Teriyaki with Fried Rice**.

g. Format the selected text as a bulleted list.

h. Save your changes.

8. Check spelling and grammar.

a. In the paragraph below About Our Kitchen, correct the spelling of the misspelled word **kitchn** by right-clicking and choosing the correct spelling from the shortcut menu.

b. Move the insertion point to the beginning of the document.

c. Open the Spelling and Grammar dialog box.

d. Review each spelling and grammar error that Word identifies, and correct or ignore it depending on what seems appropriate for this document.

e. Save your changes.

9. Preview and print a document.

a. Preview the document using the Print dialog box.

b. Return to the document and insert two blank lines above the first line of the document.

c. Move the insertion point to the end of the document, then type your name.

d. Preview the document using the Print dialog box.

e. Print the document (if your lab allows it), then save your document.

f. Compare your printed document with Figure F-25.

g. Close the document, then quit Word.

FIGURE F-25

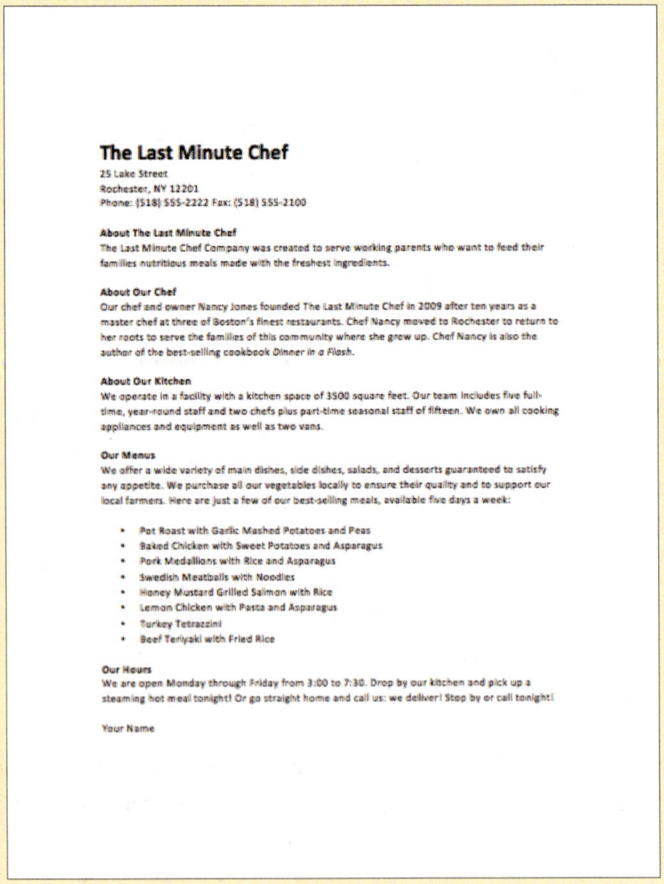

The Last Minute Chef

25 Lake Street
Rochester, NY 12201
Phone: (518) 555-2222 Fax: (518) 555-2100

About The Last Minute Chef
The Last Minute Chef Company was created to serve working parents who want to feed their families nutritious meals made with the freshest ingredients.

About Our Chef
Our chef and owner Nancy Jones founded The Last Minute Chef in 2009 after ten years as a master chef at three of Boston's finest restaurants. Chef Nancy moved to Rochester to return to her roots to serve the families of this community where she grew up. Chef Nancy is also the author of the best-selling cookbook *Dinner in a Flash*.

About Our Kitchen
We operate in a facility with a kitchen space of 3500 square feet. Our team includes five full-time, year-round staff and two chefs plus part-time seasonal staff of fifteen. We own all cooking appliances and equipment as well as two vans.

Our Menus
We offer a wide variety of main dishes, side dishes, salads, and desserts guaranteed to satisfy any appetite. We purchase all our vegetables locally to ensure their quality and to support our local farmers. Here are just a few of our best-selling meals, available five days a week:

- Pot Roast with Garlic Mashed Potatoes and Peas
- Baked Chicken with Sweet Potatoes and Asparagus
- Pork Medallions with Rice and Asparagus
- Swedish Meatballs with Noodles
- Honey Mustard Grilled Salmon with Rice
- Lemon Chicken with Pasta and Asparagus
- Turkey Tetrazzini
- Beef Teriyaki with Fried Rice

Our Hours
We are open Monday through Friday from 3:00 to 7:30. Drop by our kitchen and pick up a steaming hot meal tonight! Or go straight home and call us: we deliver! Stop by or call tonight!

Your Name

Independent Challenge 1

As the human resources director for Recycling Enterprises, Inc., you are in charge of organizing the company's summer executive retreat. You need to prepare a memo inviting the executive team to the retreat. You have already created a partially completed version of this memo, so now you need to make final edits to finish it.

a. Start Word, open the file F-3.docx from the location where you store your Data Files, then save it as **F-Executive Retreat Memo**.

b. Select the entire document, then apply the No Spacing style to the whole document.

c. In the fourth line of text, replace the text **Your Name** with your name.

d. In the sixth line of text (which begins "Our Summer Sales Offsite Meeting"), change the words **Offsite Meeting** to **Retreat**.

e. In the first line below the heading Dates and Location, delete **meeting**, then replace it with **Executive Retreat**.

f. At the end of the paragraph under Dates and Location, type the following text: **Please book your flight home anytime after 5:00 on June 17.**

g. In the first line of text under the heading Trip Planning, move the text **I look forward to seeing you there!** to the end of the paragraph.

h. Increase the font size of **Memo** in the first line of the document to 20, then apply bold formatting to it.

i. Apply bold formatting to the following headings in the memo: **Dates and Location**, **About the Hotel and Conference Center**, **Meeting Information**, **Planned Activities**, and **Trip Planning**.

j. Under the Planned Activities heading, format the lines that start with **June 15**, **June 16**, and **June 17** as a bulleted list.

k. You suddenly learn that the Orange Tree Hotel will not be able to accommodate the meeting. Fortunately, you are able to make a reservation at the Palm Grove Golf Resort, also in San Diego. Replace all instances of **Orange Tree Hotel** with **Palm Grove Golf Resort**.

l. After you enter all the text, check the spelling and grammar, and correct any errors as needed. Ignore any proper names that are flagged as misspelled words.

m. Save your changes, then preview the memo.

Advanced Challenge Exercise

These steps require an Internet connection.

■ Open the Toolbox, click the Reference Tools tab, then open the Translation group.

■ Click the pop-up menu arrows for From:, then select English.

■ Click the pop-up menu arrows for To:, then select Dutch.

■ Click Translate this document, then click Continue if the warning dialog box appears.

■ Click anywhere in the browser window, then press ⌘[A] to select all of the text. Press ⌘[C] to copy the text to the Clipboard, then click the Word icon on the Dock to return to Word. Press ⌘[N] to open a new document, then press ⌘[V] to paste the translated text from the Clipboard into the new document.

■ Save the new file as **F-Executive Retreat Memo ACE**.

n. Close all documents, then quit Word. Submit your completed documents to your instructor.

Independent Challenge 2

You own and operate an ice cream company based in Portland, Oregon. Business is booming, so you would like to expand your product line and offer new types of products. You would also like to have a better understanding of what your customers like about your ice cream products. You decide to create a simple customer survey that your customers can fill out in the store for a chance to win a prize. You have already started the survey document but need to edit it and improve its appearance before it is ready for distribution.

a. Start Word, open the file F-4.docx from the location where you store your Data Files, then save it as **F-Ice Cream Survey**.

Independent Challenge 2 (continued)

b. Replace all instances of the name **Aunt Tilly** in the survey document with your first name. In the last line of the document, replace the text **Your Name** with your full name.

c. Select all the text in the document, then apply the No Spacing style to all the selected text.

d. In the third line of text in the document, delete **weekly ice cream** and replace it with **a pint of ice cream each week**.

e. Type **Question 1:** before the first question in the document, press [spacebar], then apply bold formatting to **Question 1:**.

f. Insert **Question 2:**, **Question 3:**, and **Question 4:** to the left of the remaining three questions in the survey, insert a space, and apply bold formatting to the new text.

g. Below each of the four questions, format the list of answers as a bulleted list.

h. Reorder the bulleted items under Question 4 so that they are in alphabetical order.

i. Increase the font size of the text in the first line of the document to 20, then apply bold and italic formatting to it.

j. Check the spelling and grammar and correct all spelling and grammar errors. Ignore flagged words that are spelled correctly.

k. Save your changes to the document. Use the Print dialog box to see how the printed survey will look.

Advanced Challenge Exercise

These steps require an Internet connection.

- Save a copy of the survey document with the name **F-Ice Cream Survey ACE**.
- Replace the first line of the document with the text **Definitions**.
- Delete all other text in the document except **Butter**, **Cookie**, **Pralines**, and your name. Remove the bulleted list formatting, but keep each word on a separate line. (*Hint*: The Bulleted List button is a toggle switch. Select the text, then click the button to turn it on and click again to turn it off.)
- Type a colon after each word, then press [spacebar] after each colon.
- Right-click **Butter**, point to Look up, then click Definition to open Reference Tools to view its definition.
- Copy the first Dictionary definition of "Butter," then paste the copied definition to the right of **Butter:** in the document. (*Note*: You may need to click **here** to access online tools.)
- Use Reference Tools to look up and copy the definitions of "cookie" and "pralines," then paste them to the right of **Cookie:** and **Pralines:** in the document.
- Format **Butter**, **Cookie**, and **Pralines** in bold formatting. Format the definitions in italic.
- Close the Toolbox, then save your changes. Preview the document, then close it.

l. Submit your work to your instructor, then quit Word.

Independent Challenge 3

You are the director of marketing for a sports and fitness equipment company. You have contracted with A Plus Recruiters, an executive search firm in Chicago, to find candidates to fill the position of marketing manager, reporting to you. The recruiter you hired to locate candidates for the job has requested that you create the document shown in Figure F-26 that describes the position and the qualifications that candidates must have.

a. Start Word, open the file F-5.docx from the location where you store your Data Files, then save it as **F-Marketing Manager Job Description**.

b. Place the insertion point at the end of the document, type **Reporting Structure**, press [return], type **This position reports to the Vice President of Marketing.**, then press [return].

c. Delete the words **Vice President** in the line that you typed in Step b, then type **Director** in its place.

d. In the second line of the document, delete **Essential Duties and** as well as the space after it, so that only the word **Responsibilities** remains in this line.

e. In the third line of the document, move the first sentence that begins **Requires travel to key customer accounts** so that it is the last sentence in that paragraph.

Independent Challenge 3 (continued)

f. Apply bold formatting to the first line of text in the document, then increase the font size of this text to 24.

g. Apply bold formatting to each of the following headings in the document: **Responsibilities**, **Required Skills**, **Work Environment**, **Education and Work Experience**, and **Reporting Structure**.

h. Move the heading **Education and Work Experience** and the paragraph below it so that it is located below the Reporting Structure paragraph.

i. Check the spelling and grammar in the document, and make all appropriate changes. Ignore any occurrences of sentence fragments that Word identifies. Type your name below the last line of the document.

j. Preview the document, compare your screen with Figure F-26, then save and close the document.

k. Submit the document to your instructor, then quit Word.

FIGURE F-26

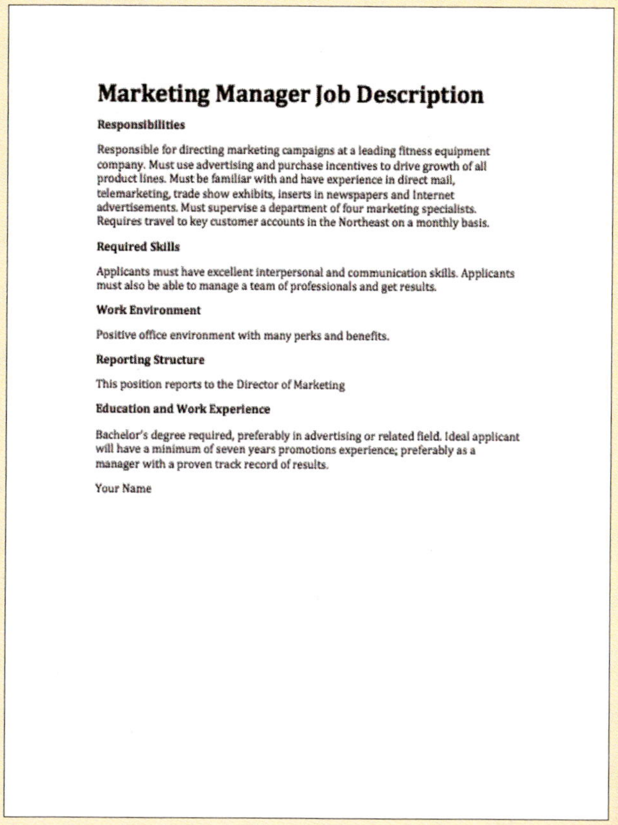

Marketing Manager Job Description

Responsibilities

Responsible for directing marketing campaigns at a leading fitness equipment company. Must use advertising and purchase incentives to drive growth of all product lines. Must be familiar with and have experience in direct mail, telemarketing, trade show exhibits, inserts in newspapers and Internet advertisements. Must supervise a department of four marketing specialists. Requires travel to key customer accounts in the Northeast on a monthly basis.

Required Skills

Applicants must have excellent interpersonal and communication skills. Applicants must also be able to manage a team of professionals and get results.

Work Environment

Positive office environment with many perks and benefits.

Reporting Structure

This position reports to the Director of Marketing

Education and Work Experience

Bachelor's degree required, preferably in advertising or related field. Ideal applicant will have a minimum of seven years promotions experience; preferably as a manager with a proven track record of results.

Your Name

Real Life Independent Challenge

When you apply for a job, it is important to make a case for why you would be ideally suited for the position for which you are applying. In this Real Life Independent Challenge, you are interested in applying for your dream job at a company for which you would love to work. The job and the company can be in any field you want—it is your choice! You have already submitted your résumé to the human resources director at this company, and she has requested that you now write a letter that states the reasons why you are ideally suited for the job.

a. Start Word, create a new blank document, then save it as **F-Dream Job Letter**.

b. Before you begin typing, apply the No Spacing style to the document. (*Hint*: Click the No Spacing button on the Home tab.)

c. Type today's date in the first line of the document, press [return] three times, then type **Marianne Johnson**, the fictional name of the human resources director at your dream company. Below Marianne's name, type the name and address of the company. (Make up this information.) Press [return] twice after typing the address.

d. Write a letter that contains three paragraphs and a closing. Make sure to insert a blank line between paragraphs. Use the guidelines in the following table to write your letter.

part of the letter	directions for what to write
First paragraph	Thank Marianne for the opportunity to apply for the specific job at your dream company. (Be sure to name a specific job and a specific company name—the company can be made up or real.)
Second paragraph	Write three or four sentences (or more) stating why you are the ideal candidate for the job.
Third paragraph	Thank Marianne for her consideration.

e. Type **Sincerely**, two lines below the third paragraph.

f. Three lines below **Sincerely**, type your name. Save your changes. Preview the letter to make sure it looks good on paper. If necessary, insert blank lines at the top of the letter so that the text is balanced on the page. Save and close the document. Submit your letter to your instructor, then quit Word.

Visual Workshop

Use the skills you have learned in this unit to create the document shown in Figure F-27. Start Word, use a Blank document to create a new untitled document, then type and format the text as shown. Set the font size of the heading text to 24, and set the font size of the body text to 14. Save the document as **F-Apartment Ad** in the location where you store your Data Files. Type your name below the last line of the document. Check the spelling and grammar in the entire document, then save and print it. When you are finished, close the document, then quit Word. Submit your completed document to your instructor.

FIGURE F-27

Apartment for Rent

Description:

LUXURY LIVING AT AN AFFORDABLE PRICE! Live in style without paying a fortune in this 2-bedroom apartment near the lake! Walk to parks and shopping. Enjoy water views from two windows.

- Modern building near the lake
- Convenient location—close to shopping, train, lake, and parks
- Great views of the water
- 2 bedrooms
- 1 full bath
- Modern appliances
- Washer/dryer in unit
- Granite countertops
- Built-in shelves
- Utilities included

Rent: $1250 per month

For more information or to schedule an appointment, call Frank at 773-555-9090

Your Name

Enhancing a Document

Microsoft Word 2011 provides a variety of tools you can use to enhance the appearance of your documents. In this unit, you learn to change the formatting of characters and paragraphs using tools on the ribbon. You also learn how to take advantage of Styles, a feature in Microsoft Word that helps you create great looking documents efficiently.  Karen Rivera, marketing director for Outdoor Designs, gives you a product fact sheet for a new canoe product. Karen asks you to format the information in the sheet so that it is attractive and easy to read.

OBJECTIVES

Change font and font size

Change font color, font style, and font effects

Change alignment and line spacing

Change margin settings

Set tabs

Set indents

Add bulleted and numbered lists

Apply Styles

Changing Font and Font Size

Choosing an appropriate font is an important part of formatting a document. The fonts you use help communicate the tone you want to set. For instance, if you are creating a report that discusses the harmful effects of global warming, you should choose a traditional font such as Times New Roman. On the other hand, if you are creating a formal wedding invitation, you should choose a font that conveys a sense of elegance and celebration, such as French Script. Table G-1 shows some examples of fonts and font sizes available in Word. To change the font and font size, you use the Font group on the Home tab of the ribbon. You can change the font and font size before you begin typing, or you can change existing text. All the text in the canoe fact sheet is the same font (Cambria) and the same font size (12 point). You decide to change the font and font size of the first two lines so that they stand out from the rest of the text in the document. First, you open the document and save it with a new name to keep Karen's original document intact.

STEPS

1. **Start Word, open the file G-1.docx from the location where you store your Data Files, then save it as G-Canoe Fact Sheet**

   The G-Canoe Fact Sheet document is now open in Print Layout view.

2. **Click the Show all nonprinting characters button ¶ to display paragraph marks, if necessary**

3. **Place the pointer to the left of Outdoor Designs in the first line until it changes to ↗, then click to select the entire line**

   To format existing text, you must first select it.

   > **QUICK TIP**
   > If the Home tab is not the active tab on the ribbon, click it.

4. **Click the Font Size pop-up menu arrow in the Font group on the Home tab, then click 20, as shown in Figure G-1**

   The Font Size pop-up menu closes, and the selected text changes to 20 point. The first line of text is now much larger than the rest of the text in the document.

5. **Select Build-Your-Own Canoe Kit in the second line of the document, click the Font Size pop-up menu arrow, then click 22**

   The second line of text increases in size to 22 point and is now larger than the first line.

6. **Click the Font pop-up menu arrow in the Font group, scroll in the Font pop-up menu until you see Arial, then point to it, but don't click**

   As shown in Figure G-2, Arial is one of many font types that has a disclosure triangle. When a disclosure triangle is displayed on a menu, it indicates that a submenu will be displayed when you point to that item.

   > **QUICK TIP**
   > To apply formatting to text as you type, select the formatting options you want, then start typing.

7. **On the submenu, click Arial, then click outside the selected text to deselect it**

   The selected text changes to the Arial font.

8. **Click the Save button 🖫 on the Standard toolbar to save your changes**

TABLE G-1: Samples of fonts and font sizes

font formats	samples
Font	Times New Roman, *Lucida Handwriting*, **Impact**, Apple Casual, **Braggadocio**, Verdana
Size	eight point, twelve point, fourteen point, eighteen point

FIGURE G-1: Changing the font size of selected text using the Font Size pop-up menu

Font Size pop-up menu arrow

Font size

Font group

Font Size pop-up menu

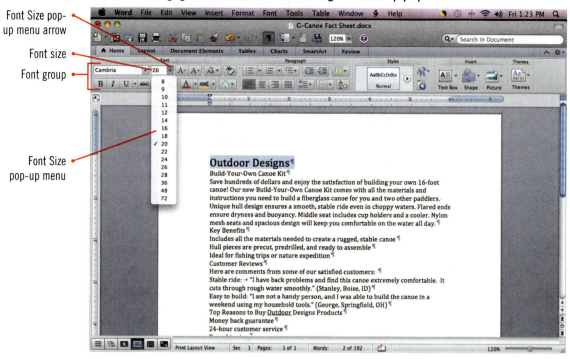

FIGURE G-2: Changing the font type of selected text using the Font pop-up menu

Font pop-up menu arrow

Font

Font pop-up menu

Disclosure triangle

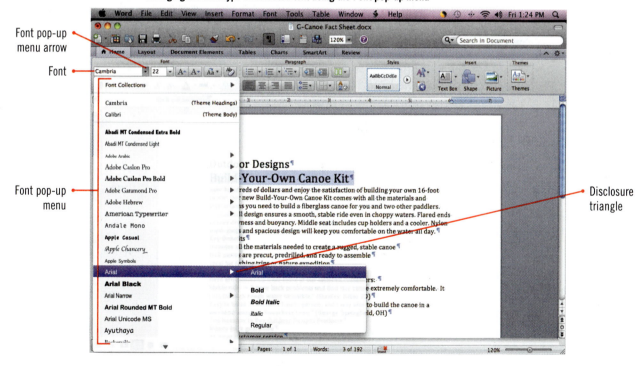

Changing Font Color, Font Style, and Font Effects

Sometimes you want to emphasize certain words, phrases, or lines of text. To do this, you can use **font styles**, which are attributes such as **bold** (darker type), *italic* (slanted type), and underline. You can also make certain words stand out by changing their color. Or, you can apply font effects to selected text. **Font effects** are special enhancements such as small caps (SMALL CAPS LOOKS LIKE THIS), shadow (shadow looks like this), or strikethrough (strikethrough looks like this) that you can apply to selected text. You can use the buttons in the Font group on the Home tab to apply formatting changes to selected text. You can apply other font effects using the Font dialog box, which you open by clicking the Font option on the Format menu. If you have text formatted the way you like, you can use the Format Painter to copy the formatting of that text to other text.  You continue to format the canoe kit fact sheet by applying font styles, colors, and effects to certain words.

STEPS

1. **Select the second line of text, Build-Your-Own Canoe Kit, then click the Font Color pop-up menu arrow**

   In the color palette that opens, you can choose from Theme Colors, Standard Colors, and More Colors. A **theme** is a predesigned set of formatting elements, including colors, which you can use to achieve a coordinated overall look in your document. **Standard colors** are the basic hues: red, orange, and so on. If you want a color you do not see in the palette, you can click More Colors to specify a particular shade.

   > **QUICK TIP**
   > To remove formatting, select the formatted text, then click the Clear Formatting button ⓐ⁄ in the Font group.

2. **Click the red color in the top row of Theme Colors (the Help Tag reads "Accent 2"), as shown in Figure G-3**

   The second line of the document is now red. The Font Color button now displays a thick, dark red underline, indicating that this is the most recently used color. Now if you were to click the Font Color button (not the pop-up menu arrow), the selected text would change to red.

3. **Select Outdoor Designs (the first line of text), then click the Text Effects button A▾ in the Font group on the Home tab**

   The Text Effects Gallery opens.

4. **Click the second option in the top row, as shown in Figure G-4**

   The selected text is now white with a red outline around it.

   > **QUICK TIP**
   > To underline text, select it, then click the Underline button U in the Font group.

5. **Scroll down until you see the line that begins Stable ride:; if necessary, select Stable ride:, click the Bold button B in the Font group, then click the Italic button I**

   "Stable ride:" is now formatted in bold and italic, and is still selected.

6. **Click the Format Painter button 🖌 on the Standard toolbar**

   Notice that the pointer shape changes to ⁺Ⅰ when you place it in the document window, indicating that you can apply the formatting of the selected text to any text you click or select next.

   > **QUICK TIP**
   > Double-clicking the Format Painter button 🖌 lets you apply the selected formatting multiple times instead of just once. To turn off the Format Painter, click the Format Painter button 🖌 once.

7. **Two lines below Stable ride:, select Easy to build:**

   The bold and italic formatting is applied to the phrase "Easy to build:."

8. **Click outside the selected text, then save your changes**

   See Figure G-5.

FIGURE G-3: Font Color pop-up menu with red selected

FIGURE G-3: Font Color pop-up menu with red selected

Bold button

Italic button

Underline button

Font Color pop-up menu arrow

In Step 2, click this shade of red

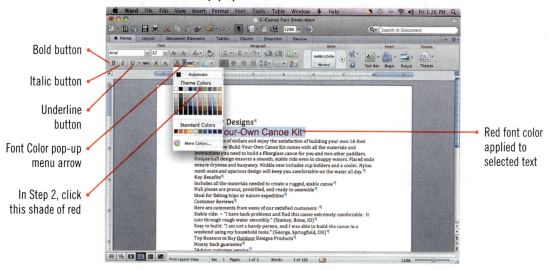

Red font color applied to selected text

FIGURE G-4: Applying a text effect

Text Effects button

In Step 4, click this option

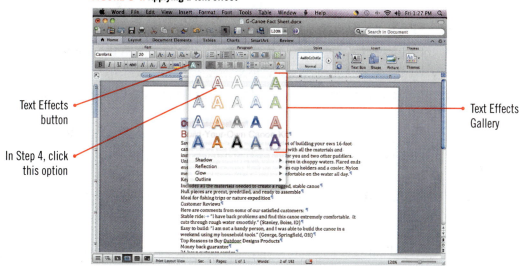

Text Effects Gallery

FIGURE G-5: Bold and italic formatting applied to text

Format Painter button

Bold button

Italic button

Text formatted in bold italic using Format Painter button

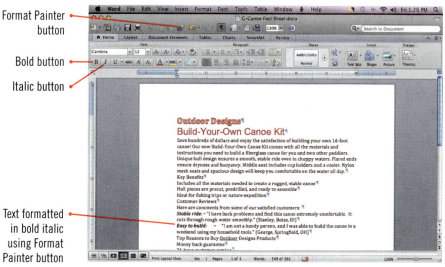

Enhancing a Document

Changing Alignment and Line Spacing

The amount of space between the edge of the page and your document text is called the **margin**. You can change the **alignment**, or position of text within a document's margins, using the alignment buttons in the Paragraph group on the Home tab of the ribbon. For example, titles are often centered, headings are usually left-aligned, and paragraphs are often **justified** (aligned equally between the left and right margins). All of the text in the canoe fact sheet is currently aligned along the left margin. You decide to center the first two lines and justify the descriptive paragraph. You also want to increase the amount of spacing between the lines in the descriptive paragraph so that it is 1.15 spaced, and you want more space both above and below the paragraph.

STEPS

1. **Press ⌘[home] to move the insertion point to the beginning of the document**
   Although you need to select text to change character formats such as font size or font style, for most paragraph formatting, such as alignment, you just need to position the insertion point anywhere in the paragraph before making the change. In Word, a **paragraph** is any text that ends with a hard return (a paragraph mark like ¶), so a paragraph can be as short as a one-word title or many pages long.

2. **Click the Center Text button ≡ in the Paragraph group on the Home tab**
   The text is centered between the two margins.

3. **Click anywhere in the second line of text (Build-Your-Own Canoe Kit), then click ≡**
   See Figure G-6.

4. **Click anywhere in the paragraph text below Build-Your-Own Canoe Kit**
   The insertion point is now set in the paragraph. Any paragraph formatting you specify will affect the entire paragraph.

5. **Click the Justify Text button ≡ in the Paragraph group**
   The paragraph's alignment changes to justified. When you select justified alignment, Word adds or reduces the space between each word so that the text is aligned along both the right and left margins. This is different from **center-aligning** text, which does not adjust spacing between words but merely places the text equally between the margins.

6. **With the insertion point still in the justified paragraph, click the Line Spacing button , then click 1.15, as shown in Figure G-7**
   The paragraph is now both justified and 1.15 spaced, making it easier to read and set off from the other text on the page.

QUICK TIP
You can also open the Paragraph dialog box by right-clicking (for a single-button mouse, press [control] and click) a paragraph, then clicking Paragraph in the shortcut menu.

7. **Click again, then click Line Spacing Options to open the Paragraph dialog box**
   The Paragraph dialog box opens with the Indents and Spacing tab in front. The Alignment is set to Justified, and Line spacing (in the Spacing section) is set to Multiple, reflecting your settings. This dialog box offers another way to change paragraph settings, including some that are not available in the Paragraph group, such as customizing the amount of space above and below a paragraph. The Preview section shows you what the paragraph will look like with the selected settings.

8. **In the Spacing section, click the Before up arrow twice to set spacing above the paragraph to 12 pt, then click the After up arrow twice to set spacing below the paragraph to 12 pt**
   See Figure G-8.

9. **Click OK, then save your changes**
   Notice that the spacing above and below the paragraph text increases.

FIGURE G-6: Center-aligned text

Center Text button

Center-aligned text

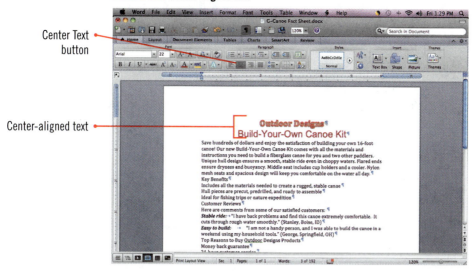

FIGURE G-7: Paragraph with justified alignment and line spacing set to 1.15

Justify Text button

Justified paragraph

Line Spacing button

Line spacing set to 1.15

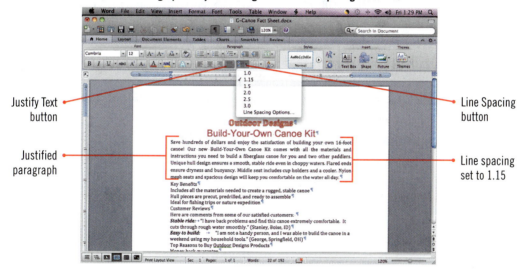

FIGURE G-8: Indents and Spacing tab of Paragraph dialog box

Alignment set to Justified

Before up arrow

After up arrow

Line spacing set to 1.15

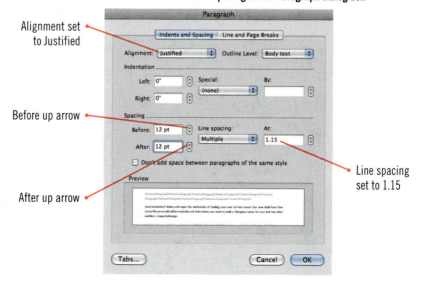

Word 2011

Changing Margin Settings

By default, Word 2011 sets page margins at 1 inch from the top and bottom of the page and 1.25 inches from the left and right sides of the page. Current margin settings are noted on the horizontal and vertical rulers by the blue-shaded measurements. If you'd like to change the margin settings, you can do so with the Margins group on the Layout tab of the ribbon. When you change the margins, Word automatically adjusts line wrapping and **repaginates** (renumbers the pages of) your document. To evaluate what margin settings to use in a specific document, you should view the document in Print Layout view so you can see and work with the margins as they will appear on the page. 🎨 The canoe fact sheet is currently formatted with the default margins. You decide to explore other margin settings to see whether a different setting would make the document look better.

STEPS

1. **Click the Layout tab**

   The margins are displayed in the Margins group and noted by the blue-shaded measurements on the rulers, as shown in Figure G-9.

2. **Click the Margins button** 📄

   The Margins pop-up menu opens and displays predefined options for margin settings, as shown in Figure G-10.

3. **Click Narrow in the Margins pop-up menu**

   The Margins pop-up menu closes, and the Narrow margins setting is applied to the document, as shown in Figure G-11. You can see that there is only a $1/2$" margin at the top, bottom, left, and right. This margin setting is too narrow for this document because the text placement is unbalanced; all the text is stretched out at the top of the document, and there is a large blank space at the bottom.

4. **Click** 📄 **, then click Wide**

   The Wide margins setting is applied to the document.

5. **Click** 📄 **again, then click Normal**

   The Normal margins setting is applied to the document.

FIGURE G-9: Margins group and rulers noting the current margin settings

Margins group

Margins button

Top margin shaded on vertical ruler

Left margin shaded on horizontal ruler

Bottom and Right margin spin boxes

Right margin shaded on horizontal ruler

FIGURE G-10: Margins pop-up menu

Your Last Custom Setting options might differ or might not appear

Normal setting

Narrow setting

Wide setting

Current (default) setting

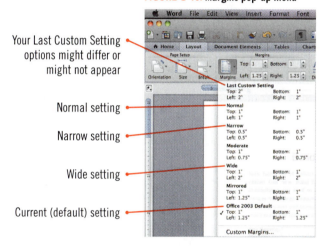

FIGURE G-11: Canoe fact sheet with Narrow margins setting applied

Narrow margins setting noted on rulers

Margin is distance between page edge and edge of document text

Narrow margins setting leaves only ½" margin

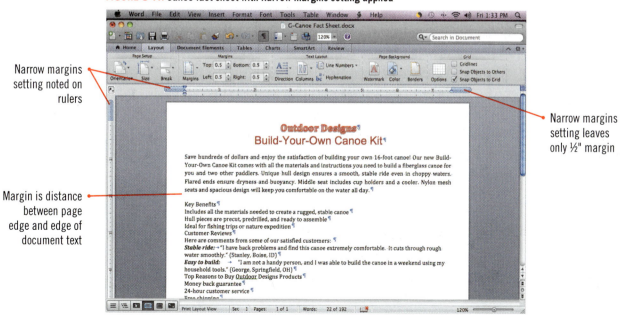

Setting Tabs

You can improve the appearance and readability of a document by using tabs to align text at specific positions on the page. A **tab** is a horizontal position within a line where text is aligned. (When the formatting marks are displayed, tabs are indicated by right-facing arrows.) The ruler makes it easy to set **tab stops** (locations the insertion point moves to when you press [tab]). By default, Word sets left-aligned tab stops every ½". The default tab stops are marked as small black slashes in the thin gray bar below the ruler. By default, any tab stop that you add is a left-aligned tab stop and appears as a ⌐ on the ruler. The new tab stop overrides the default tab stop settings. You can use the **tab indicator**, located above the vertical ruler, to align text differently, such as to the right of or centered on a tab stop. When you set tabs, they apply only to text you selected, or, if no text is selected, they apply to the paragraph containing the insertion point. ▨ You need to enter ordering information for the canoe products at the end of the document. You use tabs to align the information in columns.

STEPS

1. **Scroll down, if necessary, so that the bottom of the document is visible**

   You need to type the heading row for the product ordering information.

2. **Click to the right of Product Name in the last line of the document, press [tab], type Item Number, press [tab], type Price, then press [return]**

   You can see that the word "Item", which follows the first tab, is left-aligned at the default 1 ½" tab stop. The word "Price" is aligned at the 2 ½" mark, also a default tab stop. Notice that the tab appears as a right-arrow in the text. Now you need to enter the product information below each heading.

3. **Type Canoe Kit, press [tab], type OD-555, press [tab], type $795, then press [return]**

   You typed the first row of data. Notice that OD-555 and $795 are not aligned with the headings Item and Price at the default tab stops. Instead, OD-555 is aligned at the 1" default tab stop and $795 at the 2" tab stop.

4. **Type Canoe Paddles, press [tab], type OD-556, press [tab], then type $99**

   You entered all the product data; now you need to select the lines of text you just typed so that you can align them using tab stops.

5. **Click to the left of Product Name, press and hold [Shift], then press [down arrow] three times**

   The three lines of text are selected, from the line beginning with Product through the line beginning with Canoe Paddles, as shown in Figure G-12. Any tab stop changes you make will now apply to all three selected lines of text.

6. **Notice the tab indicator ⌐ at the top of the vertical ruler**

   The tab indicator currently displays the icon for a left tab stop. This means that clicking the ruler will add a left tab stop, which is what you want.

7. **Click the 2 ½" mark on the ruler**

   The left-aligned tab stop appears on the ruler at the 2 ½" mark, and the Item Number heading and the two item numbers below it are now all left-aligned at the 2 ½" mark. Notice that the default tab stops in the thin bar below the ruler no longer appear to the left of the new tab stop.

8. **Click ⌐ at the top of the vertical ruler, click Right to select a right tab stop, then click the 5" mark on the ruler**

   The Price heading and the two prices below it are right-aligned. When you arrange numbers in a column, it is a good idea to right-align them.

9. **Select the line of text beginning with Product Name (the column headings), click the Home tab, then click the Bold button B**

10. **Click anywhere to deselect the text, then save your changes**

    Compare your screen with Figure G-13.

FIGURE G-12: Selected text with tabs inserted

Tab indicator with left tab stop displayed

Default tab stops every ½ inch on the ruler

Selected text with tabs inserted

Right-facing arrow indicates where tabs are inserted

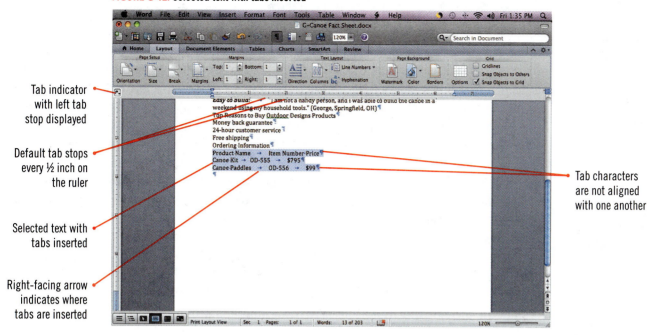

Tab characters are not aligned with one another

FIGURE G-13: Text arranged in columns using left and right tab stops

Left tab stop at 2 ½" mark on the ruler

Tab indicator with right tab stop displayed

Default tab stops every ½" to the left of the 5" mark are gone

Bolded heading row

Text left-aligned at 2 ½" tab stop

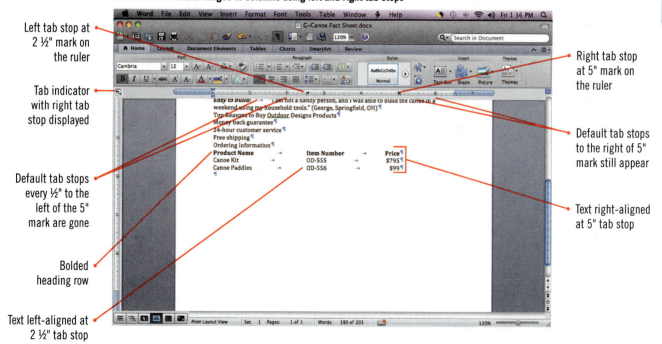

Right tab stop at 5" mark on the ruler

Default tab stops to the right of 5" mark still appear

Text right-aligned at 5" tab stop

Setting Indents

You can improve the appearance of text on a page by setting indents. An **indent** is a space between the edge of a paragraph and the right or left margin. Different types of indents are appropriate for different situations. A **first line indent** indents the first line of text in a paragraph. A **left indent** indents the left edge of an entire paragraph; a **right indent** indents the right edge of an entire paragraph. A **hanging indent** aligns the text below the first line of paragraph text. You can set indents using the sliding markers on the ruler. Table G-2 describes these markers. You can also set left and right indents at one-half inch increments using the Increase Indent and Decrease Indent buttons in the Paragraph group on the Home tab of the ribbon. The text containing the customer quotes would look neater if it were aligned under the first word after the tab. You want to set a hanging indent to improve the appearance of this text. You also decide to set a left indent to the paragraph text that describes the product.

STEPS

1. Scroll up if necessary, then select the four lines of text beginning with Stable ride: and ending with George, Springfield, OH)

2. Click the Increase Indent button 📑 in the Paragraph group

   The selected text is indented ½" on the ruler.

QUICK TIP

Make sure the Help Tag identifies the marker as Hanging Indent and not First Line Indent or Left Indent.

3. ▶ Position the pointer over the Hanging Indent marker 📑 on the ruler so that the Hanging Indent Help Tag appears, then click and hold so that a thin, vertical line appears on the screen

   This vertical line helps you position the marker in the desired location on the ruler.

QUICK TIP

When you drag an indent marker, make sure the tip of the pointer—and not the body of the pointer—is positioned over the marker; otherwise, you might have difficulty dragging it.

4. ▶ Drag 📑 to the 2" mark on the ruler

   The first line in each of the selected paragraphs remains flush left, and the text below the first line of each paragraph is now aligned at the 2" mark on the ruler, where you dragged the Hanging Indent marker, as shown in Figure G-14.

5. Drag the Right Indent marker △ (at the right margin on the ruler) to the 5 ½" mark on the ruler

   The text indents on the right side of the selected paragraphs at the 5 ½" mark. The paragraphs are narrower now, and the text in both paragraphs wraps to a third line.

6. Select the last three lines of text in the document

7. Position the pointer over the Left Indent marker ⊟ on the ruler until the Left Indent Help Tag appears, then drag ⊟ to the ½" mark on the ruler

   The product information columns are now indented by ½", as shown in Figure G-15.

8. Save your changes

FIGURE G-14: Setting a hanging indent

First Line Indent marker at ½" mark

Hanging Indent marker at 2" mark

First line of each paragraph is left-aligned at ½" mark

Lines below first line are indented at 2" mark

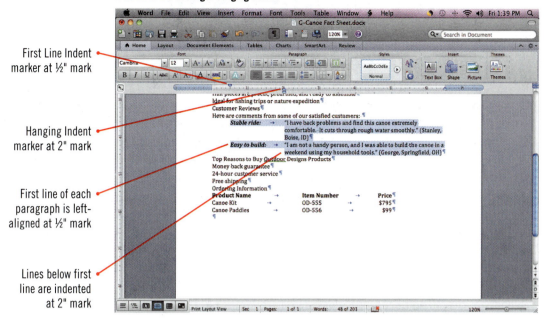

FIGURE G-15: Paragraphs formatted with left indent

Left Indent marker is positioned at ½" mark for the selected text

Paragraphs indented at ½" mark

Right Indent marker

Right indent set at 5 ½" for these paragraphs

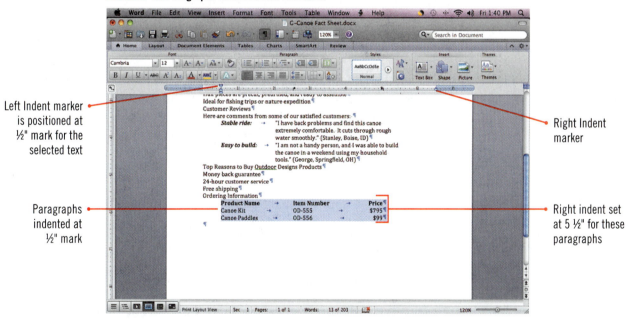

TABLE G-2: Ruler markers used for setting indents

ruler marker name	ruler marker	indents
First Line Indent marker	▽	The first line of a paragraph
Hanging Indent marker	△	The lines below the first line of text in a paragraph
Left Indent marker	▭	The left edge of an entire paragraph
Right Indent marker	△	The right edge of an entire paragraph

Adding Bulleted and Numbered Lists

Word provides many tools for organizing your text into a more orderly format. You can easily organize groups of related paragraphs into bulleted or numbered lists. You already learned how to create a bulleted list using the Bullets button in the Paragraph group on the Home tab of the ribbon. When you apply the bullet format to a paragraph, Word sets off the paragraph with a bullet and formats the text with a hanging indent. Use a numbered (ordered) list when you want to present items in a particular sequence, and use a bulleted (unordered) list when the items are of equal importance. There are many different bullet and numbering styles to choose from using the Bulleted List and Numbered List buttons or the Bullets and Numbering dialog box.  You decide to add numbered and bulleted lists to the canoe kit fact sheet to make it easier to reference.

STEPS

1. Near the top of the document, select the three lines of text under the heading Key Benefits

2. Click the Bulleted List pop-up menu arrow ⊟▾ in the Paragraph group

   The Bullet Library opens and displays bullet formatting options, as shown in Figure G-16. The Customize Bulleted List dialog box provides you with even more bullet options.

3. Click Define New Bullet

   The Customize Bulleted List dialog box opens. You use this dialog box to create a custom bullet.

4. Click Picture to open the Choose a Picture dialog box, click the Metallic Orb, as shown in Figure G-17, click Insert, click OK, then click at the end of the selected text to deselect it

   The text you selected now appears as a bulleted list. Word has indented each bullet in the list and placed a tab after each orb. You can see by the ruler that a hanging indent has been set. If any text in the bulleted list wrapped to a second line, it would align with the first line of text, not the bullet.

5. Press [return]

   A fourth orb bullet appears in the new row, ready for you to add another item to the list.

6. Type Building it yourself saves hundreds of dollars

   The text you typed is now formatted as a fourth item in the bulleted list.

7. If necessary, scroll down until you can see the bottom of the page

8. Select the three lines of text under the heading Top Reasons to Buy Outdoor Designs Products, then click the Numbered List pop-up menu arrow ⊟▾ in the Paragraph group

   The Numbering Library opens and displays different formatting options for a numbered list.

9. Click the numbered list option shown in Figure G-18 (the one with the parenthesis after each number), then save your changes

   The selected text is now formatted as a numbered list.

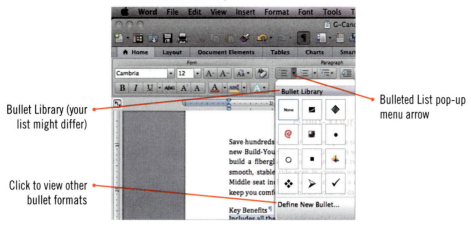

Bullet Library (your list might differ)

Bulleted List pop-up menu arrow

Click to view other bullet formats

FIGURE G-17: Choose a Picture dialog box

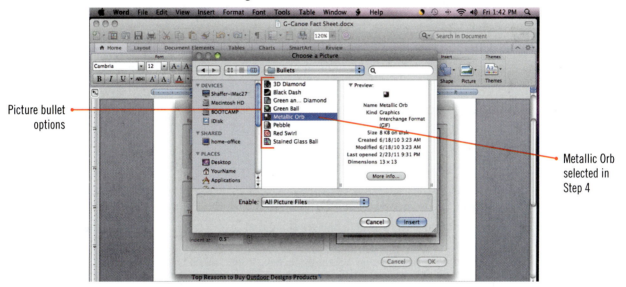

Picture bullet options

Metallic Orb selected in Step 4

Word 2011

FIGURE G-18: Canoe fact sheet with bulleted and numbered lists

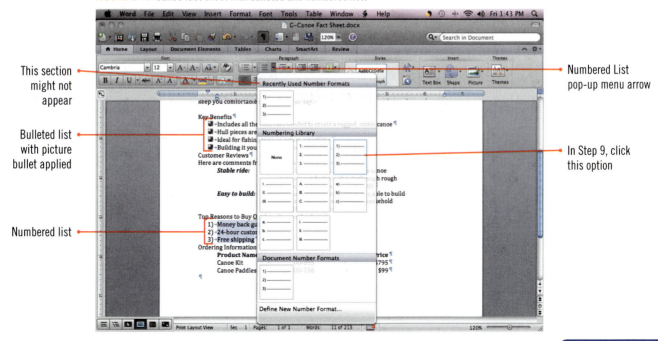

This section might not appear

Numbered List pop-up menu arrow

Bulleted list with picture bullet applied

In Step 9, click this option

Numbered list

Applying Styles

You can save a lot of formatting time and ensure that your document looks professional by applying styles to your document. A **style** is a set of predefined formatting attributes. By default, there are no styles applied to any text you type. The default settings are Cambria 12-point font with single line spacing. The Normal paragraph style changes the text to Helvetica 12-point font with single line spacing. Besides paragraph styles, you can also apply built-in styles for other types of text elements in your document, including headings, titles, and quotes. To apply a style, you can choose from styles available in the Styles group on the Home tab of the ribbon. You decide to use styles to complete the formatting of the canoe fact sheet.

STEPS

1. **Click anywhere in Key Benefits below the long paragraph**

   To apply a style to a paragraph, you first click in the paragraph to which you want to apply the style.

2. **Point to the Styles group on the Home tab of the ribbon until the Styles Gallery pop-up menu arrow [▼] appears, then click [▼]**

   The Styles Gallery opens, as shown in Figure G-19.

3. **Click the Heading 1 style**

   The Key Benefits paragraph now has the Heading 1 style applied to it and is formatted in Cambria 14-point blue, as shown in Figure G-20.

4. **Using the process you followed in Steps 1–3, apply the Heading 1 style to the following lines: Customer Reviews, Top Reasons to Buy Outdoor Designs Products, and Ordering Information**

   All of the headings in the document now have the Heading 1 style applied.

5. **Under the heading Customer Reviews, select the customer quote that begins with "I have back problems, open the Styles Gallery, then click the Quote style**

   When you want to apply a style to only part of a paragraph, you first need to select the desired text before applying the style; otherwise, the style will be applied to the entire paragraph. The selected text is now formatted in italic, the formatting specification for the Quote style. Because you selected text instead of clicking in the paragraph, the style was applied only to the characters you selected rather than to the whole paragraph.

6. **Select the customer quote that begins with "I am not a handy person, click the Quote style in the Styles Gallery, then deselect the text**

   Next, you decide to change the Quick Style settings to change the overall look of the document.

QUICK TIP
You can add additional Quick Styles sets, so you might see additional options on your Quick Styles settings pop-up menu.

7. **Click the Change Quick Styles settings button [AA▾] in the Styles group, then click Fancy**

   The Fancy style set is applied to the document. This style set specifies that the Heading 1 style includes dark red type against a light red background and bold, italic, Cambria, 11-point text.

8. **Click the Show all nonprinting characters button [¶] on the Standard toolbar to turn off paragraph marks**

9. **Press ⌘[end], type your name, then compare your screen with Figure G-21**

10. **Save your changes, close the document, then quit Word**

    Submit your document to your instructor.

FIGURE G-19: Styles Gallery

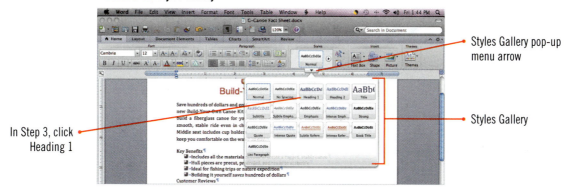

In Step 3, click Heading 1

Styles Gallery pop-up menu arrow

Styles Gallery

FIGURE G-20: Heading 1 style applied

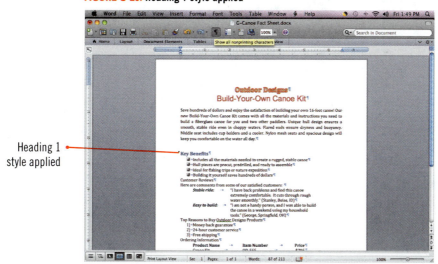

Heading 1 style applied

FIGURE G-21: Completed G-Canoe Fact Sheet

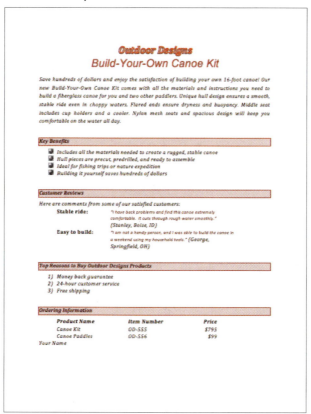

Practice

Concepts Review

Label the Word window elements shown in Figure G-22.

FIGURE G-22

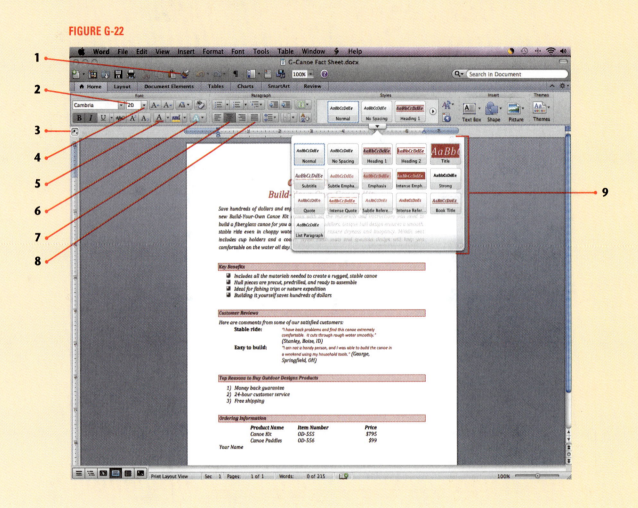

Match each button or icon with its function.

10.

11.

12.

13.

14.

a. Icon on the ruler indicating a right-aligned tab stop

b. Increases the indent by $1/2$"

c. Icon on the ruler indicating a left-aligned tab stop

d. Center-aligns the current paragraph between the right and left margins

e. Indents text following the first line in a paragraph at a specified mark on the ruler

Select the best answer from the list of choices.

15. **Which of the following tabs on the ribbon do you use to change margin settings?**
    a. Home
    b. Layout
    c. View
    d. Insert

16. **Tabs are useful when you want to:**
    a. Set line spacing for a paragraph.
    b. Organize information into columns.
    c. Set paragraph alignment.
    d. Format characters.

17. **A set of predefined formatting attributes is a:**
    a. Font.
    b. Font effect.
    c. Style.
    d. Tab stop.

18. **Which of the following methods describes how to set a hanging indent 2" from the left edge of the paper?**
    a. Drag ☰ to the 2" mark on the ruler.
    b. Use the Paragraph dialog box to specify a 2" left margin.
    c. Click at the 2" mark on the ruler.
    d. Drag ♟ to the 2" mark on the ruler.

19. **What are the default left and right margins for Word 2011?**
    a. .5"
    b. 1"
    c. 1.25"
    d. 1.5"

20. **At what increment on the ruler are tab stops set by default?**
    a. At 1-inch increments
    b. At $\frac{1}{2}$-inch increments
    c. At $\frac{1}{4}$-inch increments
    d. At $1\frac{1}{2}$-inch increments

Skills Review

1. **Change font and font size.**
    a. Start Word, open the file G-2.docx from the location where you store your Data Files, then save it as **G-Photo Exhibit Info**.
    b. Select the entire first line of the document.
    c. Change the font size to 26.
    d. Change the font to Franklin Gothic Book.
    e. Select the entire second line of the document. Change the font size to 18.
    f. Save your changes.

2. **Change font color, font style, and font effects.**
    a. Select the first line of the document again, then change the font color to dark blue (Text 2, the fourth color in the first row under Theme Colors).
    b. Format the selected blue text in bold.
    c. Select the second line of the document, open the Text Effects Gallery, then apply the orange gradient option (second option in fourth row).
    d. Select the text **Deer Park Arts Commission** in the third line of the document, then apply bold formatting to the selection. Change the font color to dark blue.
    e. Use the Format Painter to apply the formatting from Deer Park Arts Commission to the other instance of Deer Park Arts Commission in the document.
    f. Apply bold formatting to **Pete Miller** (in the 13th line of text) and **Rita Jones** (in the 15th line of text).
    g. Save your changes.

3. **Change alignment and line spacing.**
    a. Change the alignment of the paragraph located below New England Photography Exhibition to Justified.
    b. Change the line spacing to 1.15 for the justified paragraph.
    c. Use the Paragraph dialog box to add 6-point spacing before and after the paragraph.
    d. Center-align the first two lines of the document.
    e. Save your changes.

4. Change margin settings.

   a. Verify that the ruler is visible in the document window. (If it is not visible, change your settings so that it is visible.)

   b. Apply the preset Narrow margins setting to the document.

   c. Apply the preset Wide margins setting to the document.

   d. Using options in the Margins group, set both the left and right margins to 1.2".

   e. Save your changes.

5. Set tabs.

   a. Scroll down until you see the line of text that begins with **Item**, if necessary.

   b. Select this line and the three lines below it (through the line that begins with Exhibition).

   c. Set a left tab stop at the 2 ½" mark on the ruler for the four selected lines.

   d. Set a right tab stop at the 5" mark on the ruler for the four selected lines.

   e. Apply bold formatting to the line that contains **Item Description Date**.

   f. Save your changes.

6. Set indents.

   a. Select the four lines of text below Important Dates, then set the left indent to ¼".

   b. Locate the line of text that starts with Pete Miller (the 13th line of text in the document).

   c. Select the line of text that begins with Pete Miller and the three lines below it (ending with "photojournalist").

   d. Set a hanging indent at the 1" mark on the ruler for the selected lines of text.

   e. Save your changes.

7. Add bulleted and numbered lists.

   a. Format Lines 8 through 10 (**Nature** through **New Englanders at Work**) as a bulleted list using the check mark bullet.

   b. Format the last three lines in the document as anumbered list, choosing the style with a number followed by a parenthesis, as in 1) 2) 3).

   c. Save your changes.

8. Apply Styles.

   a. Apply the Heading 1 style to the text **Submissions** (Line 6 in the document).

   b. Apply the Heading 1 style to the following headings: **Judges**, **Submission Guidelines, Important Dates**, and **Awards**.

   c. Use the Change Quick Styles settings button to apply the Thatch style set to the document.

   d. Type your name in the last line of the document. (*Note*: Make sure your name is not formatted as a numbered list. If you need to remove the numbered list format from any text in the document, click in the paragraph from which you want to remove it, then click the Numbered List button to turn it off.)

   e. Save your changes.

   f. Preview the document, compare your document with Figure G-23, then quit Word. Submit your completed document to your instructor.

FIGURE G-23

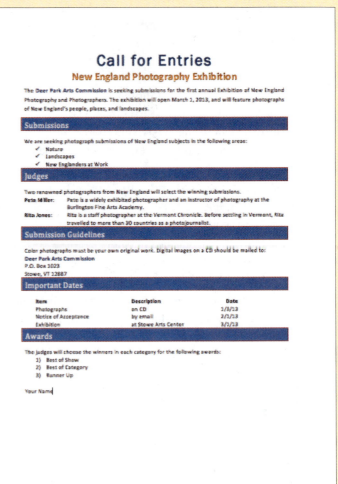

Independent Challenge 1

You work in the marketing department for the Bay City Community Center. Rhonda Johnson, the marketing manager, needs to create a one-page document that describes the programs and classes offered in October. Rhonda has already created a draft with all the necessary information; however, she is not happy with its appearance. She has provided you with her unformatted draft and has asked you to format it so that all the information is presented effectively and looks attractive and professional.

a. Start Word, open the file G-3.docx from the location where your Data Files are stored, then save it as **G-October Calendar**.

b. Center-align the first four lines of the document.

c. Change the font of **October Calendar** to Century Gothic, and increase the font size to 24.

d. Change the font color of **October Calendar** to dark orange (Help Tag reads "Accent 6"), then apply bold formatting to it.

e. Increase the font size of **Bay City Community Center** and the two lines below it to 14 point.

f. In the paragraph under What's New (Lines 6–9), align the paragraph so that it is justified, then set the line spacing to 1.15. Increase the space before and after this paragraph to 6 points.

g. Apply the Heading 1 style to the following lines of text: **What's New**, **New Resident Orientation Classes**, **Cooking Classes**, and **Adult Fitness Class**.

h. In the four lines of text that contain tabs below the heading New Resident Orientation Classes, set two left tab stops—the first at 2" and the second at 4".

i. In the four lines of text that contain tabs below the heading Cooking Classes, set a left tab stop at 2", a second left tab stop at 3 ½", and a right tab stop at 5 ½".

j. Format the last three lines in the document as a bulleted list. Choose the Picture bullet Red Swirl.

k. Apply the Simple Quick Style setting to the document.

l. Run the Spelling and Grammar check. Make corrections when appropriate. Ignore the flags for proper names.

m. Type your name at the end of the document, then right-align it. Compare your document with Figure G-24.

Advanced Challenge Exercise

- Change the color of the **What's New** heading to dark orange (Help Tag reads "Accent 6") and make it bold.

- Select the **What's New** heading and open the Toolbox. (*Hint*: Click ▦ on the Standard toolbar.) Click the Styles tab if necessary.

- Click New Style to open the New Style dialog box. Type **Calendar Heading 1** in the Name text box, then click OK to close the New Style dialog box.

- Apply the Calendar Heading 1 style to the other headings in the document.

n. Save your changes, then preview the document, close it, and quit Word. Submit the completed document to your instructor.

FIGURE G-24

October Calendar
Bay City Community Center
4500 Beech Street
Bay City, CA 94566

WHAT'S NEW
Happy October! The fall is a time for new changes, with kids back at school, and the leaves starting to turn from green to yellow and red. So why not try something new at Bay City Community Center? Our fall and winter programs offer opportunities for personal enrichment and community connections. We offer classes to help you get healthy, learn new skills, and have fun.

NEW RESIDENT ORIENTATION CLASSES
If you are new to Bay City, we recommend signing up for our 1-hour classes on Living in Bay City. Sessions for October are as follows:

Friday	October 10	5:00 PM
Saturday	October 18	10:00 PM
Wednesday	October 15	6:00 PM
Saturday	October 25	10:00 AM

COOKING CLASSES
Learn how to cook from Bay City's finest chefs. All classes meet Wednesdays starting October 1 at 7pm in the Community Kitchen. A different local chef leads each workshop.

Date	Class	Chef	Class Fee
October 1	Soups	Charles Hanson	$25.00
October 8	Bread Making	Dorothy Waters	$15.00
October 15	Italian Specialties	Georgio Martelli	$35.00

ADULT FITNESS CLASS
Drop by the Community Center every Saturday morning at 8:00 for a free fitness class led by Charlie Wong, local fitness expert. Charlie will lead the following group exercises:
- Yoga stretches
- Core strengthening exercises
- Aerobic workout

Your Name

Independent Challenge 2

You provide administrative help to the owner of Walking Adventures, a small tour company that offers walking tours in the United States, Canada, and Brazil. Raven Smith, the marketing director, has given you an unformatted document that provides information about the tours the company will offer in the summer. Raven has asked you to format the sheet so that it's attractive and easy to understand.

a. Open the file G-4.docx from the location where you store your Data Files, then save it as **G-Walking Adventures Fact Sheet**.

b. Center-align the first five lines of text in the document, which include the company name and contact information.

c. Format the Walking Adventures company name in Line 1 of the document using any font, font style, or effects you like to make it readable, attractive, and appropriate for an adventure tour company.

d. Apply the Heading 1 style to the following lines of text: **About Walking Adventures**, **Summer 2013 Walking Tours**, and **All Adventures Include**.

e. Use the Change Quick Styles setting button to apply the Simple style set to the document.

f. Justify the paragraph of text below the About Walking Adventures heading, then set line spacing for this paragraph at 1.15.

g. Select the last four paragraphs below the heading Summer 2013 Walking Tours, beginning with **Grand Canyon** and ending with **($2295)**. Set a left tab stop for these four selected paragraphs to the 2" mark on the ruler.

h. For the same four paragraphs, apply a hanging indent at the 2" mark on the ruler, so that the paragraph text wraps at the 2" mark (the same position of the tab stop that you set in Step g).

i. Apply the Strong style to the text **Grand Canyon:**, **Alaska:**, **British Columbia:**, and **Amazon Adventure:**. (*Hint*: If the Modify Style dialog box opens, click "Reapply the formatting of the Style to the selection," then click OK.)

j. Format the last four lines of text in the document as a bulleted list, choosing a Picture bullet style that looks appropriate for this document.

k. Add your name in the last line of the information sheet, then center-align it.

l. Save your changes, preview, then print the information sheet.

m. Close the document, then quit Word. Submit your completed document to your instructor.

Independent Challenge 3

You work for Stephen Wood, the marketing director of Happy Land—a family resort in Tallahassee, Florida. Stephen has asked you to create a Premium One-Day Pass for the park. The pass will be given to groups of 20 or more who buy passes to the resort. Stephen typed the information for the pass in Word and has given the document to you to format.

a. Open the file G-5.docx from the location where you store your Data Files, then save it as **G-One Day Pass**.

b. Using the skills you learned in this unit, format the pass using fonts, sizes, styles, and effects that you think are appropriate. Use your creativity to produce an attractive document.

c. Format some of the text on the pass as a bulleted list, choosing whatever bullet style you like.

d. Change the paper orientation to Landscape, and adjust the margins to different settings. (*Hint*: To specify to print the document in landscape orientation, click the Layout tab, click the Orientation button in the Page Setup group, then click Landscape.)

e. Type your name somewhere on the pass.

Independent Challenge 3 (continued)

Advanced Challenge Exercise

- Type an asterisk (*) to the right of the word **Pass** in the first line of the document. Format the asterisk with the superscript effect in the Font group.
- Move to the end of the document, type an asterisk (*) on a new line, then type **Must be at least 15 years old or accompanied by an adult to use this pass.**. Format this text and the asterisk you inserted in the previous step so that they are a different color than the rest of the text in the document.

f. Save your changes, print the pass, then close the document and quit Word. Submit your completed document to your instructor.

Real Life Independent Challenge

You are planning a party to celebrate a special occasion. The party can be for any type of event—a birthday celebration, a pizza party, or whatever you want. You need to create a flyer to hand out to your friends or invitees that announces the party, gives information about the reason for the celebration, and provides directions for how to get there.

a. Start Word, then save a new, blank document as **G-Party Flyer.docx**.

b. Type the name of the party on the first line. Format the text using a large font size, then apply a font style that is appropriate for this type of party. Center-align the party name.

c. Below the name of the party, type one line that extends an invitation to this party and explains the reason for celebrating.

d. Below the description you typed in Step c, type the date and time of the party on two separate lines.

e. On the line below the time, type the location and address of the party.

f. Center-align all the text you typed in Steps c through e.

g. Below the location and address of the party, add three highlights of the party, and format the three highlights as a bulleted list, using a Picture bullet style of your choice that is appropriate for the party's theme. Left-align the bulleted list at the 2" mark on the ruler.

h. Below the bulleted list, type **Directions:**. Left-align **Directions:** at the 2" mark on the ruler.

i. Below **Directions:**, type three lines of text that provide directions on how to get to the party from a specific location (such as from the center of town or from a main road). Format the directions as a numbered list. Left-align the numbered list at the 2" mark on the ruler.

j. Type your name on the last line of the flyer. Right-align it.

k. Format all the text in the flyer using fonts, font sizes, and formatting effects that are appropriate for the theme. Preview, save, and close the document, then quit Word. Submit your completed document to your instructor.

Visual Workshop

Open the file G-6.docx from the location where your Data Files are stored, then save it as **G-Diner Menu**. Format the document so that it appears as shown in Figure G-25. (*Hint*: A different style set has been applied to the document, and the color scheme was changed, so you might need to experiment with different combinations of Styles and Quick Style sets until you find the right mix. If you do not have or cannot find the font used in the title, apply the closest match you can find.) Add your name at the bottom of the document, then preview the document. Close the document, then quit Word. Submit the document to your instructor.

FIGURE G-25

Pete's Deli

1514 Wood Road
Atlanta, GA 30312
404-555-0765

Sandwiches

BLT	**$5.75**
Three slices of bacon with lettuce, tomatoes, and mayo on your choice of Pete's bread.	
Turkey Club	**$5.25**
Smoked turkey, bacon, avocado, lettuce, tomatoes, and mayo on triple white toast.	
Grilled Cheese	**$6.75**
Grilled cheese and tomatoes on whole wheat bread.	
Pastrami	**$5.75**
Pastrami, lettuce, and tomatoes on a bulky roll.	
Roast Beef	**$6.25**
Roast beef, lettuce, and tomatoes on a bulky roll.	

Beverages

Lemonade, juices, cola	**$2.00**

Desserts

Pete's Famous Pies	**$4.25**
Top off your lunch with one of Pete's famous pies (pecan, apple, or peach) baked fresh daily.	

Kids' Menu

Any Kids Meal (includes chips and a drink)		**$2.50**
Chicken tenders	Cheese pizza	Macaroni and cheese
Hot dog	Hamburger	Grilled cheese sandwich

Your Name

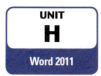

Adding Special Elements to a Document

Microsoft Word 2011 provides many tools to help you create professional looking documents, such as styles, graphics, and other special elements. For instance, you can easily change the entire look of your document in a few clicks by applying a theme. You can insert a table to present detailed information in a row-and-column format. To add visual interest to your document, Word provides a wide variety of **clip art**, which are ready-made art objects that you can insert in documents. If your document contains multiple pages, it's a good idea to insert headers and footers at the top and bottom of each page, containing the page number and other information that you want to appear on every page of your document. Word also makes it easy to insert footnotes and citations. Karen Rivera, marketing director for Outdoor Designs, has asked you to finish a report that both summarizes global corporate efforts to adopt green business practices to preserve the environment and recommends a plan for launching green initiatives at Outdoor Designs.

OBJECTIVES

Work with themes

Create a table

Insert and delete table columns and rows

Format a table

Add clip art

Insert footnotes and citations

Insert a header or footer

Add borders and shading

Format a research paper

Working with Themes

You have learned how to format individual document elements, such as a text selection or an object, and also how to use Quick Styles to change multiple formatting attributes in a selection. An even more powerful tool for making multiple formatting changes at once is the themes feature. A **theme** is a coordinated set of styles, colors, fonts, and effects that can be applied to a document. Themes ensure that your document has a consistent and professional look. To apply a theme, use the Themes button in the Themes group on the Home tab. All the same themes are available in Word, Excel, and PowerPoint, which means that a company can produce many different documents and ensure that they all have a consistent, branded look.  Karen gives you a file containing the content for the recommendation report. You begin by choosing a theme to change the overall look of the report and to go along with the Green concept by applying a theme to it.

1. **Start Word, open the file H-1.docx from the location where you store your Data Files, then save it as** H-Going Green Report

    The report opens in Print Layout view. The status bar indicates that there are four pages.

TROUBLE

If you have a laptop or small monitor, you might need to adjust your zoom to something other than 50% to see all of the pages.

2. **Click and drag the** Zoom slider **at the right end of your status bar until the zoom level is set at** 50%

    With the zoom level set at 50%, all four pages of the report are visible on screen, so you can see at a glance how your changes will affect the whole document The Zoom level can also be set by using the Reduce or enlarge display of the document spin box `100%` ▾ on the Standard toolbar.

3. **Click the** Home tab **if necessary, then click the** Themes button ▦ **in the Themes group**

    The Themes Gallery opens and displays thumbnails of available themes, as shown in Figure H-1.

4. **Scroll down, then click the** Genesis theme

    The Themes Gallery closes and the Genesis theme is applied to the report. Compare your report with Figure H-2.

5. **Click** File **on the menu bar, click** Print, **then click the** Next Page button ▶ **to preview each page of the report**

6. **Click** Cancel **to close the Print dialog box, change the zoom to** 100%, **then save your document**

Creating a custom theme

You can create your own customized themes. To do this, change the formatting of any element you want (such as the font used in headings), click the Themes button, click Save Theme, type a name for the theme, then click Save. The new theme will appear at the top of the Themes Gallery under the Custom heading.

FIGURE H-1: Zoom changed to 50% and Theme Gallery open

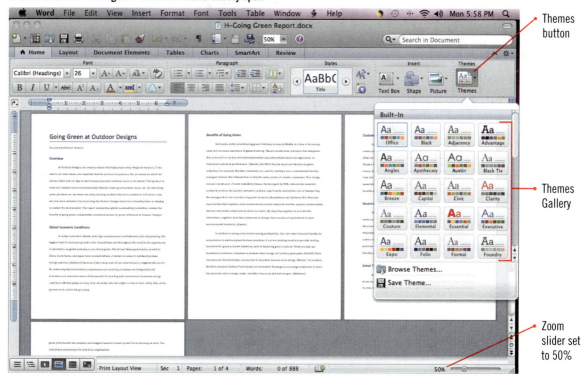

Themes button

Themes Gallery

Zoom slider set to 50%

FIGURE H-2: Genesis theme applied to document

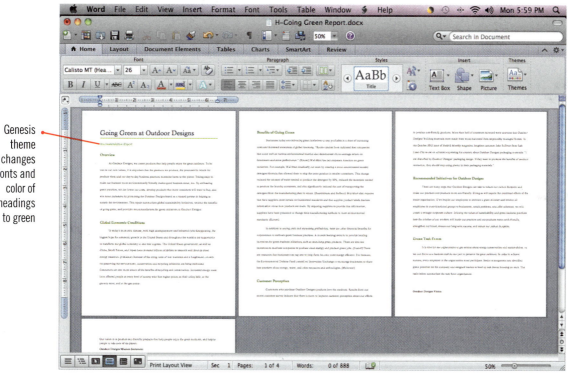

Genesis theme changes fonts and color of headings to green

Creating a Table

Certain kinds of information are best presented within a table. A **table** is a grid of rows and columns. The intersection of each row and column is called a **cell**. Cells can contain either text or graphics. You can insert a table using the New button on the Tables tab or the Table option on the menu bar. When you create a table, you specify the number of rows and columns; you can also add and delete rows and columns as you modify a table. You can use tabs to organize text into rows and columns, but working with tables is often easier. Another benefit to using tables is that Word provides a wide range of professionally designed table styles that you can apply to your table. You decide to insert a table on the third page to present the information about a new task-force organization.

STEPS

1. **Click the Show all nonprinting characters button ¶ on the Standard toolbar, click View on the menu bar, point to Sidebar, then click Thumbnail Pane**

   The Sidebar opens with the Thumbnail Pane selected on the left of your screen. You need to insert the table on page 3. You can use the Thumbnail Pane to help you move to any page quickly.

2. **Click the page 3 thumbnail**

   The top of the third page is now open on your screen, as shown in Figure H-3. You want to insert the table in the blank line above the heading "Outdoor Designs Vision" near the bottom of page 3.

3. **Scroll down so the last line of page 3 is visible, then click to the left of the paragraph mark ¶ in the blank line above Outdoor Designs Vision**

4. **Click the Tables tab, then click the New button ▦ in the Table Options group**

   The Table pop-up menu opens and displays a grid for choosing the number of rows and columns for your table.

5. **Point to the third square in the third row of the grid, as shown in Figure H-4, then click the square**

   A table with three rows and three columns appears above "Outdoor Designs Vision," and the insertion point is in the first cell. Notice that a new tab now appears on the ribbon, the Table Layout tab. This is a **contextual tab**, meaning that it appears only when a particular type of object is selected (such as the table); it is not otherwise available.

6. **Type Task Force, then press [tab]**

   Pressing [tab] moves the insertion point to the next cell. The symbol in each cell is an **end-of-cell mark**. The marks to the right of each row are **end-of-row marks**.

7. **Type Leader, press [tab], type Department, then press [tab]**

   Pressing [tab] in the last cell of a row moves the insertion point to the first cell in the next row.

8. **Type the text shown below in the rest of the table, pressing [tab] after each entry to move to the next cell, but do not press [tab] after the last entry**

Recycling	Stefanie Lin	Finance
Reducing Waste	George Fitzgerald	Operations

   All the cells in the table have data in them. Scroll as necessary and compare your screen with Figure H-5.

9. **Save your changes**

   Notice that when you move the mouse pointer over the table, the Table move handle ⊕ appears above the upper-left corner of the table. Clicking this icon selects the entire table.

FIGURE H-3: Using the Thumbnail Pane to move to page 3

Insertion point at the top of page 3

Sidebar with Thumbnail Pane selected

Page 3 thumbnail

Show all nonprinting characters button

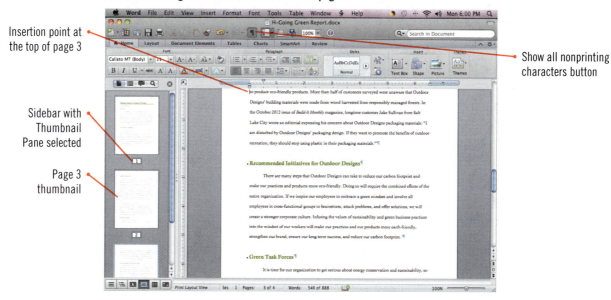

FIGURE H-4: Inserting a 3 × 3 table

Tables tab

New button

In Step 5, click this square

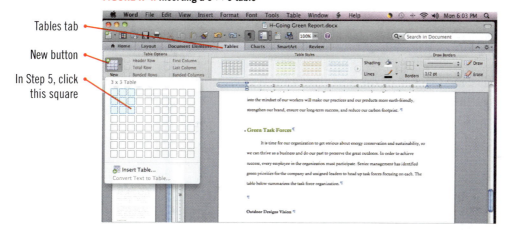

FIGURE H-5: Table with all information entered

Column

Row

End-of-cell mark

End-of-row mark

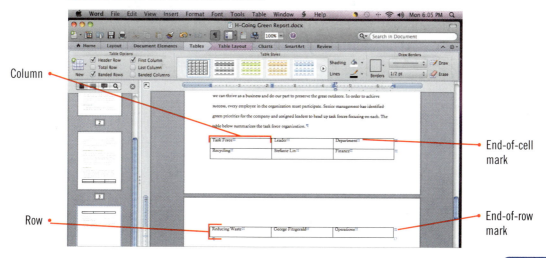

Adding Special Elements to a Document

Inserting and Deleting Table Columns and Rows

After you create a table, you might need to add more information or delete existing information. To accommodate the new information, you can add rows to the top, bottom, or middle of a table. You can add columns anywhere in a table, too. You can use buttons on the Table Layout tab to add or delete columns and rows. 🎨 You need to add two rows to the middle of the table to add information about another task force. You also need to add a column to the table that indicates each leader's job title. Finally, you need to delete one of the rows.

1. **Click Operations in the last cell of the table if necessary, then press [tab]**

   Pressing [tab] in the last cell of a table inserts a new row at the bottom of the table. The table now has four rows, and the insertion point is in the first cell of the new row.

2. **Type Green Product Packaging, press [tab], type Marco Lopez, press [tab], then type Manufacturing**

3. **Click any cell in the second row of the table, then click the Table Layout tab**

   The Table Layout tab displays tools and commands for adjusting settings in a table. Because the Table Layout tab is a contextual tab, it appears only when the insertion point is in a table or when you select a table.

4. **Click the Below button ⊞ in the Rows & Columns group on the Table Layout tab**

   A new empty row appears below the second row.

5. **Click the first cell of the new third row, type Energy Efficiency, press [tab], type Rhonda Wyman, press [tab], then type Office Management**

6. **Click the Left button ⊞ in the Rows & Columns group**

   A new empty column appears between the Leader and Department columns. Compare your screen with Figure H-6. Notice that Word narrowed the existing columns to accommodate the new column.

7. **Click the top cell of the new column, type Position, then press [↓]**

   The insertion point moves down to the second row in the third column.

8. **Type Director, press [↓], type Senior Manager, press [↓], type Director, press [↓], then type Vice President**

   You have just learned that the Recycling and Reducing Waste task forces will be combined into one. You need to delete the Reducing Waste task force row.

9. **Click any cell in the row that begins with Reducing Waste, click the Delete button ⊞ in the Rows & Columns group, click Delete Rows, then save your changes**

   The entire row is deleted, and the other rows move up to close up the space. Compare your screen with Figure H-7.

FIGURE H-6: Table with new column and rows added

Below button

Delete button

Left button

Table Layout tab

New column

New rows

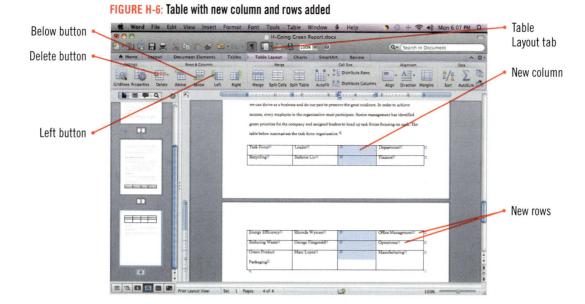

FIGURE H-7: Table after deleting row

Table Move handle

New column with text added

Reducing Waste row no longer appears

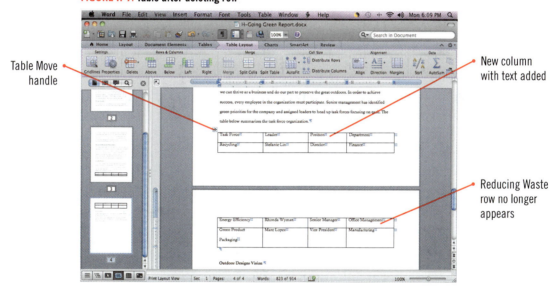

Creating a table with the Draw Table command

You can also create a table by drawing on a document using the Draw Table command. To do so, click Table on the menu bar, then click Draw Table. The pointer changes to 🖉, which you can drag in a diagonal motion to create the outside borders of the table. To create columns, click and drag vertically from the top border to the bottom border. To create rows, drag horizontally from the left border to the right border. When you're finished drawing the table, press [esc] to turn off the Draw Table feature. You can use commands in the Table Styles and the Draw Borders group on the Tables tab to change the color, line width, and style of the table borders. You can also click the Erase button 🖉 in the Draw Borders group on the Tables tab to remove columns or rows by dragging the eraser pointer over existing column or row borders. You can also use the Draw Table feature in an existing table by clicking the Draw button 🖉 in the Draw Borders group on the Tables tab. You can then add rows and columns to the currently selected table by drawing lines from border to border.

Formatting a Table

After you create a table, you can format it by applying one of many built-in table styles. A **table style** is a predefined set of formatting attributes, such as shading, fonts, and border color, which specify how a table looks. You can also format your table by choosing your own settings for each feature, but applying a table style makes your table look professionally designed. You choose a table style using the Table Styles Gallery on the Tables tab. Once you apply a table style that you like, you can further enhance and customize your table's appearance using the Shading and Lines tools in the Table Styles group and the Borders tool in the Draw Borders group. You can also improve the appearance and readability of a table by adjusting column widths and row heights. Now that the information in the task force table is complete, you decide to apply a table style to it and adjust the width of the first column so that all the task-force names fit on one line.

STEPS

1. **Click anywhere in the table if necessary, then click the Tables tab**

   The Tables tab is now active. The Table Styles group displays thumbnails of preset styles that you can apply to your table.

2. **Point to the Table Styles Gallery until the Table Styles pop-up menu arrow ▼ appears, then click ▼**

   The Table Styles Gallery opens, as shown in Figure H-8.

3. **Click the second style in the second row (Light List – Accent 1) of the Built-In section**

   The table is now formatted with a green colored top row. Notice that "Green Product Packaging" in the first column wraps to two lines. You want this task-force name to fit on one line.

4. **Position the pointer just above Task Force until it changes to ↓, then click**

   The first column is now selected, making it easy to see the right edge of the first column.

5. **Position the pointer on the right edge of the selected column until the pointer changes to ↔, drag the pointer to the right to the 2" mark on the horizontal ruler, then release the button**

   The width of the first column increases, and now the text in each first column cell fits on one line instead of two. The second column is now narrower.

6. **Click the Table Move handle ⊞ to select the entire table**

   The entire table is selected. Any formatting settings you choose at this point will be applied to all the cells in the table. You decide that you want to add column gridlines to the table.

7. **Click the Borders button ⊞▾ in the Draw Borders group, then click the All option**

   Black gridlines now outline all of the cells in the table, as shown in Figure H-9.

8. **Save your changes**

FIGURE H-8: Applying a table style

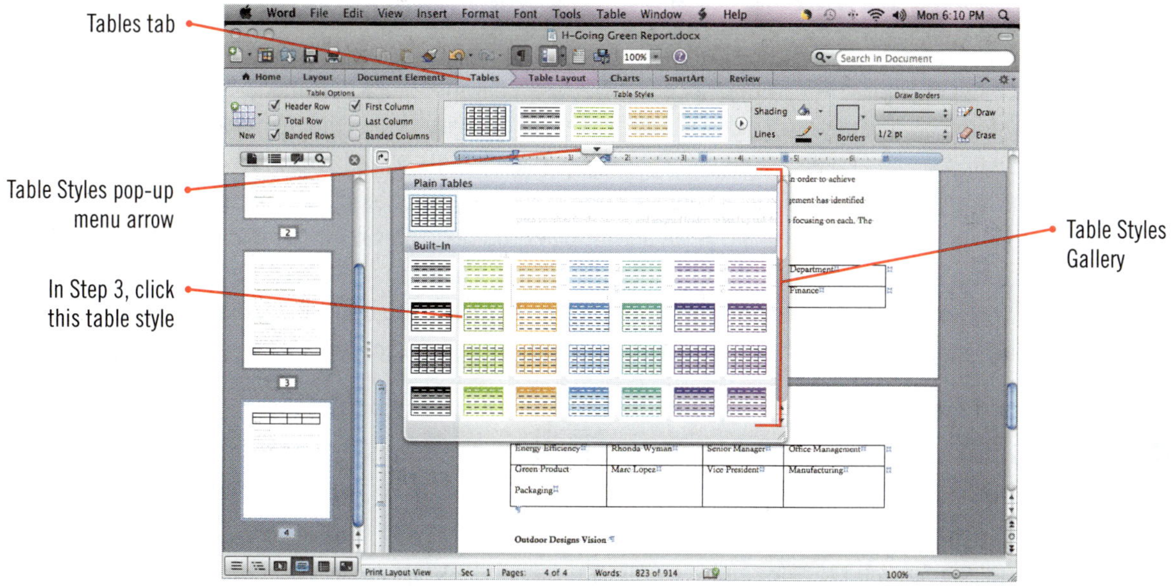

Tables tab

Table Styles pop-up menu arrow

In Step 3, click this table style

Table Styles Gallery

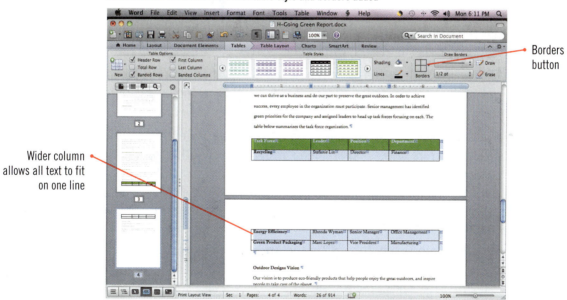

FIGURE H-9: Formatted table with table style and borders added

Borders button

Wider column allows all text to fit on one line

Adding SmartArt

Microsoft Office for Mac 2011 offers many tools for adding graphics to your documents to enhance their visual appeal and better communicate your message. **SmartArt** is a feature that lets you easily create professional looking business diagrams, such as organizational charts, process diagrams, and timelines. To create a SmartArt graphic, click the SmartArt tab on the ribbon. In the Insert SmartArt

Graphic group, click the SmartArt category from which you want to choose a graphic, then click the SmartArt thumbnail you'd like to insert. The SmartArt graphic is inserted in your document at the insertion point. You then edit the placeholder text in the graphic or use the Text Pane to suit your needs.

Adding Clip Art

Graphics can help illustrate a point or enhance the overall appeal of a document. You can insert images from files stored on disk or downloaded from the Web, add SmartArt graphics, and add shapes from the Media Browser. You can also access hundreds of ready-made images, called **clip art**, via the **Clip Gallery**. The Clip Gallery lets you search for clip art, animations, videos, and photographs, all called **clips**. Word searches the clip art folders on your hard drive and displays the search results as small pictures called thumbnails. Once you select a clip and insert it in a document, you can enhance it by applying Picture Styles, changing the way text wraps around it, moving it, or resizing it. You decide to add a picture of the Earth next to the Outdoor Designs Mission Statement heading and paragraph.

STEPS

1. **Click to the left of Outdoor Designs Mission Statement (five lines below the table), click the Home tab, click the Picture button in the Insert group, then click Clip Art Gallery**

   The Clip Gallery: Word dialog box opens with the Search text box highlighted.

2. **In the Search text box, type globe, then click Search**

   The Clip Gallery displays thumbnail previews of all available images that are associated with the word "globe."

3. **Click the image named Globe, as shown in Figure H-10, then click Insert**

   The Clip Gallery closes and the image is inserted in the report.

4. **Click the image to select it, then click the Format Picture tab on the ribbon**

   Round sizing handles in the corners and square sizing handles on the sides of the image indicate that the image is selected. Clicking and dragging the **sizing handles** allows you to manually resize the image. The Format Picture tab is a contextual tab that contains many tools to enhance the appearance of graphics, including tools to change the color of the image.

5. **Click the Recolor button in the Adjust group, then click the second option in the third row of the Recolor section (Accent Color 1 Light), as shown in Figure H-11**

   The image is now green. You can also change the look of the image by applying a Picture Style.

6. **Point to the Picture Styles Gallery until the Picture Styles pop-up menu arrow appears, click the Picture Styles pop-up menu arrow, then click the Soft Edge Oval option (sixth column, third row)**

   The image now has soft edges. The image looks awkward because its bottom edge is aligned with the paragraph heading. This is known as an **inline graphic**. To fix this so that the text flows next to the image, you need to change its **wrapping style**, or the settings for how text flows in relation to a graphic.

7. **Click the Wrap Text button in the Arrange group, then click Square**

   The image's left edge should be left-aligned with the paragraph text. Because you set the wrapping style to square, the image is now a **floating image**, which means you can drag it anywhere on the page. The anchor icon next to it indicates it is now a floating image. The image is a little large, so you need to make it smaller and move it down a little.

8. **Drag the lower-right sizing handle up and to the left diagonally until the Help Tag reads Width: 1", Height: 1"**

9. **Point to the image so that the pointer changes to ✛, drag the image down so that its bottom edge is aligned with the last line of text in the paragraph, then save your changes**

   Compare your screen with Figure H-12. You made the graphic smaller, so its top edge is aligned with the mission statement heading and the bottom edge is aligned with the last line of text.

FIGURE H-10: Clip Gallery with "globe" search results

Search button

Search field

In Step 3, click this image

Insert button

FIGURE H-11: Applying a new color to an image using Recolor

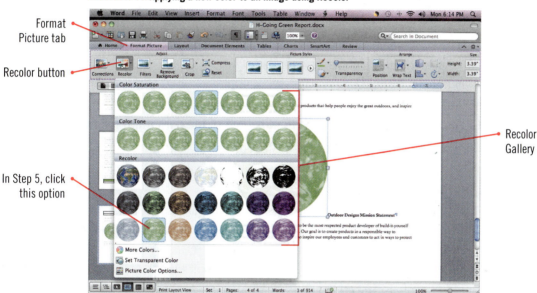

Format Picture tab

Recolor button

In Step 5, click this option

Recolor Gallery

FIGURE H-12: Recolored and resized globe image with Picture Style applied

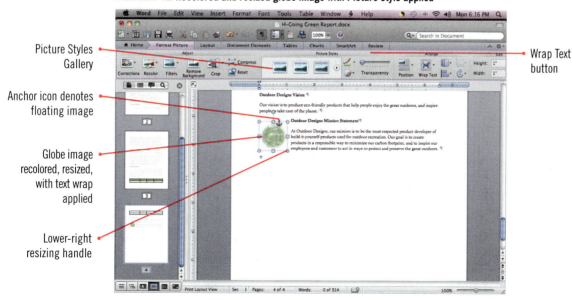

Picture Styles Gallery

Anchor icon denotes floating image

Globe image recolored, resized, with text wrap applied

Lower-right resizing handle

Wrap Text button

Inserting Footnotes and Citations

If your document includes quotes or paraphrased material from another source, you need to credit that source by inserting a citation. A **citation** is a reference to a source that usually includes the author's name and page number of the referenced material. There are different styles for using citations; MLA style is often used for research papers. Citations that follow MLA guidelines appear in parentheses after a quote or paraphrase. If a document contains citations, it must also include a **bibliography**, which is a listing of detailed source information for citations in the document. The Citations tool in Word contains tools to manage sources, insert citations, and add a bibliography. A **footnote** is a comment that appears at the bottom of a document page; it consists of two linked parts: the reference mark in the body of the document and the corresponding note text at the bottom of the page.  You need to add a footnote to the report that comments on recent energy savings. You also need to add a new source and citation and insert a bibliography.

STEPS

1. **In the Search field, type Recommended**

   All instances of the word recommended are highlighted in yellow. The search field helps you quickly locate any keyword in your document.

2. **Click to the right of footprint in the first line of the paragraph following the heading**

3. **Click Insert on the menu bar, then click Footnote**

   The Footnote and Endnote dialog box opens. By default, Footnotes is selected.

4. **Click Insert**

   The Footnote and Endnote dialog box closes, a superscript number 1 is added where the insertion point was located, and the insertion point moves to the bottom of page 3, where Word has added a partial line and footnote number 1.

5. **Type Efforts to date resulted in a 10% reduction in energy costs at our Seattle office from the prior year., as shown in Figure H-13**

   Now you need to add a citation to the quote at the end of the Customer Perception paragraph.

6. **Click page 3 in the Thumbnail Pane to go to the top of page 3, then click after materials."" at the end of the first paragraph**

QUICK TIP

The default style for citations in new documents is APA. To choose a different style, click the Citation Style pop-up menu arrow on the Citations tab of the Toolbox, then click the style you want.

7. **Click the Toolbox button 📋 on the Standard toolbar to open the Toolbox, click the Citations tab 📑, then click the Create a New Source button ➕**

   The Create New Source dialog box opens, where you can specify information about the source.

8. **Click the Type of Source pop-up menu arrow, click Article in periodical, enter the information shown in Figure H-14, then click OK**

   A reference to the source you added is inserted as "(Allen)" in the document at the insertion point and to the citation list.

QUICK TIP

To insert a page break using the menu bar, click Insert, point to Break, then click Page Break.

9. **Close the Toolbox, press ⌘ [end] to move to the end of the document, click the Layout tab on the ribbon, click the Break button 🔲, then click Page**

   Inserting a manual page break allows you to control where text flows to the top of a new page. The insertion point is now set at the top of page 5.

10. **Click the Document Elements tab on the ribbon, click the Bibliography button 📄 in the References group, click Works Cited, then scroll up to view the Works Cited section**

    See Figure H-15. Word inserts the bibliographic information for all the sources cited in the report.

11. **Save your changes**

FIGURE H-13: Footnote added to document

Toolbox button

Page 3 thumbnail

"Recommended" typed in Search field

Footnote

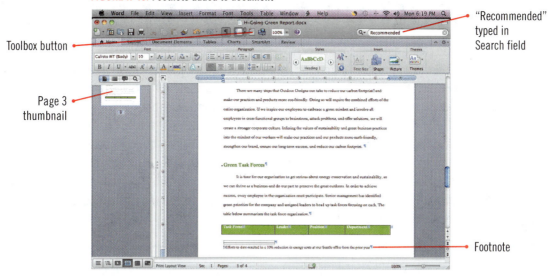

FIGURE H-14: Create New Source dialog box with source information added

Author's name, last name first

Title of article in Title text box

Year text box with publication year

Type of Source pop-up menu arrows

Title of periodical

Leave Day text box blank

Page numbers

Publication month

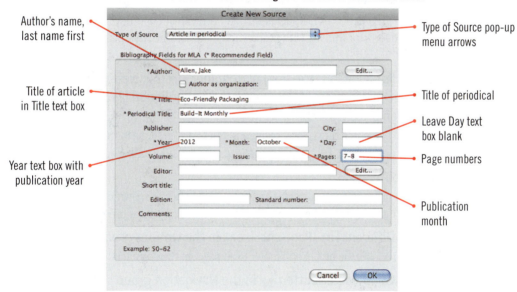

FIGURE H-15: Report with bibliography added

Document Elements tab

Bibliography inserted in MLA style; includes all sources cited in this report

Style list with MLA style selected

Bibliography button

New source appears at top of alphabetic list

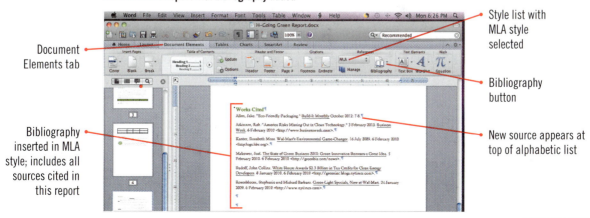

Word 2011

Inserting a Header or Footer

When you create a document that contains several pages, you might want to add page numbers and other information to the top or bottom of each page. You can do this easily by adding headers or footers. A **header** is text that appears in the top margin of a page, and a **footer** is text that appears in the bottom margin of a page. Headers and footers usually repeat from page to page, but you can have them appear on only the odd or even pages or on all the pages except the first, and so on. In addition to page numbers, headers and footers often contain such information as the date, the document author's name, or the filename. You add headers and footers using the View option on the menu bar, or you can choose from preformatted headers and footers by using the Document Elements tab on the ribbon. You can format the header and footer text in the same way you format regular text, and you can even add graphics.  You decide to add a header and a footer to the report.

STEPS

1. **Close the Sidebar, click the Document Elements tab on the ribbon if necessary, then click the Header button in the Header and Footer group**

   The Header Gallery opens, as shown in Figure H-16.

2. **Click the Basic (All Pages) style**

   The insertion point moves to the header area, which contains three [Type text] placeholders into which you can click and type text. The Header and Footer contextual tab is now available on the ribbon and contains buttons and tools for working with headers and footers. Notice that the other text on the Works Cited page is dimmed.

3. **Click the left-aligned [Type text] placeholder, press [delete], click the center-aligned [Type text] placeholder, press [delete], click the right-aligned [Type text] placeholder, type your name, then press [spacebar]**

   You deleted two of the three placeholders and inserted your name in the third placeholder.

4. **Click the Header and Footer tab on the ribbon, then click the Page # button in the Insert group**

   The header now contains your name and the page number, as shown in Figure H-17. This header will appear at the top of every page in the report. You do not want it to appear on the first page.

5. **Click the Different First Page check box in the Options group to select it**

   This option applies the header and footer to all pages in the document except the first page.

6. **Click the Go to Footer button in the Navigation group**

   The insertion point moves to the footer box.

7. **Click the Date button in the Insert group**

   The current date is inserted at the left margin in the footer.

8. **Click Close on the Footer tabs, click File on the menu bar, click Print, then click the Next Page button beneath the Quick Preview four times to view each page of the report**

   Notice that the header and footer appear on all pages except page 1. Figure H-18 shows page 3.

9. **Click Cancel to close the Print dialog box, then save your changes**

FIGURE H-16: Header Gallery

Header button

In Step 2, click Basic (All Pages) style

Header Gallery

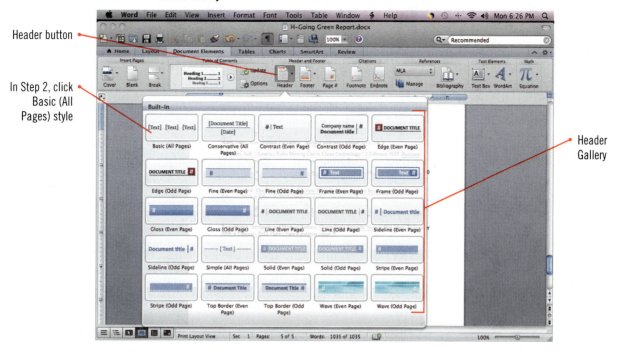

FIGURE H-17: Header with name and page number

Header and Footer tab

Page # button

Date button

Go to Footer button

Name and page number right-aligned in header

Close tab

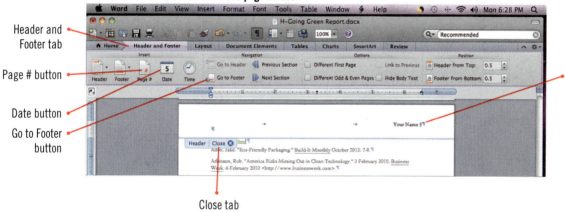

FIGURE H-18: Quick Preview showing header and footer on third page

Header

Page 3 preview

Footer

Next page button

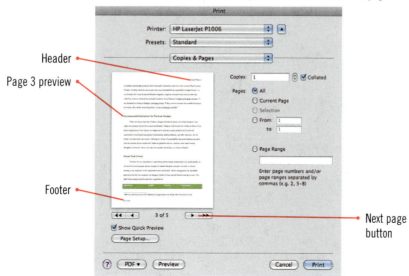

Adding Special Elements to a Document

Adding Borders and Shading

You can add visual interest to an entire document or set a block of text apart from the rest of the page by adding borders and background shading to words, paragraphs, graphics, or entire pages. To add these elements to an entire page, you can use the Borders and Shading dialog box (accessed from the Format menu); to add them to selected text or a paragraph, it is easiest to use the Shading and Borders buttons on the Table Styles tab. You can add borders to the top, bottom, left, or right edges of text or around a graphic.  You decide to add a border and shading to the "Outdoor Designs Vision" paragraph at the bottom of the fourth page to set it off from the rest of the report's text.

STEPS

1. **In the Search field, type Vision**
   The document window moves to page 4 and both instances of the word "vision" are highlighted in yellow.

2. **Select the Outdoor Designs Vision heading and the two lines of text below it**

3. **Click the Tables tab on the ribbon, click the Shading button pop-up menu arrow** 🎨 **, then click the green color in the first row of Theme colors (Help Tag reads Accent 1), as shown in Figure H-19**
   The selected text now has green shading applied to it. Notice that the Shading button displays the green shade you applied. If you wanted to apply this shade of green somewhere else, you could simply select the text and click the Shading button.

4. **Click the Lines button pop-up menu arrow** ✏️ **, then click the darkest shade of green in the Theme colors (fifth shade in the sixth row; Help Tag reads Accent 1, Darker 50%)**
   This selects the color of the lines for the borders that you want to apply.

QUICK TIP
To apply a border around the edge of an entire page, click Format on the menu bar, click Borders and Shading to open the Borders and Shading dialog box, click the Page Border tab, select the page border settings you want, then click OK.

5. **Click the Borders button** ⊞ **, then click Outside**
   The Outdoor Designs Vision heading and paragraph are now shaded in a green box with a dark green border. Compare your screen with Figure H-20.

6. **Click anywhere in the document to deselect the text, then save your changes**

7. **Close the document, quit Word, then submit your completed report to your instructor**

Tables tab

Vision typed in Search field

Shading button

In Step 3, click this color

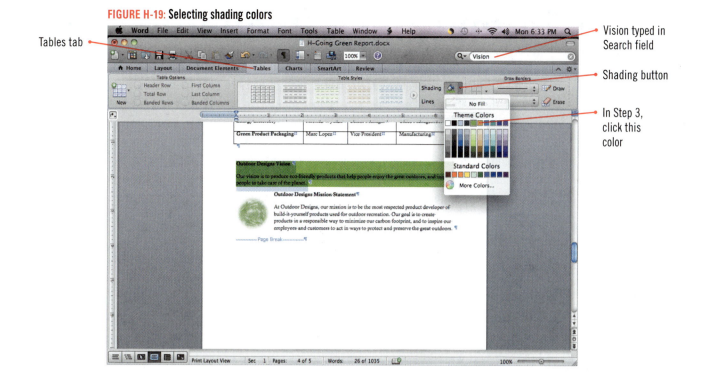

Green shading applied to selected paragraphs

Borders button

Lines button

Dark green border around selected paragraphs

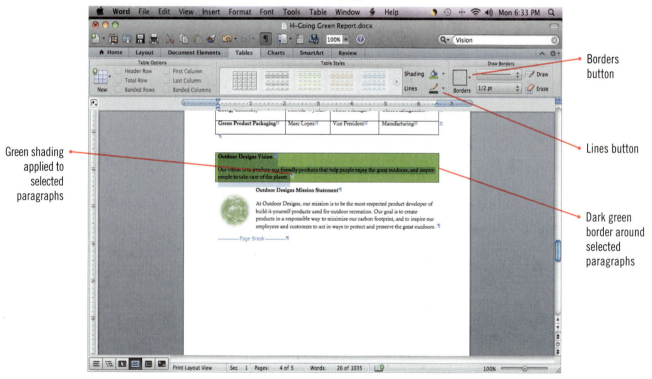

Formatting a Research Paper

Now that you have completed all the units for Word, you have learned skills to help you create many kinds of documents, including research papers. If you need to write research papers for a class, you should be aware that there are guidelines that you need to follow to format them correctly. Modern Language Association (MLA) style is a popular standard for formatting academic research papers, which many schools require. This lesson provides some basic guidelines for formatting a research paper using MLA style. Use Table H-1 and Figure H-21 to learn the guidelines for formatting the first page of a research paper using MLA style. Use Table H-2 and Figure H-22 to learn guidelines for formatting the whole paper. The guidelines provided here will just get you started; for detailed information on MLA guidelines, search online or ask your school librarian for help. (*Note*: You can format the research paper shown in this lesson by completing the Real Life Independent Challenge for this unit.)

TABLE H-1: Formatting guidelines for the first page of a research paper

required first page element	MLA guideline
Header	Your last name followed by the page number (on all pages including page 1), right-aligned
Your name	Left-aligned, 1" from top of page
Professor's name	Two lines below your name, left-aligned
Course number	Two lines below professor's name, left-aligned
Title	Two lines below course number, center-aligned
Beginning of body text	First paragraph is double-spaced below title; first line is indented ½"

TABLE H-2: Formatting guidelines for a whole research paper

setting	MLA guideline	Word quick reference
Line spacing	Double-space all text in the document	Press ⌘[A] to select all the text in the document, click the **Line Spacing button** on the Home tab, then click **2.0**
Margins	All margins set to 1"	Click the **Layout tab**, click the **Margins button**, then click **Normal**
Paragraph formatting	Indent first line of each paragraph ½"	Press [tab] at the start of a new paragraph or press ⌘[A] to select all the text in the document, then drag the **First Line Indent marker** ▽ to the ½" mark on the ruler
Font	Times New Roman	Click the **Font pop-up menu arrow** on the Home tab, then click **Times New Roman**
Font size	12 point	Click the **Font Size pop-up menu arrow** on the Home tab, then click **12**
Header	Right-aligned; your last name followed by the page number (on all pages including page 1)	Click the **Document Elements tab**, click the **Header button**, click the **Basic (All Pages) style**, delete the first and second placeholder, replace the third placeholder with your last name, press [**Spacebar**], click the **Header and Footer tab**, click the **Page Number button**, then close the header box
Citations	Insert author's name and page number in parentheses after quote or reference to work	Open the Toolbox, click the **Citations tab**, click the **source name** or click **Create New Source** to add source information
Bibliography	Include Works Cited page with sources that you reference in the paper	Insert a page break at the end of the document, click the **Document Elements tab**, click the **Bibliography button**, then click **Works Cited**

FIGURE H-21: First page of research paper formatted according to MLA style

1" top margin

Your name, professor's name, and course number appear as shown here

First line of each paragraph is indented to ½" mark

Text is double-spaced; font is 12-point Times New Roman for entire document

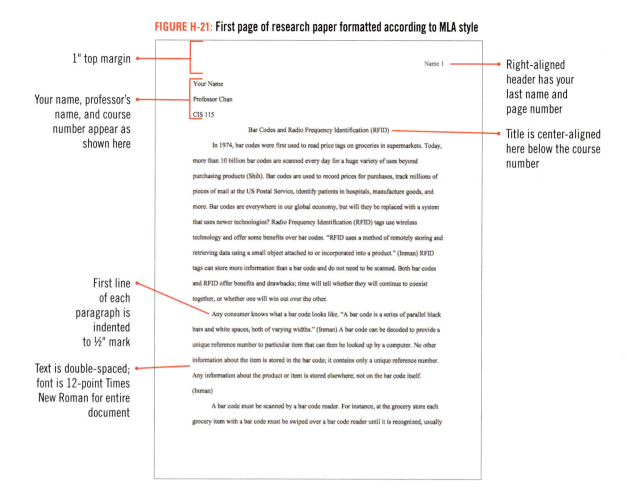

Right-aligned header has your last name and page number

Title is center-aligned here below the course number

FIGURE H-22: Page 2 of research paper and Works Cited page

Newspaper name is italicized

Quotes longer than four lines are indented to ½" and show no quotation marks

In-paragraph citation references author's last name

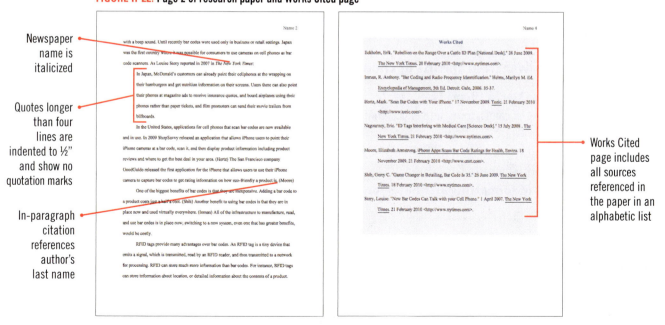

Works Cited page includes all sources referenced in the paper in an alphabetic list

Practice

Concepts Review

Label the Word window elements shown in Figure H-23.

FIGURE H-23

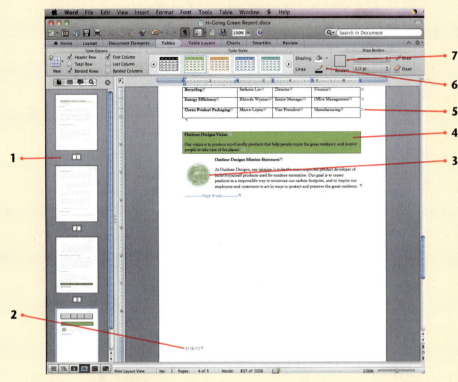

Select the best answer from the list of choices.

8. In Office 2011 for Mac, a theme is:
- **a.** A coordinated set of colors, fonts, and effects that can be applied to a document.
- **b.** Available only in Word.
- **c.** A distinctive font.
- **d.** A characteristic of a font effect.

9. A predefined set of formatting attributes for a table, such as shading, borders, and colors, is called a _____.
- **a.** SmartArt.
- **b.** Table design.
- **c.** Table style.
- **d.** Table Gallery.

10. Which of the following actions moves the insertion point to the next cell in a table?
- **a.** Pressing [tab]
- **b.** Pressing ⌘ [return]
- **c.** Pressing ⌘ [home]
- **d.** Pressing [alt] and clicking

11. Which tab is an example of a contextual tab?
- **a.** Format Picture
- **b.** Home
- **c.** Layout
- **d.** Document Elements

12. **Clip art is found in the:**
    - **a.** Clip Gallery.
    - **b.** Clip Art task pane.
    - **c.** Images folder.
    - **d.** Data Files folder.

13. **A _____ is a listing of detailed source information for citations in a document.**
    - **a.** Footer
    - **b.** Footnote
    - **c.** Header
    - **d.** Bibliography

14. **Which ribbon tab do you use to insert a header or footer?**
    - **a.** Home
    - **b.** Layout
    - **c.** Document Elements
    - **d.** Tables

15. **Borders can be applied to:**
    - **a.** Document pages.
    - **b.** Selected text.
    - **c.** Selected paragraphs.
    - **d.** All of the above

Skills Review

1. **Work with themes.**
   a. Start Microsoft Word, open the file H-2.docx from the location where you store your Data Files, then save the new document as **H-Nova Scotia Report.docx**.
   b. Set the zoom level of the document to 50% so that you can see both pages of the report.
   c. Apply the Civic theme to the document.
   d. Set the zoom level of the document to 100%.
   e. Save your changes.

2. **Create a table.**
   a. Open the Thumbnail Pane and display the thumbnails of each page in the document. Use the Thumbnail Pane to move to page 2. Set the insertion point in the blank line above Classic Walking Adventures at the bottom of page 2.
   b. Insert a table that is four columns wide and three rows high.
   c. Enter the information shown below into the table you created.

Tour Name	Start Date	End Date	Price
Senior Weekender	June 14	June 16	$1,295
Thrill Seeker	June 21	June 28	$2,195

   d. Save your changes to the document.

3. **Insert and delete table columns and rows.**
   a. Insert a new row as the last row in the table.
   b. Enter the following information into the cells in the new row:

Family Fun	July 5	July 12	$1,995

   c. Insert a new row below the row that contains the column headings, then enter the following information into the new cells:

Family Fun	June 7	June 9	$1,095

   d. Delete the row that contains the July 5 Family Fun tour.
   e. Insert a new column to the right of the Tour Name column.
   f. Enter the information from the table below into the new column.

Tour Type
Walking
Walking
Hiking and Kayaking

   g. Save your changes.

Skills Review (continued)

4. Format a table.

   a. Format the table by applying the Medium Shading 1 – Accent 6 table style.

   b. Use the AutoFit to Contents option so that all the table's contents fit neatly on one line in each cell.

   c. Apply black borders to all the cells in the table.

   d. Save your changes.

5. Add clip art.

   a. Use the Thumbnail Pane to move to page 1. Set the insertion point before the word "Nova" in the first line of paragraph text below the heading About Nova Scotia.

   b. Open the Clip Gallery, then search for an image of an apple tree.

   c. Insert the image shown in Figure H-24 (or a similar one).

FIGURE H-24

   d. Reduce the size of the image so that it is 1 $\frac{1}{2}$" wide. (*Hint*: Use the Help Tag as a guide to help you size it.)

   e. Set the wrapping style of the image to Square.

   f. Drag the image as necessary so that its bottom edge is aligned with the last line of the paragraph and its left edge is aligned with the left edge of paragraph text.

   g. Recolor the image with the Accent Color 6 Light color.

   h. Apply the Soft Edge Rectangle picture style to the image.

   i. Save your changes.

6. Insert footnotes and citations.

   a. Use the Search field to locate the heading Reasons to Offer Tours in Nova Scotia.

   b. Set the insertion point to the right of the word "survey" in the line below the Reasons to Offer Tours in Nova Scotia heading.

   c. Insert a footnote.

   d. Type the following text as footnote text: **Survey was conducted in June 2012 and completed by 124 customers.**

   e. Click the page 2 thumbnail to move to the top of page 2.

   f. Set the insertion point after the closing quotation mark that follows the word "spectacular" at the end of the paragraph, then use the Citations tab on the Toolbox to create new source. (*Hint*: Make sure the Citation Style is set to MLA.)

   g. Enter the following information in the Create New Source dialog box:

      Type of Source: Article in Periodical
      Author: Sheridan, Lindsay
      Title: Nova Scotia by Foot
      Periodical Title: The Walking Stick News
      Year: 2012
      Month: June
      Day: 26
      Pages: 10–11

   h. Close the Toolbox, scroll to the bottom of page 2, then set the insertion point in the blank line below the table.

   i. Insert a page break, then insert a bibliography using the Works Cited style.

   j. Save your changes.

Skills Review (continued)

7. Insert a header or footer.

   a. Insert a header using the Basic (All Pages) option.

   b. Delete the left-aligned and the center-aligned [Type text] placeholders. Type your name in the right-aligned [Type text] placeholder. Insert a space after your name, then insert the page number after the space.

   c. Move to the footer and insert the date at the left margin.

   d. Specify that the header and footer be different on the first page.

   e. Close the footer area, then save your changes.

8. Add borders and shading.

   a. Select the last five lines of text in the document, then apply Accent 6, Lighter 80% shading to the selection.

   b. Use the Lines button and the Borders button to apply an outside border around the selection that is Accent 6, Darker 50%.

   c. Close the Sidebar, turn off nonprinting characters if necessary, and save your changes.

   d. Compare your screen with Figure H-25, then close the document and quit Word. Submit your completed document to your instructor.

FIGURE H-25

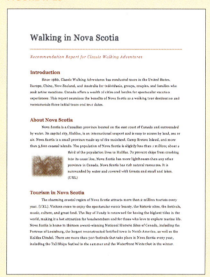  

Independent Challenge 1

You are the new marketing manager at Broad Strokes Art Studio, a small art studio in Indiana that offers art classes to the community. You need to create a one-page information sheet for prospective students. You have a partially completed document that you need to finish. You add a table containing the class schedule and a bibliography that lists titles of books that key instructors have written.

   a. Open the file H-3.docx from the location where you store your Data Files, then save it as **H-Art Classes Info Sheet**.

   b. Apply the Sketchbook theme to the document.

   c. Insert a 4 × 6 table beneath the heading Summer Classes.

   d. Enter the information below into the new table.

Class Name	Start Date	Time	Sessions
Figure Drawing	June 3	7:00-9:00	8
Studio Drawing	June 4	7:00-9:00	6
Basic Watercolor	June 5	7:00-8:30	4
Advanced Oil Painting	June 6	4:00-6:00	8
Basic Calligraphy	June 6	7:00-9:00	6

   e. Add a new row below the Studio Drawing row that contains the following information:

Basic Oil Painting	June 5	6:00-7:30	8

Independent Challenge 1 (continued)

f. Add a column to the right of the Start Date column, then enter the information from the table below into it.

Day
Monday
Tuesday
Wednesday
Wednesday
Thursday
Thursday

g. Apply the Light List – Accent 1 table style to the table.

h. Adjust the column width of the first column so that each class name fits on one line.

i. If necessary, adjust the column width of the last column so that it aligns with the 6 ½" mark on the horizontal ruler.

j. Open the Borders and Shading dialog box, click the Page Border tab, click the Box style border, then click OK to insert a border around the page.

k. Insert a clip art image appropriate for an art studio and position it to the right of the two paragraphs about the instructors. (*Hint:* You might have to search through each category to find an appropriate piece of clip art.) Apply the Square text wrapping style to it. Resize it so that it fits well and looks good in the space next to the paragraphs.

l. Insert a footer containing your name, left-aligned, and today's date, center-aligned.

m. Insert an MLA-style citation after Painting for Fun in the last line of text in the document with the following:

Type of Source:	Book
Author:	Koh, Rachelle
Title:	Painting for Fun
City:	Detroit
Publisher:	Paint Brush Press
Year:	2008

n. In the last line of the document, insert the bibliography for the source you entered. (*Hint*: Click the Bibliography button in the References group on the Document Elements tab, then click Bibliography.)

o. Replace the heading Bibliography with **Information on Rachelle Koh's Book**.

p. Delete any blank lines that cause this document to run onto a second page.

q. Save your changes, preview the document, close the document, then quit Word. Submit your completed document to your instructor.

Independent Challenge 2

You are the human resources manager at Taco Now, a Mexican fast-food chain with headquarters in Chicago. A new employee, Brenda Ingersoll, starts her first day tomorrow as an associate brand manager. You need to create a schedule for Brenda that shows the times and locations of her meetings and appointments as well as the contact people with whom she will meet.

a. Open the file H-4.docx from the location where you store your Data Files, then save it as **H-Schedule.docx**.

b. Apply a theme to the document that you think looks good and is appropriate for this type of document.

c. Set the insertion point in the blank line two lines above To: Brenda Ingersoll.

d. Type today's date in the following format: Month XX, Year.

e. In the line below To: Brenda Ingersoll, type your name to the right of From:.

Independent Challenge 2 (continued)

f. Two lines below the first long paragraph, insert a table containing the following information.

Time	Location	Contact Person	Description
9:00	Reception	Lee Allen	Benefits review
9:30	Taco Room	Juan Herrera	Orientation training
11:00	Queso Room	Sandy Landon	Team meeting
12:00	Cafeteria	Leslie Rust	Team lunch
1:30	Burrito Room	Jose Ortiz	Product overview

g. Apply a table style of your choosing to the table that is appropriate for this type of document.

h. Insert a row in the table between the 9:30 and 11:00 time slot. Enter the information shown below into the new row.

10:30	Supply Room	Julie Rosen	Get office supplies

i. Add a border around the Taco Now Philosophy heading and the paragraph below it at the bottom of the page and add shading to this text. Format the text in this box using fonts, formatting, alignment, and font styles to make it look attractive.

j. Insert a footnote to the right of Leslie Rust's name in the table. The footnote text should read **Leslie will meet you and the rest of the team in the cafeteria.** Format this footnote text so that it looks different from the main text in the document.

k. Insert a footer that contains your name, right-aligned.

l. Preview the document, then save your changes.

Advanced Challenge Exercise

- Click anywhere in the table.
- Click the Draw button in the Draw Borders group on the Tables tab, then use the pen pointer to draw a new row below the 1:30 row. (*Hint*: Drag a line from the middle of the left edge of the 1:30 cell all the way to the right edge of the cell containing Product overview.) Use the pen pointer to draw vertical lines for the cell borders in the new row. Then format the new row so that it looks like the other rows in the table. (*Hint*: Click inside the new row, then click the same table style you used to format the table.) When you are finished, click the Draw button again to turn off the pen pointer.
- Enter the following information in the new row:

4:00	Burrito Room	Karen Fogg	Get company ID card

- If necessary, remove the formatting on any text that does not match the formatted text in the same column.

m. Save, preview, and close the document. Submit the document to your instructor.

Independent Challenge 3

Serena Dunbar in the human resources department at Haskin Paper Products has asked you to create a one-page flyer for the annual company picnic. The picnic will take place at Bradley Park from 9:00 a.m. until 3:00 p.m. on July 15. Attendees can swim, compete in a volleyball tournament, play basketball, and participate in a relay race. A barbecue lunch will be served.

a. Open the file H-5.docx from the location where you store your Data Files, then save it as **H-Company Picnic Flyer.docx**.

b. Format the text in the document so that it reflects the casual, festive nature of the event. Choose fonts, font sizes, and formatting attributes that make the key information stand out.

c. Apply shading to the first line of the document (Haskin Paper Products) using a fill color and font that look good together.

Independent Challenge 3 (continued)

d. Insert a table containing the information shown below.

Activity	Time	Location
Buses Depart	9:00	Lobby
Relay Race	10:00	Field A
Volleyball Tournament	10:30	Beach
Basketball Game	11:00	Basketball Courts
BBQ Lunch	12:00	Pavilion
Buses Return	3:00	Parking Lot

e. Format the table using a table style of your choosing that is appropriate for this document and makes the information easy to read.

f. Insert an appropriate piece of clip art for the occasion, then size and position it attractively.

g. Insert a footer that contains your name, center-aligned.

h. Save your changes, preview the flyer, then close the document. Figure H-26 shows one possible solution; yours will vary depending on the formatting choices you made. Submit your flyer to your instructor.

FIGURE H-26

Haskin Paper Products

Company

Picnic!

July 15
9:00-3:00
Bradley Park

Don't miss the annual **Company Picnic** at **Bradley Park** on Friday **July 15**! Work up a sweat playing volleyball or competing in the Relay Race. Play basketball, go for a swim or simply relax on the beach. Enjoy great food with your colleagues at the barbecue lunch! See below for the schedule. See you there!

Activity	Time	Location
Buses Depart	9:00	Lobby
Relay Race	10:00	Field A
Volleyball Tournament	10:30	Beach
Basketball Game	11:00	Basketball Courts
BBQ Lunch	12:00	Pavilion
Buses Return	3:00	Parking Lot

Your Name

Real Life Independent Challenge

Research papers are frequently assigned for history and English classes in college. Knowing how to format a research paper according to standards is extremely important. A common standard used for writing and formatting research papers is MLA (Modern Language Association). Another popular standard is APA (American Psychological Association). If your professor assigns a research paper, he or she will probably specify that you write and format your paper according to MLA or APA requirements. In this Real Life Independent Challenge, you create a research paper and format it according to MLA guidelines. So that you do not have to actually research and write the paper, you use text from an existing file for the paper. Before completing the steps below, review the lesson Formatting a Research Paper located just before the end-of-unit exercises.

a. Open the file H-6.docx from the location where you store your Data Files, then save it as **H-Research Paper.docx**.

b. Change your left and right margins to 1".

c. With the insertion point set before the first line of text in the document, type your name.

d. Press [return], type **Professor Chan**, then press [return].

e. Type **CIS 115**, then press [return].

f. Center-align the title of the paper, Bar Codes and Radio Frequency Identification (RFID).

g. Find "The New York Times" on pages 1 and 2 in the text. Format both of these occurrences in italic.

h. Immediately below *The New York Times*: on page 1, select the four-line quote that begins "In Japan, McDonald's customers … ." Set the left indent at the $1/2$" mark on the ruler for this paragraph.

i. Press ⌘[A] to select all the text in the document. Set the line spacing to double-spaced (2.0).

j. Change the font for all the selected text to Times New Roman, then change the font size to 12 point.

k. Indent the beginning of each paragraph of body text in the paper to the $1/2$" mark on the ruler. Do not further indent the quote that you indented in Step h. (*Hint*: You can either press [tab] before the first character in the paragraph or create a first line indent by dragging the First Line Indent marker to the $1/2$" mark on the ruler.)

l. Remove the extra blank line between paragraphs.

m. Create a header that contains your last name followed by the page number. Right-align the header. Change the font in the header to 12-point Times New Roman if necessary.

n. Insert a citation to author R. Anthony Inman after the quote in the first paragraph of body text (which ends "… incorporated into a product"). (*Hint*: To choose this source, open the Citations tab on the Toolbox, then double-click Inman, R. Anthony.)

o. Move the insertion point to the end of the document. Insert a page break. Insert a bibliography using the Works Cited option.

p. Format all the text in the Works Cited section in 12-point Times New Roman.

q. With the Works Cited section still selected, set a hanging indent at the $1/2$" mark on the ruler.

r. Center-align the Works Cited heading.

s. Save your changes. Compare your research paper with the one shown in Figures H-21 and H-22.

Advanced Challenge Exercise

■ Save the document with the name **H-Research Paper ACE.docx**.

■ Click the Document Elements tab, click the Cover button in the Insert Pages group, then click the Cover Page 03.

■ Type **Bar Codes and Radio Frequency Identification (RFID)** in the Document Title placeholder.

■ Delete the document subtitle placeholder and the blank line that it occupied.

■ Replace the text "Your Name" with your name.

■ In the placeholder under Abstract, type a short summary that describes what the paper is about. (You will need to read the paper to write this summary.)

■ Save the document, then preview each page of the document.

t. Close the file, then quit Word. Submit the document to your instructor.

Visual Workshop

Open the file H-7.docx from the location where you store your Data Files, then save it as **H-Beach Cottage Ad.docx**. Use the skills you learned in this unit to create the flyer shown in Figure H-27. (*Hints*: Use TW Cen MT Bold for the headings and Century Gothic for the body text and table text. Select a different clip art image if the one shown in the figure is not available to you. Set the wrapping style to tight for the top image. Insert the table and apply the style shown in the figure. Apply a Box style blue border around the whole page using the Page Border tab of the Borders and Shading dialog box.) Type your name somewhere on the flyer, save your changes, preview the flyer, quit Word, then submit the document to your instructor.

FIGURE H-27

Beach Cottage for Rent

Relax and enjoy spectacular views of the Pacific Ocean on Maui's south shore. The white sandy beach is just steps away! Located on five acres of landscaped grounds, with swaying palm trees and fragrant flowering plants, this cozy 2-bedroom cottage features updated appliances, and is fully stocked to ensure you have everything you need while on vacation. Enjoy breathtaking sunsets year round. Prepare meals outside on the propane grill and dine on the lanai. Enjoy swimming, snorkeling, tennis, and windsurfing. Watch humpback whales before they migrate north. World-class restaurants are minutes away!

Property Details

Feature	Description
Location	Maui, HI
Weekly rate	$2,700
Bedrooms	2
Bathrooms	2
Outdoor grill	Yes
Lanai	Yes
Beach access	Yes
Hot tub	Yes
Air conditioning	Yes
Phone	Unlimited free local calls
Internet	Free high speed Internet access

For more details, contact:

Mindy Lee
4455 Palm Drive
Kihei, HI 96753
Phone: (800) 555-2090

Your Name

Adding Special Elements to a Document

UNIT I
Excel 2011

Creating a Worksheet

Files You Will Need:

No files needed

In this unit, you learn how to create and work with a Microsoft Excel worksheet. A **worksheet** is an electronic grid in which you can perform numeric calculations. You can use a worksheet for many purposes, such as analyzing sales data, calculating a loan payment, organizing inventory, and displaying data in a chart. An Excel file, called a **workbook**, can contain one or more worksheets. People sometimes refer to both worksheets and workbooks as **spreadsheets**. Karen Rivera, the marketing director for Outdoor Designs, asks you to help her create a worksheet that provides a sales forecast for the kite product line. You create the worksheet, enter values and labels into it, create formulas to make calculations, format it, and print it.

OBJECTIVES

Navigate a workbook

Enter labels and values

Work with columns and rows

Use formulas

Use AutoSum

Change alignment and number format

Enhance a worksheet

Preview and print a worksheet

Navigating a Workbook

Every new Excel workbook contains one worksheet. You can add more worksheets to the workbook to help organize your information. An Excel worksheet consists of a grid of rows and columns. Similar to a Microsoft Word table, the intersection of a row and a column is called a **cell**.  Before working on the sales forecast worksheet, you need to start Excel, familiarize yourself with the workbook window, and save a blank workbook.

STEPS

QUICK TIP

If the Excel icon is not visible on the Dock, click the Finder icon on the Dock, click Applications in the Finder window, locate and click Microsoft Office 2011, then double-click Microsoft Excel.

1. **Click the Microsoft Excel icon** ![X] **on the Dock**

   Excel starts and the Excel Workbook Gallery opens, as shown in Figure I-1. The Workbook Gallery provides access to all the templates available in Excel.

2. **With All selected in the left pane and Excel Workbook selected in the middle pane, click Choose**

   A blank workbook opens, as shown in Figure I-2. Excel contains elements that are in every Microsoft Office program, including the menu bar, the title bar, the Standard toolbar, the ribbon, the document window, the scroll bars, the status bar, and the View buttons.

3. **View the worksheet window**

   The cell with the blue border in the upper-left corner of this worksheet (called Sheet1) is the **active cell**. The blue border surrounding the active cell is the **cell pointer**. You must click a cell to make it active before entering data. Every cell in a worksheet has a unique **cell address**, which is a specific location of a cell in a worksheet where a column and row intersect. A cell address consists of a column letter followed by a row number (such as B33). When you first start Excel, the active cell in the new workbook (with a default file-name of Workbook1) is cell A1, where column A and row 1 intersect.

QUICK TIP

To navigate quickly to a specific cell, press [control][G] to open the Go To dialog box, type the cell address you want to navigate to in the Reference text box, then click OK.

4. **Click cell C1**

   Cell C1 becomes the active cell. Notice that the column and row headings of the active cell (column C and row 1) appear in a darker color. The **name box** shows the address of the selected cell, and the **formula bar**, located just above the column headings, shows the contents of the selected cell (it is currently empty). The pointer changes to ✛ when you move it over any cells in the workbook.

5. **Press →, press ↓, then press [tab]**

   Cell E2 is now the active cell. You can move to and select a cell by clicking it, by using the arrow keys, or by pressing [tab] (to move one cell to the right), [shift][tab] (to move one cell to the left), or [return] (to move one cell down).

6. **Click the Insert Sheet tab** ![+] **at the bottom of the worksheet**

   Another blank worksheet is added to the workbook, named Sheet2; it becomes the active sheet, and cell A1 is the active cell. To work with different sheets in a workbook, you click the sheet tab of the sheet you want to see.

7. **Drag the ✛ pointer from cell A1 to cell D5**

   Cells A1 through D5 are selected, a total of 20 cells, as shown in Figure I-3. A group of cells that share boundaries and are selected is called a **cell range**. To reference a cell range, use the cell address of the first cell in the range followed by a colon and the cell address of the last cell in the range. The cell range you selected is A1:D5.

8. **Select the cell range D8:D14**

   Cells D8 through D14 (a total of seven cells) are selected.

QUICK TIP

To rename a worksheet, right-click the tab, click Rename, type the new worksheet name, then press [return].

9. **Click the Sheet1 sheet tab, then press ⌘[home]**

   Clicking the sheet tab returns you to Sheet1, and the keyboard shortcut returns the cell pointer to cell A1.

10. **Click File on the menu bar, click Save As, navigate to the location where you store your Data Files, then save the file as I-Kite Sales Forecast**

FIGURE I-1: Excel Workbook Gallery

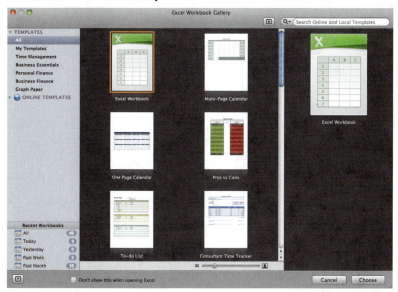

FIGURE I-2: Excel program window

Menu bar
Standard toolbar
Name box
Active cell
Formula bar
Insert Sheet tab
Sheet1 sheet tab
View buttons

Ribbon with Home tab active

Status bar

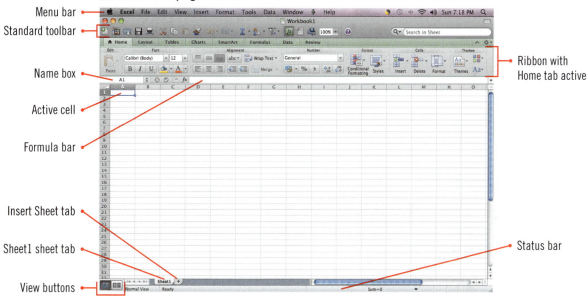

FIGURE I-3: Selecting a range of cells in Sheet2

Select All button
Row headings
Selected cell range
Sheet2 is active
Sheet1 tab

Column headings

Insert Sheet tab

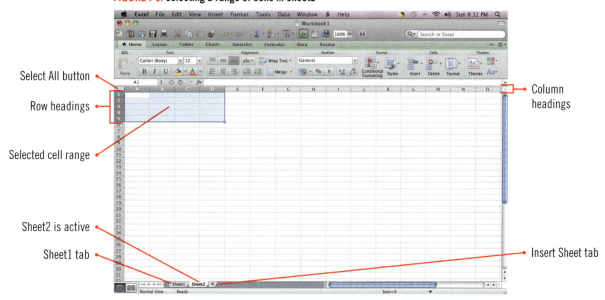

Entering Labels and Values

Entering data in a worksheet is similar to typing in a Word table. First, click the cell in which you want to enter data, and then type the data you want to enter. After typing the data, you must accept the entry by pressing [return], [tab], or an arrow key. The cells in most worksheets contain labels and values. A **label** is text that describes data in a worksheet. **Values** are numeric data that can be used in calculations. You can edit a cell entry by double-clicking the cell to put the cell in Edit mode. In Edit mode, select the part of the cell entry you do not want, and then type your corrections. Table I-1 lists several methods for selecting cells with the mouse or keyboard.  This worksheet needs to provide the names of the kite products, their net prices, the estimated first year units, and the estimated first year sales for each kite. To begin your work on the sales forecast worksheet, you decide to enter the labels and values.

STEPS

1. **In cell A1, type Product**

   As you type, the text appears both in cell A1 and in the formula bar, as shown in Figure I-4. The text you typed is a label that describes the first column of data in the worksheet.

2. **Press [tab]**

   Pressing [tab] accepts your entry and activates the next cell in the row, cell B1. The name box shows B1 as the active cell. You need to type two more labels.

3. **Type Net Price, press [tab], type Year 1 Units, then press [return]**

   Cell A2 is now the active cell. Pressing [return] accepts the entry and moves the cell pointer down one row. You need to type a kite product name in this cell.

4. **Type Apache Delta, then press ↓**

   Cell A3 is now the active cell. Pressing the [down arrow] accepted the cell entry and moved the cell pointer to the cell below. Apache Delta is too long to fit in cell A2. When data is in the next adjacent cell (in this case, cell B2), the contents of cell A2 are cut off at the column boundary. Because the adjacent cell doesn't currently contain data, the entire contents of cell A2 are displayed.

5. **Type Volcano Blaster, press [return], type Tornado Twirler, press [return], type Whirling Delta, press [return], type Rocket Stuntman, press [return], type Soaring Eagle, then press [return]**

   You have typed all the product names. Cell A8 is the active cell. You need to make an edit to one of the names.

6. **Double-click cell A4**

   Double-clicking the cell puts it in Edit mode. Notice that the insertion point is flashing in cell A4 and the status bar now displays "Edit." You can now select part of the cell entry to edit it, just like in Word.

7. **Double-click Twirler, type Trickster, then press [return]**

   Cell A4 now contains the label Tornado Trickster.

8. **Click cell B2, type 15.75, then click the Enter button  on the formula bar**

   Unlike pressing [return] on the keyboard, clicking the Enter button accepts the entry while also keeping the cell active. Notice that some of Apache Delta is cut off in cell A2 because cell B2 now contains data.

   QUICK TIP
   Pressing [control] [return] has the same effect as clicking the Enter button.

9. **Press →, type 7500, then click **

   You entered the value for Year 1 Units for the Apache Delta kite in cell C2.

10. **Enter the values shown in Figure I-5 for the range B3:C7, then save your changes**

FIGURE I-4: Worksheet text in active cell and formula bar

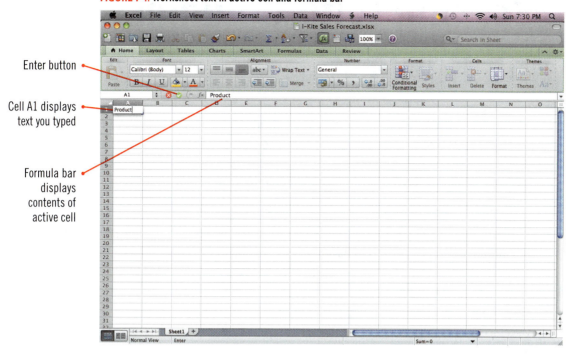

Enter button

Cell A1 displays text you typed

Formula bar displays contents of active cell

FIGURE I-5: Worksheet after entering labels and values

Labels

Column A labels are cut off on the right side because adjacent cells contain data

Enter this data as shown

	A	B	C	D	E
1	Product	Net Price	Year 1 Units		
2	Apache Delta	15.75	7500		
3	Volcano Blas	22.25	10000		
4	Tornado Tric	22.25	12000		
5	Whirling Delt	26.75	7500		
6	Rocket Stunt	29.75	7500		
7	Soaring Eagle	39.25	5000		
8					
9					
10					

Excel 2011

TABLE I-1: Methods for selecting worksheet cells

to select	with the pointing device	with the keyboard
A cell	Click the cell	Use the arrow keys
A row	Click the row heading	Select a cell in the row, then press [shift][spacebar]
A column	Click the column heading	Select a cell in the column, then press [control][spacebar]
A group of cells	Click and drag across the cells	Press [shift], then use the arrow keys
A worksheet	Click the Select all button ▢ to the left of the A column heading	Press ⌘ [A]

Working with Columns and Rows

You can adjust the width of a column or the height of a row using the mouse, the buttons on the ribbon, or a menu command. Using the mouse is a quick and easy method when you do not need an exact width or height. You can also insert or delete columns and rows using the Insert and Delete buttons in the Cells group on the Home tab.  You need to insert two rows above the labels and enter a worksheet title in the new top row. You also need to adjust the column widths so that the labels will be visible.

STEPS

1. **Position the pointer on the column boundary between column heading A and column heading B so that the pointer changes to ↔, as shown in Figure I-6**

   The boxes containing the letters A and B are **column headings**, and the boxes containing numbers in front of each row are **row headings**.

QUICK TIP

To AutoFit more than one column at a time, click and drag to select all the column headings of the columns you want to widen, then double-click any column boundary in the selection.

2. **Double-click ↔ between column heading A and B**

   Double-clicking a column boundary automatically widens or narrows it to fit the longest entry in the column using a feature called **AutoFit**. The kite names in cells A2:A7 are now fully visible. When you drag a boundary, a dotted line appears to help you position it right where you want it.

3. **Click the row 1 row heading**

   Row 1 is now selected. Clicking a row heading selects the entire row. You want to insert two rows above row 1.

QUICK TIP

To insert a column, click the column heading to the right of where you want the new one, then click the Insert button in the Cells group.

4. **Click the Insert button in the Cells group on the Home tab twice**

   Two new rows are inserted above the labels row. The cell addresses for the cells containing the labels and values you entered have all changed to reflect their new locations.

5. **Click cell A1, type Year 1 Kite Product Sales Forecast, then press [return]**

   The worksheet title now appears in cell A1.

6. **Point to the boundary between the row 2 and row 3 headings, then drag ↕ down until the Help Tag reads Height: 24.00 (0.33 inches), as shown in Figure I-7**

   The height of row 2 changes from 12 to 24 points (0.33 inches). The extra space creates a visual separation between the worksheet title and the labels. You can also use the Format button in the Cells group to adjust column width or row height if you know the precise measurement you want.

7. **Click cell A2 if necessary, click the Format button in the Cells group, then click Row Height**

   The Row Height dialog box opens, as shown in Figure I-8. The Row height text box displays the selected value 0.33", the height you specified in Step 6.

8. **Type .40, click OK, then save your changes**

   The height of row 2 increases to .4 inches to reflect the change you made.

FIGURE I-6: Changing column width in the worksheet

In Step 1, position the pointer here

Insert button

Column headings

Row headings

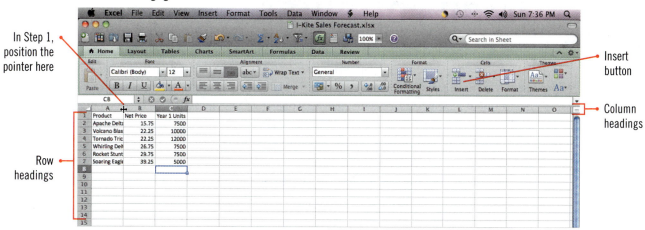

FIGURE I-7: Changing row height in the worksheet

Help Tag shows row height

In Step 6, drag the row boundary pointer down

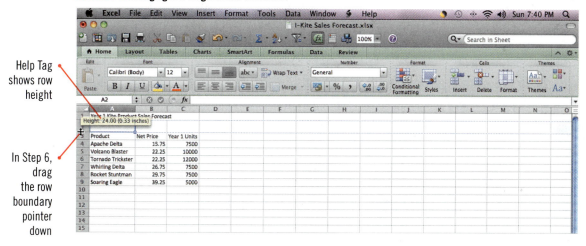

FIGURE I-8: Row Height dialog box

Using Formulas

To perform a calculation in a worksheet, you enter a formula in a cell. A **formula** is an equation that performs a calculation. Formulas start with an equal sign (=) and can contain numbers, mathematical operators, and cell references. A **cell reference** is a cell address, such as E44, that identifies the location of a value used in a calculation. Table I-2 lists some mathematical operators and sample formulas. If more than one operator is used in a formula, Excel performs the calculations in the order listed in Table I-2, the order used in math called the **order of precedence for arithmetic operations** (better known as **order of operations**). You can copy and move formulas just like other data in a worksheet. When you copy a formula to a new cell, Excel automatically replaces the original cell references with cell references that are in the *same relative position* as those in the original formula. This is called **relative cell referencing**. In the kite sales forecast worksheet, you need to create a formula that calculates the year 1 forecast for each product, which is the net price multiplied by the year 1 units. You first create a formula that calculates the year 1 sales for the first product, and then copy the formula to other cells.

STEPS

1. **Click cell D3, type Year 1 Sales, then press [return]**
   Year 1 Sales is now a label in cell D3, and the active cell is now D4.

2. **Type =**
   The equal sign (=) indicates that you are about to enter a formula in cell D4. Everything you enter in a cell after the equal sign, including any numbers, mathematical operators, cell references, or functions, is included in the formula.

3. **Click cell B4**
   A dotted border appears around cell B4, and B4 now appears in both the formula bar and cell D4.

> **QUICK TIP**
> You can also enter cell references in a formula by typing them, using either uppercase or lowercase letters.

4. **Type * (an asterisk), then click cell C4**
   See Figure I-9. In Excel, the asterisk symbol is the operator for multiplication. When Excel calculates the formula, it will multiply the value in cell B4 by the value in cell C4. Using cell references ensures that the formula will automatically update if the values in cells B4 and C4 change.

> **QUICK TIP**
> You can also double-click the fill handle to AutoFill a formula to the adjacent cells below. The formula will be copied down to the last cell that is next to a cell containing data.

5. **Click the Enter button ✓ on the formula bar**
   The result of the formula (118125) appears in cell D4. Notice that although the formula's result appears in cell D4, the formula =B4*C4 appears in the formula bar. To save time, you can copy the formula in cell D4 to cells D5:D9.

6. **Point to the small blue square in the lower-right corner of cell D5, then when the pointer changes to +, drag down to cell D9**
   Excel copies the formula in cell D4 into cells D5 through D9. Notice that cells D5:D9 display the results of the copied formulas, as shown in Figure I-10. The small blue square that you dragged is called the **fill handle**. The icon that appears after you release the button is the Auto Fill Options button, which you can click to choose additional options when copying cells.

> **QUICK TIP**
> If you want your worksheet to display formulas instead of their results in cells, click the Formulas tab, click the Show button, then click Show Formulas.

7. **Click cell D6, then save your changes**
   The formula bar shows the formula =B6*C6. Notice that the copied formula uses different cell references than those used in the original formula. When Excel copied the formula to cell D6, it adjusted the original cell references relative to the new formula location.

FIGURE I-9: Entering a formula

Enter button

Formula bar displays
the formula of the
active cell

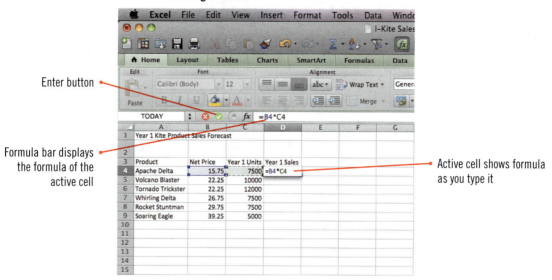

Active cell shows formula
as you type it

FIGURE I-10: Worksheet after using fill handle to copy formulas to cells D5:D9

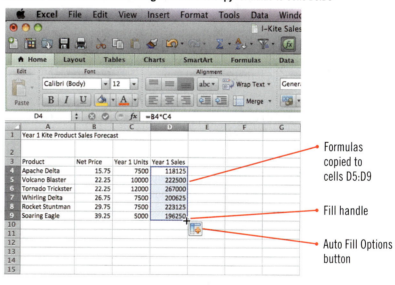

Formulas
copied to
cells D5:D9

Fill handle

Auto Fill Options
button

TABLE I-2: Useful mathematical operators and sample formulas listed in order of precedence

operator	description	sample formula	result	sample worksheet (used in sample formulas)		
( )	Parentheses	=(A2+B2)*3	$315		A	B	C
^	Exponent	=B2^2	10,000	1	Price	Quantity	
*	Multiplication	=B2*2	200	2	$ 5.00	100	
/	Division	=B2/2	50	3			
+	Addition	=B2+10	110	4			
-	Subtraction	=B2-20	80				

Using AutoSum

Excel comes with a wide variety of **functions**, which are prewritten formulas designed for particular types of calculations. The most frequently used worksheet function, **SUM**, totals all numbers and cell references included as function arguments. An **argument** is information a function needs to make a calculation, and can consist of values (such as 100 or .02), cell references (such as B3), or range references (such as A9:G16). Functions save time and help ensure accuracy, and they are available for both simple calculations and extremely complex ones. Each Excel function has a name that you usually see in all capital letters, such as AVERAGE or DATE. Because the SUM function is so commonly used, it has its own button on the Standard toolbar (it is also known as the AutoSum button). You are now ready to add up the Year 1 Units and Year 1 Sales columns. You decide to use the AutoSum button.

STEPS

1. **Click cell C10**

   Cell C10 is now the active cell. You want cell C10 to display the total year 1 units for all of the kite products, which is the sum of the range C4:C9.

QUICK TIP

The AutoSum button ∑ ▾ is also available on the Formulas tab of the ribbon.

2. **Click the AutoSum button ∑ ▾ on the Standard toolbar**

   A flashing dotted border appears around the cells in the range C4:C9, as shown in Figure I-12, indicating that these are the cells that Excel assumes you want to add together. The function =SUM(C4:C9) appears in cell C10 and in the formula bar, ready for you to edit or accept. When you use a function, Excel automatically looks for cells containing values to include in the calculation. First it looks above the cell containing the function. If there aren't any cells containing values, it then looks to the left. Excel will suggest the cells containing values to use as arguments in the function.

3. **Click the Enter button ✓ on the formula bar**

   Excel accepts the formula and the result, 49500, appears in cell C10.

4. **Click cell D10, click ∑ ▾, then click ✓**

   When you clicked the AutoSum button, Excel correctly assumed that you wanted to calculate the sum of cells D4:D9, the cells directly above cell D10. See Figure I-13.

5. **Click cell B4, type 22.25, then click ✓**

   Changing cell B4 automatically changed the formula results in cell D4 (for the Apache Delta Year 1 Sales) and also for the total sales in cell D10, as shown in Figure I-14, because these formulas referenced the value in cell B4. You can see what a valuable tool Excel is; changing one value in a cell changes the results in any cell that contains a cell reference to that cell.

6. **Save your changes**

Changing the number format

You can format numbers using the Number Format list or the Format Cells dialog box. The Number group contains buttons for common number formats such as the Accounting Number Format button, the Percent Style button, and the Comma Style button. The Number Format list in the Number group contains other useful number formats, including Time, Fraction, and Scientific, which formats numbers in scientific notation. For specific formatting options in the number categories, you need to use the Format Cells dialog box. To access the Format Cells dialog box, click Format on the menu bar, and then click Cells. The Number tab usually opens by default, but you might need to click it. The number categories are listed in the left pane and the category types are listed in the main pane, as shown in Figure I-11.

FIGURE I-11: Format Cells dialog box

FIGURE I-12: Using the AutoSum button

AutoSum button

SUM function in formula bar with selected range as argument

Excel suggests the range you want to sum

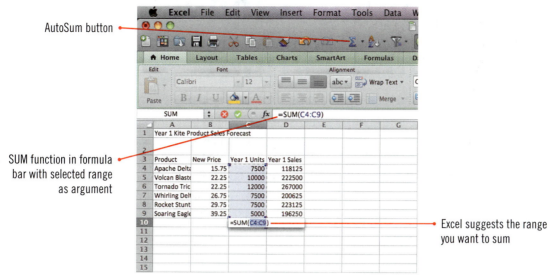

FIGURE I-13: Worksheet with totals calculated using the SUM function

Formula bar displays formula of active cell (D10)

Cell D10 displays result of AutoSum

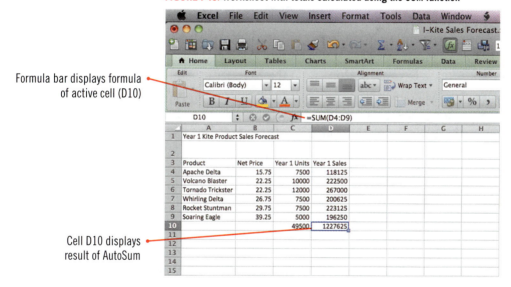

FIGURE I-14: Worksheet after changing the net price in cell B4

Cell B4 with new price

Value in cell D4 automatically updated

Value in cell D10 automatically updated

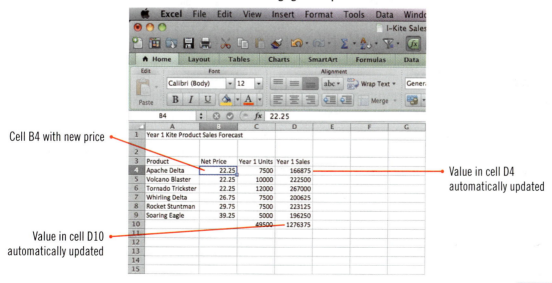

Excel 2011

Changing Alignment and Number Format

When you enter data in a cell, Excel automatically left-aligns text and right-aligns values. You can change the alignment to left-, right-, or center-align cell contents using the buttons in the Alignment group on the Home tab. You can also use the Merge button to combine several cells into one cell and center the text in the merged cell. Using the Merge button is helpful for formatting a worksheet title so that it is centered above the worksheet data. You can also change the format of numbers to make your worksheet easier to read by using the buttons in the Number group. For instance, you can quickly format a value or range of cells as currency or as a date, or format numbers so that they contain commas, decimals, or both. You can also insert rows and columns in your worksheet; when you do so, any cell references are updated to reflect the change. 🎨🖌️ You decide to apply number formats and adjust alignments to improve the worksheet's appearance. You also need to add a new column that includes the release date for each kite, format the column labels in bold, and merge and center the worksheet title.

STEPS

1. **Select the range C4:C10, then click the Comma Style button** ⎡›⎤ **in the Number group**

   The numbers in column C are now formatted with a comma and include two decimal places. The decimal places are not necessary for the unit estimates because all the values are whole numbers.

2. **Click the Decrease Decimal button** ⎡.00→.0⎤ **in the Number group twice**

   The numbers in column C now appear without decimals.

3. **Select the range B4:B9, press and hold ⌘, select the range D4:D10, then click the Accounting Number Format button** ⎡💲⎤ **in the Number group**

   Pressing and holding ⌘ when you select cells lets you select nonadjacent cell ranges. The Net Price values in column B and Year 1 Sales values in column D are now formatted as accounting, with the $ at the left edge of the cell, as shown in Figure I-15.

4. **Click the column C heading, then click the Insert button** ⎡📋⎤ **in the Cells group**

   A new column is inserted to the left of the Year 1 Units column. You need to enter a label in cell C3.

5. **Click cell C3, type Release Date, click the Enter button** ⎡✓⎤ **on the formula bar, click the Wrap Text button in the Alignment group, then click Wrap Text**

   Using the Wrap Text feature wrapped the Release Date text to two lines. Now the entire label is visible in cell C3.

6. **Click cell C4, type March 1, 2013, then click** ⎡✓⎤

   Excel recognized that you typed a date in cell C4 and changed the format to 1-Mar-13. You can use the Number Format list in the Number group to change the date format.

7. **Click the Number Format pop-up menu arrow, as shown in Figure I-16, then click Date**

   The format of the date in cell C4 is now 3/1/13. You can copy this date to the other cells in column C using the Copy and Paste commands.

8. **Click the Copy button** ⎡📋⎤ **on the Standard toolbar, select the range C5:C9, click the Paste button** ⎡📋⎤ **on the Standard toolbar, then press [esc]**

   Now all cells in the range C5:C9 display the date 3/1/13.

9. **Click the row 3 heading, click the Center Text button** ⎡≡⎤ **in the Alignment group, then click the Bold button** ⎡B⎤ **in the Font group**

   Each label in row 3 is now center-aligned and bold, making them stand out from the data in the worksheet.

10. **Select the range A1:E1, click the Merge button** ⎡ Merge ▾⎤ **in the Alignment group, then save your changes**

    As shown in Figure I-17, the worksheet title is centered across the five selected cells, which have merged into one cell. Note that the cell address for this cell is still A1.

FIGURE I-15: Worksheet after using the Accounting, Comma, and Decrease Decimal buttons

Accounting Number Format button

Values formatted as Accounting with $

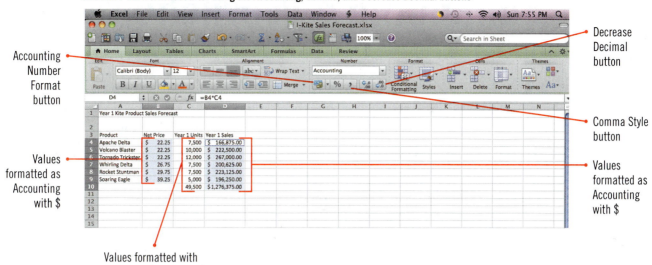

Decrease Decimal button

Comma Style button

Values formatted as Accounting with $

Values formatted with comma and no decimals

FIGURE I-16: Applying a date format using the Number Format list

Wrap Text button

New label wraps to two lines

Active cell

New column inserted

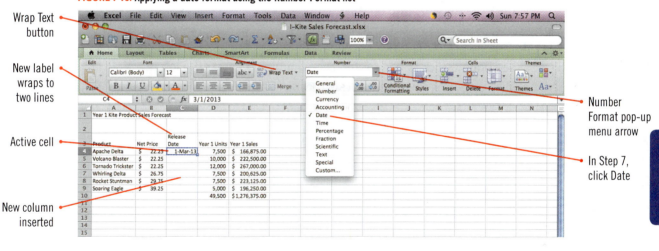

Number Format pop-up menu arrow

In Step 7, click Date

FIGURE I-17: Worksheet after changing alignment and number formats

Copy button

Paste button

Worksheet title is centered in a merged cell A1

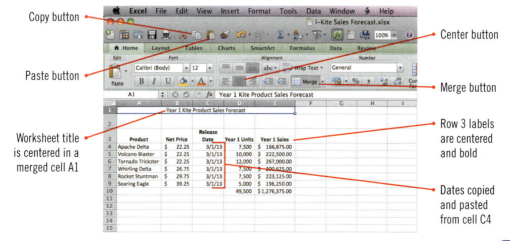

Center button

Merge button

Row 3 labels are centered and bold

Dates copied and pasted from cell C4

Excel 2011

Enhancing a Worksheet

You can enhance an Excel worksheet to make it look more professional and increase its visual appeal. In Page Layout view, you can add headers and footers containing information that you want to include at the top or bottom of each page. You can also apply a theme, and you can add shading and borders to set apart titles, labels, and values.  You decide to add a header that contains your name and a footer that contains the date and filename. You also decide to apply a theme and add borders and shading.

STEPS

1. **Click the Page Layout View button ▦ on the status bar, point to the center of the header area above row 1 until you see "Double-click to add header", then double-click**

   The worksheet is now in Page Layout view, and the insertion point is above the worksheet title in the middle of the header's three sections. If you double-click at the left side of the header area, the insertion point will be in the left section. If you double-click at the right side of the header area, the insertion point will be in the right section. Headers and footers can be inserted in Normal view, but will not be displayed in Normal view.

2. **Click the right section of the header area, then type your name**

   Your name appears in the right section of the header, right-aligned, and the Header and Footer floating toolbar appears, as shown in Figure I-18.

3. **Click the Close button on the floating toolbar**

4. **If necessary, scroll down to the footer area at the bottom of page 1, point to it until you see Double-click to add footer, then double-click near the left margin**

   The footer area opens with the insertion point in the left section and the Header and Footer floating toolbar reappears.

5. **Click the Insert Date button ▦ on the floating toolbar**

   Excel inserts the code "&[Date]" into the left section of the footer area. When you click outside of this section, the current date will appear here.

6. **Click the right section of the footer area, click the Insert File Name button ▦ on the floating toolbar, then click the Close button on the floating toolbar**

   The filename appears in the right section, and the date is in the left section of the footer area, as shown in Figure I-19.

7. **Press ⌘[home], click the Themes button ▦ in the Themes group, then click the Slipstream theme**

   The Slipstream theme is applied to the worksheet.

8. **Select the range A1:E10, click the Borders button ▦▾ in the Font group, then click All Borders**

   Cells A1:E10 now have borders applied to them.

9. **Select the range A3:E3, click the Fill Color pop-up menu arrow ▦▾ in the Font group, click Background 2 (third square in top row), then click cell A1**

   The column labels are now shaded in light blue. Compare your screen with Figure I-20.

10. **Click the Normal View button on the status bar, then save your changes**

FIGURE I-18: Header with text added

Insert File Name button

Insert Date button

Header and Footer floating toolbar

Your name entered in header area

Close button

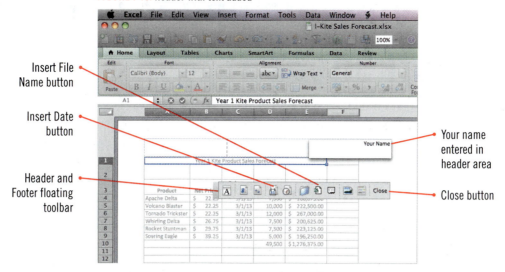

FIGURE I-19: Footer with current date and filename added

Current date appears here

Filename replaces &[File] code when you click in the worksheet

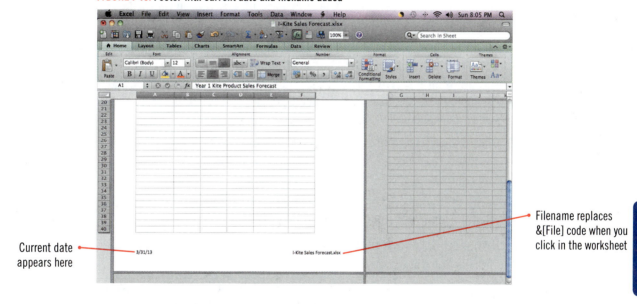

FIGURE I-20: Worksheet with Slipstream theme, borders, and shading applied

Borders button with All Borders selected

Fill Color button

Cell range A1:E10 now has borders

Page Layout View button

Normal View button

Themes button

Shading applied to cells A3:E3

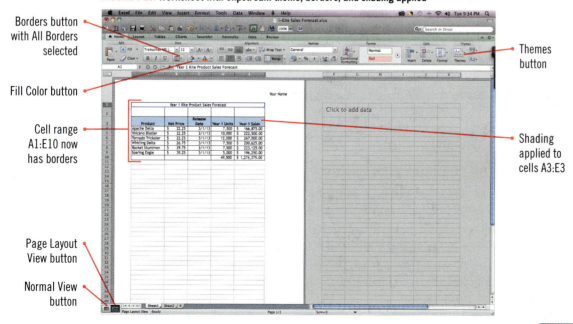

Previewing and Printing a Worksheet

When you finish working with a worksheet and have saved your work, you are ready to print it. Just like in Word, you can use the Print dialog box to preview the printed worksheet and specify settings. You can specify the printer, specify the paper size, change the orientation, scale your worksheet to fit on one page, and more.  You have finished working with the worksheet, and are ready to preview and print it. (*Note*: Many schools limit printing in order to conserve paper. If your school restricts printing, click Cancel in Step 5.)

STEPS

1. **Click File on the menu bar, then click Print**
   The Print dialog box opens and the sales forecast worksheet appears in the Quick Preview box, as shown in Figure I-21. Notice that the header and footer text you entered in the last lesson appear at the top and bottom of the page. The worksheet is set to print in **portrait orientation** (where the page is taller than it is wide); you can change this to **landscape orientation** (where the page is wider than it is tall).

2. **Click the Page Setup button, click the Page tab if necessary, then click the Landscape option button in the Orientation section, as shown in Figure I-22**
   The Page Setup dialog box contains tabs for Page, Margins, Header/Footer, and Sheet. By having this tab in the Print dialog box, these items can be changed prior to printing. The Page tab allows you to change orientation, scaling, and print quality.

3. **Click OK, and compare your screen with Figure I-23**
   The Page Setup dialog box closes and the screen returns to the Print dialog box, showing the worksheet in landscape orientation.

4. **Verify that your printer is on and connected to your computer, and that the correct printer appears in the Printer spin box**

5. **If your school allows printing, click the Print button; otherwise, click Cancel**
   The Print dialog box closes and the document prints.

6. **Save your changes, click Excel on the menu bar, then click Quit Excel**
   The worksheet is saved, and the worksheet and Excel both close.

7. **Submit your completed worksheet to your instructor**

Exploring alternatives to printing

The Print dialog box offers two alternatives to printing your worksheet or document. Click the Preview button to open Preview, a Mac OS X program for displaying images and Portable Document Format (PDF) documents. Using Preview, you can zoom in on sections of your document and add or remove pages. Preview can also be opened from the Applications folder in the Finder window.

Click the PDF button in the Print dialog box to open a list of specialized commands for saving your document in different formats; the first option is to save as PDF. Other commands on the list may differ, depending on which programs you have installed on your computer. Saving an Excel workbook as a PDF document can be helpful when you need to e-mail it or post it to the Web, or if you don't know whether the recipient has access to Excel.

FIGURE I-21: Print dialog box for Excel

Selected printer
(yours will differ)

Quick Preview

Page Setup
button

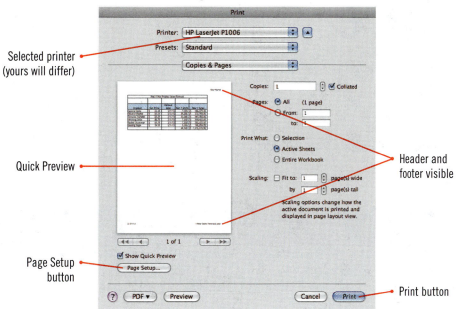

Header and
footer visible

Print button

FIGURE I-22: Page Setup dialog box

Page tab

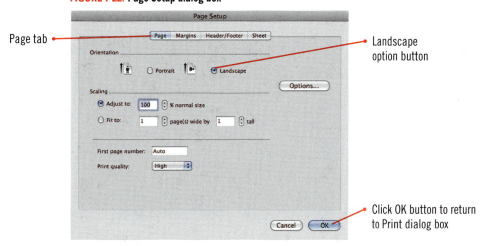

Landscape
option button

Click OK button to return
to Print dialog box

FIGURE I-23: Completed worksheet as shown in the Print dialog box

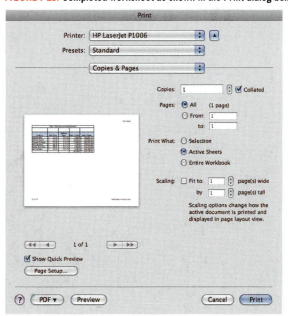

Practice

Concepts Review

Label each item shown in Figure I-24.

FIGURE I-24

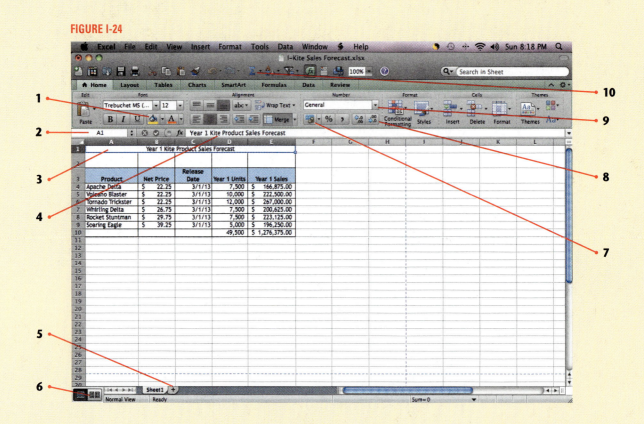

Match each pointer or button to its appropriate description.

11.

12.

13.

14.

15.

16.

17.

a. Pointer shape when it is placed over a worksheet cell

b. Normal View button

c. Page Layout View button

d. Button used to apply shading to selected cells

e. Pointer shape when it is positioned over a fill handle

f. Pointer shape used to change the width of a column

g. Pointer shape used to change the height of a row

Select the best answer from the list of choices.

18. The name of the cell located at the intersection of column F and row 223 is:
    a. 223F
    b. F223
    c. F222
    d. 22F3

19. Which of the following operators do you use to begin typing a formula in a cell?
    a. =
    b. +
    c. -
    d. *

20. Which of the following formulas is *not* correctly written?
    a. B7+A5=
    b. =A5*B7
    c. =7+B55
    d. =B21/7

21. Which view do you need to work in to add a header?
    a. Normal view
    b. Page Layout view
    c. Header/Footer view
    d. Page Setup view

22. For which of the following tasks would you use the fill handle?
    a. To apply shading to selected cells
    b. To apply a border to selected cells
    c. To copy a formula from cell A2 to cell F7
    d. To copy a formula from cell A2 to cell A3

Skills Review

1. **Navigate a workbook.**
   a. Start Microsoft Excel and open a new workbook.
   b. Identify the program window elements without referring to the lesson material.
   c. Click cell H22, then click cell B25.
   d. Use the keyboard to place the cell pointer in cell A1.
   e. Save the workbook as **I-Weekly Sales** in the location where you store your Data Files.

2. **Enter values and labels.**
   a. Starting in cell A1, type the following labels in the range A1:D1:
      Bread Type　　**Quantity Sold**　　**Unit Price**　　**Total Sales**
   b. Enter the following labels for Bread Type in the range A2 through A8: **White**, **Whole Wheat**, **Rye**, **Pumpernickel**, **Bagels**, **Muffins**, **Specialty Breads**.
   c. Use the following table as a guide to enter the values for Quantity Sold (in the range B2:B8) and Unit Price (in the range C2:C8):

Quantity Sold	Unit Price
1217	2.25
1457	2.95
122	2.95
87	2.95
1356	.75
1785	.95
102	5.95

3. **Work with columns and rows.**
   a. Increase the size of column A by dragging the appropriate column boundary so that the column is wide enough to fit all the labels in the range A1:A8.
   b. Increase the width of column B by double-clicking the appropriate column boundary.
   c. Insert two rows above row 1.
   d. Enter the label **Uncle Bob's Bread Shop Weekly Sales** in cell A1. Apply bold formatting to cell A1.
   e. Increase the height of row 2 to 0.33 inches using the drag method. Open the Row Height dialog box to verify that the row height is 0.33".
   f. Save your changes.

Skills Review (continued)

4. Use formulas.

a. Enter a formula in cell D4 that multiplies the value of cell B4 and the value of cell C4, then use a button on the formula bar to accept the entry. When you create the formula, add the cell references to the formula by clicking the cells.

b. Type a formula in cell D5 that multiplies the value of cell B5 and the value of cell C5, then use a keyboard command to accept the entry.

c. Use the fill handle to copy the formula you entered in cell D5 to the range D6:D10.

d. Save your changes.

5. Use AutoSum.

a. Use the AutoSum button to enter a formula in cell B11 that adds the values in the cell range B4:B10.

b. Use the AutoSum button to enter a formula in cell D11 that adds the values in the cell range D4:D10.

c. Change the Quantity Sold value for Pumpernickel to **99**, then view the changes in cells D7 and D11.

d. Save your changes.

6. Change alignment and number format.

a. Apply the Comma Style number format to the cell range B4:B11. Use a button to remove the decimals for the selected range.

b. Apply the Accounting number format to the cell range C4:D11.

c. Insert a column to the left of column D. Enter the label **Close Date** in cell D3.

d. Enter the date **May 4, 2013** in cell D4. Use the Number Format list to change the format of the date to 5/4/13. Use the fill handle to copy cell D4 to the range D5:D10. Widen column D, if necessary, so that all the dates are visible.

e. Center the labels in the cell range A3:E3. Apply bold formatting to cells A3:E3.

f. Merge and center cells A1:E1.

g. Save your changes.

7. Enhance a worksheet.

a. Change to Page Layout view.

b. Type your name in the right section of the header.

c. Switch to the footer, then insert the current date in the left section of the footer. Insert a code for the filename in the right section of the footer.

d. Move the cell pointer to cell A1, then change the view to Normal view.

e. Apply the Angles theme to the worksheet.

f. Change the height of row 3 to .42".

g. Apply the Accent 2, Lighter 80% fill color to the labels in row 3 (range A3:E3).

h. Apply the All Borders border style to the range A1.E11.

i. Save your changes.

8. Preview and print a worksheet.

a. Preview the worksheet using the Print dialog box.

b. Change the orientation to Landscape.

c. Change the orientation back to Portrait.

d. If your school permits printing, verify that the printer settings are correct, then print the worksheet. Compare your completed worksheet with Figure I-25.

e. Save your changes, close the workbook, exit Excel, then submit your completed workbook to your instructor.

FIGURE I-25

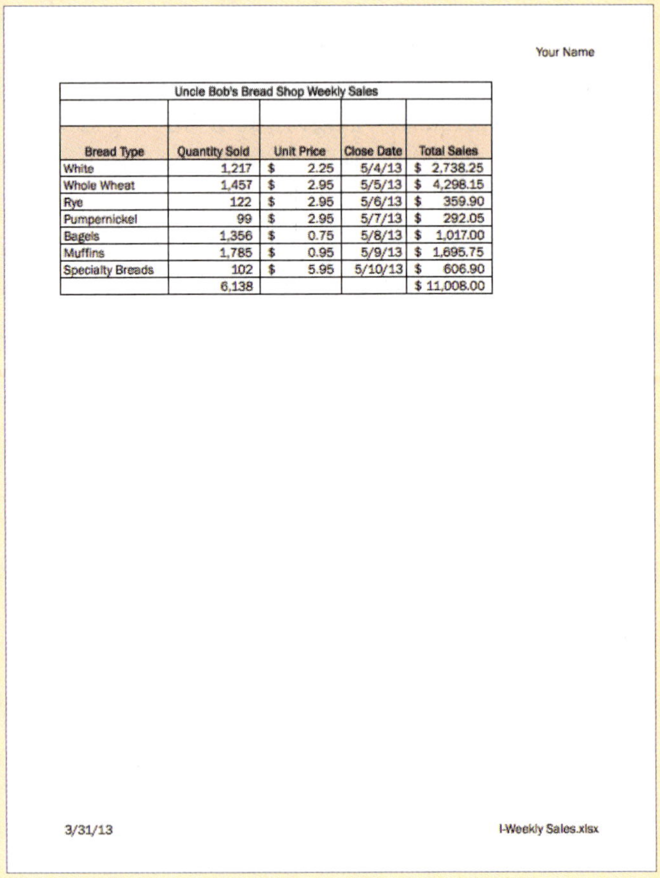

Your Name

	Uncle Bob's Bread Shop Weekly Sales				
Bread Type	Quantity Sold	Unit Price		Close Date	Total Sales
White	1,217	$	2.25	5/4/13	$ 2,738.25
Whole Wheat	1,457	$	2.95	5/5/13	$ 4,298.15
Rye	122	$	2.95	5/6/13	$ 359.90
Pumpernickel	99	$	2.95	5/7/13	$ 292.05
Bagels	1,356	$	0.75	5/8/13	$ 1,017.00
Muffins	1,785	$	0.95	5/9/13	$ 1,695.75
Specialty Breads	102	$	5.95	5/10/13	$ 606.90
	6,138				$ 11,008.00

3/31/13

I-Weekly Sales.xlsx

Independent Challenge 1

You are a sales representative at Green Earth Stationery, Inc., a small environmentally friendly paper products company based in Chicago. Your manager, Anne Badders, has asked you to provide her with a worksheet that shows the top five orders in your region for the month of April. The summary needs to include the order number, account name, order date, order total, and payments received. The worksheet also needs to show the monthly sales total and the outstanding balance due.

a. Start Excel, open a new workbook, then save it as **I-Top Five Orders** in the location where you store your Data Files.

b. Enter the title **Top Five Orders for April, Midwest Region** in cell A1.

c. Enter the information shown in the following table, starting in cell A3.

Order Number	Account Name	Date	Total	Paid
4596	Card Giant, Inc.	April 10, 2013	15946	7865
4597	Office Hub	April 17, 2013	7247	0
4987	Stationery, Etc.	April 19, 2013	6534	5024
5094	Paper Mega Store	April 22, 2013	12259	8540
5895	Office Champ	April 30, 2013	4095	4095

d. Widen or narrow each column as necessary so that all the labels and data in the range A3:E8 are visible.

e. Add the label **Balance Due** in cell F3. Apply bold formatting to the range A3:F3. Widen the columns if necessary.

f. Enter a formula in cell F4 that subtracts cell E4 from cell D4, then use the fill handle to copy the formula to cells F5:F8.

g. Use the AutoSum button to enter a formula in cell D9 that adds the values in the range D4:D8. Then change the amount in cell D6 to **9544**.

h. Use the fill handle to copy the formula in cell D9 to cells E9 and F9.

i. Center-align the order numbers in cells A4:A8, then center-align the labels in row 3.

j. Apply the Accounting number format to cells D4:F9.

k. Merge and center cells A1:F1. Apply bold formatting to the merged cell. Increase the font size of the title in cell A1 to 14 point. (*Hint*: Select cell A1, click the Font Size pop-up menu arrow, then click 14.)

l. Change the date format in the range C4:C8 to MM/DD/YY.

m. Apply bold formatting to the totals in row 9.

n. Add your name in the right section of the header. Add the filename to the right section of the footer.

o. Apply the Solstice theme to the workbook. (*Hint*: If you see any cells containing ######, you'll need to increase the column width to view the contents.)

p. Apply All Borders to the range A3:F9, then apply a Thick Box Border around the range A3:F8.

q. Apply a fill color to the range A9:F9, choosing the lightest shade of green (Accent 4, Lighter 80%). Apply this same shading to the range A3:F3.

Advanced Challenge Exercise

- Select cells A1:F8, then click the Copy button.
- Add a new worksheet.
- On the new worksheet, click the Paste button.
- Click the Formulas tab, click the Show button in the Function group, and then click Show Formulas. Adjust column widths so that all of the cells fit in the screen without scrolling. Notice that all the formulas are showing in the cells that contain formulas.
- Right-click the Sheet2 tab, click Rename, type **Show Formulas**, then press [return]. Preview the Show Formulas worksheet in the Print dialog box, change the orientation to Landscape for this worksheet, then save your changes.

r. Save the workbook, then preview it using the Print dialog box.

s. Close the workbook, quit Excel, then submit the workbook to your instructor.

Independent Challenge 2

You are the national franchise manager for Relax Now Day Spa, which has five spas in California and the Pacific Northwest. You need to create a worksheet that analyzes second quarter sales by franchise. Your worksheet needs to compare second quarter sales for the current year (2013) to those of the previous year (2012). You also want to show how second quarter actual sales compare with the forecast. Each franchise was forecast to meet a sales increase of 10% over the prior year.

a. Start Excel, open a new workbook, then save it as **I-Q2 Sales Analysis** in the location where you store your Data Files.

b. Enter the company name **Relax Now Day Spa** in cell A1, then enter **Q2 2013 Sales Analysis** in cell A2.

c. Enter the information shown in the following table in the worksheet, starting with the **Franchise** label in cell A4. First type the values, then apply the proper number formatting and adjust decimal places so that your data matches the table.

Franchise	Q2 2013	Q2 2012
Los Angeles	$25,500	$20,675
Portland	$12,750	$15,645
San Diego	$17,010	$14,563
San Francisco	$21,663	$23,087
Seattle	$21,876	$19,843

d. Enter **Increase** in cell D4, then enter a formula in cell D5 that calculates the increase in sales in Q2 2013 over Q2 2012 for the Los Angeles franchise. (*Hint*: The formula should subtract cell C5 from cell B5.)

e. Copy the formula in cell D5 to cells D6 through D9. Apply the Accounting number format to the range D5:D9. Remove the decimal places in the range D5:D9.

f. Enter **Forecast** in cell E4, then enter a formula in cell E5 that multiplies the Q2 2012 sales by 1.10. (*Hint*: The formula should use the * operator to multiply cell C5 by 1.10.) Copy this formula to cells E6 through E9. Apply the Accounting number format to the range E5:E9. Remove the decimal places in the range E5:E9.

g. Enter the label **Actual vs. Forecast** in cell F4. Format the label so that it wraps to two lines. Enter a formula in cell F5 that subtracts the amount in cell E5 from the amount in cell B5. Copy this formula to cells F6 through F9. Apply the Accounting number format to the range F5:F9. Remove the decimal places in the range F5:F9.

h. Enter **Totals** in cell A10, then use the AutoSum button to enter a formula in cell B10 that calculates the total of cells B5 through B9. Copy this formula to the range C10:F10.

i. Apply the Accounting number format to the range B10:F10 and remove the decimal places.

j. Increase the row height of row 3 to 0.33 inches. Center-align the labels in row 4.

k. Merge and center cells A1:F1, so that the worksheet title is centered in the merged cell A1. Then merge and center cells A2:F2, so that the worksheet subtitle is centered in the merged cell A2.

l. Apply bold formatting to the worksheet title, the labels in row 4, the city labels in the range A5:A9, and the Totals label and values in row 10.

m. Apply a theme of your choosing to the workbook. Enhance the worksheet further by applying fill colors and borders where appropriate to make the worksheet visually appealing. Increase column widths as necessary so that all labels and values are visible in each cell.

n. Insert your name in the left section of the header.

o. Preview the worksheet in the Print dialog box. Save your changes, close the workbook, and quit Excel. Submit your completed workbook to your instructor.

Independent Challenge 3

You own a used car business called Joe's Used Autos. You buy preowned vehicles, pay contractors to fix them up, and then resell them for a profit. You decide to create a spreadsheet to track your profits for cars you have sold in the first quarter.

a. Create a new workbook and save it as **I-Q1 Profits** in the location where you store your Data Files.

b. Enter the company name **Joe's Used Autos** in cell A1. Enter **Q1 Profits** in cell A2.

c. Enter the labels and data shown in the following table, starting in cell A4. Use Currency number formatting for the cells that contain dollar amounts.

Vehicle	**Purchase Price**	**Cost to Fix**	**Sale Price**	**Date Sold**
Toyota Corolla	**$750**	**$350**	**$1,750**	**January 15, 2013**
Nissan Sentra	**$2,025**	**$764**	**$7,995**	**February 1, 2013**
Ford Taurus	**$2,250**	**$578**	**$5,995**	**February 8, 2013**
Honda Civic	**$2,015**	**$1,095**	**$7,775**	**March 1, 2013**
Mazda Protege	**$1,725**	**$775**	**$7,995**	**April 1, 2013**

d. Adjust the width of the columns as necessary, so that all the data is visible.

e. Insert a new column to the left of Sale Price. Enter the label **Total Investment** in cell D4. Format the label and adjust the column width so that the label is on one line in the cell.

f. Enter a formula in cell D5 that sums cells B5 and C5.

g. Copy the formula in cell D5 to cells D6:D9.

h. Type the label **Profit** in cell G4. Enter a formula in cell G5 that calculates the total profit for the Toyota Corolla. (*Hint*: The formula needs to subtract the value in the Total Investment cell from the Sale Price cell.)

i. Copy the formula in cell G5 to cells G6:G9.

j. Add the label **Total** to cell A10. Enter a formula in cell B10 that sums cells B5:B9. Use the Copy and Paste commands to copy this formula to cells C10:E10 and to cell G10.

k. Center-align the labels in row 4, then apply bold formatting to these cells. Apply bold formatting to row 10.

l. Change the number format of the Date Sold values to MM/DD/YY.

m. Format the worksheet by applying a theme, adding borders, and adding fill colors to enhance its appearance. Format the worksheet title in cell A1 so that the font size is larger than that in the rest of the worksheet.

n. Add your name to the center section of the header. Add the filename to the right section of the header. Save your changes.

o. Preview the worksheet in the Print dialog box. Change the orientation to Landscape. Save your changes. Figure I-26 shows the completed worksheet with possible formatting options applied (your formatting will look different).

FIGURE I-26

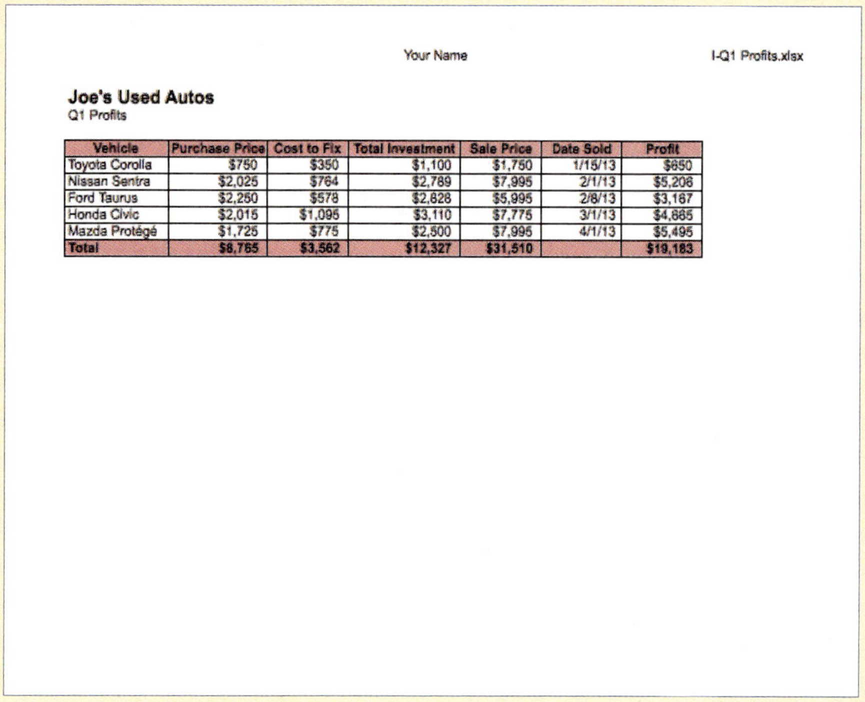
Your Name I-Q1 Profits.xlsx

Joe's Used Autos
Q1 Profits

Vehicle	Purchase Price	Cost to Fix	Total Investment	Sale Price	Date Sold	Profit
Toyota Corolla	$750	$350	$1,100	$1,750	1/15/13	$650
Nissan Sentra	$2,025	$764	$2,789	$7,995	2/1/13	$5,206
Ford Taurus	$2,250	$578	$2,828	$5,995	2/8/13	$3,167
Honda Civic	$2,015	$1,095	$3,110	$7,775	3/1/13	$4,665
Mazda Protégé	$1,725	$775	$2,500	$7,995	4/1/13	$5,495
Total	$8,765	$3,562	$12,327	$31,510		$19,183

Independent Challenge 3 (continued)

Advanced Challenge Exercise

■ Enter the label **Profit as %** in cell H4. Use the Format Painter button to copy the formatting of cell G4 to cell H4. Widen column H if necessary so that the entire label fits in cell H4.

■ Enter a formula in cell H5 that calculates the percent of the profit made. (*Hint*: Divide cell G5 by cell D5.)

■ Copy the formula in cell H5 to cells H6:H10.

■ Select cells H5:H10, then click the Percent Style button in the Number group on the Home tab.

■ Apply the same border style and fill colors that are applied to cells G5:G10 to the cells in range H5:H10. Save your changes.

p. Close the workbook, quit Excel, then submit your completed workbook to your instructor.

Real Life Independent Challenge

You just got a new job that pays more than your current position. You have decided to move into a better apartment, without roommates, and you have found a new apartment that looks perfect. However, you are concerned that the new apartment will hurt your ability to save for a house. Not only will the new apartment cost more to rent, but you will need to pay additional money for other living expenses that will be necessary in this new situation. For instance, you currently walk to work, but the new job will require you to lease a car and pay for gas and insurance. You will also have to pay more for utilities and cable TV because you will not be sharing these expenses anymore. You decide to create a budget spreadsheet that compares your current living expenses with your expected new expenses in the new apartment and determine what impact this will have on your monthly savings.

a. Start Excel, open a new workbook, then save it as **I-Budget Comparison** in the location where you store your Data Files.

b. Enter the title **Budget Comparison** in cell A1. Merge cells A1:D1 and center the contents.

c. Enter the following labels in cells A3:A5:
   New Monthly Salary
   Current Monthly Salary
   Salary Increase

d. Adjust the width of column A so that all labels fit.

e. Enter a formula in cell B3 that calculates your new weekly net salary (which is $725) multiplied by 4.

f. Enter a formula in cell B4 that calculates your current weekly salary (which is $550) multiplied by 4.

g. Enter a formula in cell B5 that calculates the difference between your new monthly salary and your current salary.

h. Enter the following labels and values in cells A7 through C17:

Expense	Current Cost	New Cost
Rent	$675	$1,200
Food	$400	$400
Utilities	$50	$100
Car Payment	$0	$225
Car Insurance	$0	$100
Gas/Parking	$0	$90
Student Loan	$100	$100
Cable	$50	$100
Phone	$95	$95
Entertainment	$140	$140

Real Life Independent Challenge (continued)

i. Format all the cells in the range B8:B17 with the Accounting number format. Display decimals in the formatting.

j. Enter the label **Change** in cell D7, then enter a formula in cell D8 that calculates the difference between the new cost for rent and the current cost for rent. Copy this formula to cells D9:D17. Format cells C8:D17 with the Accounting number format. Keep decimal formatting.

k. Add the label **Total Expenses** to cell A18. Enter a formula in cell B18 that calculates the total expenses in the Current Cost column. Copy this formula to cells C18 and D18.

l. Enter the label **Available for Savings** in cell A21. Apply bold formatting to this label.

m. Type the label **Current** in cell A22. Type the label **New** in cell A23.

n. In cell B22, type a formula that subtracts B18 from B4.

o. In cell B23, type a formula that subtracts C18 from B3.

p. Apply a theme of your choosing to the worksheet. Then, format the worksheet using fonts, borders, shading, and alignment so that it is visually appealing and easy to read. Make sure to use formatting to emphasize the key cells in the worksheet, such as the title, labels, and totals.

q. Insert a header that contains your name in the center section and the current date in the left section.

r. Save the worksheet, print it, quit Excel, then submit your completed workbook to your instructor.

Visual Workshop

Create the worksheet shown in Figure I-27 using the commands, formulas, and formatting skills you learned in this unit. Use formulas in cells D5:D12 to calculate the June total revenue for each cottage. Use formulas in the range G5:G12 to calculate the July total revenue for each cottage. Use the AutoSum button for the totals shown in row 13. Enter a formula in cell B15 that sums the June and July weeks. Use a formula in cell B17 that sums the total revenue for June and July. Apply the Apothecary theme, and apply the borders and shading shown. Save the workbook as **I-Summer Rental Revenue** in the location where you store your Data Files, with your name in the center section of the footer. Save and preview the worksheet, then submit it to your instructor.

FIGURE I-27

	A	B	C	D	E	F	G	H
1	Castaway Cottage Rentals							
2	June and July Rental Revenue							
3								
4	Cottage Name	June Weekly Rate	June Weeks Rented	June Total Revenue	July Weekly Rate	July Weeks Rented	July Total Revenue	
5	Bird's Nest	$ 695	2	$ 1,390	$ 995	4	$ 3,980	
6	Cozy Cabana	$ 795	3	$ 2,385	$1,095	3	$ 3,285	
7	Bear Cave	$ 645	4	$ 2,580	$ 945	4	$ 3,780	
8	Sunset Hideaway	$ 1,095	2	$ 2,190	$1,395	3	$ 4,185	
9	Sunshine Cabin	$ 1,125	1	$ 1,125	$1,495	4	$ 5,980	
10	Blossom Cottage	$ 725	2	$ 1,450	$1,025	4	$ 4,100	
11	Munchkin Castle	$ 695	3	$ 2,085	$ 995	3	$ 2,985	
12	Captain's Nook	$ 895	3	$ 2,685	$1,195	4	$ 4,780	
13	Totals		20	$ 15,890		29	$33,075	
14								
15	Total Weeks	49						
16								
17	Total Revenue:	$48,965						
18								
19								
20								

Using Complex Formulas, Functions, and Tables

In addition to the simple, single-operator formulas you learned about in the previous unit, Microsoft Excel includes powerful data analysis tools. One of these tools is complex formulas, which perform more than one calculation at a time. Functions are prewritten formulas that can contain multiple operators, which you can use in your formulas to save time typing all the parts of a complicated formula. Excel also provides **tables** to let you quickly analyze rows of data that have the same kind of information, such as customer or transaction lists. To analyze table data, you can **sort** the information to put it in a more helpful order and you can **filter** it to display only the type of data you specify. You can also make certain data stands out in your worksheets by applying conditional formatting.  Serena Henning, director of sales for Outdoor Designs, has given you a worksheet that shows sales for the company's western region for January and February. She has asked you to perform some calculations on the data, organize it so that it is easier to read, and highlight important information.

OBJECTIVES

Create complex formulas

Use absolute cell references

Understand functions

Use date and time functions

Use statistical functions

Apply conditional formatting

Sort rows in a table

Filter table data

Creating Complex Formulas

When you create worksheets that contain many calculations, you often need to create formulas that contain more than one mathematical operator. For instance, to calculate profits for a particular product, a formula would first need to calculate product sales (product price multiplied by number of products sold) and then subtract costs from that result. Formulas that contain more than one operator are called **complex formulas**. When a formula contains multiple operators, Excel uses standard algebraic rules, such as order of operations, to determine which calculation to perform first. Calculations in parentheses are always evaluated first. Next, exponential calculations are performed, then multiplication and division calculations, and finally addition and subtraction calculations. If there are multiple calculations within the parentheses, they are performed according to this same order. Table J-1 lists the common mathematical operators and the order in which Excel evaluates them in a formula. Serena provides you with a worksheet showing January and February sales for the western region and year-to-date returns. She asks you to add a new column that calculates the adjusted sales total for both months.

STEPS

1. **Start Excel, open the file J-1.xlsx from the location where you store your Data Files, then save it as J-Western Region Sales**

    A copy of Serena's partially completed worksheet is open and saved with a new name.

2. **Click cell F6**

    You need to enter a formula in this cell that calculates Brenda Simpson's total sales for January (cell C6) and February (cell D6), then subtracts Brenda's returns (cell E6).

3. **Type =, click cell C6, type +, click cell D6, type -, click cell E6, then click the Enter button** ☑

    See Figure J-1. The formula bar displays the formula =C6+D6-E6, and cell F6 displays the formula result, $33,575. This formula added the value in cell C6 (Brenda's January sales) to the value in cell D6 (Brenda's February sales), then subtracted the value in cell E6 (the returns). In effect, Excel calculated $22,045+$13,876-$2,346. Now you need to copy the formula to the range F7:F13, to calculate the total sales less returns for the other sales reps.

    > **QUICK TIP**
    > You can also double-click the fill handle to copy the formula to the range F7:F13.

4. **Drag the cell F6 fill handle pointer ✛ down through cell F13 to copy the formula to the range F7:F13**

    The results of the copied formula appear in cells F7 through F13, as shown in Figure J-2.

5. **Click the Save button 🖫 on the Standard toolbar**

    Excel saves your changes to the workbook.

FIGURE J-1: Complex formula and its returned value

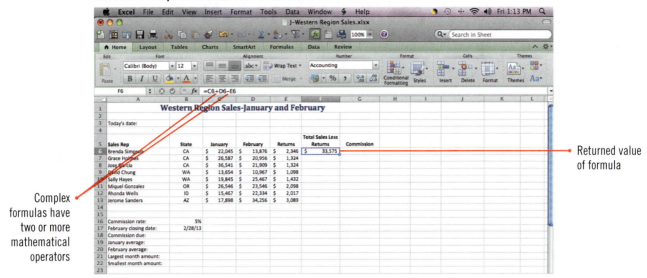

Complex formulas have two or more mathematical operators

Returned value of formula

FIGURE J-2: Copying a formula to a range of cells

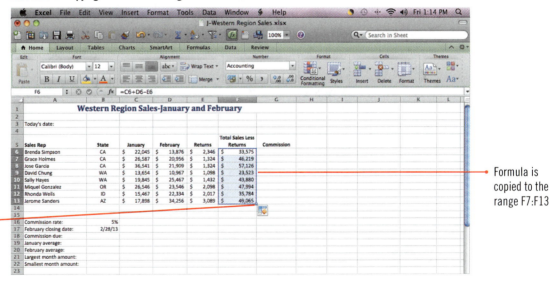

Formula is copied to the range F7:F13

Drag fill handle to cell F13 to copy the formula in cell F6 to the range F7:F13

TABLE J-1: Review of order of operations

order of operations	operators
1. Calculate items in parentheses	( )
2. Calculate exponents	^
3. Multiply or divide (from left to right)	* or /
4. Add or subtract (from left to right)	+ or -

Using Absolute Cell References

When you copy a formula from one cell to another, Excel automatically adjusts the cell references in the copied formula to reflect the new formula location. For example, a formula in cell D5 that reads "=B5*C5" changes to "=B6*C6" when you copy the formula to cell D6. As you learned in Unit I, a relative cell reference changes when you move it to reflect its relative location to the new cell. There may be times when you want a cell reference in a formula to refer to a specific cell, even when you copy the formula to a different cell. In this case, you use an absolute cell reference in the formula. An **absolute cell reference** is a cell reference that stays the same even when you copy a formula that contains it to a new location. An absolute cell reference contains a $ symbol before the column letter and row number (such as $A$1). You need to create a formula for the cells in the Commission column that multiplies the commission rate (5%) in cell B16 by the Total Sales Less Returns value in column F. You use the absolute cell reference $B$16 for the commission rate in the formula.

1. **Click cell G6, then click the Formulas tab**

    You need to enter a formula in this cell that calculates Brenda Simpson's commission. The formula needs to multiply the commission rate contained in cell B16 (5%) by the Total Sales Less Returns value in cell F6. You begin the formula by entering the absolute cell reference $B$16.

2. **Type =, click cell B16, then click the Switch Reference button** ⊞ **in the Function group**

    The formula bar and cell G6 display =$B$16. Clicking the Switch Reference button automatically added two $ symbols to the B16 cell reference to format it as an absolute cell reference. Now you need to complete the formula.

3. **Type *, then click cell F6**

    The formula bar and cell G6 display the formula =$B$16*F6, as shown in Figure J-3. Cells B16 and F6 are highlighted because they are referenced in the formula.

4. **Click the Enter button** ✓

    Cell G6 shows the formula result of $1,678.75, the commission amount for Brenda Simpson. Excel formats the number using the Accounting number format because the cells referenced in the formula are formatted with the Accounting number format. You want to round the result to the nearest whole number.

5. **Click the Home tab, then click the Decrease Decimal button** ⊞ **in the Number group twice**

    The value in cell G6 is now formatted as currency with no decimal places. You need to copy the formula to the range G7:G13, to calculate the commission amounts for the other sales reps.

6. **Double-click the cell G6 fill handle** ⊞ **to copy the formula to G7:G13**

    Double-clicking the fill handle automatically filled cells G7:G13. Double-clicking a fill handle automatically fills adjacent cells down a column or across a row; this method can be faster and more efficient than dragging the fill handle. Now cells G6:G13 display the commission amounts for all the sales reps.

7. **Click cell G7, then save your changes**

    As shown in Figure J-4, the formula bar displays =$B$16*F7, which is the formula for cell G7. Notice that the formula contains the absolute cell reference $B$16; it was copied exactly from cell G6. The other cell reference in the formula, F7, is a relative cell reference, which changed when the formula was copied to cell G7. Cell G7 displays the value $2,311, the commission for Grace Holmes.

FIGURE J-3: Using an absolute cell reference in a formula

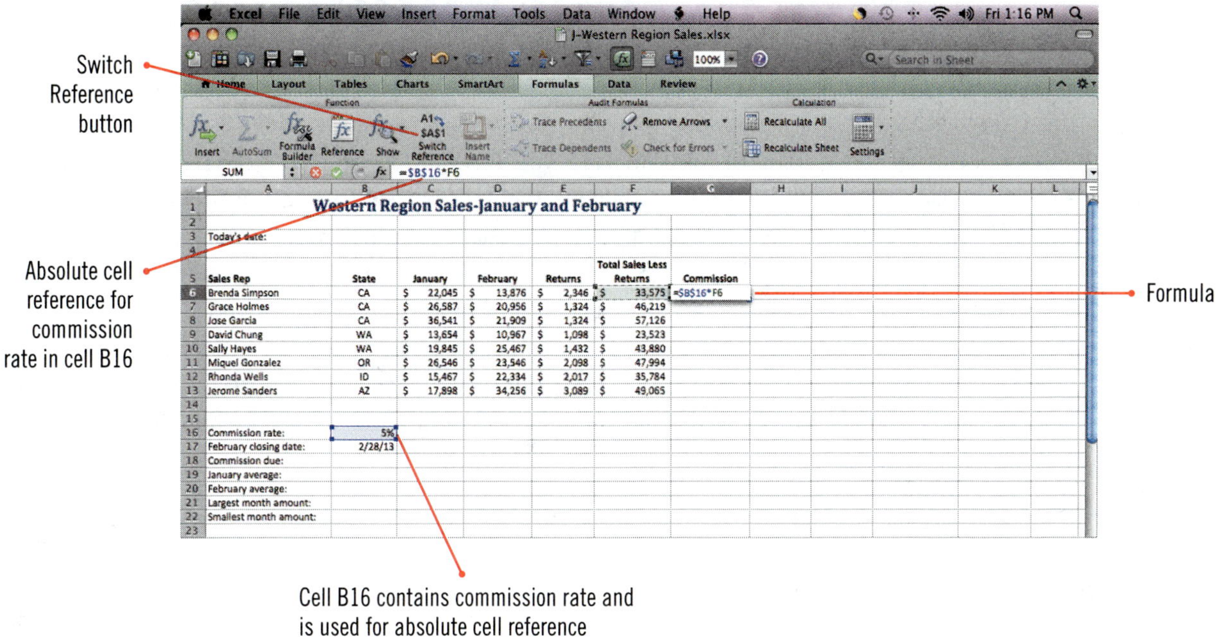

Switch Reference button

Absolute cell reference for commission rate in cell B16

Formula

Cell B16 contains commission rate and is used for absolute cell reference

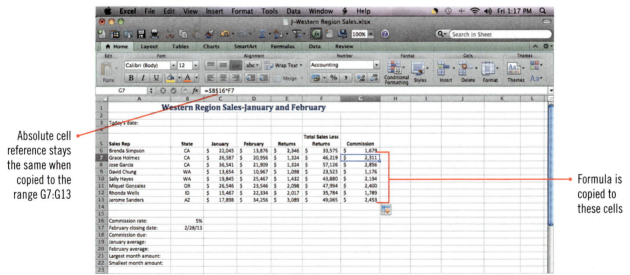

FIGURE J-4: Viewing an absolute cell reference in a copied cell

Absolute cell reference stays the same when copied to the range G7:G13

Formula is copied to these cells

Excel 2011

Understanding Functions

Functions are prewritten formulas that come with Excel. Instead of figuring out which calculations you need to achieve a particular result—and what order in which to type them so the final result is accurate—you can use a function to compose the formula for you. Functions save time and help ensure accuracy, and they are available for both simple calculations and extremely complex ones. Each Excel function has a name usually written in capital letters. The SUM function, for example, adds values; the AVERAGE function calculates the average value of a specified range of cells or values; and so on. There are four parts to every function: an equal sign, the function name, a set of parentheses, and arguments. Arguments are all the information a function needs to perform a task, and can be values (such as 100 or .02), cell references (such as B3), or range references (such as A9:G16). You want to familiarize yourself with functions so that you can use them in the Western Region Sales worksheet, so you decide to practice this new skill in a blank worksheet.

STEPS

1. **Click the Insert Sheet tab** ⊞

   The Sheet2 worksheet opens; this sheet contains no data and is a perfect place to practice using functions.

2. **Click cell A5, type =, then type s**

   See Figure J-5. A list of functions beginning with the letter S appears. Anytime you type an equal sign followed by a letter, a list of valid functions beginning with that letter appears. This feature is called **Formula AutoComplete**.

3. **Type u**

   Typing the letter U shortens the list, so that only the functions beginning with SU are listed. The SUM function is one of the most commonly used functions.

4. **Click SUM from the list of functions**

   Now SUM is entered into cell A5. A Help Tag appears below cell A5 showing the proper structure for the SUM function. The placeholders "number1" and "number2" indicate arguments, which should be separated by commas. You can insert values, cell references, or ranges. The ellipsis (...) indicates that you can include as many arguments as you want.

5. **Type 1,2,3 then click the Enter button** ✓ **on the formula bar**

   The formula bar displays the function =SUM(1,2,3), and cell A5 displays the value 6, which is the result of the SUM function. See Figure J-6.

6. **Click the Formulas tab**

   The Formulas tab contains commands for inserting and working with formulas and functions. The Function group lets you choose a function by category or by using the Insert Function command.

7. **Click cell A7, then click the Formula Builder button** *fx* **in the Function group**

   The Toolbox opens with the Formula Builder tab selected. The Formula Builder helps you select which function to use and how to structure the function's arguments so that it yields correct results. If you're unsure of which function to use, the Search field allows you to search for functions by description or name. To use a function from the Formula Builder list, double-click its name.

8. **Type loan payment in the Search field**

   As soon as you start typing, Excel displays a list of functions related to your search criteria, calculating a loan payment. The results are listed under categories, with Most Recently Used listed first. Any other function categories that contain a function that meet your search criteria are then listed.

9. **Click PMT from the list of functions**

   When you click a function in the list, a description of the function appears below the search results, as shown in Figure J-7.

10. **Press [esc], click the Sheet1 tab, then save your changes**

Using Complex Formulas, Functions, and Tables

FIGURE J-5: Entering a formula using Formula AutoComplete

List of functions that begin with S

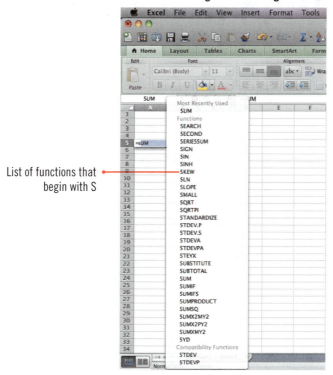

FIGURE J-6: Completed formula containing the SUM function

Function in formula bar

Returned value of formula containing function

Arguments

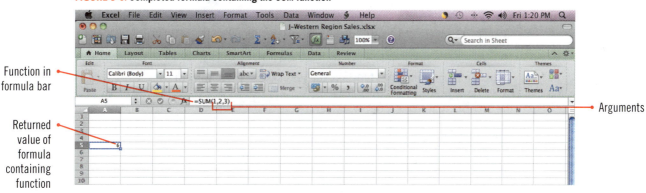

FIGURE J-7: PMT function description

Formula Builder button

Toolbox with Formula Builder tab selected

Description of selected function (PMT)

Search field

PMT function selected in function list

Syntax — example of what to include in parentheses of function

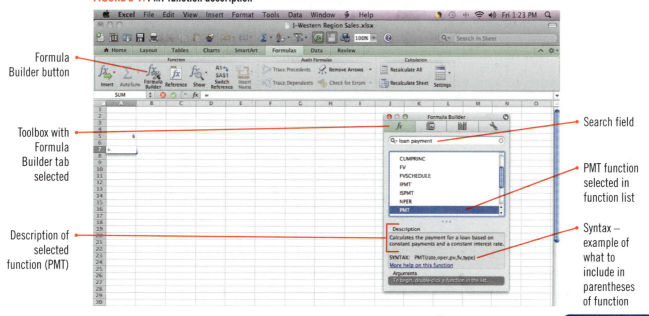

Using Date and Time Functions

There are many categories of functions in Excel. See Table J-2 for a list of common ones. The Excel date and time functions let you display the current date and/or time in your worksheet and can help you calculate the time between events. Some date and time functions produce recognizable text values that you can display as is in your worksheets. Other date and time functions produce values that require special formatting. Serena wants the Western Region Sales worksheet to calculate the date that commission checks are scheduled to be issued. To accomplish this, you decide to use the TODAY function to enter the current date in the worksheet, and you want to enter a formula that uses this information to calculate the check issue date, which is 30 days from today.

STEPS

1. **Click cell B3**

   This cell is to the right of the label Today's date. You want to enter a function in this cell that returns today's date.

2. **Type today in the Formula Builder Search field, then click TODAY in the functions list**

   The description of this function explains that the TODAY function returns the current date formatted as a date. The syntax shows empty parentheses, meaning that the TODAY function requires no arguments, so you don't need to add values or cell references between the parentheses in the formula.

3. **Double-click TODAY in the functions list, compare your screen with Figure J-8, then press [return]**

   When you double-click TODAY, the function, =TODAY(), appears in cell B3 and in the formula bar. After you press [return], the result of this function, the current date, appears in cell B3.

4. **Click cell B18**

   You want to enter a formula in this cell that returns the date that is 30 days from the date in cell B17, which was the closing date for February.

5. **Type =, press [↑] to select cell B17, then type +30**

   The formula you entered, =B17+30, calculates the day when commission checks should be issued, which is 30 days after the date in cell B17 (2/28/13).

6. **Click the Enter button ✓ on the formula bar, then save your changes**

   The commission due date (3/30/13) now appears as a date in cell B18, as shown in Figure J-9.

TABLE J-2: Categories of common worksheet functions

category	used for	examples
Financial	Loan payments, appreciation, and depreciation	PMT, FV, DB, SLN
Logical	Calculations that display a value if a condition is met	IF, AND, NOT
Text	Comparing, converting, and reformatting text strings in cells	FIND, REPLACE
Date and Time	Calculations involving dates and times	NOW, TODAY, WEEKDAY
Lookup and Reference	Finding values in lists or tables or finding cell references	ADDRESS, ROW, COLUMN
Math and Trigonometry	Simple and complex mathematical calculations	ABS, ASIN, COS

Using Complex Formulas, Functions, and Tables

FIGURE J-8: Inserting the TODAY function

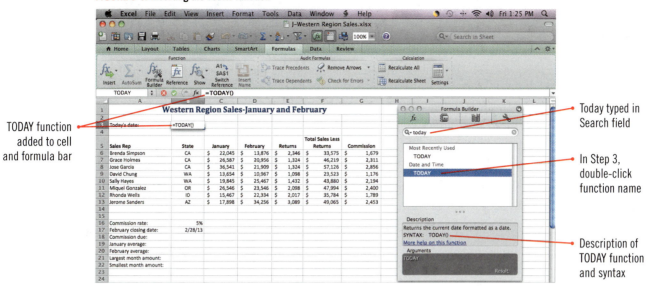

TODAY function added to cell and formula bar

Today typed in Search field

In Step 3, double-click function name

Description of TODAY function and syntax

FIGURE J-9: Western Region Sales worksheet after adding date functions

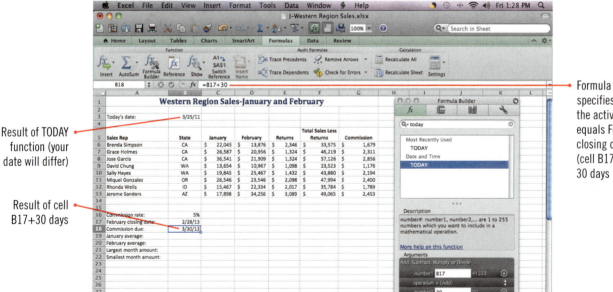

Result of TODAY function (your date will differ)

Result of cell B17+30 days

Formula specifies that the active cell equals February closing date (cell B17) plus 30 days

Understanding how dates are calculated using serial values

When you enter a date in a worksheet cell, the date is actually stored as a serial value, regardless of whether it appears in a familiar format (such as March 15, 2013). A **serial value** is a number in a sequential series of numbers. Date serial values represent the number of days since January 1, 1900. Dates are stored as serial values so they can be used in calculations. For example, in this lesson you added 30 days to the current date. To Excel, the formula in cell B18 in Figure J-10 is really =41333+30. This is useful to know if you remove the formatting from a cell previously formatted as a date, or apply the General format to a cell containing a date. Instead of displaying the date, Excel displays the serial value that represents that date. To make the cell contents recognizable again, click the cell, click the Format Number pop-up menu arrow, then click Date.

Using Statistical Functions

Excel includes many statistical functions that let you assemble, classify, and tabulate numeric data. The most popular statistical functions, AVERAGE, MIN, and MAX, are available on the AutoSum pop-up menu. You can calculate the average of a range of cells using the **AVERAGE** function, and you can identify the lowest or highest value in a range of cells using **MIN** or **MAX**. These functions are also available in the Statistical category of the Insert Function button on the Formulas tab, and you can also access them using the Formula Builder on the Toolbox.  Serena wants you to include the average sales amounts for each month in the Western Region Sales worksheet. She also wants you to indicate the largest and smallest order amounts for the whole region. You decide to use functions to add the necessary calculations to the worksheet.

STEPS

1. **Click cell B19, type Average in the Formula Builder Search field, then click AVERAGE in the functions list**

   Excel provides the description of what the AVERAGE function does. You want the Formula Builder to help you use the AVERAGE function to produce accurate results.

2. **Double-click AVERAGE in the functions list**

   The function =AVERAGE() is entered in cell B19 and in the formula bar. The Formula Builder changes to display the arguments section, where the insertion point is now located, as shown in Figure J-10. Arguments can be typed here or you can click the appropriate cells to make the selection on the worksheet.

3. **Select the range C6:C13, then click the Enter button** ✓

   The formula =AVERAGE(C6:C13) is added to the arguments section and entered in the formula bar. The active cell (B19) displays the result of the formula ($22,323). This is the average sales amount among the sales reps for January. Next you need to enter a formula in cell B20 that calculates the average for February sales.

4. **Click cell B20, click the AutoSum pop-up menu arrow ∑· in the Function group, then click Average**

   Notice that Excel highlights cell B19. Excel assumes that you want to calculate the average of the cells containing numbers directly above the active cell. This is not what you want to do; you want to calculate the average February sales amounts in the range D6:D13.

5. **Select the range D6:D13, then click** ✓

   The average sales amount for February ($21,664) now appears in cell B20. The formula =AVERAGE(D6:D13) appears in the formula bar. Now you need to enter a formula in cell B21 that returns the highest sales amount in both months.

6. **Click cell B21, click the AutoSum pop-up menu arrow in the Function group, then click Max**

   Notice that Excel highlights cells B19 and B20. Excel assumes that you want to calculate the highest value in the cells containing numbers directly above the active cell (B19 and B20). This is not what you want to do; you want to find the highest sales amounts in the range C6:D13.

7. **Select the range C6:D13, then click** ✓

   The formula =MAX(C6:D13) appears in the formula bar, as shown in Figure J-11. The active cell B21 displays the formula's result ($36,541), which is the largest sales amount for January and February. This amount, found in cell C8, is the January sales for Jose Garcia.

8. **Click cell B22, click the AutoSum pop-up menu arrow in the Function group, click Min, select the range C6:D13, then click** ✓

   The formula =MIN(C6:D13) appears in the formula bar. This formula returns the lowest value contained in the cell range C6:D13. The active cell B22 displays the formula's result ($10,967), which is the lowest sales amount. This amount, found in cell D9, is the February sales for David Chung.

9. **Close the Toolbox, then save your changes to the workbook**

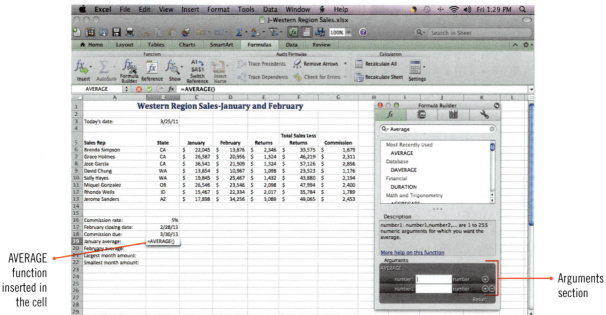

AVERAGE
function
inserted in
the cell

Arguments
section

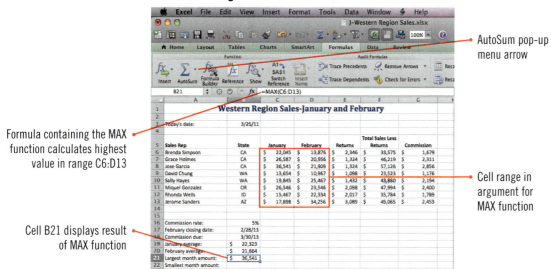

AutoSum pop-up
menu arrow

Formula containing the MAX
function calculates highest
value in range C6:D13

Cell range in
argument for
MAX function

Cell B21 displays result
of MAX function

Excel 2011

Using the status bar to view calculated data

The status bar calculates data using the Average, Count, Count Nums, Max, Min, and Sum functions on any selected range. When a range of cells containing values is selected, by default the status bar displays the sum of the values in the selected cells. To display the calculated data as the Average, Count, Count Nums, Max, or Min functions, click the pop-up menu arrow next to the value on the status bar, as shown In Figure J-12, then click the appropriate function.

FIGURE J-12: Using the functions on the status bar

None

Average
Count
Count Nums
Max
Min
✓ Sum

Applying Conditional Formatting

Sometimes you might want to highlight certain cells in a worksheet that contain significant data points. For instance, if your worksheet lists customer orders, you might want to highlight the cells containing orders that exceed a certain amount. If your worksheet shows product sales, you might want to highlight cells containing the highest and lowest product revenues. Instead of manually formatting each highlighted cell, you can use conditional formatting. Excel applies **conditional formatting** to cells when specified criteria are met. For instance, you could apply green, bold formatted text as conditional formatting to all sales orders greater than $50,000. You can specify your own customized conditional formats, or you can use one of the built-in conditional formatting options available in Excel 2011, such as data bars, color scales, and icon sets.  Serena wants the worksheet to highlight the high and low total amounts in the Western Region Sales worksheet. You'll explore different conditional formatting options to find the right effect.

STEPS

1. **Click the Home tab, then select the cell range F6:F13**

   You selected the cells in the Total Sales Less Returns column. These cells display the total sales amounts for each rep (minus returns).

2. **Click the Conditional Formatting button ▦ in the Format group, point to Color Scales, then click the Green - Yellow - Red Color Scale option (first option, top row), as shown in Figure J-13**

   Color scales are shading patterns that use two or three colors to show the relative values of a range of cells. The selected cells now contain shading gradations of three different colors. The green shades highlight the cells containing the higher values, the yellow shades highlight the values in the middle, and the red shades highlight the lower values. You decide to remove this shading so that you can explore other conditional formats.

> **QUICK TIP**
> You can also apply red, yellow, and green icons as conditional formats to indicate low, medium, and high values in a selected range. Click the Conditional Formatting button, point to Icon Sets, then click the icon set you want.

3. **Click the Conditional Formatting button ▦, point to Clear Rules, then click Clear Rules from Selected Cells**

   With the conditional formatting rules cleared, the color scales no longer appear in the selected cells.

4. **Click ▦, point to Data Bars, then click the Green Data Bar option in the Gradient Fill section, as shown in Figure J-14**

   The cells in the selected range now contain green shaded bars. The cells with the highest values have the widest bars, and the cells with the lowest values have the thinnest bars. **Data bars** make it easy to quickly identify the high and low values in a range of cells and also highlight the relative value of cells to one another.

> **QUICK TIP**
> After selecting the Highlight Cells Rules criteria, you can apply your own custom formatting choices in the New Formatting Rule dialog box by clicking the pop-up menu arrows for Format with, clicking custom format, choosing the options you want from the Format Cells dialog box, and then clicking OK.

5. **Select cells C6:D13, click ▦, point to Highlight Cells Rules, then click Less Than**

   The New Formatting Rule dialog box opens. You decide to apply a light red fill with dark red text to cells containing values less than $15,000.

6. **Type 15000 in the text box, compare your screen with Figure J-15, then click OK**

   The cells containing values less than $15,000 in cells C6:D13 are now shaded in red with red font, making it easy to pick out the lowest sales amounts. It is now easy to see that David Chung's sales for January and February and Brenda Simpson's sales for February are less than $15,000.

7. **Save your changes to the worksheet**

FIGURE J-13: Selected cells with color scales applied

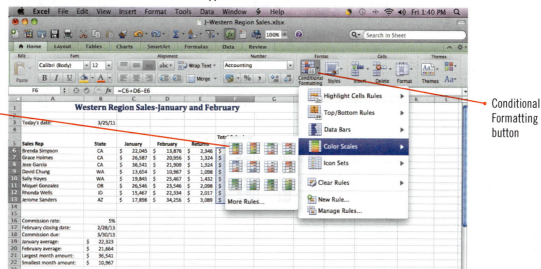

Green – Yellow – Red Color Scale option

Conditional Formatting button

FIGURE J-14: Applying data bars to selected cells

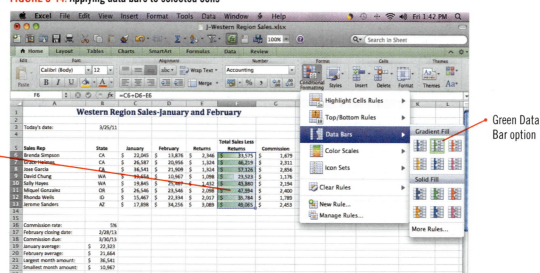

Green data bars show relative value of cells in range

Green Data Bar option

FIGURE J-15: New Formatting Rule dialog box with conditional formatting rules specified

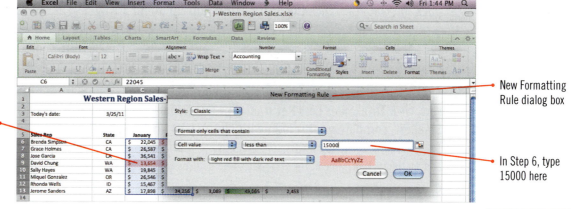

New Formatting Rule dialog box

Cells with values less than $15,000 have red fill with dark red text

In Step 6, type 15000 here

Using Complex Formulas, Functions, and Tables

Sorting Rows in a Table

Excel lets you analyze a separate range of worksheet data called a **table**, or rows and columns of data with a similar structure. When you designate a cell range as a table, you can manage and analyze its data separately from other parts of the worksheet. For instance, you can **sort**, or change the order of the table rows, by specifying that the rows be arranged by a particular column in the table. An Excel table is similar to a table in a database because you can sort data in much the same way. You can use the Table Styles Gallery to define a table and choose an appropriate table style. Serena wants the data sorted alphabetically by state, and then within each state, by total sales amount from largest to smallest. You decide to format the data as a table in order to sort it.

STEPS

QUICK TIP

To remove the header row, deselect the Header Row check box in the Table Options group on the Tables tab.

QUICK TIP

Excel automatically formats all adjacent cells that contain data as a table. If you do not want all adjacent cells with data to be formatted as a table, select the range of cells to be included in your table before selecting the Table Style.

TROUBLE

Remember that the fill handle is in the lower-right corner of cell G14. Drag the fill handle to the left to cell C14, just as you would drag it down to fill a column or to the right to fill a row.

QUICK TIP

To undo the results of a sort immediately after performing it, click the Undo button on the Standard toolbar.

1. **Click cell A5, click the Tables tab on the ribbon, point to the Table Styles Gallery until the pop-up menu arrow appears, then click the arrow**
   The Table Styles Gallery opens to display the options for Table Styles.

2. **Click the Table Style Light 9 style (second style in the second row), as shown in Figure J-16**
   Table Style Light 9 is applied to the cell range A5:G13. In the Table Options group, Header Row and Banded Rows are selected. In a table, the **header row** is the row at the top that contains column headings. Rows with borders are considered banded rows. To add borders for your columns, you must select Banded Columns in the Table Options group.

3. **Click any cell in the table**
   Cells A5:G13 are now defined as a table. Notice that each cell in the header row contains a pop-up menu arrow on its right edge. In the Table Options group, notice that the Total Row check box is not selected. A **Total Row** is an extra row at the bottom of a table that Excel adds. You want to add a Total Row to the table.

4. **Click the Total Row check box in the Table Options group, then click cell G14**
   Excel inserted a new row 14 that contains a Total label (in cell A14). By default, the last cell in the Total Row contains the SUBTOTAL function, which calculates the sum total of the table's last column of data.

5. **Position the pointer over the fill handle in the lower-right corner of cell G14 until it changes to ✚, then drag ✚ to cell C14**
   You copied the formula that summed cells G6:G13 from cell G14 to cells C14:F14. Now cells C14:G14 display the sum totals for the data in columns C through G.

6. **Click the State pop-up menu arrow ▼ in cell B5, click Ascending, as shown in Figure J-17, then click ⊗**
   The items in the table are now sorted by state in alphabetical order, with the Arizona rep at the top and the Washington reps at the bottom. Notice that the State pop-up menu arrow has now changed to ▾▴. This symbol lets you know that this table column has the ascending sort applied to it. Serena also wants the list to be sorted by totals within each state, from largest to smallest.

7. **Click the Data tab, click the Sort button pop-up menu arrow ▾ in the Sort & Filter group, then click Custom Sort**
   The Sort dialog box opens. Because you already performed one sort on this data, your sort criteria is listed in the dialog box. You can use this dialog box to add additional sort criteria.

8. **Click the Add Level button ＋, click the Column pop-up menu arrows in the Then by row, click Total Sales Less Returns, click the Order pop-up menu arrows, click Largest to Smallest, compare your screen with Figure J-18, then click OK**
   The list is now sorted first by the State column in alphabetical order. Within each state listing, the cells containing the highest value in the Total Sales Less Returns column are listed first, as shown in Figure J-19.

9. **Save your changes**

Using Complex Formulas, Functions, and Tables

FIGURE J-16: Choosing a table style and defining a table

Tables tab

In Step 4, click this check box

Table Style pop-up menu arrow

In Step 2, select this table style

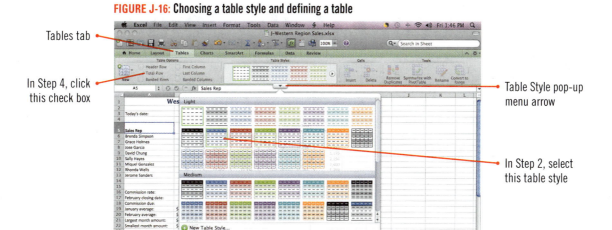

FIGURE J-17: Column sort options

Data tab

Close button

In Step 6, click this option

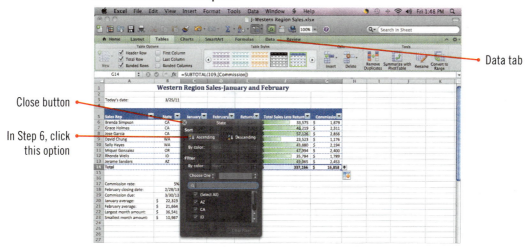

FIGURE J-18: Sort dialog box

Additional sort criteria added as a level

Column pop-up menu arrows

Add Level button

Order pop-up menu arrows

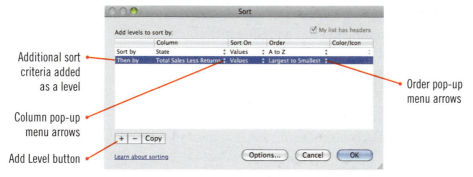

FIGURE J-19: Table sorted by two sort criteria

Arrows indicate sort order is applied

AZ is listed first

WA is listed last

Within each state grouping, sales figures are listed from highest to lowest by Total Sales Less Returns column

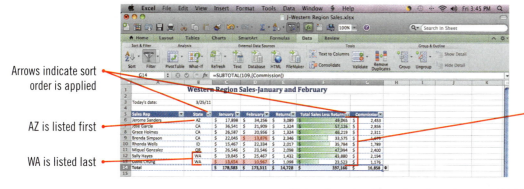

Filtering Table Data

If your Excel table contains a large amount of data, you might want to **filter** it to display only the data you need. Applying a filter tells Excel to show only those rows that meet specific requirements, such as customers with a particular zip code, or orders that exceed a certain dollar amount. When you tell Excel which rows in a table you want to see, you are specifying the **criteria** for your filter. Just as when you sort data in a table, you can apply a filter to a table by using the filter pop-up menu arrows that appear to the right of each column heading. Unlike a sort, a filter does not change the order of the items in your table; instead, it temporarily hides the rows that do not meet your criteria.  Serena wants you to filter the table data so that it shows only the sales reps for California and Washington whose sales amounts are less than $50,000.

STEPS

1. **Click the State list sort arrow** ▾↑ **in cell B5**

   The Sort and Filter menu opens and displays the list of available sort and filter options for this column. Excel creates filters for each of the values in the column, plus filters to automatically select all entries, custom values, specified text, or numeric values. You can even filter a table by cell color.

2. **Click the (Select All) check box to deselect it**

   The check marks are now removed from all the check boxes. You want to check the CA and WA check boxes, to specify that only rows containing CA or WA in the States column are displayed. When you apply a filter, it filters out, or hides, the data that do not meet your criteria.

> **QUICK TIP**
>
> To remove an applied filter, click the Data tab on the ribbon, select the table, then click the Filter button ▽▾ in the Sort & Filter group to deselect it.

3. **Click the CA check box, scroll down and click the WA check box, compare your screen with Figure J-20, then click** ⊗

   You have applied a filter that shows only the rows that contain the values CA and WA in the State column (five rows). You can tell that the table is filtered because the sort arrow next to State has changed to ▾▼, which indicates a sort and filter has been applied to this column.

4. **Click the Total Sales Less Returns sort arrow** ▾↑ **in cell F5, click the Choose One pop-up menu arrows, click Less Than, type 50000 in the spin box next to Less Than, then compare your screen with Figure J-21**

   You use the Sort and Filter menu to specify one or more criteria for a filter. The Choose One filter option displays "Less Than" and the amount is set to 50,000.

5. **Click** ⊗ **to close the Sort and Filter menu**

   The table is filtered to show sales reps whose Total Sales Less Returns amounts are less than $50,000. Now the table displays only four rows.

> **QUICK TIP**
>
> To change a table back to a normal range, click anywhere in the table, click the Convert to Range button in the Tools group on the Tables tab, then click Yes.

6. **Type your name in cell A25, click** ✓, **then compare your screen with Figure J-22**

7. **Click File on the menu bar, then click Print**

   The Print dialog box opens and the worksheet appears in the Quick Preview box. You can see that the last two columns in the worksheet (Total Sales Less Returns and Commission) do not fit on the page. You can fix this by changing the Scaling settings.

> **QUICK TIP**
>
> In Normal view, you can also adjust how pages break by clicking and dragging the dotted, vertical line that denotes where the page breaks are.

8. **Click the Scaling check box**

   By default, the Scaling spin boxes are set to 1 page wide by 1 page tall. The worksheet shrinks down just enough so that all the columns fit on the page, as shown in Figure J-23.

9. **Click Print if your lab allows printing; if not, click Cancel**

10. **Save your changes, quit Excel, then submit the completed workbook to your instructor**

Using Complex Formulas, Functions, and Tables

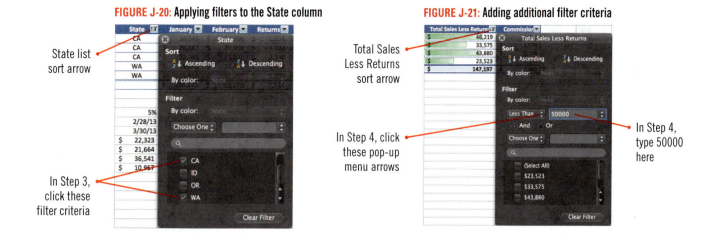

FIGURE J-20: Applying filters to the State column

State list sort arrow

In Step 3, click these filter criteria

FIGURE J-21: Adding additional filter criteria

Total Sales Less Returns sort arrow

In Step 4, click these pop-up menu arrows

In Step 4, type 50000 here

FIGURE J-22: Worksheet with two filters applied

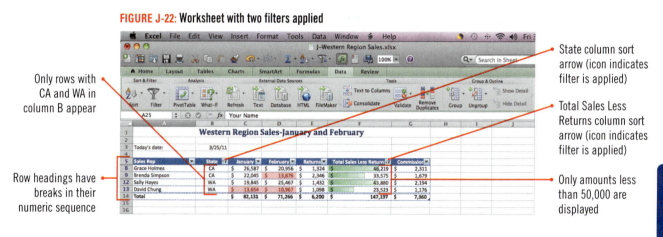

Only rows with CA and WA in column B appear

Row headings have breaks in their numeric sequence

State column sort arrow (icon indicates filter is applied)

Total Sales Less Returns column sort arrow (icon indicates filter is applied)

Only amounts less than 50,000 are displayed

FIGURE J-23: Completed worksheet as shown in the Print dialog box

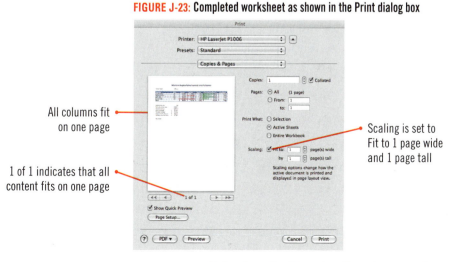

All columns fit on one page

1 of 1 indicates that all content fits on one page

Scaling is set to Fit to 1 page wide and 1 page tall

Using Complex Formulas, Functions, and Tables

Practice

Concepts Review

Label each of the elements of the Excel worksheet window shown in Figure J-24.

FIGURE J-24

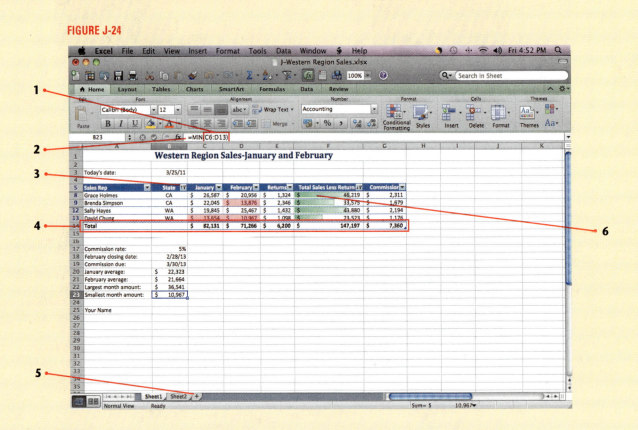

Match components of the formula =MIN(D2:H7,J2:L7) with their descriptions.

7. **J2:L7**

8. **MIN**

9. **=**

10. **C2:C10**

11. **,**

a. Second argument in the function

b. Symbol that separates arguments in functions

c. Symbol that indicates that the subsequent text is a formula

d. First argument in the function

e. Function name

Select the best answer from the list of choices.

12. **Which of the following is a complex formula?**
    a. =SUM(A2:A10)
    c. =F2+1400
    b. =(E2+E3)*.20
    d. =MIN(A7:24)

13. **In a complex formula, which of the following is evaluated first?**
    a. ( ) Items in parentheses
    c. + Addition
    b. * Multiplication
    d. – Subtraction

14. **Which of the following functions is correctly structured and calculates the sum of 5 plus the values in cells C3, C4, and C5?**
    a. =SUM(5,C3,C5)
    c. =SUM(5,C3:C5)
    b. =SUM(5:C5)
    d. =SUM(5,C3:C4:C5)

15. **In the formula =AVERAGE(C3:C10,D3:D10), which of the following are the arguments?**
    a. C3:D10
    c. C3 and D3
    b. C10 and D10
    d. C3:C10 and D3:D10

16. **Which of the following functions returns a date value?**
    a. =TODAY()+60
    c. =AVERAGE(B7:C10)
    b. =MIN(J5:K20)
    d. =MAX(A2:A50)

17. **What value would Excel return in calculating the formula =SUM(5,AVERAGE(10,30))?**
    a. 35
    c. 25
    b. 20
    d. 45

18. **What value would Excel return in calculating the formula =MIN(22,(2*3),770,(4+3),200)?**
    a. 22
    c. 7
    b. 6
    d. 200

19. **If you want an Excel table to display only rows containing values less than 50 in the Revenue column, which of the following actions should you take?**
    a. Sort the rows from largest to smallest in the Revenue column.
    b. Use the Sort and Filter menu to specify to show only rows where the Revenue field is less than 50.
    c. Choose the 50 filter on the Revenue filter list.
    d. Sort the rows from smallest to largest in the Revenue column.

Skills Review

1. **Create complex formulas.**
   a. Start Excel, open the file J-2.xlsx from the location where you store your Data Files, then save it as **J-May Orders**.
   b. Enter a complex formula in cell G6 that calculates the sum of cells D6 and E6 minus the value in cell F6.
   c. Copy the formula from cell G6 to the range G7:G14.
   d. Save your changes to the workbook.

2. **Use absolute cell references.**
   a. In cell H6, enter a formula that multiplies the value in cell D6 by the value in cell B17, using an absolute cell reference for cell B17.
   b. Use the fill handle to copy the formula in cell H6 to cells H7:H14.
   c. Save your changes to the workbook.

3. **Use date and time functions.**
   a. Use the TODAY function to enter today's date in cell B22.
   b. Enter a formula in cell J6 that calculates the date that is 30 days later than the Order Date for Harold's Tea Shop.
   c. Use the fill handle to copy the formula in cell J6 to cells J7:J14.
   d. Save your changes to the workbook.

Using Complex Formulas, Functions, and Tables

Skills Review (continued)

4. Use statistical functions.

   a. Enter a formula in cell B18 that uses the AVERAGE function to determine the average May Order Amount for the range D6:D14.

   b. Enter a function in cell B19 that determines the smallest May Order Amount for the range D6:D14.

   c. Enter a function in cell B20 that determines the largest May Order Amount for the range D6:D14.

   d. Save your changes to the workbook.

5. Apply conditional formatting.

   a. Select the range D6:D14.

   b. Apply a Color Scales conditional formatting to the selected range, choosing any style you like.

   c. Clear the conditional formatting rules you applied in Step 5b.

   d. Apply Gradient Fill Light Blue Data Bars conditional formatting to the range D6:D14.

   e. Select the range G6:G14, then apply conditional formatting to the cells in this range, specifying that all cells containing values that are greater than 1000 be formatted in Light Red Fill with Dark Red Text.

   f. Save your changes to the worksheet.

6. Sort rows in a table.

   a. Format the cell range A5:J14 as a table, applying Table Style Light 11 (fourth style in second row of Table Styles Gallery).

   b. Specify to add a Total Row to the table. Delete the value in cell J15 of the Total Row (because it refers to cells containing dates).

   c. Select cell D15, click the pop-up menu arrows, then click Sum.

   d. Drag the cell D15 fill handle to cell H15.

   e. Sort the table in alphabetical order by Town.

   f. Use the Sort dialog box to sort the list data first by Town in alphabetical order, then by May Order Amount in largest to smallest order. (*Hint*: Click the Sort button pop-up menu arrow in the Sort & Filter group, then click Custom Sort.)

   g. Save your changes to the workbook.

7. Filter table data.

   a. Apply a filter so that only the rows containing Bay City and Gulfwood appear.

   b. Enter your name in cell A25 of the worksheet.

   c. View the worksheet in the Print dialog box, change the orientation to landscape, then adjust the scaling so that all columns fit on one sheet.

   d. Save your changes, close the worksheet, then quit Excel. Submit your completed worksheet to your instructor. Compare your completed worksheet with Figure J-25.

FIGURE J-25

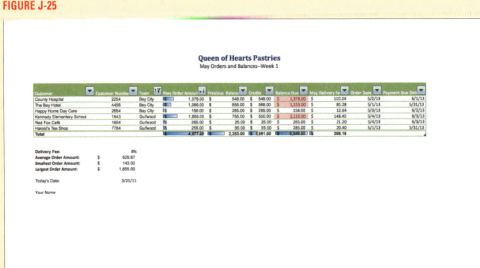

Using Complex Formulas, Functions, and Tables

Independent Challenge 1

You are the sales manager for the Midwest Region at Plushkin Fine Linens and Towels Inc. You need to create a worksheet that analyzes sales results for each state in your region. In addition, you need to highlight the total sales, the average sales, and the best- and worst-performing sales regions. You also need to calculate the bonuses for each sales rep. A sales rep is eligible for a bonus only if his or her average sales increase for each state exceeds 10%. If a sales rep is eligible for a bonus, his or her bonus is calculated by multiplying total sales by 3%.

a. Start Excel, open the file J-3.xlsx from the location where you store your Data Files, then save it as **J-Midwest Q1 Sales**.

b. In cell E5, enter a formula that subtracts the value in cell D5 (Q1 Sales Prior Year) from the value in cell C5 (Q1 Sales). Use the fill handle to copy the formula to cells E6:E16.

c. Enter a formula in cell F5 that calculates the percentage that Q1 Sales increased over Q1 Sales in the prior year. (*Hint*: Your formula needs to divide the value in cell E5 by the value in cell D5.) Use the fill handle to copy the formula to cells F6:F16.

d. In cell B18, use the AVERAGE function to compute the average sales for all states in Q1. (*Hint*: Specify the range C5:C16.)

e. In cell B19, use the MAX function to calculate the maximum (or highest) Q1 sales for the states.

f. In cell B20, use the MIN function to compute the minimum (or lowest) Q1 sales for the states.

g. Define the range A4:F16 as a table and apply a table style that you like. Include a Total Row. Delete the value in cell F17. Click cell E17, click the down arrow in cell E17, then click Sum. Drag the E17 fill handle to cells D17:C17.

h. Sort the data in the table by the Sales Rep column (column B) in order from A to Z. Using the Sort dialog box, apply a second sort level that sorts by Q1 Sales vs. Prior Year Q1 ($) from largest to smallest.

i. In cell B23, use the AVERAGE function to compute the average Q1 increase (as a percentage) for Jonathan Stephens' states. (Use the range F5:F9.)

j. In cell B24, use the AVERAGE function to compute the average Q1 increase (as a percentage) for Patricia Morley's states. (Use the range F10:F13.)

k. In cell B25, use the AVERAGE function to compute the average Q1 increase (as a percentage) for Ricardo Juarez's states. (Use the range F14:F16.)

l. Apply Data Bars conditional formatting to the range E5: E16. Choose any Data Bars style you like; make sure that the color you choose contrasts well with the colors in the table style you chose.

m. If Jonathan Stephens' average Q1 increase (shown in cell B23) exceeds 10%, then enter a formula in cell F23 that calculates his bonus amount. (*Hint*: The formula needs to multiply cell F20 by the sum of cells C5:C9.)

n. If Patricia Morley's average Q1 increase (shown in cell B24) exceeds 10%, then enter a formula in cell F24 that calculates her bonus amount. (*Hint*: The formula needs to multiply cell F20 by the sum of cells C10:C13.)

o. If Ricardo Juarez's average Q1 increase (shown in cell B25) exceeds 10%, then enter a formula in cell F25 that calculates his bonus amount. (*Hint*: The formula needs to multiply cell F20 by the sum of cells C14:C16.)

p. Preview the worksheet in the Print dialog box. Change the orientation to landscape, then adjust the scaling so that all columns fit on one sheet. Save your changes.

Advanced Challenge Exercise

- Select the range C5:C16.
- Click the Conditional Formatting button, then apply the icon set 3 Stars under the Ratings section.
- Save your changes.

q. Save your changes, close the workbook, then quit Excel. Submit your completed worksheet to your instructor.

Independent Challenge 2

The sales director at Wexler Organics Inc. has just received the raw sales data for the month of August. She has asked you to finish creating a worksheet that she started. She wants you to highlight key information on this worksheet, including the highest individual sale, the overall sales total, and the number of sales reps who logged individual sales transactions greater than $5,000 for the month.

a. Open the file J-4.xlsx from the location where you store your Data Files, then save it as **J-August Sales Rep Report**.

b. Enter a formula in cell E7 that calculates the commission owed to the rep. (*Hint*: Multiply cell D7 by the absolute reference cell B4.) Use the fill handle to copy the formula to cells E8:E39.

c. Create a formula in cell F7 that subtracts the rep's commission in cell E7 from the Sales amount in cell D7.

d. Copy the formula in cell F7 to the range F8:F39.

e. Create a table from the range A6:F39. Apply a table design style that you like to the table. Include a Total Row. Use the fill handle to copy the formula in cell F40 to cells E40:D40.

f. Sort the table data by sales in order from largest to smallest. Look at the sorted list, then enter the name of the rep that has the largest sales amount in cell B42.

g. Enter a formula in cell B43 that uses the MAX function to identify the highest individual sale in the month. Apply the Accounting number format to cell B43 with no decimal places.

h. Enter a formula in cell B44 that calculates the average for all sales in cells D7:D39. Apply the Accounting number format and remove all decimals.

i. Apply Data Bars conditional formatting to the range D7:D39, choosing any data bar color you like.

j. Enter your name in cell A3.

k. Preview the worksheet in the Print dialog box. Adjust the scaling so that all columns fit on one sheet in portrait orientation.

l. Save your changes, close the workbook, then quit Excel. Submit your completed worksheet to your instructor.

Independent Challenge 3

You own and operate The Last Minute Chef, a restaurant and caterer that serves busy families in Rochester, New York. You are building an Excel spreadsheet to calculate your profits for the previous year. You have entered sales and most of the expense data in the worksheet. Now you need to enter the necessary formulas to calculate the delivery costs and the profits for each month.

a. Open the file J-5.xlsx from the location where you store your Data Files, then save it as **J-Restaurant Profits**. Enter your name in cell A26.

b. The Last Minute Chef pays for food deliveries through a delivery service, which charges a $7.00 flat fee per delivery. The delivery fee is in cell B20. Enter a formula in cell I5 that calculates the cost of deliveries for the month of January. (*Hint*: The formula needs to multiply cell H5—the cell that contains the number of deliveries for January—by cell B20, with B20 as an absolute cell reference.)

c. Enter a complex formula in cell J5 that calculates profits for January. The formula should subtract the sum total of cells C5:G5 and cell I5 from cell B5 (Sales for January). (*Hint*: Start the formula with cell B5 followed by the - mathematical operator, followed by the SUM function to add the range C5:G5 and cell I5. You will need to use two sets of parentheses—one set around the arguments and the other around the whole SUM function part of the formula.)

d. Select cells I5 and J5, then use the fill handle to copy the formulas down the columns.

e. Enter a formula in cell B21 that identifies the highest profit amount.

f. Enter a formula in cell B22 that identifies the smallest profit amount.

g. Enter a formula in cell B23 that calculates the average monthly profit for the entire year.

h. Apply conditional formatting to the cell range J5:J16 to format any cells containing values greater than 55,000 with green fill and dark green text.

Independent Challenge 3 (continued)

i. Format the range A4:J16 as a table, choosing any table style you like. Add a Total Row. Use the fill handle to copy the formula in cell J17 to cells I17:B17.

j. Sort the table in the Profits column by Largest to Smallest.

k. Preview the worksheet in in the Print dialog box. Change the orientation to landscape, then adjust the scaling so that all columns fit on one sheet.

Advanced Challenge Exercise

- Click cell A17 (the Total label), then type Average.
- Click cell B17, click the down arrow that appears in the right side of the cell, then click Average.
- Copy the new formula in cell B17 to cells C17:J17 by dragging the fill handle. Save your changes.

l. Save your changes, close the workbook, then quit Excel. Submit your completed worksheet to your instructor.

Real Life Independent Challenge

You can take advantage of dozens of prebuilt Excel worksheets that are available as templates in the Excel Workbook Gallery. These templates provide a wide range of tools for helping you with school, work, and life tasks. For instance, you can find templates for creating invoices, memos, calendars, and time sheets. You can even find templates for helping you plan a party or clean your house. In this Real Life Independent Challenge, you use a loan calculator to calculate monthly payments for a car loan.

a. Start Excel. When the Excel Workbook Gallery opens, select Personal Finance in the left pane.

b. Select Loan Calculator in the middle pane, then click Choose.

c. Save the workbook as **J-Loan Calculator** in the location where you store your Data Files.

d. In cell D4, enter 10000 as the loan amount.

e. In cell D5, enter 5 as the annual interest rate amount.

f. In cell D6, enter 5 as the number of years you want to pay off your loan.

g. In cell D7, enter a formula that returns a date that is 30 days from today. Leave cell D8 blank.

h. Enter your name in cell A16.

i. Save your changes, then preview the worksheet in the Print dialog box. Close the workbook, quit Excel, then submit the workbook to your instructor.

Visual Workshop

Open the file J-6.xlsx and save it as **J-Spring Classes Profits** in the location where you store your Data Files. Modify the worksheet so that it contains all the formulas, functions, and formatting shown in Figure J-26. The Total Student Fees cells need to include formulas that multiply the number of students by the student fee by the number of classes. The Instructor Cost cells need to include formulas that multiply the number of classes by the instructor fee ($75.00) in cell B19. (*Hint*: Use an absolute cell reference.) The Profit cells need to subtract the Instructor Cost from the Total Student Fees. Convert the range A4:H17 to a table, then resize column widths to match the figure. Sort the table as shown. Enter appropriate formulas in the range E19:E20. Change alignments and font styles to match the figure. Add your name to cell A21. Adjust the print settings to landscape orientation. Save and close the workbook, quit Excel, then submit your finished workbook to your instructor.

FIGURE J-26

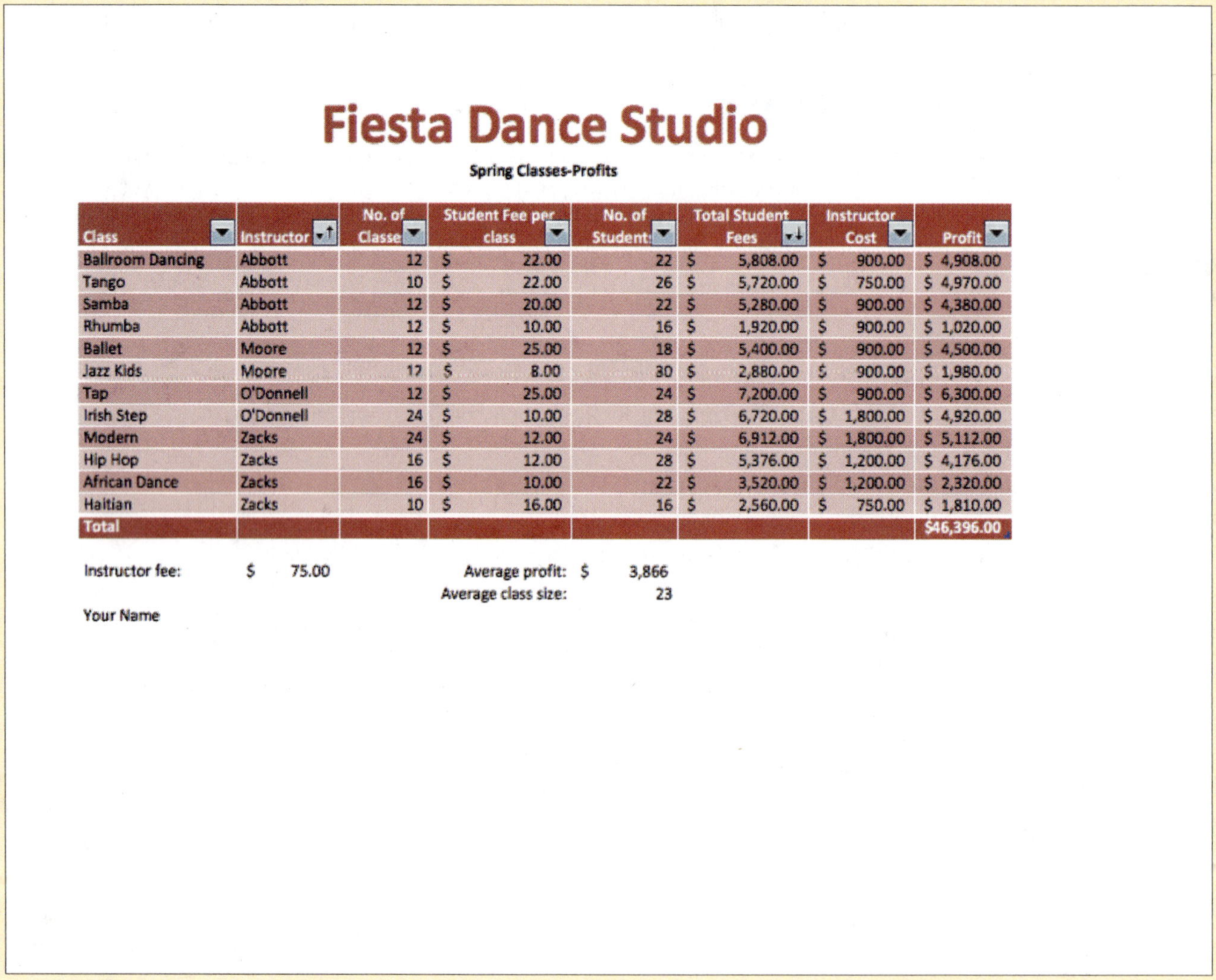

Fiesta Dance Studio

Spring Classes-Profits

Class	Instructor	No. of Classes	Student Fee per class	No. of Students	Total Student Fees	Instructor Cost	Profit
Ballroom Dancing	Abbott	12	$ 22.00	22	$ 5,808.00	$ 900.00	$ 4,908.00
Tango	Abbott	10	$ 22.00	26	$ 5,720.00	$ 750.00	$ 4,970.00
Samba	Abbott	12	$ 20.00	22	$ 5,280.00	$ 900.00	$ 4,380.00
Rhumba	Abbott	12	$ 10.00	16	$ 1,920.00	$ 900.00	$ 1,020.00
Ballet	Moore	12	$ 25.00	18	$ 5,400.00	$ 900.00	$ 4,500.00
Jazz Kids	Moore	17	$ 8.00	30	$ 2,880.00	$ 900.00	$ 1,980.00
Tap	O'Donnell	12	$ 25.00	24	$ 7,200.00	$ 900.00	$ 6,300.00
Irish Step	O'Donnell	24	$ 10.00	28	$ 6,720.00	$ 1,800.00	$ 4,920.00
Modern	Zacks	24	$ 12.00	24	$ 6,912.00	$ 1,800.00	$ 5,112.00
Hip Hop	Zacks	16	$ 12.00	28	$ 5,376.00	$ 1,200.00	$ 4,176.00
African Dance	Zacks	16	$ 10.00	22	$ 3,520.00	$ 1,200.00	$ 2,320.00
Haitian	Zacks	10	$ 16.00	16	$ 2,560.00	$ 750.00	$ 1,810.00
Total							$46,396.00

Instructor fee:	$ 75.00		Average profit:	$ 3,866
			Average class size:	23

Your Name

Using Complex Formulas, Functions, and Tables

Working with Charts

A worksheet is great for organizing and calculating data, but interpreting numbers in rows and columns takes time and effort. A much more effective way to communicate worksheet data to an audience is to present the data as a chart. A **chart** is a visual representation of worksheet data. For example, a chart can illustrate the growth in sales from one year to the next in a format that makes it easy to see the increase. Microsoft Excel provides many tools for creating charts to help you communicate key trends and facts about your worksheet data. In this unit, you learn how to create and work with charts. Serena Henning, director of sales for Outdoor Designs, has asked you to create a chart from worksheet data that shows first-quarter sales of the Canoe Kit by region. You create and customize two different types of charts for Serena. You also add sparklines, which are miniature charts, to help illustrate the sales trends for each region in the worksheet.

OBJECTIVES

Understand and plan a chart

Create a chart

Move and resize a chart and chart objects

Apply chart layouts and styles

Customize chart objects

Enhance a chart

Create a pie chart

Create sparklines

Understanding and Planning a Chart

Before you create a chart, you need to understand some basic concepts about charts. You also need to determine what data you want your chart to show and what chart type you want to use.  Before you create the chart that Serena has requested, you decide to review your data and think about which chart type best represents the information you want to convey.

DETAILS

When planning and creating a chart, it is important to:

- **Understand the various parts of a chart**

  The chart in Figure K-1 shows sales of the Canoe Kit by region for January, February, and March. This chart is based on the range A4:D8 in the worksheet. Like many charts, the one shown here is two-dimensional, meaning it has a horizontal axis and a vertical axis. The **horizontal axis** (also called the **x-axis** or the **category axis**) is the horizontal line at the base of the chart that shows categories. The **vertical axis** (also called the **y-axis** or the **value axis**) is the vertical line at the left edge of the chart that displays values. In Figure K-1, the vertical axis provides values for sales, and the horizontal axis shows months. The **axis titles** identify what is shown on each axis. The blue, red, green, and orange bars each represent a data series. A **data series** is a sequence of related numbers that shows a trend. For example, the blue data series shown in Figure K-1 represents Canoe Kit sales for the West region. A **data marker** is a single chart symbol that represents one value in a data series. For example, the orange data marker on the far right of the chart represents the Canoe Kit sales in March for the Northeast region. A chart **legend** identifies what each data series represents. The **gridlines** in the chart are vertical and horizontal lines that help identify the value for each data series. The **plot area** is the part of the chart contained within the horizontal and vertical axes; in the figure, the plot area is yellow. The **chart area** is the entire chart and all the chart elements.

- **Identify the purpose of the data and choose an appropriate chart type**

  You can use Excel to create many different kinds of charts; each chart type is appropriate for showing particular types of data. Before you create a chart, decide what aspect of your data you want to emphasize, such as making a comparison between two categories, so that you can choose the appropriate chart type. Table K-1 provides descriptions of common Excel chart types and examples of what each type looks like. As the chart in Figure K-1 demonstrates, column charts are good for comparing values. This chart shows that all regions except the Midwest had sales increases in March. It also shows that the Northeast region (represented by the orange bars) had the highest overall sales for February and March, and that the West region (represented by the blue bars) had the highest sales for January.

- **Design the worksheet so Excel creates the chart you want**

  Once you have decided on the chart type that best conveys your meaning, you might want to arrange your rows and columns so that the chart data illustrates the points you want to make. In the figure, notice that the region with the highest revenues in March (Northeast) appears on the right. Serena arranged the data series in this order in the underlying worksheet, so that the chart would show the Northeast's revenues in the far-right column.

FIGURE K-1: Example of a column chart

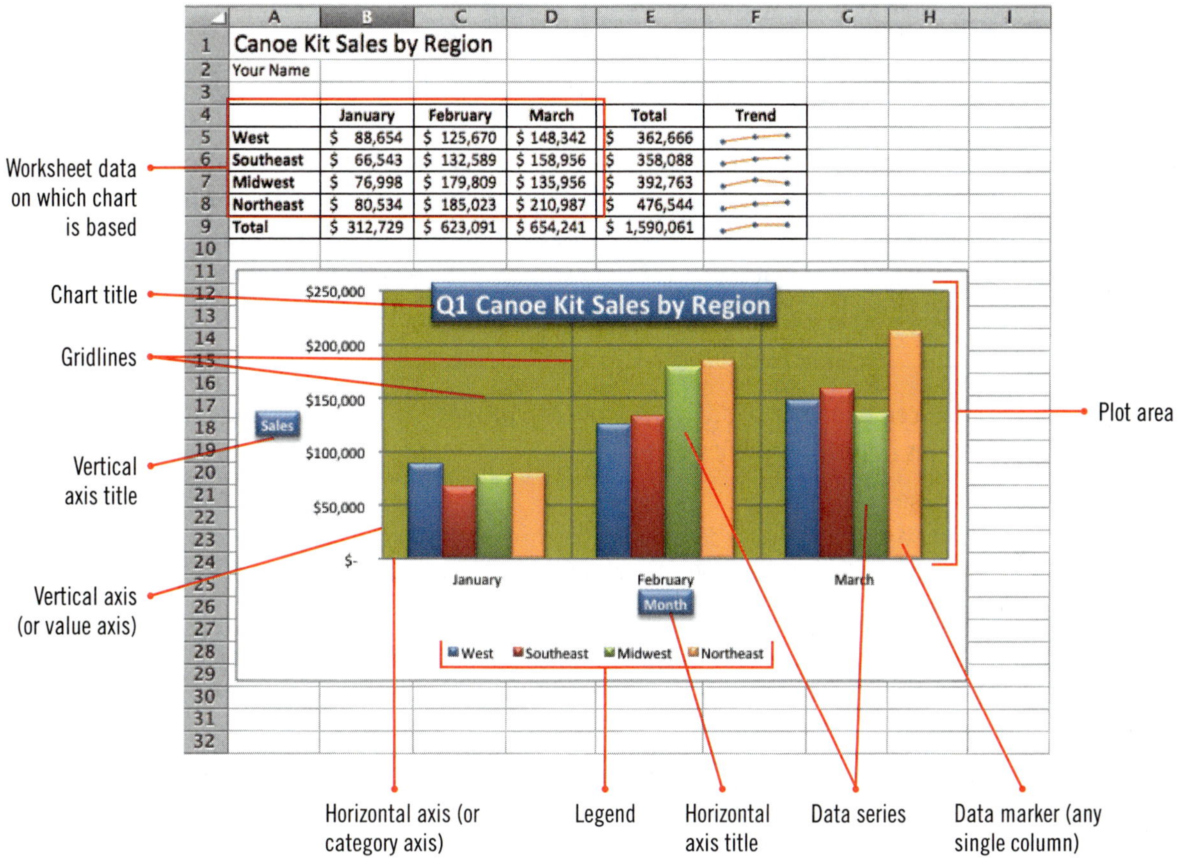

Worksheet data on which chart is based

Chart title

Gridlines

Vertical axis title

Vertical axis (or value axis)

Horizontal axis (or category axis)

Legend

Horizontal axis title

Data series

Data marker (any single column)

Plot area

TABLE K-1: Common chart types in Excel

chart type	description	example
Area	Shows relative importance of values over a period of time	
Bar	Compares values among individual items	
Column	Compares values across categories over time	
Line	Shows trends by category over time	
Pie	Describes the relationship of parts to the whole	
Radar	Shows changes in data or data frequency relative to a center point	
X Y (Scatter)	Shows the relationship between two kinds of related data	

UNIT
K
Excel 2011

Creating a Chart

You can create Excel charts from your worksheet data automatically. In a worksheet, you select the cells that contain the data you want to chart, then use commands in the Insert Chart group on the Charts tab to specify the chart type you want to add. Any changes you make to the worksheet data are automatically reflected in the chart. You can change the chart type to explore different options until you find the type that best illustrates your data. Serena has just compiled the first-quarter sales results for the Canoe Kit. She has a worksheet that shows sales for each month by region. You need to create a chart based on her worksheet data.

STEPS

1. **Start Excel, open the file K-1.xlsx from the location where you store your Data Files, then save it as K-Canoe Kit Sales by Region**

2. **Select the range A4:D8**
   The range A4:D8 contains the data you want to chart. Notice that you selected the row and column labels but not the column totals. When you select cells for most charts, you should avoid including totals.

3. **Click the Charts tab**
   The Insert Chart group on the Charts tab contains buttons for inserting common types of charts, including Column, Line, Pie, Bar, Area, Scatter, and Other. The Line chart type is good for showing trends in data over time.

TROUBLE

There are two Line buttons on the Charts tab; be sure to click the one in the Insert Chart group.

4. **Click the Line button 〰 in the Insert Chart group, as shown in Figure K-2**
   The Line chart menu opens and displays two subcategories, 2-D Line and 3-D Line. The thumbnails provide a visual guide for what each chart subtype looks like.

QUICK TIP

Depending on your screen resolution, your vertical (value) axis might show different values or numeric intervals.

5. **Click the Line option (first thumbnail under 2-D Line)**
   A line chart is inserted into the current worksheet, as shown in Figure K-3. The region names from the worksheet are on the chart's horizontal axis, and sales amounts are on the chart's vertical axis. Colored lines representing the sales data for January, February, and March appear in the chart. The blue border and sizing handles around the chart indicate that the chart is selected. Notice that the Chart Layout and Format tabs are available on the ribbon; these contextual tabs become available when a chart is selected. To select another chart type, simply click the button for the chart type you'd like to use. Excel will convert the existing chart type to the new selection.

6. **Click the Column button 📊, then click the 2-D Clustered Column option, as shown in Figure K-4**
   The chart in the worksheet changes to a clustered column chart, with three data series (blue, red, green) representing January, February, and March sales for each region. See Figure K-5.

7. **Click the Save button 💾 on the Standard toolbar**
   The chart is saved as part of the workbook file.

FIGURE K-2: Choosing a Line chart type

Charts tab

Line button

In Step 5, click the Line option

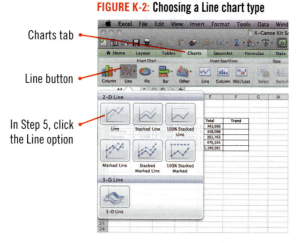

FIGURE K-3: Line chart in the worksheet

Chart Layout and Format tabs are available when chart is selected

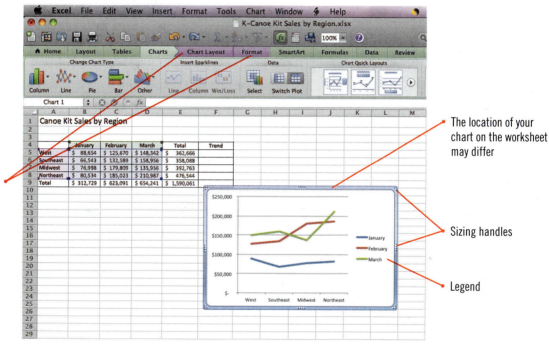

The location of your chart on the worksheet may differ

Sizing handles

Legend

FIGURE K-4: Column chart types

2-D Clustered Column option

Column button

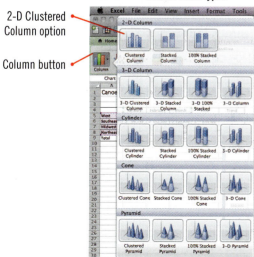

FIGURE K-5: Column chart inserted into worksheet

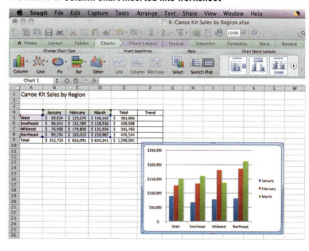

Excel 2011

Moving and Resizing a Chart and Chart Objects

You can easily move a chart if it obscures your worksheet data, and you can resize it if it is too large or too small. You can also move or resize many of the individual components of a chart—called **chart objects**—such as the chart background or the legend. To move a chart object, select it and drag it to a new location. To resize a chart object, drag one of its sizing handles. Note that some chart objects (such as the chart axis) cannot be moved, and that others (such as the chart title) cannot be resized by dragging. To improve the overall appearance of the worksheet, you decide to move the chart directly below the worksheet data and make it larger. You also decide to move the legend so that it is aligned with the top edge of the chart.

STEPS

1. If the chart is not selected, click the chart border to select it

2. Point to the top edge of the chart so that the pointer changes to ✛, drag the chart so that its upper-left corner is aligned with the upper-left corner of cell A11, then release the button

   The chart is now directly below the worksheet data. As you dragged the chart, a white box representing the chart moved with the pointer.

3. If necessary, scroll down until you can see row 29

   QUICK TIP
   If you make a mistake when moving or resizing a chart, click the Undo button on the Standard toolbar, then try again.

4. Position the pointer over the chart's lower-right sizing handle so that the pointer changes to ⬊, drag the sizing handle down so that the chart's lower-right corner is aligned with the lower-right corner of cell H29, then release the button

   The chart enlarges to the new dimensions. If you drag a corner sizing handle, you increase or decrease a chart's height and width simultaneously. To increase or decrease only the height or width of a chart, drag a side, top, or bottom sizing handle. Compare your screen with Figure K-6.

   QUICK TIP
   To delete a chart or chart object, select it, then press [delete].

5. Click the chart legend

   Sizing handles appear around the edge of the legend, indicating that it is selected. Note that the sizing handles on the legend—and on all chart objects—are circular at the legend corners and square on the border midpoints. This is different from the sizing handles on the chart itself, where they appear as groups of dots.

6. Point to any border of the legend (but not to a sizing handle) until the pointer changes to ✛, then drag the legend up to the position shown in Figure K-7

   The legend is now positioned to the right of the upper-right corner of the chart.

7. Save your changes to the worksheet

FIGURE K-6: Resizing a chart

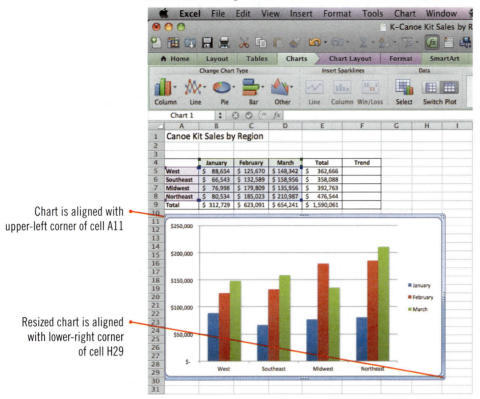

Chart is aligned with upper-left corner of cell A11

Resized chart is aligned with lower-right corner of cell H29

FIGURE K-7: Moving the legend

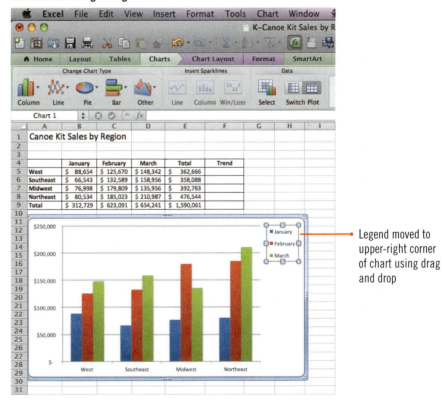

Legend moved to upper-right corner of chart using drag and drop

Applying Chart Layouts and Styles

When you create a chart, it has default layout and style settings for the chart type applied. A **chart layout** is a predefined arrangement of chart elements, such as the placement of the legend and the chart title. A **chart style** is a predefined set of chart colors and fills. Instead of modifying individual chart elements, such as moving the legend or changing the color of a data series, you can instantly change the way chart elements are positioned and whether certain elements are displayed or hidden by choosing a different layout. Chart layouts are available from the Chart Quick Layouts Gallery on the Charts tab. You can change fill colors and textures by choosing a chart style from the Chart Styles Gallery on the Charts tab. You can also get a different view of your data by reversing the rows and columns. You decide to experiment by switching the rows and columns of the chart to see the effect. You also want to improve the appearance of your chart by applying a different chart layout and style.

STEPS

1. **Click the Switch Plot button in the Data group (Help Tag reads "Plot series by row")**

   See Figure K-8. The chart now shows only three clusters of data series (instead of the original four), one for each month. Each data series now represents the revenue for each region (instead of each month), so there are four data points for each cluster instead of three. The horizontal axis labels now list the three months of the first quarter (instead of the regions). This view of the data shows more clearly the overall growth trend for each month.

2. **Point to the Chart Quick Layouts Gallery until the pop-up menu arrow appears, then click the pop-up menu arrow**

   The Chart Quick Layouts Gallery displays an assortment of thumbnails of different layouts. Some have gridlines, some have data labels, and a few have chart and axis titles. You want a layout that has a chart title, axis titles, and a legend.

3. **Click Layout 9**

   Your chart now has placeholder text for a chart title, a vertical axis title, and a horizontal axis title, along with the legend. You need to replace the placeholder text for these titles with appropriate text for your chart.

4. **Click Chart Title, then type Q1 Canoe Kit Sales by Region**

   As you type, the words "Chart Title" are replaced with "Q1 Canoe Kit Sales by Region."

5. **Click Axis Title in the vertical axis, then type Sales**

   The vertical axis label now reads "Sales," clarifying that each data series represents sales figures.

6. **Click Axis Title in the horizontal axis, then type Month**

   The horizontal axis label changes to "Month." The chart and axis titles make it easier to interpret the meaning of the chart. Compare your screen with Figure K-9.

7. **Point to the Chart Styles Gallery until the pop-up menu arrow appears, click , then click the second style in the fourth row**

   The new style is applied to the chart, as shown in Figure K-10. This style has a three-dimensional appearance and makes your chart more visually appealing.

8. **Save your changes**

FIGURE K-8: Chart rows and columns switched

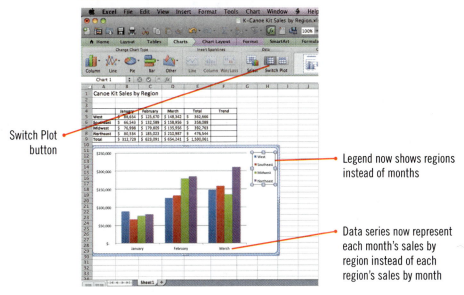

Switch Plot button

Legend now shows regions instead of months

Data series now represent each month's sales by region instead of each region's sales by month

FIGURE K-9: Chart with layout applied and customized chart axis titles

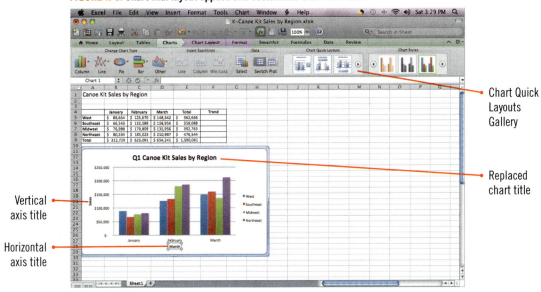

Chart Quick Layouts Gallery

Replaced chart title

Vertical axis title

Horizontal axis title

FIGURE K-10: Applying a chart style using the Chart Styles Gallery

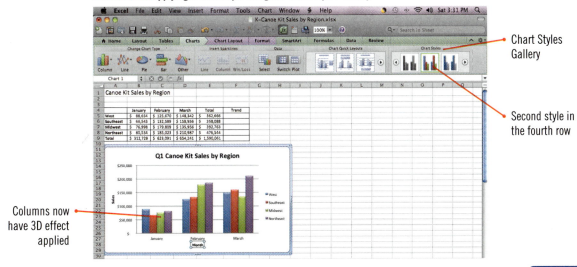

Chart Styles Gallery

Second style in the fourth row

Columns now have 3D effect applied

Customizing Chart Objects

When you create a chart, each chart object has default layout settings applied. For instance, the clustered column chart with the layout you applied positions the title above the chart and positions the legend to the right of the chart. You can easily change the positioning and attributes of individual chart objects by choosing from additional preset options on the Chart Layout tab, or by making custom choices in the Format dialog box. Chart elements that can be modified include the title, axis titles, legend, data labels, axes, gridlines, plot area, and data table. A **data table** in a chart is a grid containing the chart's underlying worksheet data, which is added below the x-axis in certain types of charts. You decide to position the chart title so that it is inside the plot area. You also want to position the legend at the bottom of the chart to make more room for the data series, and you change the orientation of the vertical axis title so that it is easier to read. You also decide to explore other options to improve the chart's appearance.

STEPS

1. **Click the Chart Layout tab**

   The Chart Layout tab contains buttons and commands for changing the layout of a selected chart. You use this tab to work with individual chart elements.

2. **Click the Chart Title button in the Labels group, then click Overlap Title at Top**

   The chart title is now positioned in the chart just above the tallest data series. This arrangement increases the size of the plot area without requiring you to enlarge the chart.

3. **Click the Axis Titles button in the Labels group, point to Vertical Axis Title, then click Horizontal Title**

   See Figure K-11. The vertical axis title changes from a vertical to a horizontal position.

   QUICK TIP

   A Format dialog box is available for every chart object; it offers many options beyond the presets available on the ribbon. To open the Format dialog box for any chart object, right-click it (or press [control] and click for a single button mouse), then click Format [name of the object] or select the object, click Format on the menu bar, then click Format [name of object].

4. **Click the Legend button , then click Legend at Bottom**

   The legend now appears below the chart, and the chart expands to fill the empty space on the right, as shown in Figure K-12.

5. **Click the Data Labels button in the Labels group, then click Outside End**

   Labels for each worksheet value in cells B5 through D8 now appear above each data marker. Unfortunately, the values are too big to fit in the chart and the labels overlap, making them look cluttered and difficult to read.

6. **Click , then click No Data Labels**

   The data labels are removed.

7. **Click the Gridlines button in the Axes group, point to Vertical Gridlines, then click Major Gridlines**

   Vertical gridlines now appear in the chart, enclosing the monthly sales for each region. This effect helps to visually separate each region's monthly sales.

   QUICK TIP

   Data tables are helpful when your chart contains data from another worksheet or location.

8. **Click the Data Table button in the Labels group, then click Data Table with Legend Key**

   See Figure K-13. A data table is inserted, with a legend in the first column that identifies the data series in each row. Data tables are helpful when you want to show both the chart and the underlying worksheet data. Because this worksheet already contains the data for the chart, you don't need the data table here; it makes the worksheet look cluttered.

9. **Click , click No Data Table, then save your changes**

FIGURE K-11: Chart with repositioned vertical axis title and chart title

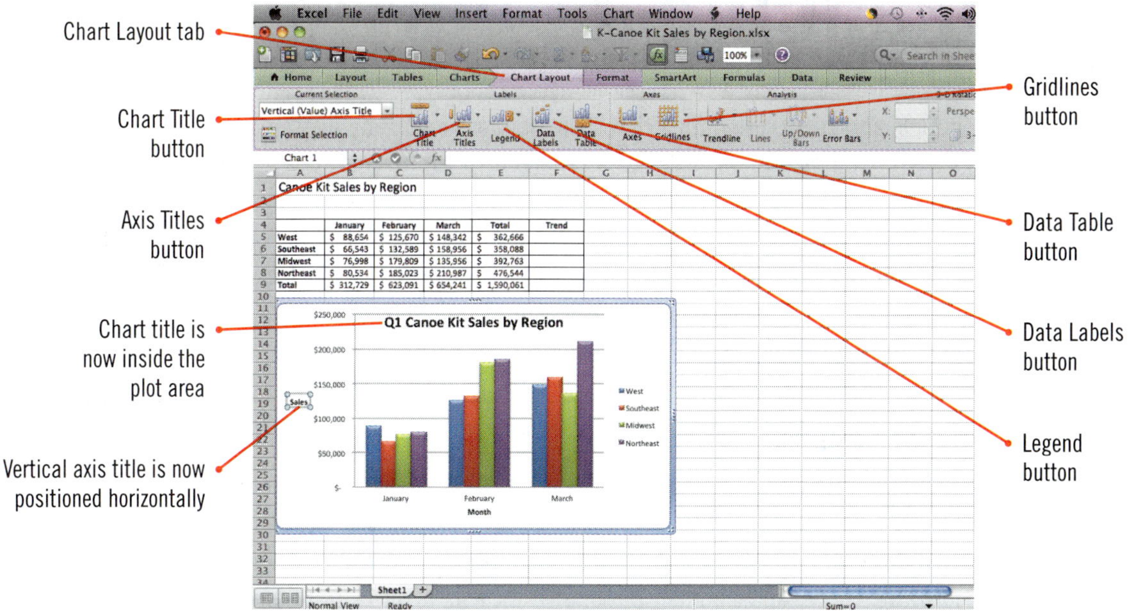

Chart Layout tab

Chart Title button

Axis Titles button

Chart title is now inside the plot area

Vertical axis title is now positioned horizontally

Gridlines button

Data Table button

Data Labels button

Legend button

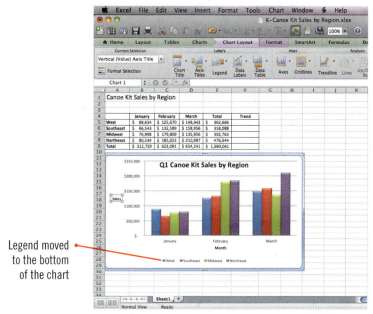

FIGURE K-12: Chart with legend in a different location

Legend moved to the bottom of the chart

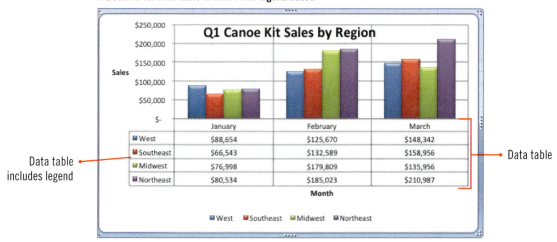

FIGURE K-13: Data table in chart with legend added

Data table includes legend

Data table

	January	February	March
West	$88,654	$125,670	$148,342
Southeast	$66,543	$132,589	$158,956
Midwest	$76,998	$179,809	$135,956
Northeast	$80,534	$185,023	$210,987

Enhancing a Chart

You can choose from a variety of styles and effects to improve the effectiveness of a chart and increase its visual appeal. In addition to using the Chart Layout tab to modify any selected chart object, you can choose from a variety of commands and galleries on the Format tab to make further enhancements and adjustments. For instance, you can apply a chart element style to a chart or axis title and then adjust the fill, outline, and shape effect to your liking. You can apply text styles to any text to make it stand out. You can also align and reposition multiple objects. To format an object, you first must select it. Serena asks you to change the color of the Northeast data series and to add visual effects to the chart and axis titles to make the chart more visually appealing.

STEPS

1. **Click the Format tab**

   The Format tab is active. You can use either the Format Series dialog box or the Format tab to apply special styles and effects to selected chart objects.

2. **Click any one of the purple Northeast data markers in the chart**

   Round sizing handles and a border surround all the data markers in the Northeast data series. Clicking a single data marker selects all the data markers in that series. You decide to change the selected data series color to orange.

   > **QUICK TIP**
   > You can also open the Format Data Series dialog box by double-clicking a data marker.

3. **Click the Format Selection button** 🖼 **in the Current Selection group on the Format tab**

   The Format Data Series dialog box opens, providing options you can select to enhance and change the appearance of the selected data marker. You need to adjust the Fill setting.

4. **Click Fill in the left pane, click the Solid tab if necessary, click the Color pop-up menu arrows, click the Accent 6 color, as shown in Figure K-14, then click OK**

   The Northeast data series color changes to orange and the Format Data Series dialog box closes.

5. **Click the chart title to select it, point to the Chart Element Styles Gallery until the pop-up menu arrow appears, then click the pop-up menu arrow** ⬇ **to open the gallery**

   The Chart Element Styles Gallery displays styles that you can apply to the selected chart title.

6. **Click the style shown in Figure K-15**

   The chart title is now formatted with a three-dimensional blue background and white font. You decide to add a special effect so that the title matches the style of the data series.

7. **Click the Effects button** ⬜ **in the Chart Element Styles group, point to Shadow, then click Outside Bottom in the Outer category (second option in the first row)**

   The chart title now has a shadow along its bottom edge, further enhancing the impression that it is three-dimensional.

8. **Click the vertical axis title (Sales), then apply the same chart element style as applied to the chart title in Step 6**

9. **Click the horizontal axis title (Month), apply the same chart element style as applied to the chart title and vertical axis title, then save the worksheet**

   Compare your screen with Figure K-16.

Using text styles in a chart

You can use text styles in Excel to create stylized text in your charts. The Text Styles Gallery provides a selection of preset text styles that you can apply to make text look exciting and eye-catching. To apply a text style, select the chart text you want to enhance, point to the Text Styles Gallery until the pop-up menu arrow appears, then click the pop-up menu arrow to open the gallery. If the Text Styles Gallery is not visible, click the Quick Styles button to display it. To apply a style from the gallery, click it. You can then use additional commands in the Text Styles group to further enhance the selected text.

FIGURE K-14: Format Data Series dialog box

Solid tab

Fill category

Accent 6 color

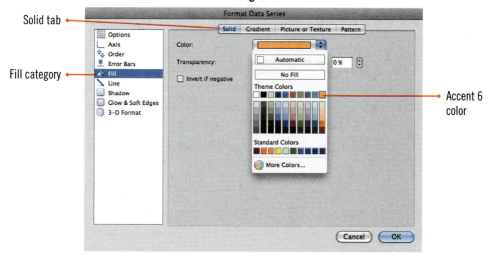

FIGURE K-15: Applying a chart element style to a chart object

Format tab

Chart Element Styles Gallery pop-up menu arrow

In Step 6, click this option

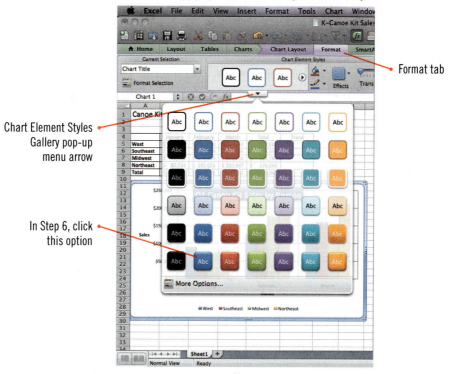

FIGURE K-16: Completed chart with formatting enhancements

Chart title has style applied

Axis titles have style applied

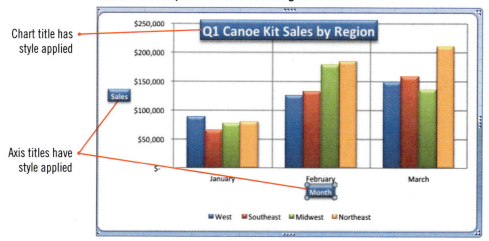

Creating a Pie Chart

Column charts are great for comparing values across categories, but they are not very useful for comparing percentages or parts to a whole. For instance, the column chart does not convey the West region's percentage of total first-quarter sales. A pie chart is an effective tool for comparing the relative values of parts to a whole. Just like any other type of chart, you can add it to a worksheet, or you can add it on a separate chart sheet. A **chart sheet** is a sheet in a workbook that contains only a chart; it contains no worksheet cells.  Serena wants you to create a pie chart on a separate chart sheet that compares total first-quarter revenues of the Canoe Kit by region.

STEPS

1. **Select the range A5:A8, press and hold ⌘, then select the range E5:E8**

   You selected two nonadjacent ranges (the region names and total first-quarter sales for each region); this is the only worksheet data you want reflected in the pie chart. You want to create a pie chart that shows each region's percentage of total sales.

2. **Click the Charts tab, click the Pie button ⬤ in the Insert Chart group, then click the 3-D Pie option**

   See Figure K-17. A 3D style pie chart now appears in the worksheet and covers part of the column chart. The pie chart shows that the purple pie wedge (representing the Northeast region) is slightly bigger than the others, and the blue pie wedge (representing the West region) is the smallest. You decide to move the pie chart to a new chart sheet in the workbook, so that it can be viewed separately from the column chart.

3. **Click Chart on the menu bar, then click Move Chart**

   The Move Chart dialog box opens.

4. **Click the New sheet option button, type Q1 Canoe Kit Sales % in the New sheet text box, as shown in Figure K-18, then click OK**

   The pie chart moves to a new chart sheet called "Q1 Canoe Kit Sales %".

5. **Point to the Chart Quick Layouts Gallery until the pop-up menu arrow appears, click [▼], then click Layout 1**

   Each pie slice in the chart now contains a label for the region and the region's percentage of total sales. A chart title placeholder is displayed above the chart.

6. **Click the chart title placeholder, then type Q1 Canoe Kit Sales by Region**

7. **Click Northeast on the purple pie slice and verify that the labels on all the slices are now selected**

   When you click to select one data label, all data labels are selected.

8. **Click the Home tab, click the Font Size menu arrow in the Font group, then click 20**

   The data labels are now larger and easier to read.

9. **Click File on the menu bar, then click Print**

   A preview of the chart sheet is displayed in the Print dialog box, as shown in Figure K-19. Notice that the orientation is set to Landscape, the default setting for chart sheets.

10. **Click Cancel to close the Print dialog box, then save your changes**

Two cell ranges selected as data to be charted

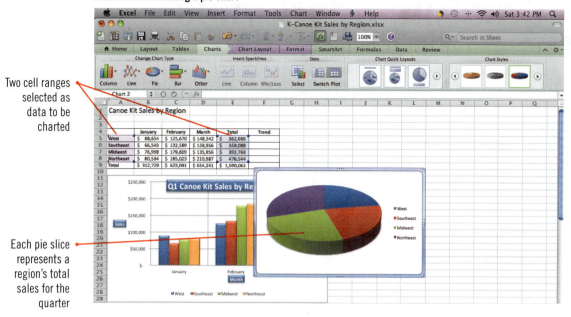

Each pie slice represents a region's total sales for the quarter

New sheet option button

Name of new chart sheet

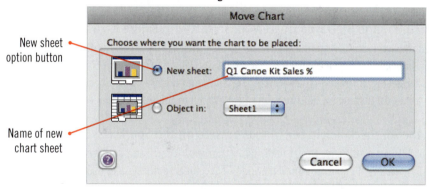

Chart title

Landscape orientation is indicated by longer width than height in the preview

Data labels show region name and percentage of that region's sales

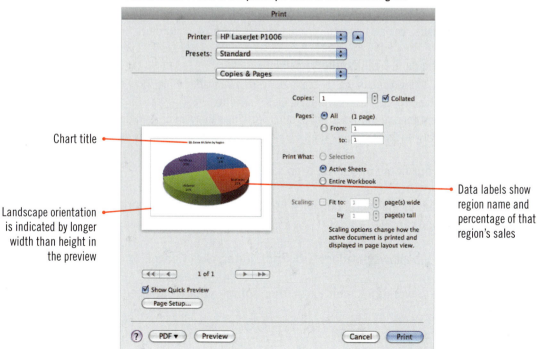

Creating Sparklines

In addition to charts, you can also add sparklines to a worksheet to communicate patterns or trends visually. **Sparklines** are tiny charts that fit in one cell and illustrate trends in selected cells. There are three types of sparklines you can add to a worksheet. A **line sparkline** is a miniature line chart that is ideal for showing a trend over a period of time. A **column sparkline** is a tiny column chart that includes a bar for each cell in a selected range. A **win/loss sparkline** shows only two types of bars: one for gains and one for losses. Table K-2 provides descriptions and examples of sparkline types. You should place sparklines close to the cells containing the data they illustrate. You decide to create sparklines next to your worksheet data to illustrate sales trends in the quarter for each of the regions.

STEPS

1. Click the Sheet1 sheet tab, then click cell F5

This is where you will insert a sparkline for the range B5:D5, the data series for the West region sales from January to March.

2. Click the Charts tab, then click the Line button 🗠 in the Insert Sparklines group

The Insert Sparklines dialog box opens. You need to select the cells for which you want to create a sparkline: the range B5:D5.

3. Select the range B5:D5, compare your screen with Figure K-20, then click OK

Cell F5 now contains a sparkline that starts in the lower left of the cell and slants upward to the upper-right corner, indicating an increase from cell B5 to C5 to D5. At a glance, the sparkline communicates that sales increased steadily from January to March. The Sparklines tab now appears on the ribbon. You'll use this tab to add markers on the line to indicate values for each cell in the selected range.

4. Click the All check box in the Markers group on the Sparklines tab

The sparkline now displays three small square markers. The left marker represents the West region's January sales (B5), the middle marker represents the West region's February sales (C5), and the far-right marker represents the West region's March sales (D5). You want to change the sparkline to a different color.

5. Point to the Format Style Gallery until the pop-up menu arrow appears, click ▼, then click Sparkline Style Accent 6, Darker 25% (last style in second row)

The sparkline color is now orange, and the sparkline markers are blue.

6. Drag the cell F5 fill handle to cell F9

Cells F6:F9 now contain orange sparklines with blue markers that show sales trends for the other regions, as well as the total sales, as shown in Figure K-21. Notice that the sparkline in cell F7 shows a downward trend from the second to third marker. All other sparklines show an upward direction. You can see how sparklines make it easy to see at a glance the sales performance of each region for the quarter.

7. Enter your name in cell A2, then save your changes

8. Click File on the menu bar, click Print, then preview the worksheet in the Print dialog box

9. If your lab allows printing, click Print; if not, click Cancel

10. Close the workbook, quit Excel, then submit your completed worksheet to your instructor

Working with Charts

FIGURE K-20: Insert Sparklines dialog box

Charts tab

Line button

In Step 3, select the range B5:D5

Range you selected appears here

FIGURE K-21: Completed worksheet with sparklines added

Sparklines tab

This sparkline style is applied to sparklines in the range F5:F9

All Markers check box

Sparklines show upward trend for each region except the Midwest

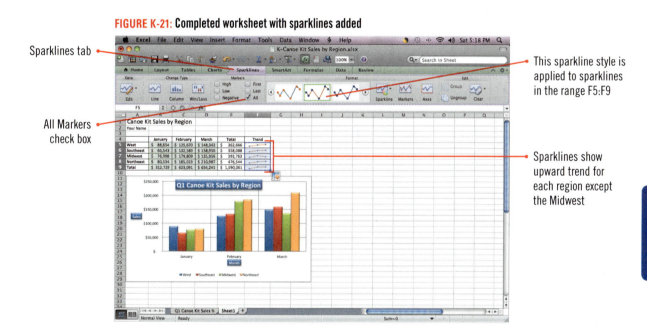

TABLE K-2: Sparkline types and their uses

sparkline type	used for	example
Line	Showing trends over time	
Column	Comparing values over time	
Win/Loss	Showing gains and/or losses over time	

Practice

Concepts Review

Label each chart element shown in Figure K-22.

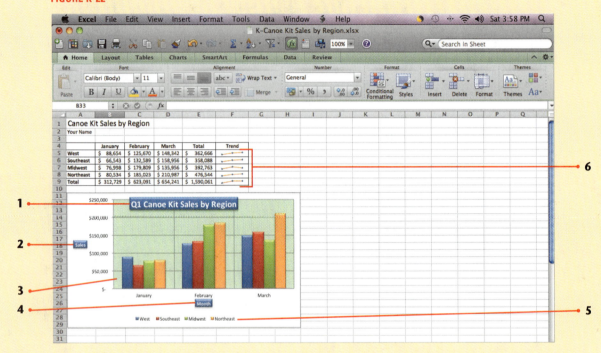

Match each chart type with its description.

7. **Line chart**	**a.** Shows trends by category over time
8. **Pie chart**	**b.** Compares values across categories
9. **Area chart**	**c.** Shows relative importance of values over a period of time
10. **Column chart**	**d.** Describes the relationship of parts to a whole

Select the best answer from the list of choices.

11. A symbol that represents a single data point on a chart is called a(n):

    a. Data bar.

    b. Data marker.

    c. Data series.

    d. Axis.

12. Which of the following axis titles would most likely be shown on a vertical axis in a chart?

    a. Years

    b. Costs

    c. Months

    d. Countries

13. Which of the following tabs on the ribbon do you use to add a data table to your chart?

    a. Charts

    b. Chart Layout

    c. Format

    d. Tables

14. You just finished a 10-week math class, in which you had a quiz every week. You want to create a chart that shows each quiz score for each week. Which of the following charts would *not* be a good choice for your chart?

    a. Pie chart

    b. Bar chart

    c. Column chart

    d. Line chart

15. Where should you place a sparkline in a worksheet?

    a. In a chart below its underlying data

    b. In a separate chart sheet, away from its underlying data

    c. In a single cell adjacent to the cells containing its underlying data

    d. In a group of cells below its underlying data

Skills Review

1. Understand and plan a chart.

    a. Open the file K-2.xlsx from the location where you store your Data Files, then save it as **K-Recycling Revenue**.

    b. Examine the worksheet data, then consider what Excel chart types would best present this type of information.

    c. Is the worksheet designed in such a way that it will be easy to create a chart? Why or why not?

2. Create a chart.

    a. Select the range A4:D9.

    b. Display the tab on the ribbon that contains commands for inserting charts.

    c. Insert a 3-D Clustered Column chart.

    d. Save your changes to the workbook.

3. Move and resize a chart and chart objects.

    a. Drag the chart so that the upper-left corner of the chart is aligned with the upper-left corner of cell A12.

    b. Use the lower-right corner sizing handle to align the lower-right corner of the chart with the lower-right corner of cell G28.

    c. Move the legend so that its top edge aligns with the top of the tallest data marker in the chart.

    d. Save your changes.

4. Apply chart layouts and styles.

    a. Use a button on the Charts tab to reverse the columns and rows and get a different view of the data. Examine the chart and identify what new meaning this new structure conveys.

    b. Apply the Layout 3 chart layout to the chart.

    c. Replace the placeholder chart title with **Recycling Revenue, 2011-2013**.

    d. Apply the multicolor chart style with the black background to the chart.

    e. Save your changes.

5. Customize chart objects.

    a. Display the Chart Layout tab.

    b. Add a horizontal axis title to the chart below the axis. Replace the placeholder axis title with **Years**.

    c. Add a vertical axis rotated title. Replace the placeholder axis title with **Revenue**.

Skills Review (continued)

d. Add major gridlines for the vertical axis.

e. Save your changes.

6. Enhance a chart.

   a. Display the Format tab.

   b. Select one of the West data markers in the chart.

   c. Open the Format Data Series dialog box.

   d. In the Format Data Series dialog box, select the Fill category, specify a solid fill, choose Accent 6 from the Theme Colors, then click OK to close the dialog box.

   e. Select the chart title, open the Chart Element Styles Gallery, then apply the last option in the fifth row to the chart title.

   f. Apply the same chart element style used in Step e to the vertical axis title and the horizontal axis title.

   g. Save your changes.

7. Create a pie chart.

   a. Select cells A5:A9, then press and hold ⌘ while selecting cells E5:E9.

   b. Insert a pie chart, choosing the 3-D Exploded pie option.

   c. Move the pie chart to a new sheet in the workbook. Name the sheet **Revenue by Region**.

   d. Apply the Layout 6 chart layout to the chart.

   e. Increase the font size of the percentage amounts on the pie slices to 24.

   f. Click the chart title placeholder, then type **Recycling Revenue by Region, 2011-2013**.

   g. Save your changes.

8. Create sparklines.

   a. Click the Sheet1 sheet tab to return to the worksheet.

   b. Add a line sparkline to cell F5 that is based on the data range B5:D5.

   c. Specify to add data markers to the sparkline.

   d. Apply the Sparkline Style Dark #5 to the sparkline. (*Hint.* This style is located in the fifth row, fifth column.)

   e. Use the fill handle to copy the sparkline in cell F5 to the range F6:F10.

   f. Enter your name in cell A30. Save your changes.

   g. Preview the worksheet in the Print dialog box. Change the scaling settings to Fit to one page wide by one page tall, then save your changes. Compare your completed worksheet and chart sheet with Figures K-23 and K-24.

   h. Close the workbook, quit Excel, then submit your completed workbook to your instructor.

FIGURE K-23

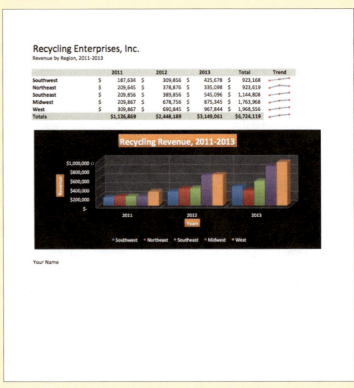

FIGURE K-24

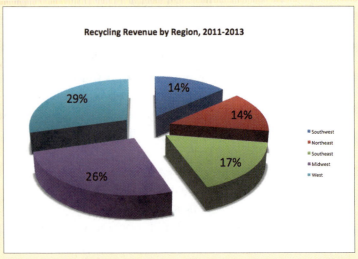

Independent Challenge 1

You work for a landscaping services company called Landscapes for Good Living, located in the Midwest. The company offers landscaping services, including brick paving, landscape design, sodding and seeding, landscape lighting, and irrigation. Frank Langdon, the general manager, has created a worksheet that contains revenue data for the five categories of services that the company offers. He has asked you to create a chart using the worksheet data to show the results for each quarter.

a. Open the file K-3.xlsx from the location where you store your Data Files, then save it as **K-Landscape Revenue**.

b. Create a stacked area chart based on the data in the range A4:E9.

c. Move the chart so that it is positioned directly below the worksheet data, then enlarge it so that the lower-right corner of the chart is aligned with cell G30.

d. Switch the rows and columns, so that May, June, July, and August are on the x-axis.

e. Apply the Layout 3 chart layout to the chart, then apply a chart style that you like.

f. Replace the chart title placeholder with **Revenue, May-August**.

g. Add a rotated vertical axis title **Revenue**. Add a horizontal axis title with the text **Months**. Apply a chart element style that you like to the vertical and horizontal axis titles.

h. Apply a chart element style that you like to the chart title.

i. Add line sparklines to the range G5:G10. Include all markers in the sparklines. Apply a sparkline style of your choosing.

j. Create a 2-D Exploded Pie chart by selecting the noncontiguous ranges A5:A9 and F5:F9. Move the pie chart to a separate chart sheet named **Revenue by Service Type**. Apply the Layout 2 chart layout to the pie chart. Change the chart title to **Revenue by Service Type**. Increase the font size of the percentage amount labels on each pie slice to 20.

k. Open Sheet1, then type your name in cell A32. Format the worksheet data and worksheet title using fonts, font sizes, borders, alignments, and shading to make the worksheet look professional and easy to understand. Choose formatting options that are complementary to the colors and style of the chart.

l. Preview the Sheet1 worksheet in Print Preview. Change the scaling settings to Fit to one page wide by one page tall, then save your changes. Figure K-25 shows one possible solution for the worksheet and area chart.

FIGURE K-25

Landscapes for Good Living, Inc.
Revenue, May-August

	May	June	July	August	Total	Trend
Brick Paving	$65,423	$90,456	$95,934	$25,987	$277,800	
Landscape Design	$50,927	$75,874	$98,567	$145,769	$371,137	
Sodding & Seeding	$20,978	$48,765	$65,345	$96,542	$231,630	
Landscape Lighting	$17,645	$35,645	$48,763	$15,432	$117,485	
Irrigation	$50,987	$79,867	$54,323	$32,312	$217,489	
Total	$205,960	$330,607	$362,932	$316,042	$1,215,541	

Revenue, May-August

Your Name

Advanced Challenge Exercise

- Open the Revenue by Service Type chart sheet.
- Click one of the data labels on the pie chart (such as 10%) to select all the data labels.
- Click the Format tab, point to the Text Styles Gallery until the pop-up menu arrow appears, click the pop-up menu arrow, then click the third option in the second row.
- Select the legend, then increase the font size of the legend font to 14.
- Click View on the menu bar, click Header and Footer, click Customize Footer, type your name in the Right section, click OK, then click OK.

m. Save your changes, then preview the chart sheet in the Print dialog box. Close the workbook, quit Excel, then submit your completed workbook to your instructor.

Independent Challenge 2

You work for Thelma Watson, the general manager of an online bakery retailer. Thelma has created an Excel worksheet showing product sales for June and the revenue generated by each product category. She has asked you to create a chart in the worksheet that shows the percentage of total sales each category represents.

a. Open the file K-4.xlsx from the location where you store your Data Files, then save it as **K-June Product Sales**.

b. Create a pie chart using the data in the range A5:B9. Choose the 3-D Pie chart type.

c. Move the chart below the worksheet data.

d. Resize the chart so that its lower-right corner is aligned with the lower-right corner of cell G29.

e. Change the value in cell B9 (the number of pies sold) to **5,275**. Observe the change in the chart.

f. Apply the Layout 1 chart layout to the chart. Apply a chart style that you like.

g. Display the Chart Layout tab, select Chart Area in the Current Selection pop-up menu if necessary, then click the Format Selection button to open the Format Chart Area dialog box. Choose a solid fill that you think will look good. Experiment by choosing different settings, then click OK to close the dialog box to view the settings. Repeat this process until you are satisfied with how the chart area looks.

h. Increase the font size of the labels and percentage amounts in each pie slice to 12.

i. Format the worksheet data and worksheet title using fonts, font sizes, borders, alignments, and shading to make the worksheet look professional, visually pleasing, and easy to understand. Choose formatting options that are complementary to the colors and style of the chart. Make any other formatting enhancements to the chart and to the worksheet data to make it attractive and more professional looking. Enter your name in cell A31 in the worksheet.

j. Save your work, then preview the worksheet and chart in the Print dialog box. Close the workbook, quit Excel, then submit your completed workbook to your instructor.

Independent Challenge 3

You work for Stephen Briggs, the manager of an art gallery. In September, the gallery opened an exhibit of paintings from a private collector. The paintings included never-before-seen masterpieces by several famous artists. Gallery attendance increased dramatically in that month due to the high public interest in the exhibit and a strong marketing campaign. Stephen is preparing to meet with the gallery's board of directors to discuss the increased attendance. He has asked you to create a chart that shows the number of people who visited the gallery from May through September. He also needs the chart to show a breakdown of children, adults, and seniors who attended. The data you need to create the chart has already been put into a worksheet.

a. Open the file K-5.xlsx from the location where you store your Data Files, then save it as **K-Gallery Visitors**. Enter your name in cell A9.

b. Create a 2D line chart of all three customer categories during the months May through September. Choose the 2-D Marked Line chart type. Choose a chart style that you like.

c. Move the chart to a new chart sheet in the workbook. Name the chart sheet **Gallery Visitors, May Sept**.

d. Apply the Layout 9 chart layout to the chart. Change the chart title to **Gallery Visitors, May-Sept**.

e. Add minor vertical gridlines to the chart. Add an appropriate vertical axis title that is rotated, then add an appropriate horizontal axis title.

f. Apply a solid color fill to the plot area, choosing a color you think looks good. (*Hint*: To select the plot area, open the Chart Layout tab. In the Current Selection group, click the pop-up menu arrow next to Chart Area, and click Plot Area. Then click the Format Selection button to open the Format Plot Area dialog box and specify a fill color.)

Independent Challenge 3 (continued)

g. Apply a chart element style of your choosing to the chart title, axis titles, and legend. Figure K-26 shows one possible example of the completed chart.

FIGURE K-26

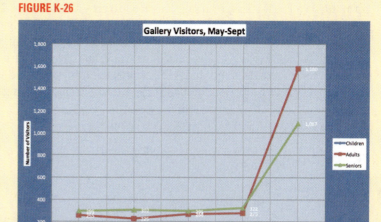

Advanced Challenge Exercise

- Switch to the Sheet1 worksheet that contains the chart data. Enter **Trend** in cell H3. Notice that the label you entered is formatted like the label in cell G3.
- Click cell H4, click the Charts tab, click the Column button in the Insert Sparklines group, select the range B4:F4, then click OK. Notice the column sparkline that appears in cell H4.
- Use the fill handle in cell H4 to copy the column sparkline in cell H4 to the range H5:H7.

h. Save your changes, preview the worksheet and chart sheet, close the workbook, then quit Excel. Submit your completed workbook to your instructor.

Real Life Independent Challenge

Creating a personal budget is a great way to keep your finances in order. In this Real Life Independent Challenge, you will create a personal budget for monthly expenses. For the purposes of this exercise, imagine that you earn $2,500 per month. Your budget needs to include categories of expenses and the amounts for each expense. The total expenses in the worksheet must add up to $2,500. Once you enter all your monthly expenses in the worksheet, you will then create a pie chart that shows the percentage of each individual expense.

a. Start a blank Excel workbook, and save it as **K-My Budget** in the location where you store your Data Files.
b. Enter **My Budget** in cell A1. Format the title so that it stands out. Enter your name in cell A2.
c. Enter the label **Expense** in cell A3, and enter the label **Amount** in cell B3.
d. Enter the following labels for the expenses in cells A4:A12: **Housing**, **Utilities**, **Car Payment**, **Insurance**, **Student Loans**, **Food**, **Entertainment**, **Gas**, **Savings**.
e. Enter appropriate amounts for each expense in cells B4:B12.
f. When you have entered all your expenses in the worksheet, enter the label **Total** in cell A13. Enter a formula in cell B13 that totals all the expense amounts in cells B4:B12. If the returning value in the formula cell does not add up to $2,500, then adjust the numbers in your budget so that the total adds up to $2,500.
g. Insert a pie chart based on the data in your chart. (*Hint*: Remember not to include the Total row when you select the data; select only the labels and expense amounts.) Choose any pie chart option that you like. Move the chart so that it is located below the worksheet data.
h. Apply a chart layout and chart style that you like. If the chart layout that you choose does not include a chart title, add one to the chart using the appropriate options on the Chart Layout tab. Replace the chart title placeholder with the title **My Monthly Expenses**.
i. Save your changes, preview the worksheet with the chart, close the file, then quit Excel. Submit your completed workbook to your instructor.

Visual Workshop

Open the Data File K-6.xlsx, then save it as **K-Charity Challenge Results** in the location where you store your Data Files. Make formatting changes to the worksheet so that it looks like Figure K-27, then add the two charts so that they match the figure, using the commands and techniques you learned in this unit and previous units. You will need to make formatting changes to both charts so that they match the figure. Enter your name in cell A3 as shown. (*Hint*: You will need to merge and center the ranges A1:G1, A2:G2, and A3:G3 so that the company name, worksheet title, and your name match the figure.) Save your changes, preview the worksheet and charts, close the file, then quit Excel. Submit your completed workbook to your instructor.

FIGURE K-27

Haskell-Barnes Insurance, Inc.
Employee Charity Challenge Results

Your Name

	2012	2013	Total	Trend
San Francisco	$ 5,287	$ 5,026	$ 10,313	
Chicago	$ 5,845	$ 6,248	$ 12,093	
Boston	$ 4,576	$ 6,542	$ 11,118	
New York	$ 5,324	$ 7,543	$ 12,867	
Los Angeles	$ 6,342	$ 9,087	$ 15,429	
Total Revenue	$ 27,374	$ 34,446	$ 61,820	

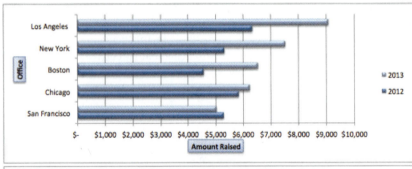

Creating a Presentation

Files You Will Need:

L-1.pptx
L-2.pptx
L-3.pptx

PowerPoint is a **presentation graphics program** that allows you to create dynamic slide shows, which are made up of on-screen pages called **slides**. You can select from an array of templates and themes, and you can add media such as photographs, clip art, sound, and video. PowerPoint also has features that convert ordinary text into stunning graphics. You can create handouts, notes, and outlines to augment the presentation and ensure its success when delivering it to an audience. Once your presentation is complete, you can show it on a computer or video projector, burn it to a CD, or publish it to a Web page. Karen Rivera, marketing director for Outdoor Designs, has asked you to create a presentation to educate the company's sales reps on this year's product line. The presentation will name each product line to better brand it to customers.

OBJECTIVES

View a presentation

Use a theme

Enter text on a slide

Format text

Add a text box

Create SmartArt

Add a header and footer

Print handouts

Viewing a Presentation

PowerPoint includes several different ways to view a presentation. When you start PowerPoint, the workspace opens by default in **Normal view** and is divided into three areas that allow you to concentrate on specific information. The largest area, the **Slide pane**, shows the full layout of the selected slide. To the left side of the Slide pane is the **Slides and Outline pane**. It contains the **Slides tab** and **Outline tab**, which show slide thumbnails and text-only hierarchical versions of the slides, respectively, and are useful for navigating through the presentation. The third area in Normal view is the **notes pane** at the bottom of the window, where you input text relevant to a specific slide; you can use these notes as part of your audience handouts or as reference notes during your presentation. You can also switch to other views. **Slide Sorter view** shows thumbnails of the entire presentation across the workspace and is very useful for reordering and deleting slides. To preview a presentation, you can switch to **Slide Show** to view the slide show as your audience will see it. PowerPoint also includes a dedicated **Notes Page view**, which displays a large preview of the slide on the top half of the page and speaker notes on the bottom half of the page; **Presenter view**, a view for practicing and delivering presentations; and three Master views for working with recurring elements within a presentation, such as headers and footers. Before you get started using PowerPoint, you view a presentation from an installed template to become familiar with the workspace.

STEPS

QUICK TIP

If the PowerPoint icon is not on the Dock, click the Finder icon on the Dock, click Applications in the Finder window, locate and click Microsoft Office 2011, then double-click Microsoft PowerPoint.

1. **Click the Microsoft PowerPoint icon 🅟 on the Dock**

   The PowerPoint Presentation Gallery opens, as shown in Figure L-1. You want to open an installed template.

2. **Under Templates in the left pane, click Presentations, in the middle pane click Introducing PowerPoint 2011, then click Choose**

   The presentation opens in Normal view and is titled Presentation1. See Figure L-2. Scroll bars in each pane allow you to move within the sections of the workspace. The status bar includes buttons for switching among the three most commonly used views: Normal view, Slide Sorter view, and Slide Show. The notes pane is where you can add notes to remind you of important points about the slide for use when presenting a slide show.

3. **Click the Next Slide button ⬇ in the Slide pane**

   Slide 2 becomes the active slide. You can move to the next or previous slides by clicking the Next Slide button ⬇ or Previous Slide button ⬆, or by pressing ▼ or ▲, respectively, on the keyboard.

TROUBLE

Depending on your computer's display settings, you may not see ≣ in the left pane. Your tabs may be identified as Slides and Outline. If this is the case, click the Outline tab.

4. **Click the Outline tab ≣, then click anywhere in the text for Slide 4**

   You can also move to a slide by clicking it in the Slides tab or in the Outline tab. The presentation appears as a text outline in the Outline tab. Viewing a presentation in this form makes it easy to read and move text.

5. **Click the Slide Sorter View button ⊞ on the status bar**

   The view changes to Slide Sorter view, as shown in Figure L-3. The slides are arranged in rows across the window. The currently selected slide, Slide 4, is outlined with an orange box. To move a slide, click and hold the pointer on the selected slide, and then drag it to its new location. You can also switch to a different view using the View option on the menu bar.

6. **Click Slide 1, then click the Slide Show button ⬛ on the status bar**

   The currently selected slide fills the screen.

QUICK TIP

Pressing [esc] while in Slide Show returns the presentation to the previous view.

7. **Press [return] until you reach the end of the presentation**

   The slide show advances. After the last slide of the presentation, pressing [return] returns to the last view selected. In this example, it's Slide Sorter view.

8. **Click File on the menu bar, then click Close**

   The Presentation1.pptx file closes, with PowerPoint still open and running.

FIGURE L-1: PowerPoint Presentation Gallery

In Step 2, click Presentations

In Step 2, click this template

Choose button

FIGURE L-2: Presentation template open in Normal view

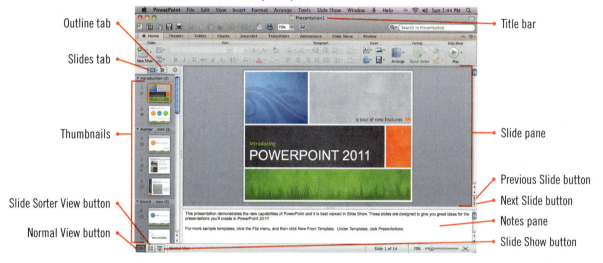

Outline tab

Slides tab

Thumbnails

Slide Sorter View button

Normal View button

Title bar

Slide pane

Previous Slide button

Next Slide button

Notes pane

Slide Show button

FIGURE L-3: Viewing a presentation in Slide Sorter view

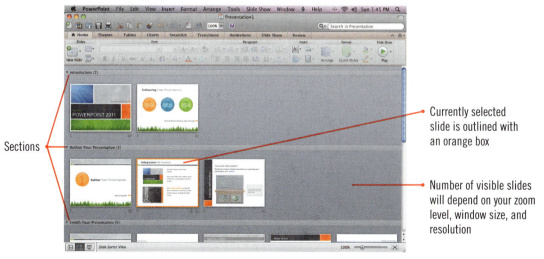

Sections

Currently selected slide is outlined with an orange box

Number of visible slides will depend on your zoom level, window size, and resolution

Navigating in Slide Show

When you're in Slide Show, you can advance to the next slide in a slide show by pressing [return], clicking the screen, or by pressing [page down], [spacebar], [down arrow], [right arrow], or [N]. To go to the previous slide in the slide show, press [left arrow], [up arrow], or [P]. To move to a specific slide during a slide show, right-click the screen, point to Go to Slide, and then click the slide you want to see. To exit the slide show and return to the previous view at any time during the presentation, press [esc].

Creating a Presentation

Using a Theme

When you create a new presentation, you need to consider how the slide show will help convey your message. Even the most interesting subject matter can be lost on an audience if the visual presentation is monotonous or overpowering. PowerPoint themes can give a distinctive look to the text, bullets, background colors, and graphics in a presentation. Using a theme is a big time-saver and immediately adds a professional touch to any presentation. You can apply a theme when you create a new presentation, and/or you can change the theme after creating one. It is also easy to customize themes by changing the background, colors, or fonts, giving you a great deal of flexibility while developing your presentation.  You are ready to create the presentation Karen requested, and you begin by selecting a theme and changing its background style.

STEPS

1. **Click File on the menu bar, then click New Presentation**

   A new, blank presentation opens on your computer screen.

2. **Click the Themes tab on the ribbon, point to the Themes Gallery until the pop-up menu appears, then click the pop-up menu arrow** [▼]

   The **Themes Gallery** opens, as shown in Figure L-4. Here you can find themes used in the open presentation, any custom themes you have created, and all built-in themes on this computer. At the bottom of the gallery, you can browse your computer for additional themes. The Themes group on the ribbon also contains the Save Theme button ![button] to save themes you create (either from scratch or from changes you make to existing themes).

   > **QUICK TIP**
   >
   > Themes are listed in alphabetical order after White and Black in the Built-In category.

3. **Scroll down, then click the Pushpin theme**

   The Pushpin theme is applied to the new presentation.

4. **Click File on the menu bar, click Save As, type L-Product Branding in the Save As text box, navigate to the location where you store your Data Files, then click Save**

   The Save As dialog box closes and the presentation is saved to the designated location. Although you like the Pushpin theme, you decide you want a more subtle look for the presentation.

   > **QUICK TIP**
   >
   > To apply a theme to two or more slides but not the entire presentation, select the slides in the Slide pane in Normal view or in Slide Sorter view, open the Themes Gallery, then select the theme you'd like to apply to the selected slides. However, keep in mind that too many themes in a single presentation can be visually overwhelming and diminish the presentation's effectiveness.

5. **Open the Themes Gallery, then click the Hardcover theme**

   The Hardcover theme is applied to the presentation, as shown in Figure L-5. When you point to a theme, its name appears in a Help Tag. You want to explore how to customize this theme to add your own personal touch.

6. **Click the Background button ![button] in the Theme Options group**

   The Background menu opens, displaying thumbnails of the background options for the Hardcover theme.

7. **Click Style 10 (the second option in the third row), then save your changes**

   The Style 10 background is applied to the presentation, as shown in Figure L-6.

FIGURE L-4: Viewing the Themes Gallery

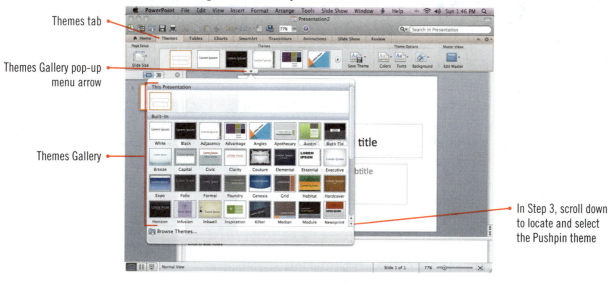

Themes tab

Themes Gallery pop-up menu arrow

Themes Gallery

In Step 3, scroll down to locate and select the Pushpin theme

FIGURE L-5: Hardcover theme applied to presentation

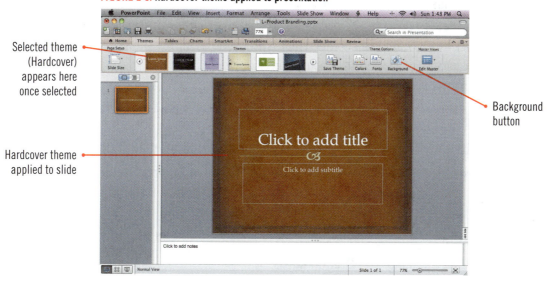

Selected theme (Hardcover) appears here once selected

Background button

Hardcover theme applied to slide

FIGURE L-6: Style 10 background applied to presentation

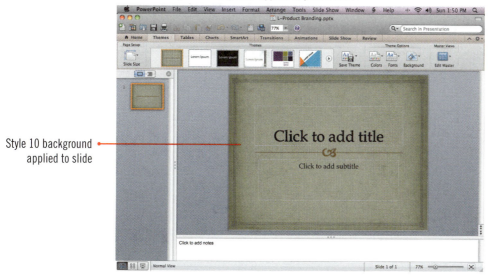

Style 10 background applied to slide

Entering Text on a Slide

You can add text to a slide in the Slide pane or in the Outline tab. Working in the Slide pane shows you exactly how the text will look on the slide, while Outline view can be useful when you have a lot of text to edit and rearrange among several slides. When you create a new presentation, the first slide is a **title slide**. The Title Slide layout contains two placeholders: a title placeholder that reads "Click to add title" and a sub-title placeholder that reads "Click to add subtitle." When you add a new slide, the default placeholders adjust to new content. By default, subsequently added slides are Title and Content layout; they have a title place-holder and a content placeholder that supports bulleted text, graphic elements, and other media. Once you fill in a placeholder of any type—text, table, graphics, or any combination thereof—the placeholder becomes an editable **object** in the slide. You begin your presentation by adding text to the title slide. You fill in the substance of the presentation by adding three content slides and adding text to them.

1. **Click the Home tab, then click the title placeholder**

   A light blue **selection box** surrounds the title placeholder, the placeholder text is hidden, and a blinking vertical insertion point indicates where the new text will be entered, as shown in Figure L-7.

2. **Type Sustainable Lifestyle & Fun**

   The title text appears in the title font and style, and it automatically wraps in the title placeholder.

3. **Click the subtitle placeholder, then type Green, Healthy, and Profitable**

   The subtitle text appears in the subtitle font and style.

   > **TROUBLE**
   > Be sure to click the main area of the New Slide button, not the pop-up menu arrow.

4. **Click the New Slide button [icon] in the Slides group**

   A new slide with the Title and Content layout appears in the Slide pane. A **slide layout** is an arrangement of placeholders and formatting configured to support a particular type of content.

   > **QUICK TIP**
   > The default format-ting for text in a content placeholder is a bulleted list.

5. **Click the title placeholder, type Recyclable Bird Houses, then click the content placeholder**

6. **Type Meet the Peeps, press [return], type Wings Aloft, press [return], then type Sky Condo**

   Each time you press [return], the insertion point moves to a new bulleted line, as shown in Figure L-8.

   > **QUICK TIP**
   > Except for when you are on a title slide, each time you click [icon], PowerPoint inserts a new slide with the same slide layout as the selected slide. To insert a new slide with a different slide layout, click the New Slide button pop-up menu arrow, then click the layout you'd like for the new slide. To change the layout of an existing slide, click the Layout button [icon] in the Slides group, then select the layout you'd like to apply.

7. **Click [icon], then enter the text shown below**

Title:	Bullets:
Fitness Paddling	• Dragon Kayak
	• Trident Canoe
	• Loch Ness Hybrid

8. **Click [icon], enter the text shown below, then save your changes**

Title:	Bullets:
Lounge Chairs	• Sustained Relaxation
	• Kick Back
	• Tranquility Base

   Each completed slide thumbnail appears in the Slides tab, as shown in Figure L-9. The presentation has four slides total.

Creating a Presentation

FIGURE L-7: Entering text in a placeholder

Selection box surrounds title placeholder

Insertion point

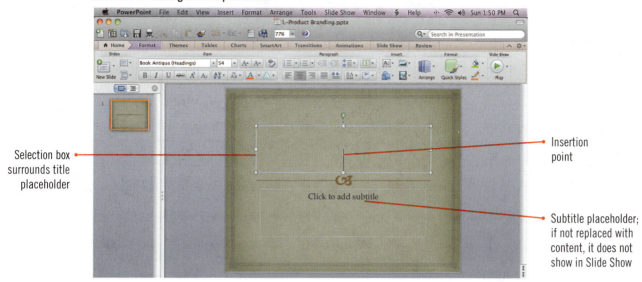

Subtitle placeholder; if not replaced with content, it does not show in Slide Show

FIGURE L-8: Entering bulleted text

New Slide button

Title and Content layout contains a title placeholder and a content placeholder

Press [return] to create a new bulleted line

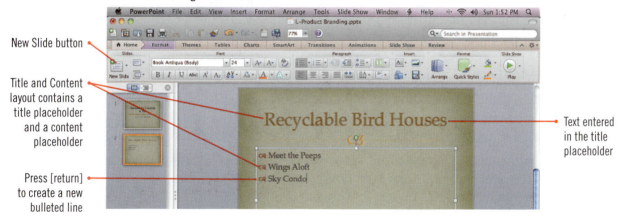

Text entered in the title placeholder

FIGURE L-9: Four completed slides

Completed slides

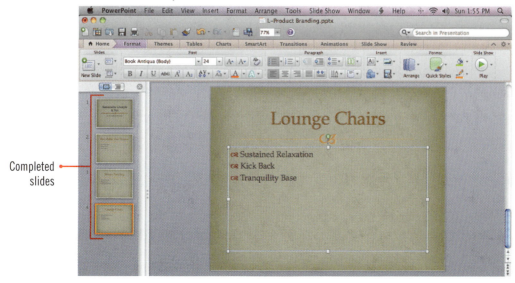

Formatting Text

You can format presentation text to emphasize specific words or phrases, or to improve the way text appears in a slide. For example, in a bulleted list, you might want to enhance one bullet point by changing its color or by increasing its font size. Formatting text in a slide is similar to formatting text in other Microsoft Office programs, particularly Word. You can use commands on the Home tab of the ribbon to alter the font type, size, and color. You can also change the fonts in a presentation by using the Fonts button in the Theme Options group on the Themes tab. Karen wants you to make a few changes to the text in the presentation. You also show her the effect of changing the theme fonts in the presentation.

STEPS

QUICK TIP
To select a single word, double-click the word.

1. **Click Slide 1 in the Slides tab, then triple-click the subtitle**
   The phrase "Green, Healthy, and Profitable" is selected.

2. **Click the Bold button B in the Font group, then click a blank area of the slide to deselect the text**
   The text is deselected and bolded.

3. **Click just before the word and in the subtitle, then press [return]**
   The words "and Profitable" are centered on their own line, as shown in Figure L-10.

4. **Click Slide 2 in the Slides tab, select the letter R in "Recyclable," then click the Increase Font Size button A▴ in the Font group twice**
   The text increases in size from 54 pt to 66 pt.

QUICK TIP
If the Font Color button displays the color you want to apply, you can click the button instead of the pop-up menu arrow to apply the color to a selection.

5. **Select the three lines of bulleted text in the content area, click the Font Color button pop-up menu arrow A▾ in the Font group, then click the Accent 1, Darker 50% color (Theme Colors, bottom row, fifth column from the left), as shown in Figure L-11**
   The text color changes to a shade of dark red/brown.

6. **Move to Slide 3, increase the size of the letter F in "Fitness" twice, select the bulleted list, then click A▾ in the Font group to apply the dark red/brown color used in Step 5**
   The formatting of text in Slide 3 is a duplicate of the text in Slide 2.

7. **Move to Slide 4, increase the size of the letter L in "Lounge" twice, select the bulleted list, then click A▾**
   The formatting of text in Slide 4 is the same as in Slides 2 and 3.

8. **Click the Themes tab, click the Fonts button Aa in the Theme Options group, scroll down, click Urban Pop, click a blank part of the slide to deselect the object, then compare your screen with Figure L-12**
   The title and bulleted fonts change to a different font style. Changing theme fonts changes all the text in a presentation instantaneously, which can be a big time-saver.

9. **Save your changes, click Slide 1 in the Slides tab, click the Slide Show button 🖵 on the status bar, view the presentation, then return to Normal view**

Using sections in a presentation

Long presentations can become difficult to manage, especially if you need to find a particular slide or group of slides quickly. You can easily organize slides by inserting sections into a slide show. You can apply formatting, themes, animations, transitions, and other presentation enhancements to entire sections. To create a section, select the slide that you'd like the section to start with. Next, click the Section button 🗒 in the Slides group on the Home tab, and then click Add Section. The Rename Section dialog box opens. Type your chosen name for the section, and then click Rename. You can also click the Section button to rename, remove, collapse, or expand sections. In both the Slides tab and Slide Sorter view, you can right-click a section name to access these commands.

FIGURE L-10: Bold and formatted subtitle text

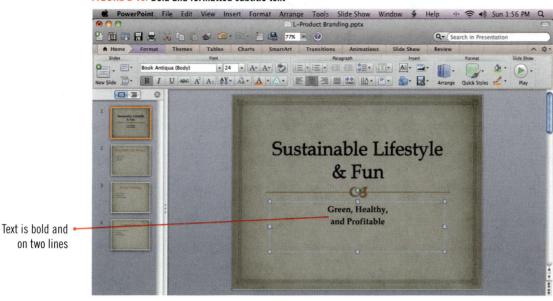

Text is bold and
on two lines

FIGURE L-11: Selecting a theme color

Increase Font
Size button

Font color
pop-up
menu arrow

In Step 5, click
this color

FIGURE L-12: Different theme fonts applied to presentation

Theme fonts
modify title and
content text

Fonts
button

Creating a Presentation

Adding a Text Box

There may be times when you want to add text to a slide but format it outside the confines of a text place-holder, such as in a label or as part of a graphic. You can add a text box, apply a style to it, and place it anywhere on the slide (including aligning it to other objects on the slide). As with any object, you can modify a text box by moving, resizing, and realigning it. As in Word, PowerPoint includes Quick Styles that you can use to apply multiple formatting attributes at once.  Karen wants you to add a slide about the Outdoor Designs' Community Partner Award and create a colorful text box that reminds sales reps to play up the award with their clients.

STEPS

1. **Click** Slide 4 **in the Slides tab, click the** Home tab**, click the** New Slide **pop-up menu arrow in the Slides group, click the** Title Only **layout, click the** title placeholder**, click the** Decrease Font Size button Ⓐⁱ **in the Font group twice, then type** Community Partner Award
   The new slide has only a title text placeholder at the top.

> **QUICK TIP**
> To insert a text box using the menu bar, click Insert on the menu bar, click Text Box, then click the slide where you want to place the text box.

2. **Click the** Text button Ⓐⁱ **in the Insert group, click** Text Box**, then click the approximate center of the slide**
   A blank text box appears on the slide.

3. **Type** Prepare media kit**, press** [return]**, then type** Upload video of awards ceremony
   The text appears in the text box, as shown in Figure L-13.

> **TROUBLE**
> The right side of the text box may extend past the edge of the slide. This will be corrected in a later step.

4. **Select the** text**, then click the** Center Text button ⬚ **in the Paragraph group**
   The text is centered in the text box.

5. **Click the** Font Size **pop-up menu arrow in the Font group, then click** 28

6. **Click the** Quick Styles button ⬚ⁱ **in the Format group, then click the** style option in the second row and second column**, as shown in Figure L-14**
   This Quick Style is applied to the text box.

7. **Click the** Arrange button ⬚ⁱ **in the Format group, point to** Align or Distribute**, then click** Align Center
   The text box is center-aligned beneath the title object.

> **QUICK TIP**
> To align a single object on the slide, verify that Align to Slide has a check mark; to align multiple objects to each other, select Align Selected Objects.

8. **Click** ⬚ⁱ**, point to** Align or Distribute**, click** Distribute Vertically**, click a blank area in the slide to deselect the text box, then save your changes**
   The object is distributed vertically on the slide, as shown in Figure L-15.

Creating a custom theme

In addition to applying a predefined theme to a presentation, you can create a truly unique theme from an existing theme, theme colors, theme fonts, and background options. To customize theme colors, click the Colors button in the Theme Options group of the Themes tab, and then click Create Theme Colors. Select colors for the text/background, accent, and hyperlink boxes, and then type a Colors Theme name in the Name text box. The unique name you assign to the theme colors will be visible in the Colors Gallery. To create a custom theme, apply the theme and theme colors, and choose fonts as desired. Click the Save Theme button ⬚ⁱ in the Themes group. In the dialog box that opens, type a unique name in the Save As text box, and then click Save. Your new theme will appear in the Themes Gallery under the Custom category; it can be applied to any presentation.

FIGURE L-13: Creating a text box

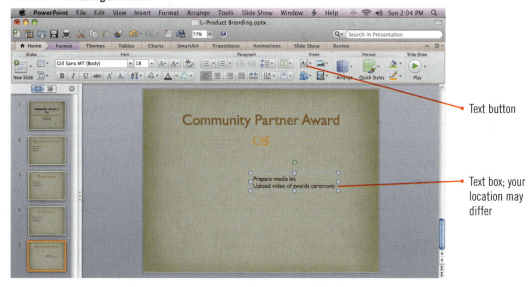

Text button

Text box; your location may differ

FIGURE L-14: Applying a Quick Style to a text box

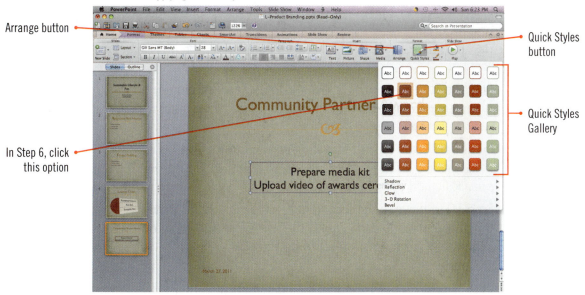

Arrange button

In Step 6, click this option

Quick Styles button

Quick Styles Gallery

FIGURE L-15: Completed text box

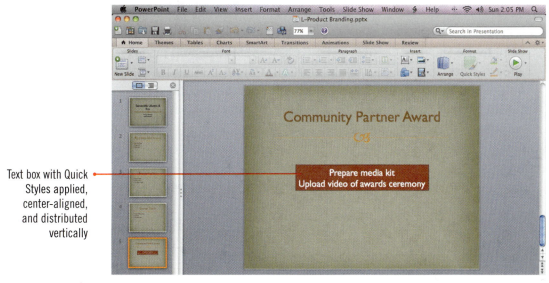

Text box with Quick Styles applied, center-aligned, and distributed vertically

UNIT
L
PowerPoint 2011

Creating SmartArt

Although regular or bulleted text can be effective in capturing a viewer's attention, there may be times when you need something more visually striking. You can convert text or transform photographs to **SmartArt** and instantly create visually rich and professional looking diagrams. SmartArt includes dozens of layouts organized by category, as listed in Table L-1. For example, you can show proportional or hierarchical relationships, various processes, and directional flows. You can also include photos with the graphics. Once you create a SmartArt graphic, you can modify its style just as you can with any object. You want to create another slide about the Community Partner Award and decide to use SmartArt to create a diagram for the text. You also want to convert some existing text to SmartArt.

STEPS

1. **Select Slide 5 if necessary, click the New Slide pop-up menu arrow in the Slides group, click Duplicate Selected Slides, select the text box on the new slide in the Slide pane, then press [delete]**

   A duplicate of Slide 5 is inserted, and the text box is deleted. Duplicating a slide is a quick way to reuse content. On the new Slide 6, you want to use the title text but not the content placeholder.

2. **Click the SmartArt tab, then click the Process button in the Insert SmartArt Graphic group**

   The Process Gallery opens, as shown in Figure L-16. Each category of SmartArt has many options, viewable in its gallery.

TROUBLE
If the Text Pane does not open by default, click the Text Pane button.

3. **Click the Step Up Process layout (first row, second column)**

   A blank SmartArt object appears in the slide using the current theme colors, and the Text Pane is open and active, as shown in Figure L-17. Notice the insertion point is placed next to the first bullet.

QUICK TIP
You can also enter text in the text placeholders on the SmartArt graphic.

4. **In the Text Pane, type ID Stakeholders next to the first bullet**

   As you type, the first placeholder on the graphic is replaced with your text. The text automatically wraps and resizes to fit the first graphic element. Notice that the text in the other placeholders resizes as well.

QUICK TIP
To open the Text Pane, click the Text Pane button on the upper-left corner of the SmartArt graphic.

5. **Press [↓] to move to the second bullet, type Spotlight Activities, press [↓] to move to the third bullet, type Engage Public, click the Close button on the Text Pane, then click outside of the SmartArt object to deselect it**

   The SmartArt object is complete.

6. **Click Slide 4, click anywhere in the bulleted text, click the Relationship button in the Insert SmartArt Graphic group, then click the Target List layout (fourth row, first column)**

   The Target List layout is applied to the bulleted list, and the Format tab is now available. You do not have to first select all the bulleted text you want to convert to SmartArt; you only need to click in the bulleted text object you want to convert.

QUICK TIP
To add an additional element to a SmartArt graphic, use the Text Pane and press [return] to add another bullet point. To remove an element, select the element in the graphic, then press [delete].

7. **Point to the SmartArt Graphic Styles Gallery until the pop-up menu arrow appears, click ▼ , click the Sunset Scene style (second row, third option), click outside the SmartArt object to deselect it, then save your changes**

   The objects appear three-dimensional with an engraved texture, as shown in Figure L-18.

PowerPoint 286   Creating a Presentation

FIGURE L-16: SmartArt Process Gallery

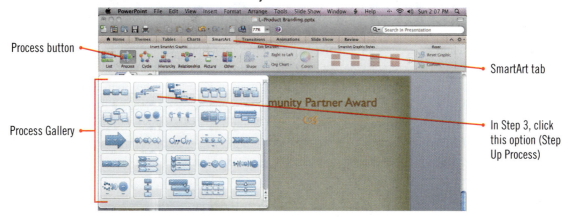

Process button

Process Gallery

SmartArt tab

In Step 3, click this option (Step Up Process)

FIGURE L-17: SmartArt inserted in a slide

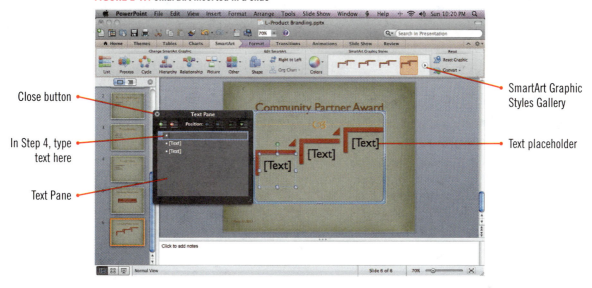

Close button

In Step 4, type text here

Text Pane

SmartArt Graphic Styles Gallery

Text placeholder

FIGURE L-18: Style applied to SmartArt

TABLE L-1: SmartArt categories

type	use
List	Nonsequential information
Process	Directional flow and connections between parts of a process
Cycle	Repeating or circular processes
Hierarchy	Decision tree, chain of command, and organizational chart
Relationship	Connections between two or more sets of information
Picture	Highlight photographs with or without text
Other	Complex relationships relating to a whole (Matrix) or proportional/hierarchical relationships (Pyramid)

Adding a Header and Footer

You can add a header and/or footer to a presentation if you want certain information to appear on each slide, such as the current slide number; the presentation date or location; a copyright disclaimer; or the presenter's name and company, organization, or college. Because the text in headers and footers appears on every slide, it can help the audience (and presenter) keep track of and focus on the presentation. Footers can be applied to the slides to be displayed in Slide Show, and can be applied to the hard copy when you print notes, outlines, or handouts. Headers are visible only when you print notes and handouts.  Karen wants everyone to know that this information is not yet finalized. You decide to add a header and footer to the presentation to include this and other useful information.

STEPS

QUICK TIP

You can also add headers and footers using the menu bar. Click View on the menu bar, then click Header and Footer.

1. **Click the Home tab, click the Text button**  **in the Insert group, then click Header and Footer**

   The Header and Footer dialog box opens with the Slide tab active. You use this tab to specify the information you want visible in the slide's footer. The Preview box shows the location of the footer information. As you select each item, the appropriate text box will be bold in the Preview box.

QUICK TIP

You can add footers and headers to the presentation from any slide.

2. **Click the Date and time check box to select it, click the Update automatically pop-up menu arrows, then click the fourth option in the list (for example, March 23, 2013), then compare your dialog box with Figure L-19**

   The date will appear in a formal date style. The Update automatically selection means that the date on the slide is dynamic and will always update to the date the presentation is opened. To select a date that doesn't change, select the Fixed option and type the date you want shown in the slide.

3. **Click the Slide number check box, click the Footer check box, then in the Footer text box, type DRAFT – Do Not Distribute**

4. **Verify that the Don't show on title slide check box is not selected, click Apply to All, compare your screen with Figure L-20, then press [page up] three times to move to the title slide**

   The dialog box closes, and the footer information is applied to every slide. Because you did not select the Don't show on title slide check box, the footer information appears on the title slide. Usually, the title slide is not numbered. You decide to customize the footer for the title slide and remove the page number and footer text.

5. **Click**  **in the Insert group, then click Header and Footer**

6. **Click the Slide number check box and the Footer check box to deselect them, click Apply, then save your changes**

   Only the date appears in the title slide. Because you clicked Apply instead of Apply to All, the change affects only the title slide, as shown in Figure L-21.

FIGURE L-19: Header and Footer dialog box

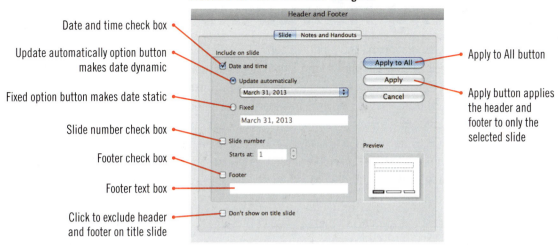

Date and time check box

Update automatically option button makes date dynamic

Fixed option button makes date static

Slide number check box

Footer check box

Footer text box

Click to exclude header and footer on title slide

Apply to All button

Apply button applies the header and footer to only the selected slide

FIGURE L-20: Date, footer text, and page number applied to slides

Date

Slide number

Footer text

FIGURE L-21: Footer applied to title slide only

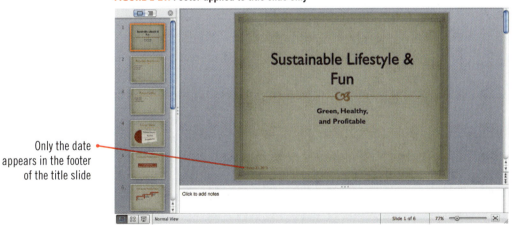

Only the date appears in the footer of the title slide

Editing the Slide Master

Themes and templates come with default settings. However, there may be times when you want to make a design change to every slide, such as changing the alignment or font size of text throughout the entire presentation, or adding a logo or other graphic to every slide. Instead of making the change manually on each slide, you can modify the Slide Master. Every PowerPoint presentation contains a Slide Master. The **Slide Master** contains the layouts, design elements, and other formatting attributes for a presentation. After you apply a theme or a template, you can customize the Slide Master and save it for future use. To modify the Slide Master, click the Themes tab on the ribbon, click the Edit Master button in the Master Views group, and then click Slide Master. In Master view, the template for each layout is displayed in the left pane, the Title and Content layout is displayed in the right pane, and the Slide Master tab is active on the ribbon. You can select additional Slide Masters, insert placeholders, apply multiple themes, and change backgrounds and layouts. To create a new Slide Master, click the New Master button in the Slide Master group, and then customize the Slide Master as desired. To save the new layout with a unique name, click the Rename button, type a name, and then click the Rename button. To exit Master view, click the Close button in the Master View group on the Slide Master tab.

Printing Handouts

When you give a presentation, having a printed copy to which you can refer and on which your audience can take notes is helpful. You can print a few different types of supporting materials. For example, you can print the actual slides, one to a page. You can also print **handouts**, which contain one or more slides per page and can include blank lines for audience members to use for notes. **Notes pages** contain a thumbnail of each slide plus any speaker notes you added in the notes pane, as well as any header and footer information. Before printing any document, it is always a good idea to preview it. You have completed the draft of the slide show for Karen. Now, you want to preview the presentation, select a handout layout, add a header, and print out a handout for her to review. *Note*: Many schools limit printing to conserve paper. If your school restricts printing, skip Step 8.

STEPS

1. Click the Home tab if necessary, click the Text button 🔠 in the Insert group, click Header and Footer, then click the Notes and Handouts tab, as shown in Figure L-22

   The Notes and Handouts tab is active and looks similar to the Slide tab used in the previous section. This tab allows you to add headers and footers to the printed copy when you print handouts, notes, or an outline.

2. Click the Header check box, type Karen's Review in the Header text box, then click Apply to All

   The Header and Footer dialog box closes.

3. Save your changes

> **QUICK TIP**
> To select all, a range of slides, or selected slides to print, click the appropriate option button.

4. Click File on the menu bar, then click Print

   The Print dialog box opens. To save wear and tear on your printer and minimize use of ink and paper, you want to print more than one slide per page.

> **QUICK TIP**
> To see a full-screen preview, click the Preview button at the bottom of the Print dialog box to open the Preview program.

5. Click the Print What pop-up menu arrows and compare your screen with Figure L-23

6. Click Handouts (3 slides per page), view the Quick Preview box, then click the Next Page button ▶ under the Quick Preview box to view the next handout page

   The Quick Preview box displays three slides per page with note lines. This Handouts option is the only one that provides note lines. All other Handouts options provide slide thumbnails only.

> **QUICK TIP**
> If you do not have a color printer selected, the preview will display in grayscale by default.

7. Click the Output pop-up menu arrows, then click Grayscale

   The handouts will print in shades of white and black. Compare your screen with Figure L-24.

> **QUICK TIP**
> To select another printer, click the Printer pop-up menu arrows, then click a printer.

8. If your school allows printing, click the Print button to print the handouts; if not, click the Cancel button

9. Save your changes to the presentation, close it, then quit PowerPoint

FIGURE L-22: Notes and Handouts tab of the Header and Footer dialog box

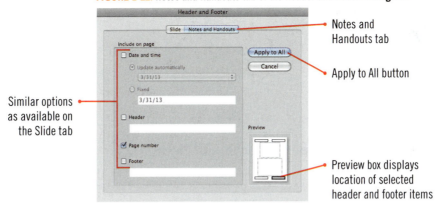

Notes and Handouts tab

Apply to All button

Similar options as available on the Slide tab

Preview box displays location of selected header and footer items

FIGURE L-23: Viewing a handout in the Print dialog box

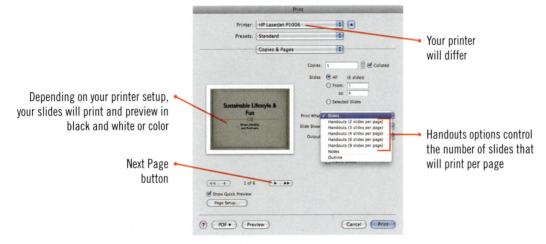

Your printer will differ

Depending on your printer setup, your slides will print and preview in black and white or color

Handouts options control the number of slides that will print per page

Next Page button

FIGURE L-24: Previewing handouts

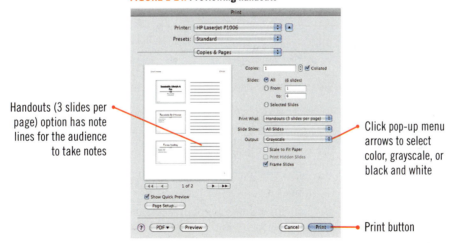

Handouts (3 slides per page) option has note lines for the audience to take notes

Click pop-up menu arrows to select color, grayscale, or black and white

Print button

Sharing a presentation

The ultimate goal of creating a slide show is to have viewers watch it. To examine the many avenues PowerPoint offers for sharing a presentation, click File on the menu bar, and then point to Share. Here you can save your presentation to SkyDrive or to a SharePoint site; or you can e-mail it as an attachment, send it to iPhoto, or broadcast it on Windows Live. To reach online users, you can either post your presentation online to Windows SkyDrive, where viewers can access it using the PowerPoint Web App, or you can broadcast a copy of your presentation in real time, where viewers just need a free Windows Live ID to be able to experience your presentation as you give it—just as if you were in the same room. Sending it to iPhoto saves your slides individually with the .jpg file extension and makes it available from the Media Browser in all Microsoft Office for Mac 2011 programs.

Practice

Concepts Review

Label the PowerPoint window elements shown in Figure L-25.

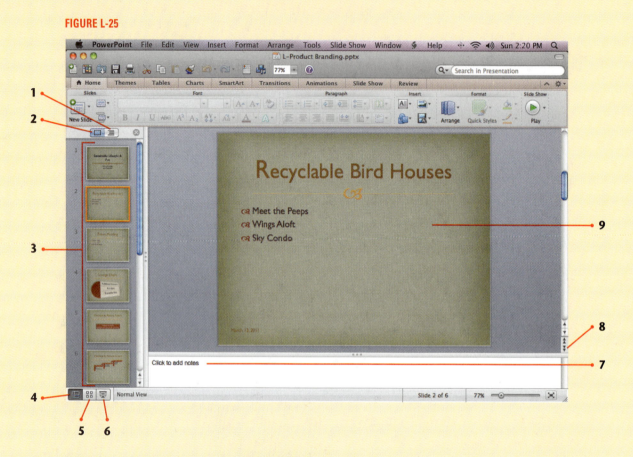

Match each term with the statement that best describes it.

10. Slide Sorter view
11. Placeholders
12. Notes pane
13. Themes Gallery
14. Handouts

a. Allows you to choose how many slide thumbnail images are displayed on a printed page

b. Contains a collection of predefined colors and styles you can apply to a presentation

c. Displays slides as thumbnails, for easy rearranging of slides

d. Contains text written specifically to the audience or for the speaker's reference

e. Boxes in slide layouts where you can enter text or add graphics

Select the best answer from the list of choices.

15. Which view allows you to see the presentation as your audience will?

a. Normal view

b. Slide Sorter view

c. Slide Show

d. Presenter view

16. Which of the following best describes SmartArt?

a. Transforms graphics to bullets

b. Formats text into rich graphical shapes

c. Transforms theme colors

d. Converts the theme's font colors

17. Which of the following is *not* true about printing PowerPoint presentations?

a. You can print a range of slides.

b. You can print one or more slides per page.

c. You can save your presentation before printing.

d. You can print handouts only in color.

Skills Review

1. View a presentation.

a. Start Microsoft PowerPoint, view the sample templates in the PowerPoint Presentation Gallery, then create a presentation using the Contemporary Photo Album template. (*Hint*: Select All under the Templates category.)

b. Move to Slide 4 using the Next Slide button.

c. Make the Outline tab active, then move to Slide 5.

d. View the presentation in Slide Sorter view, then click Slide 1.

e. Select Slide Show, then view each slide in the presentation.

f. Return to Normal view.

g. Close the presentation.

2. Use a theme.

a. Click File on the menu bar, then click New Presentation.

b. Apply the Breeze theme to the presentation.

c. Save the presentation as **L-Telecommunicate** in the location where you store your Data Files.

d. Apply the Slipstream theme to the presentation.

e. Apply the Style 7 background to the presentation.

f. Save your changes.

3. Enter text on a slide.

a. Type **Factoids** in the title placeholder.

b. Type **Hold the Phone & Pass the Technology** in the subtitle placeholder.

c. Use a command on the Home tab to add a new slide.

d. Type **19th Century Tech** in the title placeholder on the new slide.

e. Type **Telegraph**, **Phonograph**, **Telephone**, and **Radio** as separate bullets in the content placeholder.

Skills Review (continued)

f. Add Slides 3 and 4 to the presentation, and enter the following information on the slides:

Slide	Title	Bullets
3	20th & 21st Century Tech	Television
		Satellite Communication
		Computer/E-mail
		Text Messaging
		Twitter
4	First Messages	Telegraph: What hath God wrought?
		Telephone: Mr. Watson, come here. I want to see you.
		Phonograph: Mary had a little lamb
		E-mail: QWERTYUIOP
		Text message: Merry Christmas
		Tweet: just setting up my twttr

g. Save your changes.

4. Format text.

a. Move to Slide 1, select the title text, then make the text italic.

b. Move to Slide 3, select the title text, then change the font size to 40.

c. Move to Slide 4, select the title text, then use a button on the Home tab to change the font color to the sixth option in the first row of Theme Colors (Help Tag reads "Accent 2").

d. On Slide 4, select the bulleted text, change the font size to 24, then italicize the text following each colon in the bulleted list.

e. Use a command on the Themes tab to apply the Waveform Theme Fonts to the presentation.

f. View the slide show, return to Normal view, then save your changes.

5. Add a text box.

a. Following Slide 4, insert a new slide with the Blank layout.

b. Insert a text box in the approximate center of the slide, type **"I think there is a world market**, press [return], type **for maybe five computers."**, press [return], then type **Thomas Watson, President IBM, 1943**. (*Hint*: Make the "f" lowercase in "for" after you type it.)

c. Select the first two lines of text, then change the font size to 32.

d. Select all the text, then make it italic and right-aligned.

e. Use a command on the Home tab to apply the Quick Style option in the first row, third column of the Quick Styles Gallery to the text box.

f. Use commands on the Home tab to arrange the text box with the Align Middle and Distribute Horizontally settings.

g. Save your changes.

6. Create SmartArt.

a. Following Slide 5, insert a new slide with the Blank layout.

b. Use a button on the SmartArt tab to insert a Cycle SmartArt. Insert the Circle Arrow Process layout in the slide.

c. Type **Design** in the first text placeholder, then type the following text in the two remaining text placeholders: **Test** and **Implement**. Use the Text Pane to add another bullet, then type **Modify** next to the new bullet. (*Hint*: To add another bullet, click after Implement, then press [return].)

d. Close the Text Pane.

e. Apply the Intense Effect SmartArt style to the SmartArt graphic, then increase the height of the SmartArt graphic approximately one inch. (*Hint*: Use the Help Tag to help you measure.)

f. Select Slide 2, then convert the bulleted text to a Vertical Bullet List SmartArt layout.

g. Select Slide 3, then repeat Step f for the bulleted text.

h. Save your changes.

Skills Review (continued)

7. Add a header and footer.

a. Use a button in the Insert group on the Home tab to open the Header and Footer dialog box.

b. Select the Date and time check box, then select the top option in the Update automatically date list.

c. Select the Slide number check box and the Don't show on title slide check box.

d. Add a footer with your name, then click Apply to All.

e. Save your changes.

8. Print handouts.

a. Use a button in the Insert group on the Home tab to open the Header and Footer dialog box and select the Notes and Handouts tab.

b. Click the Header check box, type **Brown Bag Lunch** in the header text box, then click Apply to All.

c. Open the Print dialog box and use an option to select Handouts (2 slides per page).

d. Use the Previous Page button in the Print dialog box to move to the first page, if necessary, then compare your Quick Preview box with Figure L-26.

e. Click the Output pop-up menu arrows, then select Black and White.

f. Print the handouts if your lab allows printing.

g. Save your changes, close the L-Telecommunicate presentation, then quit PowerPoint. Submit your completed presentation (and printed handouts) to your instructor.

FIGURE L-26

Independent Challenge 1

You are the fitness director for CoreWerks, a trendy health club and spa in the LoDo section of Denver. The club is updating its Web page, and you are responsible for briefing the Web designer and other marketing staff on the fitness classes the club offers. You will be presenting to the entire staff at a company meeting and want to encourage input from the audience.

a. Start PowerPoint, open the file L-1.pptx from the location where you store your Data Files, then save it as **L-CoreWerks**.

b. Apply the Executive theme to the presentation.

c. On Slide 1, change the subtitle font attributes to font size 32 and bold.

d. Change the background style in the presentation to Style 11.

e. Change the font color of the title in Slide 3 to black (Text 1 or Background 1) and make it bold.

f. Convert the bulleted text in Slide 3 to SmartArt and apply the Horizontal Multi-Level Hierarchy layout to it. (*Hint*: It's in the Hierarchy category.)

g. Change the SmartArt style to Metallic Scene.

h. Insert a new slide at the end of the presentation and enter the following information:

Title	Bullets
Aerobics	Salsa
	Hip Hop
	General Dance

Independent Challenge 1 (continued)

i. Add a slide number to every slide except the title slide.

j. View the presentation in Slide Sorter view, then compare your screen with Figure L-27.

Advanced Challenge Exercise

- On Slide 2, move Pilates to the end of the list, then move Slide 6 after Slide 7, so that the Pilates slide is the last slide.
- On Slides 2 and 7, type **& Yoga** after the word Pilates.
- On the Indoor Cycling slide, add a new bullet after Century Training, press [tab], then type **Prepare for the Old Santa Fe Trail Trek**.
- Press [return], press [tab], then type **100 miles of great scenery and companionship**.

k. Add your name as a header to the handout, then print the presentation as handouts (nine slides per page) if your lab allows printing.

l. Save your changes, close the presentation, then quit PowerPoint. Submit your completed presentation (and printed handouts) to your instructor.

FIGURE L-27

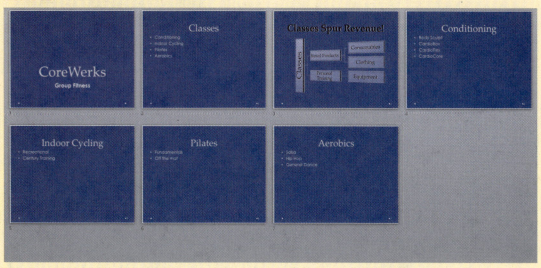

Independent Challenge 2

You are curator of the Sauce and Marinade Museum. Along with cosponsors from the food industry, you are creating a traveling exhibit on vinegars from around the world. The exhibit will also feature classes on making flavored vinegars. The first step is to provide an overview of vinegar to the people involved in creating the exhibit. You decide to create a PowerPoint presentation to educate your staff.

a. Start PowerPoint, open the file L-2.pptx from the location where you store your Data Files, then save it as **L-Vinegar**.

b. Apply the theme of your choice to the presentation. Select a background style if desired.

c. Select fonts and font sizes, and apply formatting attributes to slides as desired, to add a professional touch and enhance the look and feel of the presentation. (*Hint*: Italicize foreign or unfamiliar words.)

d. Use the text in the sub-bullet in Slide 6 to create and format a text box in that slide. (*Hint*: Resize the content placeholder, create a text box, then copy and paste or type the text from the sub-bullet.)

e. Use SmartArt shapes at least twice in the presentation, either by creating from scratch or by converting existing text. (*Hint*: Add slides as desired.)

f. Insert a slide number in the footer of the presentation, and add your name to the header of the Notes and Handouts tab.

g. Print handouts using the layout of your choice if your lab allows printing, then save your changes.

h. Close the presentation, then quit PowerPoint. Submit your completed presentation (and printed handouts) to your instructor.

Independent Challenge 3

You are the new regional marketing director for Belongings, a niche retail chain that specializes in crafts from around the world. The previous year was a bit tumultuous for the company, with individual stores implementing their own sales strategies and policies with varying success. At the upcoming annual meeting, you want to implement company-wide best business practices. You need to create a PowerPoint presentation that centers on this theme.

a. Start PowerPoint, open the file L-3.pptx from the location where you store your Data Files, then save it as **L-Best Practices**.

b. Apply the Grid theme to the presentation.

c. Apply the Style 6 background style to the presentation.

d. Apply the Couture Color theme to the presentation. (*Hint*: Use the Colors button in the Theme Options group.)

e. After Slide 1, insert a Title Only slide, then type **Mission Statement** in the placeholder. (*Hint*: Click the New Slide pop-up menu arrow.)

f. Insert a text box with the following text: **Build trade partnerships based on economic justice and sustainable development**.

g. Center-align the text in the text box, change the font to Courier, then change the font size to 32.

h. Apply the Quick Style of your choice to the text box, then resize and arrange the text box so that it is aligned attractively on the slide.

i. Select Slide 7, then change the font color of the text **green** to Green and make it bold. (*Hint*: Use Standard Colors.)

j. Select Slide 1, replace the text **Your Name** with your name, then make the title text bold.

k. Insert a slide number and a date to each slide except the title slide, then preview handouts for two slides.

Advanced Challenge Exercise

- Select Slide 1, then arrange the Belongings logo on the slide so that it is left-aligned.
- Select the Belongings logo, then apply a 3-D Rotation Picture Effect style of your choice to the logo. (*Hint*: On the Format Picture tab, click the Effects button in the Picture Styles group.)

l. View the presentation in Slide Show.

m. Save your changes, print handouts with two slides per page if your lab allows printing, close the presentation, then quit PowerPoint. Submit your completed presentation (and printed handouts) to your instructor.

Real Life Independent Challenge

You are organizing your upcoming family reunion. You have been collecting facts about your family's history and want to create a PowerPoint presentation that uses this information creatively. You create a presentation about your ancestors using a template that displays information in a quiz format.

a. Start PowerPoint, create a new presentation based on the installed template Quiz Show, then save it as **L-Family Quiz Show** in the location where you store your Data Files.

b. In the subtitle placeholder, replace the words "Question and Answer" and "Samples and Techniques" with your family information.

c. Apply a theme or change the background style as desired.

d. Modify theme colors and theme fonts in the presentation as needed.

e. Delete the content in Slide 2 and insert a text box with your own content. (*Hint*: Delete the existing placeholders.)

f. Replace the content in Slide 3 with a hierarchical SmartArt graphic representing part of your family tree.

g. Modify the content in the remaining slides so that it is appropriate for your own family. For Slides 7 and 8, view the slides in Slide Show so that you know where to put the correct answers.

h. Insert a slide number, date, and footer on all slides except the title slide.

i. Insert your name in the handout header.

j. Save your changes, then if your lab allows printing, print handouts with nine slides per page and an outline.

k. Close the presentation, then quit PowerPoint. Submit your completed presentation (and printed handouts) to your instructor.

Visual Workshop

Using the skills you learned in this unit, create and format the slide shown in Figure L-28. Create a new, Title Only, one-slide slide show. Apply a theme with default settings, and change the background style; for the SmartArt, look in the List category and apply a layout. (*Hint*: It's the Vertical Circle List.) You may need to scroll to the end. Add your name to the slide footer, then save the file as **L-Condiments We Love** to the location where you store your Data Files. Print the slide of your presentation if your lab allows printing. Save your changes, close the presentation, then quit PowerPoint. Submit your completed presentation (and printed slide) to your instructor.

FIGURE L-28

Polishing and Running a Presentation

Files You Will Need:

M-1.pptx
birdhouse.jpg
duck_1.au
BaldEagle.mov
M-2.pptx
sisal.jpg
afghanrug.mov
M-3.pptx
Books.mov
Coffee.mov
coffee_grinder.mp3
Playground Noises
  .mp3
M-4.pptx
fedgovt.mov
Gavel Banging.mp3
M-5.pptx
sandcastle.jpg

You can enhance a PowerPoint presentation by adding media—such as shapes, clip art, photographs, sounds, and movies—or by customizing the way slides appear on the screen. Adding graphics, such as images and photographs, and movies to your slides can enhance your slide content. You can embed sound effects and music clips to narrate or add excitement. Jihong Chen, assistant sales manager, is preparing detailed background information about each kit. She believes that the sales representatives will have more success if they are familiar with the finer points of each kit. To kick off the training, she asks you to create a distinctive, attention-getting presentation for the sales reps. You begin with the birdhouse kit.

OBJECTIVES

Add a shape

Add clip art

Work with pictures

Add sound and video

Edit a movie

Set slide timing and transitions

Animate slide objects

Create speaker notes

Adding a Shape

PowerPoint has dozens of built-in shapes you can use to present, highlight, or connect information, or to simply add visual interest to a slide show. Shapes have the same formatting properties as other Office objects: You can alter various attributes, such as style, fill, and so on. You can also add text to a shape. Among the many ways you can align an object on a slide is to use rulers; with precise measurements you can insert a shape in the same location in multiple slides. You want to add a shape to a slide in the birdhouse kit presentation to reinforce the impact of bulleted text. You want to augment the shape's impact, so you also change its style and fill it with a texture.

STEPS

1. **Start PowerPoint, open the file M-1.pptx from the location where you store your Data Files, then save it as M-Birdhouse.pptx**

2. **Move to Slide 6**

3. **Click View on the menu bar, then click Ruler**
The horizontal and vertical rulers appear in the Slide pane.

4. **On the Home tab of the ribbon, click the Shape button [icon] in the Insert group, point to Basic Shapes, then click the Bevel shape (fourth option in the sixth row), as shown in Figure M-1**
You can select from a variety of shape styles, including Lines and Connectors, Rectangles, Basic Shapes, Block Arrows, Equation Shapes, Flowchart shapes, Stars and Banners, Callouts, and Action Buttons. After you click the shape you want, the palette closes and the pointer changes to ﹢ so that you can draw the shape on the slide.

5. **Position ﹢ so that it aligns with the 2" mark on the right side of the horizontal ruler and the 1.5" mark on the top of the vertical ruler, then click**
The shape is inserted on the slide. Because you clicked without dragging to add the shape, it was added at the default size. If you click and drag to add a shape, you can make it as large or small as you'd like.

6. **Click the Format tab, point to the Shape Styles Gallery until the pop-up menu arrow [▼] appears, click [▼], then click the first option in the fourth row, as shown in Figure M-2**
The style is applied to the shape.

7. **Click the Fill button pop-up menu arrow [Fill ▼] in the Shape Styles group, then click Fill Effects**
The Format Shape dialog box opens.

8. **Click the Picture or Texture tab, click the From texture pop-up menu arrows, click Walnut, as shown in Figure M-3, then click OK**
The texture is applied to the shape.

9. **With the shape selected, type Build, select the text, click the Home tab, click the Bold button [B] in the Font group, click the Font Color pop-up menu arrow [A ▼], then click the white color (the Help Tag reads "Background 1")**
A shape can accept text whenever it is selected in the slide. The text appears centered and bold on the shape.

10. **Click outside the shape to deselect it, compare your screen with Figure M-4, then click the Save button [icon] on the Standard toolbar**

FIGURE M-1: Selecting a shape

Shape button

Shape categories

Ruler

In Step 4, click this shape

FIGURE M-2: Adding a style to a shape

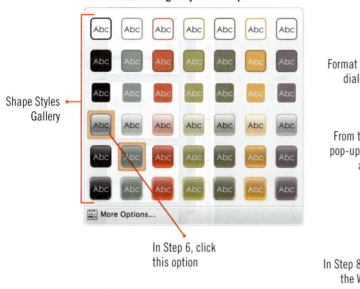

Shape Styles Gallery

In Step 6, click this option

FIGURE M-3: Selecting a Shape Fill texture

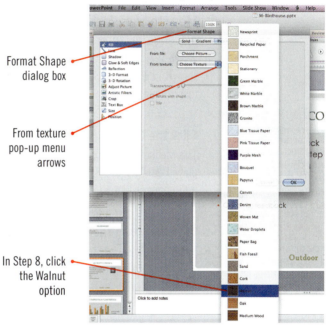

Format Shape dialog box

From texture pop-up menu arrows

In Step 8, click the Walnut option

FIGURE M-4: Style, texture, and text added to shape

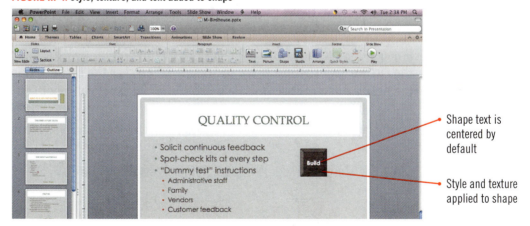

Shape text is centered by default

Style and texture applied to shape

Resizing graphics and images

To resize an image, you can adjust sizing handles of the graphic in the slide. To resize a graphic proportionally, select the image, and then drag a corner sizing handle inward or outward; to resize only the height or width, drag a sizing handle on one side of the image.

To resize an image using precise measurements, use the Size group on the Format Picture tab of the ribbon. For additional size and position options, open the Format Shape dialog box and then click Crop, Size, or Position in the category list.

Adding Clip Art

You can insert a clip art image or photograph in a slide using the Clip Art Browser or the Clip Art Gallery. The Clip Art Browser provides access to the thumbnail cache of clip art that comes with Office for Mac 2011. The Clip Art Gallery provides access to the clip art package installed with Office for Mac 2011 and also provides keyword searches. To open either option, click the Picture button in the Insert group on the Home tab of the ribbon (or click Insert on the menu bar and point to Clip Art), and then select either Clip Art Browser or Clip Art Gallery. Clicking the Clip Art Browser button in a content placeholder opens the Clip Art Browser. Once you've inserted a piece of clip art into your presentation, you can resize or crop it, or add an effect to enhance its appearance. To tie a new slide in with the birdhouse motif, you decide to add clip art and then format it to make it stand out.

STEPS

1. **Move to Slide 1, click the New Slide button in the Slides group, click the title placeholder, then type Avian Construction Crew**

   When you add a new slide after Slide 1, PowerPoint applies the Title and Content layout by default, as shown in Figure M-5. This layout provides a title placeholder and a content placeholder with icons for inserting media.

   > **QUICK TIP**
   > For instructions to insert clip art using the Clip Art Gallery, refer to Unit H, pages 182–183.

2. **Click the Clip Art Browser button in the content placeholder**

   The Media Browser opens with the Clip Art tab selected. Thumbnail images of the built-in clip art are displayed. All Images is selected by default; however, you can filter the clip art images by category by clicking the pop-up menu arrows next to All Images.

   > **TROUBLE**
   > If the clip art image of a duck is not available, click and drag a different image of a duck or bird.

3. **Click and drag the duck image onto the content placeholder, then release the button**

   The duck clip art is inserted in the content placeholder, and three buttons appear in a floating toolbar beneath it. You use these buttons to reposition, resize, or crop a picture; crop a picture to fill the placeholder; and resize the picture to fit inside the placeholder.

4. **Click the Resize picture to fit inside placeholder button beneath the content placeholder**

   The image is resized to fit inside the placeholder. Next, you want to add a shadow to the image.

5. **If necessary, click the Format Picture tab on the ribbon, click the Effects button in the Picture Styles group, point to Shadow, then click the first effect in the first row under the heading Perspective (the Help Tag reads "Perspective Upper Left"), as shown in Figure M-6**

   Options for Shadow are organized into the categories Outer, Inner, and Perspective.

6. **Close the Media Browser, compare your screen with Figure M-7, then save your changes**

FIGURE M-5: Inserting media using the content placeholder

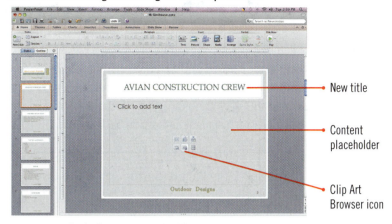

New title

Content placeholder

Clip Art Browser icon

FIGURE M-6: Duck clip art inserted in slide

Format Picture tab

Resize picture to fit inside placeholder button

Effects button

In Step 5, click this effect

FIGURE M-7: Completed clip art image with effect applied

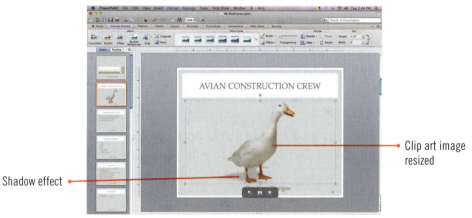

Clip art image resized

Shadow effect

Understanding adjustment effects

PowerPoint contains substantial graphics-editing features that give you more creative control over the appearance of your photographs and graphics. First, select the image to activate the Format Picture tab. Use the buttons in the Adjust group to highlight, contrast, or complement design elements in your presentation (note that not all features are available for each file type). You can isolate an object by removing the background areas around it; sharpen or soften the edges of an image; adjust an object's brightness and contrast; recolor an image by changing the amount of saturation and hue; and apply artistic effects that emulate painting, sketching, or drawing styles. The Corrections and Filters Galleries are shown in Figure M-8.

FIGURE M-8: Understanding picture adjustment features

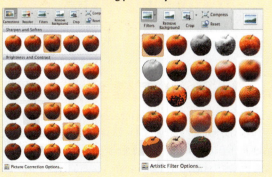

Working with Pictures

While you may commonly think of "picture" to mean a piece of clip art or a photograph, in PowerPoint a picture can be an image created and saved in any number of file formats. You can use features on the Format Picture tab to adjust the color, add effects and styles to photos, and crop portions of a picture to keep the parts you want. 🎨 You insert a photograph in a slide and modify it using several drawing features so that it appears transparent in the slide background.

STEPS

QUICK TIP

When a graphic is selected and you move to another slide, PowerPoint automatically selects the Home tab on the ribbon.

1. **Move to** Slide 5, **click the** Picture button 🖼 **in the Insert group on the Home tab, then click** Picture from File

   The Choose a Picture dialog box opens.

2. **Navigate to the location where you store your Data Files, click** birdhouse.jpg, **then click** Insert

   A photograph of a birdhouse is inserted on top of the bulleted text, and the Format Picture tab is active. The photograph obscures a considerable amount of text, so you need to modify it. You begin by deleting the image background.

QUICK TIP

To remove parts of an image from the top, bottom, or either side, click the Crop button 🔲 in the Adjust group, then drag an edge to crop.

3. **Click the** photo **to select it, click the** Remove Background button 🖼 **in the Adjust group, click and drag an** edge **of the selection rectangle over the birdhouse, then drag the** sizing handles **on the selection rectangle until it surrounds the birdhouse, as shown in Figure M-9**

   The areas that will be removed are highlighted in magenta. The Remove Background feature consists of an adjustable selection rectangle and tools that you can use to fine-tune the areas to keep or remove.

4. **Click** 🖼

   The background is removed, and only the birdhouse is visible.

5. **Click the** Recolor button 🖼 **in the Adjust group, then click the** Washout thumbnail **in the Recolor section (first row, fourth column), as shown in Figure M-10**

   The Washout option adjusts the **opacity**, or the opaqueness or transparency of the image. The washout effect is perfect to use as a background image. Now, you want to move it behind the text.

6. **Click the** Reorder button 🔲 Reorder ▾ **in the Arrange group, then click** Send to Back

   The photo is behind the bulleted items, visible but not concealing the text. You want to balance the slide visually by moving the photo.

QUICK TIP

To further optimize the images in your presentation, click the Compress button 🔲 in the Adjust group to open the Reduce File Size dialog box.

7. **Click the** Align button 🔲 Align ▾ **in the Arrange group, click** Align Right, **click away from the photo to deselect it, compare your screen with Figure M-11, then save your changes**

Understanding file types

Each file format supports images differently. For example, most photographs are saved in **Joint Photographic Experts Group (JPEG)** because the format uses and compresses color so well, whereas line art (such as clip art) is best suited for **Graphics Interchange Format** **(GIF)**. Images created using Preview, a Mac OS X program for editing and displaying images, are created in **Portable Network Graphics (PNG)** format, which was developed for image use on the Internet.

FIGURE M-9: Setting the rectangle for the Remove Background tool

Remove Background button

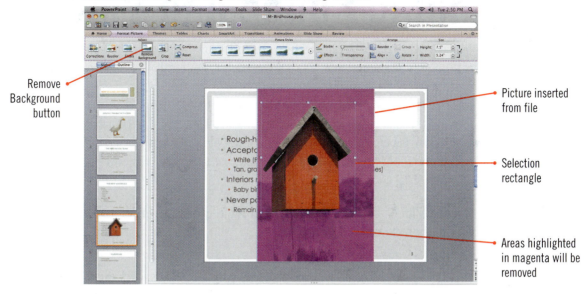

Picture inserted from file

Selection rectangle

Areas highlighted in magenta will be removed

FIGURE M-10: Recoloring a photo

Recolor button

In Step 5, click the Washout thumbnail

Reorder button

FIGURE M-11: Completed slide with washed-out photo in the background

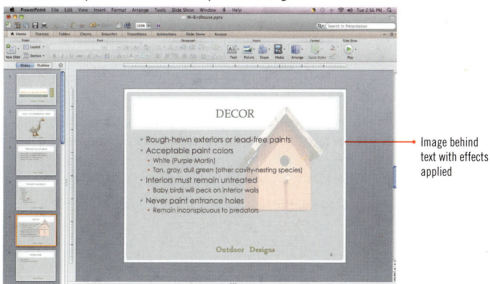

Image behind text with effects applied

Adding Sound and Video

Adding sound and video to a presentation can help your viewers remember it—and your message. You can insert movies and sound from any storage device, you can link to a video on the Web, or you can record your own audio for your presentation. You can use features on the Format Audio tab to access audio tools or on the Format Movie tab to access movie tools to adjust characteristics of a sound or movie file. Keep in mind that your Mac will not play all video file types. The default video file is a **QuickTime Movie**, or **.mov** file type. See Table M-1 for a list of file types that are supported by your Mac without additional software. You decide to add a movie and an accompanying sound effect to a slide.

STEPS

QUICK TIP
To open the Choose Audio dialog box, you can also click Insert on the menu bar, point to Audio, then click Audio from File.

1. **Move to Slide 2, click the Media button** 🖼 **in the Insert group on the Home tab of the ribbon, then click Audio from File**

   The Choose Audio dialog box opens.

2. **Navigate to the location where you store your Data Files, click duck_1.au, then click Insert**

   The sound clip appears on the slide as a sound icon above a set of playback controls, and the Format Audio tab is active on the ribbon. You can choose to hide or display the sound icon during the slide show. When inserting a sound, you can have it play automatically when the slide show advances to that slide, or have it play only when you click its icon during the slide show.

QUICK TIP
You can also select a sound on a slide, then click the Play button ⏵ in the Preview group on the Format Audio tab to listen to a sound.

3. **Click the Play button** ⏵ **on the playback controls to hear the sound effect**

4. **Click the Playback Options button** 🔊 Playback Options **in the Audio Options group on the Format Audio tab, click Hide Icon During Show, click the Start pop-up menu arrows, click Automatically, then compare your screen with Figure M-12**

QUICK TIP
You can also click Insert on the menu bar, point to Movie, then click Movie from File to open the Choose a Movie dialog box.

5. **Move to Slide 6, click** 🖼, **click Movie from File, navigate to the location where you store your Data Files in the Choose a Movie dialog box, click BaldEagle.mov, then click Insert**

   The movie file is inserted in the slide, as shown in Figure M-13, and the Format Movie tab is active on the ribbon. You can preview the movie using the playback controls beneath the image or by using the Play button on the ribbon.

6. **Click the Play button** ⏵ **in the Preview group, watch for a few seconds, press the Pause button** ⏸, **then click the Play button** ⏵ **on the playback controls to watch the rest of the movie**

   The movie file plays and then stops at the last frame. By default, you will need to click the movie placeholder to start the movie file when you are presenting to an audience. The size of the movie placeholder is a little large for the slide, so you want to resize it.

7. **Double-click the Height spin box in the Size group, type 3, press [return], then drag the movie to the location shown in Figure M-14**

   PowerPoint automatically resizes the movie proportionally. You want to preview the slide show as your audience will see it.

QUICK TIP
To start the slide show with the current slide, click the Slide Show button 🖥 on the status bar.

8. **Click the Slide Show tab, click the From Start button** 🔄 **in the Play Slide Show group, click to advance the slides, then click anywhere in the movie placeholder to play the movie file**

   The sound plays in Slide 2, and the movie plays when you click the movie placeholder in Slide 6.

TROUBLE
If you are playing the movie and you press [esc], the movie will stop. Press [esc] again to exit the slide show.

9. **Press [esc] to exit the slide show, then save your changes**

FIGURE M-12: Inserting a sound from file

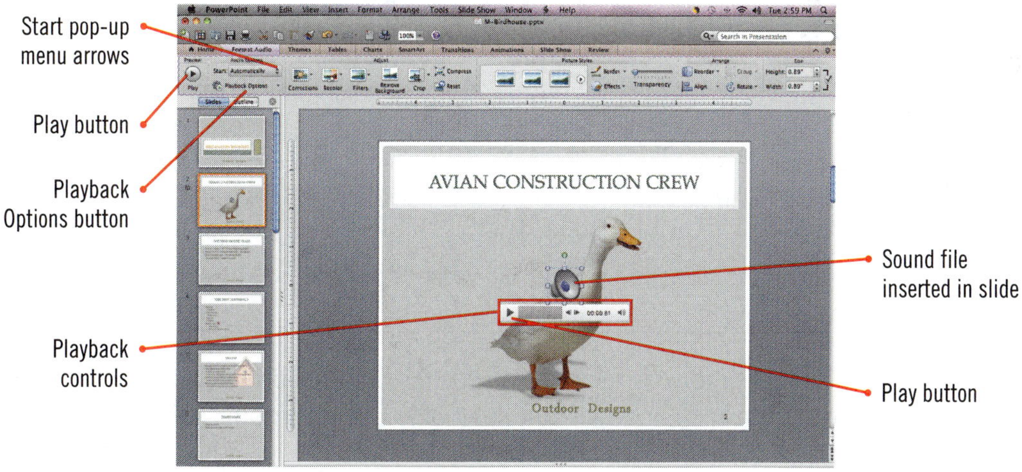

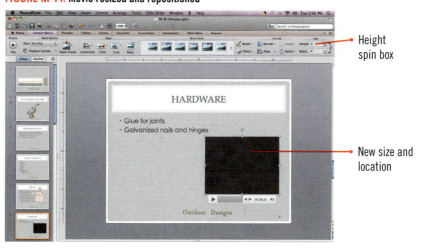

Start pop-up menu arrows

Play button

Playback Options button

Playback controls

Sound file inserted in slide

Play button

AVIAN CONSTRUCTION CREW

Outdoor Designs

FIGURE M-13: Inserting a movie in a slide

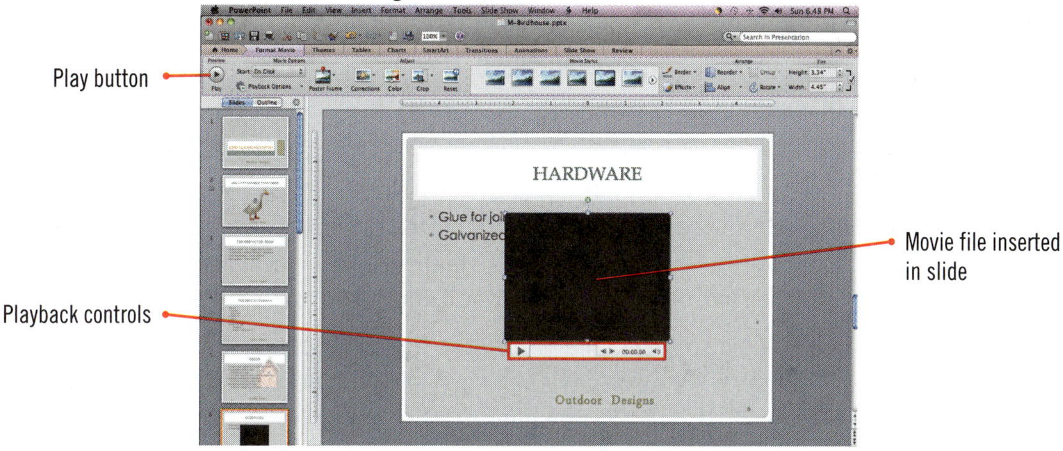

Play button

Playback controls

Movie file inserted in slide

HARDWARE

- Glue for joints
- Galvanized

Outdoor Designs

FIGURE M-14: Movie resized and repositioned

Height spin box

New size and location

HARDWARE

- Glue for joints
- Galvanized nails and hinges

Outdoor Designs

TABLE M-1: Audio and movie file types supported by Macs

file type	formats supported
Audio	.m4a, .aif, .aiff, .aifc, .alaw, .auu, .snd, .ulaw, .au, .al, .caf, .gsm, .wave, .wav, .mpa, .mp2v, .mp2, .mp3, .mpeg, .mpg, .midi, .mid, .kar, .rmi, .qcp, .sd2
Movie	.mov, .moov, .qt, .mpg, .mpeg, .mpe, .m1v, .mpv, .mp4, .dv, .flc, .gif, .smil, .avi
	Please note: QuickTime Virtual Reality (QTVR) files, which have a file extension of .mov or .qt, do not play in PowerPoint 2011.

Editing a Movie

You can edit a movie file from within PowerPoint to create the perfect visual event for your audience. Features on the Format Movie tab allow you to adjust the movie's appearance. For example, you can select a **poster frame**—an image stored on your computer or an image from a movie frame to serve as the movie's "cover," or preview image, on the slide. You can also play the movie full screen during your presentation. To have the movie best match your theme, you can add styles, borders, or effects to it.  Jihong asks you to adjust the movie so it will play full screen and to choose a poster frame that she can use in a flyer.

STEPS

1. **Make sure the movie is selected in Slide 6, click the Format Movie tab, click the Playback Options button** `Playback Options` **in the Movie Options group, then click Play Full Screen, as shown in Figure M-15**

   The Playback Options pop-up menu closes; the movie will now fill the screen when clicked. You'd like a close-up image of the bald eagle to select as the poster frame.

   TROUBLE
   You do not need to click the Pause button at exactly 00:17.00 on the timer. The close-up images of the bald eagle last for over 15 seconds and can be backed up or moved forward .25 seconds at a time by clicking the Move back button ◄ or the Move forward button ►️ located to the left of the timer in the playback controls.

2. **Click the Play button ▶ beneath the movie placeholder to play the movie until the timer reaches approximately 00:17.00, then click the Pause button ⏸ beneath the movie placeholder**

   This section of the movie contains close-up images of a bald eagle, which will make a great poster frame for this movie file.

3. **Click the Poster Frame button 🖼 in the Adjust group, then click Current Frame**

   The bar in the playback controls indicates that the poster frame is set, as shown in Figure M-16. To complete the movie's appearance in the presentation, you decide to add a style to it.

4. **Point to the Movie Styles Gallery until the pop-up menu arrow ▼ appears, click ▼ to open the Movie Styles Gallery, click the Beveled Frame, Gradient style in the Subtle section (first row, fourth column), click a blank area of your slide, then compare your screen with Figure M-17**

   The movie now has a white-and-gray frame around it.

5. **Watch the entire slide show, making sure you click the movie poster frame on Slide 6 to start the movie, return to Normal view, then save your changes**

Downloading media files from the Microsoft Office Web site

In addition to clip art, you can download animations and sounds from the Microsoft Office Web site using the Clip Gallery. To access this feature in PowerPoint, click the Picture button 🖼 in the Insert group on the Home tab of the ribbon, click Clip Art Gallery to open the Clip Gallery, click the Online button, then click Yes when prompted "We will now launch your default Internet browser. Is this OK?" When the Microsoft Office Web site opens, use the search box to enter keywords to locate Illustrations, Photos, Animations, and Sounds that match your keywords.

FIGURE M-15: Playing a movie full screen

Playback
Options button

Play Full
Screen option

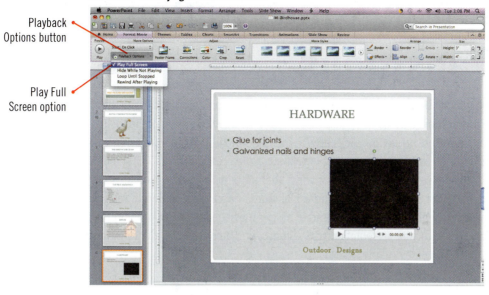

FIGURE M-16: Setting a poster frame

Poster Frame
button

Play button

Movie Styles
Gallery

Indicates
poster frame
has been set

Click to move
backward or forward
.25 seconds

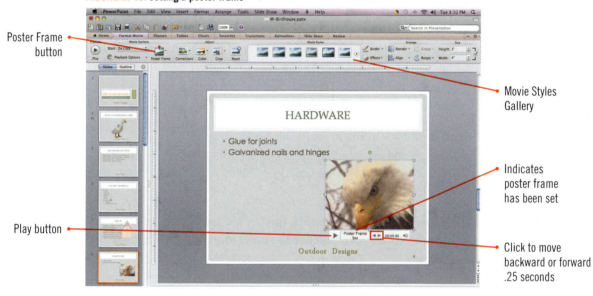

FIGURE M-17: Applying a movie style to a movie

Beveled Frame,
Gradient style
applied to movie

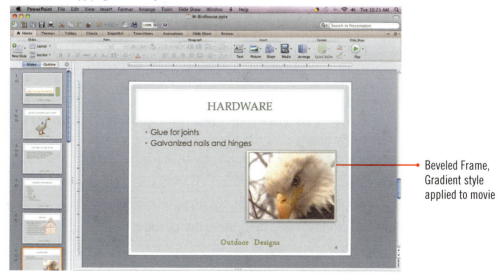

Setting Slide Timing and Transitions

There may be times when you want to run a presentation automatically, without manually controlling the slide progression, such as when you want the presentation to run unattended at a kiosk or booth. You might also want to customize how slides appear in a slide show. To accomplish this, you can set slide timings and transitions. A **timing** is the number of seconds a slide remains on the screen before advancing to the next one, while a **transition** is a special effect that determines how a slide appears as it enters or leaves the screen. You can adjust settings for individual slides or apply one setting to multiple slides. You want to make it easy for Jihong to concentrate on her message instead of running the slide show. You decide to set the timing for the presentation to 8 seconds, add a consistent slide transition, and add an audio transition to the last slide.

STEPS

QUICK TIP

PowerPoint 2011 has many new transitions, such as Ripple, Honeycomb, Glitter, Vortex, and Shred.

1. **Move to Slide 1, click the Transitions tab, point to the Transition to This Slide Gallery until the pop-up menu arrow [▼] appears, then click [▼]**

   The Transition to This Slide Gallery is shown in Figure M-18. You decide to add a transition to the first slide.

2. **Click the Cube transition in the second row of the Exciting section**

   The Cube transition is applied to the slide. When a slide has a transition applied to it, a small transition icon appears beneath the slide number in the Slides and Outline pane. Now that you have selected a transition, you want to apply these settings to the entire presentation.

QUICK TIP

To adjust the timing or transition for an individual slide, select the slide, then adjust the settings as desired.

3. **Click the All Slides button in the Apply To group**

   The transition you applied to Slide 1 is now applied to all slides in the presentation. The transition icon appears next to every slide in the Slides and Outline pane. You now want to set the slide show to advance automatically after a set amount of time.

QUICK TIP

To remove a transition for the current slide, open the Transition to This Slide Gallery, then click None.

4. **In the Advance Slide group, click the On Mouse Click check box to deselect it, click the After check box to select it, click the up arrow until 8.00 appears in the After spin box, then click**

   Each slide will remain on the screen for 8 seconds before advancing to the next slide. During a presentation, you can manually override these settings by using any navigation method: pressing [spacebar], pressing [return], or clicking the Next Slide button on the Slide Show toolbar. Because you deselected On Mouse Click, the only option that will *not* advance your slide is clicking the left button.

5. **Click the Slide Sorter View button on the status bar, then adjust the zoom as needed so that all slides are easily visible**

   The slide timing and transition icons are visible beneath each thumbnail.

QUICK TIP

You can also play the effects applied to a slide by clicking the transition icon.

6. **Move to Slide 8, click the Sound pop-up menu arrow in the Transition to This Slide group, click Drum Roll, compare your screen with Figure M-19, then click the Play button in the Preview group**

   A preview of the Drum Roll sound that will play during the transition to Slide 8 is heard. You can preview any special effects added to a slide in Slide Sorter view.

QUICK TIP

Be aware that you can easily overwhelm or distract your audience if you apply several different slide transitions or insert too much media in a presentation.

7. **Move to Slide 1, click the Slide Show button on the status bar, view the slide show, switch to Normal view, then save your changes**

   The slide transitions, timing, and sounds play in the slide show.

Polishing and Running a Presentation

FIGURE M-18: Selecting a slide transition

Transitions tab

Transition to This Slide Gallery

In Step 2, click this transition

On Mouse Click check box

All Slides button

After spin box

After check box

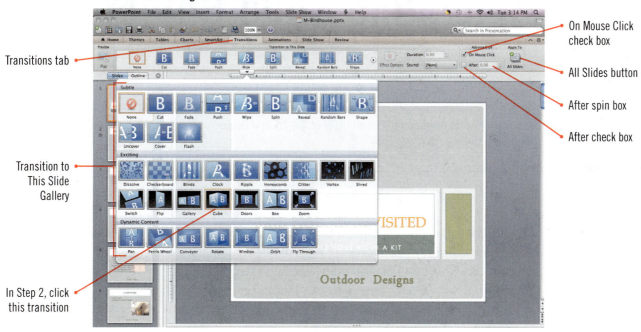

FIGURE M-19: Inserting a transition sound in a slide in Slide Sorter view

Play button

Transition icon

Sound pop-up menu arrow

Zoom slider

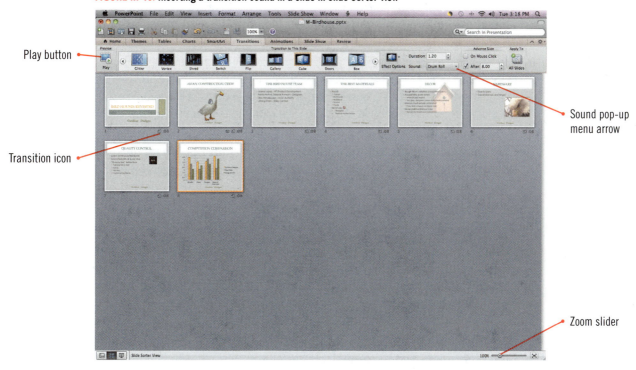

Animating Slide Objects

Just as transitions animate the way slides advance on-screen during a slide show, you can animate individual text objects and images in a slide, such as clip art, photos, illustrations, and charts. An **animation** is the movement (entrance, for emphasis, or exit effect) that can be applied to any object in a slide. You select an animation from the Animations tab and adjust how and when the animation effect plays. You can also apply multiple animations to an object.  You decide to animate the bulleted text in Slide 6 and the text in Slide 3.

STEPS

1. **Select Slide 6, then click anywhere in the bulleted text**

> **QUICK TIP**
> When a special effect has been added to a slide, like an audio file or animation, a star icon appears beneath the selected slide's number (or transition icon if one has been applied) in the Slides and Outline pane when the Slides tab is selected.

2. **Click the Animations tab, point to the Entrance Effects Gallery until the pop-up menu arrow ▼ appears, click ▼ to display the gallery, as shown in Figure M-20, then click Bounce animation in the Exciting category**
The bullets "bounce" in. When you animate a bulleted list, each bulleted item animates separately. You want to adjust the animation so that both items bounce in at the same time but have a slight delay before entering the slide.

3. **Click the Toolbox button 🖽 on the Standard toolbar, then click the Custom Animation tab, if necessary**
The Custom Animation tab displays a list of animation effects added to the selected slide in the order they will animate.

> **QUICK TIP**
> You can modify other effect options and timing for an animation by opening the Effect Options group, the Timing group, and the Text Animations group in the Custom Animation tab on the Toolbox.

4. **Verify that Animation is selected on the Toolbox, click the Effect Options button in the Animation Options group on the ribbon (you may have to move the Toolbox), then click All at Once**
The two lines bounce in together. If you have multiple animations, you can adjust when they play by using the Start options in the Animation Options group on the Animations tab: Select On Click to have the animations start when you click a mouse button, select With Previous for them to play simultaneously, or select After Previous for them to play in a sequence. You want the animation to be delayed.

5. **Click the Timing group on the Toolbox, click the Start pop-up menu arrows, click With Previous, type 1.5 in the Delay spin box, then compare your screen with Figure M-21**

6. **Click the Play button 🌟 in the Preview group**
The bulleted items bounce in all at once after a short time. You want to apply these settings to another object.

> **QUICK TIP**
> You can also apply a sound effect with an animation effect by opening the Effect Options group on the Toolbox, then selecting a sound effect from the Sound pop-up menu.

7. **Move to Slide 3, click anywhere in the bulleted text, repeat Steps 2 through 5 to apply the same animation, then compare your screen with Figure M-22**
The delayed bounced animation is added to the bulleted list of names.

8. **Click the Slide Show tab, click 🅖 to view the slide show from the beginning, then press [esc] to return to Normal view**
The slide show plays with the transitions and animation effects that you applied.

9. **Close the Toolbox, then save your changes**

Polishing and Running a Presentation

FIGURE M-20: Selecting an animation

Animations tab

In Step 2, click this animation

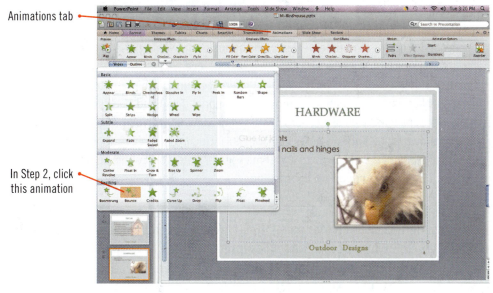

FIGURE M-21: Using the Toolbox to alter animation effects

Toolbox button

Icon that represents a special effect has been added to this slide

Effect Options button

Toolbox with Custom Animation tab selected

Selected animation is highlighted

Timing group

Start pop-up menu arrows

Delay spin box

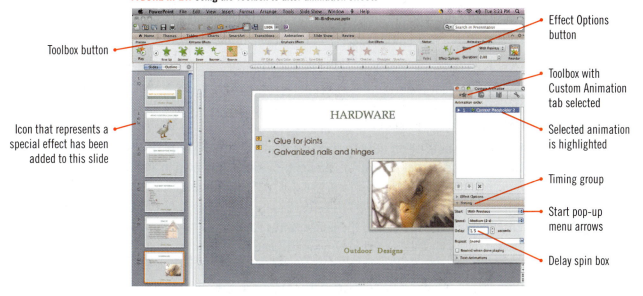

FIGURE M-22: Additional animation applied

Play button

Additional animations added to bulleted text in Slide 3

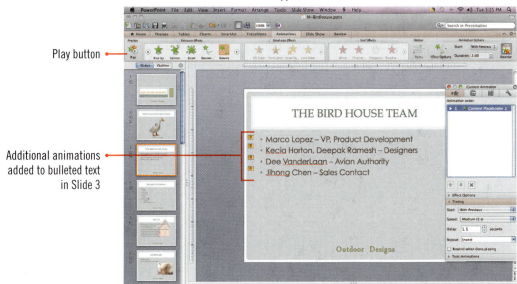

THE BIRD HOUSE TEAM

- Marco Lopez – VP, Product Development
- Kecia Horton, Deepak Ramesh – Designers
- Dee VanderLaan – Avian Authority
- Jihong Chen – Sales Contact

Outdoor Designs

Creating Speaker Notes

Even experienced speakers sometimes feel nervous or anxious giving a presentation. As a presenter, having notes on hand that list key points can be very helpful, even if you just glance at them from time to time. **Speaker notes** contain key points you can reference during the presentation. For your audience, distributing speaker notes with handouts provides additional detail and background. You enter speaker notes in the Notes pane in Normal view or in Notes Page view. When you print speaker notes, each slide is printed on its own page, and the notes you added—including graphics—appear beneath the slide on the page.  Jihong has asked you to add some speaker notes to a couple of slides in the presentation to ensure she does not miss important information.

STEPS

1. Move to **Slide 1**, click the **Notes pane**, then type **Many companies make recycled plastic products – here's why wood kits are still supreme.**

   The text appears in the Notes pane. Jihong has also given you notes to add to the team slide.

2. Move to **Slide 3**, click the **Notes pane**, type **Marco: Won 1st place at the Fiery Food Show for Green Chili Enchiladas**, then type the following text, each on its own line:

   Kecia: Won a local Emmy for a pet safety ad when she was 17

   Deepak: Has a first-edition collection of Octavia Butler novels

   Dee: Taught her parrot to say "I'm really a dinosaur"

   Jihong: Was first-chair clarinet in her college marching band

   The default space allotted to the Notes pane is not sufficient to view all of your notes. You want to resize the Notes pane so that you can see all the text.

3. Position the pointer on the **top border** of the Notes pane until the pointer changes to [↕], then drag the **border** up until all the text is visible, as shown in Figure M-23

   All of the text is visible in the Notes pane. Now that you've entered all the speaker notes, you want to preview how the notes will look when printed with the slide.

4. Click **View** on the menu bar, then click **Notes Page**

   The slide opens in Notes Page view, as shown in Figure M-24, and displays the slide on the top half of the window and notes on the bottom half of the window. You want to print only the pages that have notes.

5. Click 🖳 to return to Normal view, click **Slide 1** in the Slides and Outline pane, press and hold ⌘, then click **Slide 3**

   Holding ⌘ while clicking another slide allows you to select multiple slides that are not adjacent to one another.

6. Click **File** on the menu bar, then click **Print**

   The Print dialog box opens, allowing you to make changes to how the presentation will print.

7. Click the **Selected Slides option button** in the Slides section, click the **Print What pop-up menu arrows**, click **Notes**, then compare your screen with Figure M-25

   Only Slides 1 and 3 are selected to print as Notes pages.

8. Click **Cancel**, save your changes, close the presentation, then quit PowerPoint

FIGURE M-23: Resized Notes pane

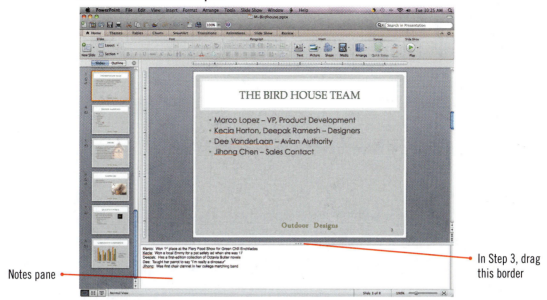

Notes pane

In Step 3, drag this border

FIGURE M-24: Viewing a slide and notes in Notes Page view

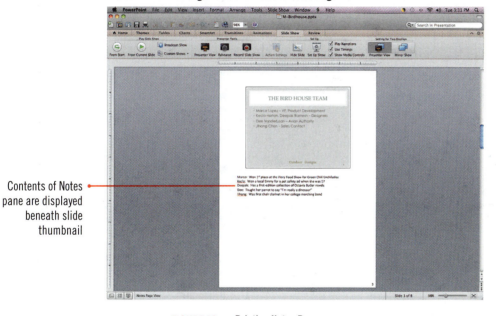

Contents of Notes pane are displayed beneath slide thumbnail

FIGURE M-25: Printing Notes Pages

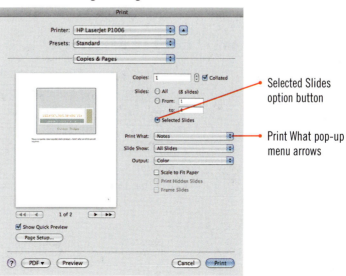

Selected Slides option button

Print What pop-up menu arrows

Practice

Concepts Review

Label the PowerPoint window elements shown in Figure M-26.

FIGURE M-26

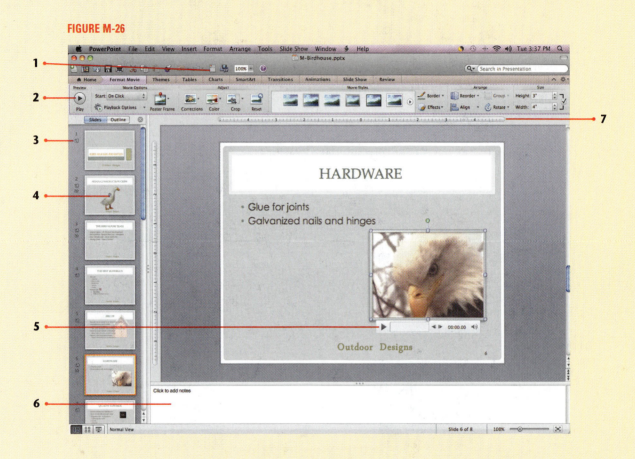

Match each term with the statement that best describes it.

8. **Poster frame**
9. **Transition**
10. **Animation**
11. **Crop**
12. **Transition sound**

a. A tool that is often used to hide or trim part of a picture

b. An image from your computer or an image created from a movie frame that serves as the movie's "cover," or preview image, on the slide

c. A special effect that determines how a slide advances on the screen

d. A sound effect that plays as one slide advances to the next slide in a presentation

e. An effect that triggers movement of a specific element in a slide

Select the best answer from the list of choices.

13. Which of the following about animations is *not* correct?

    a. You can apply them only to clip art.

    b. You can apply multiple animations to an object.

    c. You can control the speed at which they play.

    d. You can easily edit them.

14. Which of the following best describes a transition?

    a. Determines the amount of time a slide is visible

    b. Determines how long an animated object plays

    c. Determines whether media plays automatically or needs to be clicked

    d. Determines how a slide appears as it enters or leaves the screen

15. Which of the following views does *not* have a view icon on the status bar?

    a. Slide Sorter view

    b. Slide Show

    c. Notes Page view

    d. Normal view

16. Which of the following is true about audio files inserted in a slide?

    a. They cannot be clicked to start playing.

    b. The speaker icon cannot be hidden during Slide Show.

    c. They can be added to a slide by clicking the Media button on the Home tab of the ribbon.

    d. Audio files cannot be inserted in a slide.

Skills Review

1. Add a shape.

    a. Start PowerPoint, open the file M-2.pptx from the location where you store your Data Files, then save it as **M-Natural Fiber Rug Sales.pptx**.

    b. Move to Slide 6.

    c. Make sure that the rulers are visible; if necessary, use a tool on the View menu to display them.

    d. Insert a Down Ribbon shape on the slide. Place the shape at the 2" mark at the right on the horizontal ruler and the 2.5" mark at the top of the vertical ruler. (*Hint*: This shape is located in the Stars and Banners section in the Shapes Gallery.)

    e. Open the Shape Styles Gallery, then apply the style that is the second option in the second row.

    f. Select the shape if necessary, click the Fill pop-up menu arrow in the Shape Styles group, click Fill Effects to open the Format Shape dialog box, click the Picture or Texture tab, then apply the Green Marble texture to the shape.

    g. Type **Banner Year** in the shape, make the text bold, resize and position the shape if necessary, then compare your shape with Figure M-27.

    h. Save your changes.

FIGURE M-27

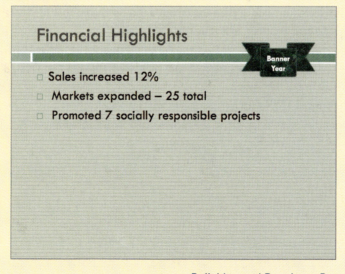

PowerPoint 2011

2. **Add clip art.**
   a. Move to Slide 7, then insert a new Title and Content slide.
   b. Click the title placeholder, then type **To the Future….**
   c. Click the Clip Art Browser button in the content placeholder.
   d. Change the category on the Clip Art tab of the Media Browser from All Images to Photos, then insert the clip art photo shown in Figure M-28.
   e. Open the Picture Styles Gallery, then click the Rotated, White style. (*Hint:* The effect is in the third row.)
   f. Close the Media Browser, then save your changes.

FIGURE M-28

3. **Work with pictures.**
   a. Move to Slide 2, then use a command on the Home tab to open the Choose a Picture dialog box.
   b. Insert the file **sisal.jpg** from the location where you store your Data Files.
   c. Use a command in the Arrange group to send the object to the back of the slide.
   d. Verify that the sisal image is selected, click the Crop button in the Adjust group, drag the top border of the photograph down below the green bar, then click the Crop tool to turn it off.
   e. Click the Recolor button, then recolor the photo to Accent Color 5 Light. (*Hint:* The effect is in the bottom row.)
   f. Save your changes.

4. **Add sound and video.**
   a. Download a music file of your choice from the Microsoft Office Web site. (*Hint:* Follow the instructions in the Clues to Use at the bottom of page 308. In the search box, type music and click the Sounds check box.)
   b. Move to Slide 1, then use a command on the Home tab to insert the downloaded music file.
   c. On the Format Audio tab, select the Playback Options to hide the sound icon during the show and to loop until stopped.
   d. Select Play Across Slides from the Start pop-up menu in the Audio Options group, then play the sound.
   e. Move to Slide 3, then use a command on the Home tab to insert a movie from file.
   f. Navigate to the location where you store your Data Files, insert the movie **afghanrug.mov**, then play it.
   g. Change the size of the movie to 3" high by 4" wide, then move the movie to the lower-right corner of the slide.
   h. View the slide show from the beginning, then save your changes.

5. **Edit a movie.**
   a. Make sure the movie is selected in Slide 3, then use a command on the Format Movie tab to play the movie full screen.
   b. Play the movie, then pause it at approximately the 00:06.00 mark.
   c. Use a command on the Format Movie tab to select the current frame as the poster frame.
   d. Open the Movie Styles Gallery on the Format Movie tab, then apply the Beveled Oval, Black style in the Moderate section.
   e. Use a command on the Format Movie tab to start the movie automatically.
   f. Start the slide show from the beginning, watch the movie, then save your changes.

Skills Review (continued)

6. Set slide timing and transitions.

   a. Open the Transition to This Slide Gallery on the Transitions tab.

   b. Select the Cover transition, then apply it to all the slides. (*Hint*: The transition is in the second row of the Subtle section.)

   c. In the Advance Slide group, deselect the On Mouse Click check box, click the After check box, set the time to 3 seconds, then apply the timing to all the slides.

   d. Change to Slide Sorter view.

   e. Move to Slide 8, then add the Ricochet transition sound to the slide.

   f. View the slide show from the beginning, then save your changes.

7. Animate slide objects.

   a. Switch to Normal view, move to Slide 6, then click anywhere in the bulleted list.

   b. Apply the Wipe animation as an entrance effect to the list. (*Hint*: This effect is located in the Basic category.)

   c. Click the Effect Options button, then click From Top.

   d. Open the Toolbox, click the Custom Animation tab if necessary, then change the animation delay to .25 seconds.

   e. Move to Slide 8 and apply the same animation effect (Steps 7b–d) to the clip art photo.

   f. Close the Toolbox, view the slide show, then save your changes.

   g. Switch to Slide Sorter view, then compare your screen to Figure M-29.

8. Create speaker notes.

   a. Move to Slide 2, then type in the Notes pane: **Weaving started in Egypt at least 8,000 years ago**.

   b. Move to Slide 6, then type in the Notes pane: **Green building and government projects have been very successful**

      Working with international groups is very promising

      New podcasts bring in many visitors to the Web site

   c. If necessary, increase the size of the Notes pane to accommodate the notes text.

   d. View the slides in Notes Page view, then return to Normal view.

   e. Select Slides 2 and 6 only.

   f. Click File on the menu bar, click Print, then print the selected slides as Notes (if your lab allows printing).

   g. Save your changes, close the presentation, then quit PowerPoint.

   h. Submit your completed presentation (and printed notes) to your instructor.

FIGURE M-29

Independent Challenge 1

You work at A Fine Ruse—a local, independent weekly newspaper. To boost readership, you have decided to host an Annual Best of Ruse contest, honoring a host of different categories. Readers will send in their winning entries, and the paper will devote an issue to the contest. Your job is to come up with categories that are distinctive, interesting, and sure to elicit a response. You want to present your ideas to your colleagues for feedback and fine-tuning.

a. Start PowerPoint, open the file M-3.pptx from the location where you store your Data Files, then save it as **M-Best of Ruse.pptx**.

b. Insert a shape in Slide 1 and add text of your choosing to the shape. (*Hint*: Modify the shape fill, outline, and effects as desired.)

c. Insert clip art in Slides 5, 6, 7, 8, and 9, choosing clips that pertain to each topic, and apply styles as desired.

d. Move to Slide 3 and insert the movie file **Books.mov**, stored with your Data Files. Reposition and resize the movie as desired.

e. Add a poster frame to the movie in Slide 3.

f. Move to Slide 4 and insert the movie file **Coffee.mov**, one of your Data Files. Reposition and resize the movie as desired.

g. Add a poster frame to the movie in Slide 4.

h. On the same slide, insert the audio file **coffee_grinder.mp3**. Change the start to Automatically (instead of "On Click") and hide the icon during the show.

i. Move to Slide 8 and insert the audio file **Playground Noises.mp3**, one of your Data Files. Change the start to Automatically and hide the icon during the show.

j. Apply the Checkerboard slide transition to all slides in the presentation, and advance all slides after 3 seconds.

k. Add the Yeehaw transition sound to Slide 2.

l. Add the Curve Up entrance animation to the title in Slide 2. Change the animation option to start With Previous.

m. Add the Faded Zoom entrance animation to the SmartArt in Slide 2, then change when it starts to After Previous. (*Hint*: Select the SmartArt object, then select the Faded Zoom entrance effect.)

n. Add the Flip entrance animation to the text beneath the title in Slide 1 and customize settings as desired.

o. Add the following notes to Slide 2:
   Allow readers to submit their own categories and winners
   Include side pieces from local personalities listing their favorites

p. Add your name to the slide footer on all slides except the title slide, switch to Slide Sorter view, then compare your presentation with the sample shown in Figure M-30.

Advanced Challenge Exercise

- Add an exit effect animation to at least one object.
- Use your imagination to come up with speaker notes to add to Slide 9.

q. Save your changes, print the Notes page for Slides 2 and 9, close the presentation, then quit PowerPoint.

r. Submit your completed presentation (and printed notes) to your instructor.

FIGURE M-30

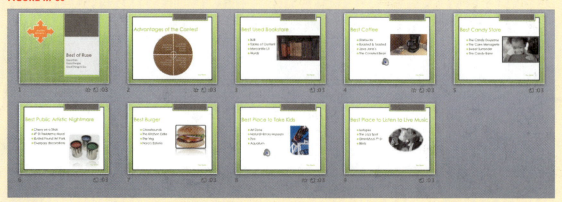

Independent Challenge 2

Your graphics and Web design company, Grafik Traffic, just merged with another large graphics business, Pipeline Design. As you have begun to work on joint projects, you have realized that members of the Pipeline Design staff are not well versed in copyright law. You decide to create a PowerPoint presentation for in-house training on the basics of copyright law.

a. Start PowerPoint, open the file M-4.pptx from the location where you store your Data Files, then save it as **M-Copyright 101.pptx**.

b. Using the Clip Art Browser, insert a photograph in Slide 3, then apply attractive styles and appropriate effects to it.

c. Move to Slide 2 and select a clip art photo image from the Clip Art Browser that relates to a myth listed on this slide. Add a style and effect if desired.

d. In Slide 1, insert the movie file **fedgovt.mov** from the location where you store your Data Files. Resize the movie and move it to the center, above the title.

e. Using the Clip Art Gallery, search for a clip art image using the keyword **law**, then insert it in Slide 9. Adjust the image as desired so that it complements the look of the slide.

f. In Slide 9, insert the audio file **Gavel Banging.mp3** from the location where you store your Data Files. Have it play automatically, and hide the icon during the show.

g. Animate the bulleted text in the first six slides with bulleted lists.

h. Apply the Doors slide transition to all slides, then adjust the slide timing as desired. Deselect the On Mouse Click check box in the Advance Slide group.

i. Add the following notes to Slide 5:
The copyright holder (who may not be the creator) has rights over work: reproduce, prepare derivative works, distribute copies, perform, and display the work

j. Add your name and the slide number to all slides as a footer, view the slide show, then compare your Slide 9 with the sample shown in Figure M-31.

Advanced Challenge Exercise

- Add a photo from the Clip Art Browser of your choosing to a slide in the presentation, then apply two different animations to the object.

k. Save your changes, print Slide 5 as Notes, close the presentation, then quit PowerPoint.

l. Submit your completed presentation (and printed notes) to your instructor.

FIGURE M-31

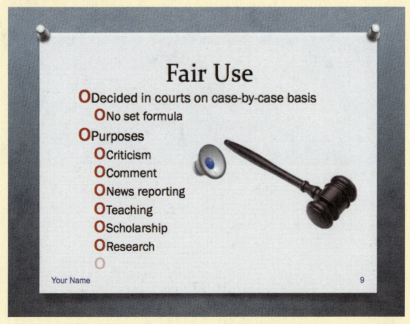

PowerPoint 2011

Independent Challenge 3

You are a business consultant specializing in customer relations. You have been hired to do a workshop for a small business that has a great product, but the company's internal processes need some improvement. You create a PowerPoint presentation that emphasizes customer relationships.

a. Start PowerPoint, open the file M-5.pptx from the location where you store your Data Files, then save it as **M-Customer Trust.pptx**.

b. On Slide 1, add the Wipe Entrance animation to the subtitle that starts With Previous.

c. Move to Slide 4. Using the Clip Art Browser, insert a clip art image from the People category, then send it to the back of the bulleted text. Resize the clip art as necessary. Refer to the sample shown in Figure M-32.

d. Move to Slide 5, insert the image file **sandcastle.jpg** from the location where you store your Data Files, move it behind the text, than apply the effects and styles of your choice.

e. Add one clip art image to Slide 7, and add a photo or clip art image to a slide of your choice. Add effects and styles as desired.

f. Add the transition of your choice to all slides and add the transition sound of your choice to Slide 7.

g. Add at least one shape to a slide of your choice. Modify the shape fill, outline, and effects as desired.

h. Adjust slide timing as desired.

i. Animate at least one text object or image on a slide.

j. Animate each slide title in Slides 2–7, then add an additional animation to the title of the presentation.

k. Add notes to at least two slides.

l. Add your name to the slide footer on all slides, then switch to Slide Sorter view.

m. Save your changes, close the presentation, then quit PowerPoint.

n. Submit your completed presentation to your instructor.

FIGURE M-32

Real Life Independent Challenge

Take advantage of your new skills in PowerPoint to create a presentation for friends, family, or coworkers. Create a slide show about your favorite hobby or topic of interest, and intersperse the slides with related facts or stories.

    a. Start PowerPoint, create a new file from an installed theme or template, then save the file as **M-My Personal Favorite.pptx** in the location where you store your Data Files.

    b. On the title slide, add your name as a subtitle.

    c. Insert photos of your topic, either from your computer or from the Clip Art Browser. (*Hint*: Apply various Picture Styles to the photos.)

    d. Create slides describing the item, person, or creature, or relating to something in the photos, then insert relevant clip art and a movie. (*Note*: You'll need to locate a .mov file to use either from the Internet or from one of your home movies. If you use a movie found on the Internet, remember to cite your source.)

    e. Apply slide transitions, sounds, and slide timings to the presentation.

    f. Add at least one shape to the presentation.

    g. Add notes to at least two slides.

    h. Animate objects as desired.

    i. Add the slide number and your name to the slide footer on all slides except the title slide.

    j. Save your changes, then print the Notes pages if your lab allows printing.

    k. Close the presentation, then quit PowerPoint.

    l. Submit your completed presentation (and printed notes) to your instructor.

Visual Workshop

Create a slide that resembles Figure M-33. Save the presentation as **M-Networking Smarts.pptx** in the location where you store your Data Files. Use default settings for each element. (*Hint*: Start with a blank presentation; after you apply the design theme, add a new Title and Content slide, then delete the Title slide.) Add the animation shown. Add your name to the slide footer, then print the slide. Save your changes, close the presentation, then quit PowerPoint. Submit your completed presentation to your instructor.

FIGURE M-33

Social networking smarts

- Keep private information private

- Think before you post

- Control your profile

- Monitor your tagged photos

Your Name

Integrating Office for Mac 2011 Programs

So far you've created many documents, worksheets, and presentations using individual Microsoft Office programs. You can also create documents that combine information from different Office programs; for example, you can write a newsletter with Microsoft Word and add a chart created with Microsoft Excel. You can also capture a screen or part of a screen to paste into a document or presentation, or to save as an image file. Jihong Chen, assistant sales manager for Outdoor Designs, needs you to insert an Excel chart into a presentation she created, create Microsoft PowerPoint slides from a Word outline, and insert a screen capture into a slide. She also has a letter for the shareholders; she needs you to paste a linked chart into the letter, and then send it out as a mail merge form letter. You use several Office programs to accomplish these tasks.

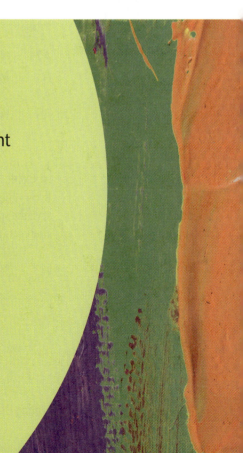

OBJECTIVES

Insert an Excel chart into a PowerPoint slide

Insert PowerPoint slides from a Word document

Share a clip using the Toolbox

Insert text from a Word file into an open document

Link an Excel chart to a Word document

Update a linked Excel chart in a Word document

Insert placeholders in a Word document

Perform a mail merge

Inserting an Excel Chart into a PowerPoint Slide

An Excel chart is an excellent tool for communicating numerical data visually. You can create an Excel chart right from a PowerPoint slide to convey financial results or trends to your audience. When you create a chart in PowerPoint, you embed data from Excel into the presentation. When you **embed** data, the data becomes part of the new file, regardless of what program the data came from. Once the chart is inserted into a presentation, you can update it when you open the spreadsheet in Excel or from the Chart Tools tab in PowerPoint. Jihong has given you a presentation she created for the quarterly sales meeting and a hard copy of sales figures. You need to insert a chart comparing sales, so you decide to create the chart directly in PowerPoint.

STEPS

1. **Start PowerPoint, open the file N-1.pptx from the location where you store your Data Files, then save it as N-Sales and Projections.pptx**

QUICK TIP
You can also insert a chart without using the Insert Chart icon in the content placeholder by clicking the Charts tab on the ribbon, clicking the appropriate Chart button, then clicking the appropriate chart type.

2. **Move to Slide 2, then click the Insert Chart icon 📊 in the content placeholder**
   PowerPoint opens the Charts tab, where you select the chart type that you would like to insert in this slide.

3. **Click the Column Chart button 📊 in the Insert Chart group, then click the Clustered Cylinder in the Cylinder category, as shown in Figure N-1**
   Excel opens in front of PowerPoint with sample data in a new spreadsheet, as shown in Figure N-2. In PowerPoint, a chart based on the sample data appears in the slide and the Chart Layout and Format tabs appear on the ribbon. You replace the sample data in Excel with data from Jihong's report.

QUICK TIP
If you want to use only certain cells from the Excel worksheet in your PowerPoint chart, delete the cells containing the unused sample data in Excel; if you want to add additional data to a chart, continue typing data in adjacent cells on the Excel worksheet.

4. **Replace the data in the worksheet with the data in the following table:**

cell	data	cell	data	cell	data	cell	data
		B1	Q4 2012	C1	Q4 2013	D1	Projected Q4 2014
A2	Northeast	B2	525,000	C2	544,100	D2	579,000
A3	Midwest	B3	478,300	C3	491,000	D3	516,000
A4	Southwest	B4	389,600	C4	400,000	D4	419,200
A5	West	B5	415,700	C5	427,500	D5	453,000

   As you enter the data in Excel, the chart data in the slide is updated

5. **In Excel, click Excel on the menu bar, then click Quit Excel**
   Excel closes and the chart in PowerPoint is updated in Slide 2, as shown in Figure N-3. It is not necessary to save the spreadsheet in Excel; the data is embedded in Slide 2 in PowerPoint. If you later decide to edit the chart data from PowerPoint, the data opens in a new spreadsheet to give you access to Excel tools.

6. **Save your changes to the presentation**

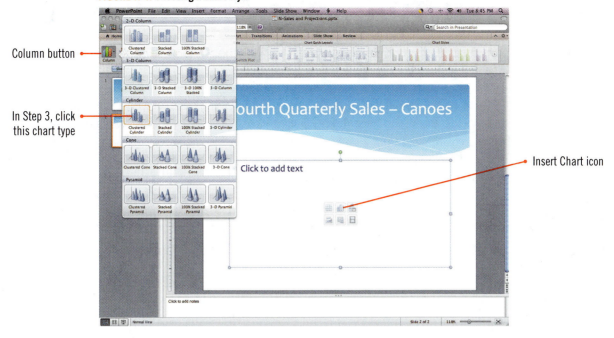

Column button

In Step 3, click this chart type

Insert Chart icon

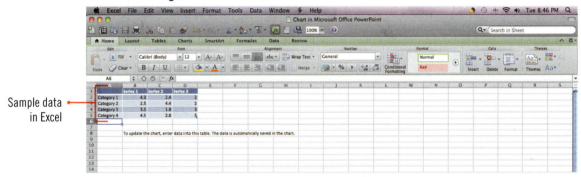

Sample data in Excel

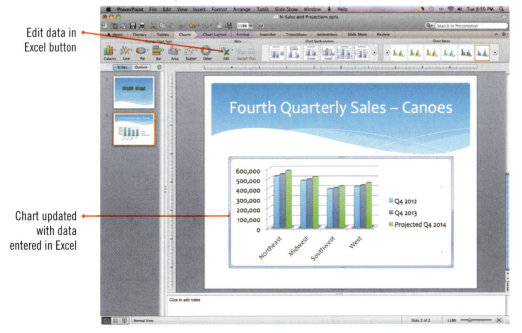

Edit data in Excel button

Chart updated with data entered in Excel

Integration 2011

Inserting PowerPoint Slides from a Word Document

You can use an outline that you've created in Word as a starting point for a new PowerPoint presentation or to add slides to an existing presentation. Outline view makes it easy to see how a document is organized. When you create slides from a Word document, Outline view in PowerPoint lets you easily see how the structure will translate to the levels in a slide. Level-1 lines of text from Word appear as slide titles, and lower-level Word text appears as bulleted text. 🎨 Jihong wants you to use one of her outlines as a starting point for several new slides in the presentation. First, you want to view the document in Word.

1. **Start Word, then open the file N-2.docx from the location where you store your Data Files**

2. **Click the Outline View button** 🔲 **on the status bar**

   The text appears in a hierarchical structure using headings and subheadings—perfect for a PowerPoint presentation. You can use Outline view any time you need to organize topics or restructure a document. You can adjust the outlining structure by selecting a line or paragraph and clicking the Promote button 🔲, Demote button 🔲, Move Up button 🔲, or Move Down button 🔲. You can change the view by clicking the Expand button 🔲 or Collapse button 🔲 in the Outline Tools group, as shown in Figure N-4.

3. **Click File on the menu bar, then click Save As**

   The Save As dialog box opens.

4. **If necessary, navigate to the location where your Data Files are stored, click the Format pop-up menu arrows in the Save As dialog box, click Rich Text Format (.rtf), then click Save**

   Word saves the file as a Rich Text Format document with the filename N-2.rtf (same filename, but a new extension).

5. **Click Word on the menu bar, then click Quit Word**

   The Word document and the Word program close.

6. **In PowerPoint, click Slide 2 in the Slides and Outline pane if necessary, click the Home tab, click the New Slide pop-up menu arrow in the Slides group, then click Insert Slides from Outline (the last option on this menu)**

   The Choose a File dialog box opens.

7. **Navigate to the location where you store your Data Files, click N-2.rtf, as shown in Figure N-5, then click Insert**

   Three new slides are inserted in the presentation, as shown in Figure N-6. Each Level-1 line of the outline appears as the slide title, and lower-level text appears as bulleted text. The new slides have the theme that was applied to the original Word document. When the theme of the original Word document differs from the theme of the presentation into which its outline is inserted, you'll need to reset the slides' layout so the new slides are formatted with the theme used in PowerPoint.

8. **Select the three newly added slides in the Slides and Outline pane, click the Layout button** 🔲 **in the Slides group, then click the Reset Layout to Default Settings button**

   The newly added slides are formatted with the theme of the presentation.

9. **Add your name to the slide footer, click Apply to All, then save your changes**

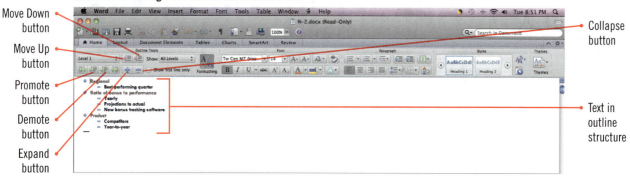

FIGURE N-4: Viewing a Word document in Outline view

Move Down button

Move Up button

Promote button

Demote button

Expand button

Collapse button

Text in outline structure

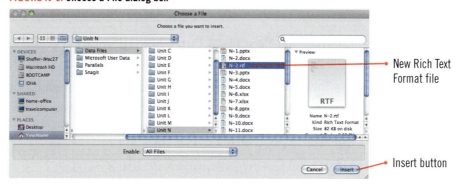

FIGURE N-5: Choose a File dialog box

New Rich Text Format file

Insert button

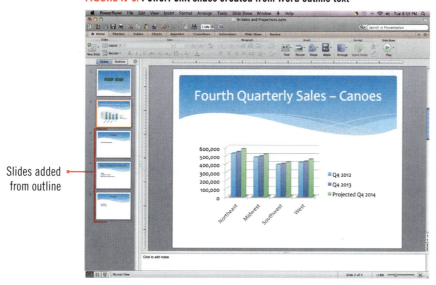

FIGURE N-6: PowerPoint slides created from Word outline text

Slides added from outline

Fourth Quarterly Sales – Canoes

Using outlines in Word and PowerPoint

If you want to create an outline in Word that you can use as the basis for a PowerPoint presentation, it is best to create or structure a document that is formatted for this purpose. Start a new document in Word, then click the Outline View button [icon] on the status bar. As you type your outline text, use the Promote and Demote buttons in the Outline Tools group to apply a level for each line. Word applies the Heading 1 style for slide titles, Heading 2 for the first level of indented text, and so on. It's important to use the built-in heading styles in Word when you create your outline because the heading tags determine the structure of the outline when it is inserted into

PowerPoint. When the outline is complete, be sure to save the file as a Rich Text Format (.rtf) so you won't have any problems converting the file for use in PowerPoint.

You can also reverse this process: You can use a PowerPoint presentation in outline format to create an outline in Word. To do this, click File on the PowerPoint menu bar, click Save As, click the Format pop-up menu arrows, and then click Outline/Rich Text Format (*.rtf) under Specialty Formats. Next, open the document in Word. From there, you can add or delete text, promote or demote outline levels, and resize or reformat the text as desired.

Sharing a Clip Using the Toolbox

The Screenshot feature, available in Word and PowerPoint, allows you to capture an image from another active program window on your screen and insert it into an open Word document or PowerPoint presentation. You can take a screen shot of an entire window or part of a window, which gives you a quick way to include graphics or data you could not otherwise insert.  Jihong wants to include a screen shot from a PowerPoint presentation as a logo in a letter to shareholders. You use the Screenshot tool to capture a clip of the slide as it plays in Slide Show view.

STEPS

1. **In PowerPoint, open the file N-3.pptx from the location where you store your Data Files, watch the animation play in Slide Show view, then press [esc]**

2. **Click the Toolbox button 📷 on the Standard toolbar, then click the Scrapbook tab 📇**

   The Scrapbook opens, as shown in Figure N-7. The Scrapbook is a useful tool that makes it easy to share text or graphics among the Office programs. Each item stored on the Scrapbook is known as a "clip." You want to add a slide in this presentation to the Scrapbook so you can use it as a logo for a Word document.

3. **In the Slides and Outline pane, click Slide 1 to select it**

   Even though it appears that the slide was selected when you opened the Toolbox, none of the options are available on the Scrapbook tab until you select the item after opening it. Once you click Slide 1, the Add button ⊕ Add on the Scrapbook becomes active and available for use.

4. **Click the Add button ⊕ Add on the Scrapbook, then compare your screen with Figure N-8**

   Slide 1 is added to the Scrapbook as a clip. All clips added to the Scrapbook remain on the Scrapbook until deleted, even after you quit the Office program. This clip can now be inserted into any Office document, regardless of what program created it.

5. **Start Word, open the file N-4.docx from the location where you store your Data Files, then save it as N-Shareholder letter.docx**

6. **If necessary, press [⌘][home] to move to the top of the document, press [return] to insert a new line, press [▲] to move up a line, then click the Center Text button ▤ in the Paragraph group**

   You set the insertion point at the top center of your document. You want the clip of the PowerPoint slide to appear here as a logo.

7. **Click the Toolbox button 📷 on the Standard toolbar, then click 📇 if necessary**

   The Toolbox does not automatically open when you start an Office program.

8. **Click the clip of the PowerPoint slide on the Scrapbook, then click the Paste button 📋 Paste**

   The clip of the PowerPoint slide is inserted at the top of the document. You can adjust its color and apply styles to the clip. The image of the ocean canoeist is a little large for the letter, so you resize it.

9. **Click the image in the Word document to select it, click the Format Picture tab on the ribbon, double-click the Height spin box in the Size group, type 2, press [return], click a blank area of the document, then compare your letter with Figure N-9**

   The image is resized and centered between the margins at the top of your document. You can adjust the image and apply styles to it as you would any photograph.

10. **Close the Toolbox, save your changes to the document, close the presentations in PowerPoint, then quit PowerPoint**

FIGURE N-7: Viewing the Scrapbook

Scrapbook tab

Clips (your Scrapbook might contain different images or might not contain any images)

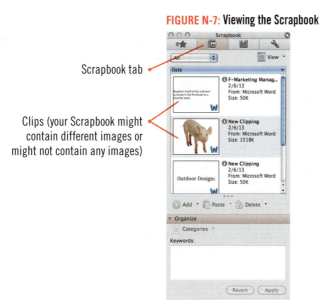

FIGURE N-8: Adding a clip to the Scrapbook

Selected slide

Selected slide added to the Scrapbook as a clip

Paste button

Add button

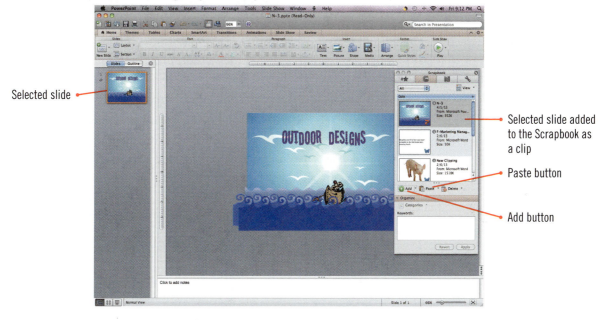

FIGURE N-9: Clip inserted into a Word document

Inserted and resized clip

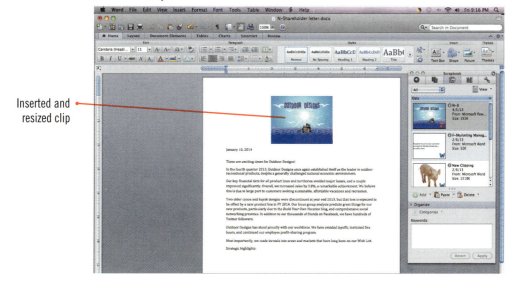

Inserting Text from a Word File into an Open Document

As you work, you might want to combine two files into one, or insert one document into another. Although you can easily copy and paste information between two or more open documents, it is sometimes easier to insert the contents of a file without having to open it first.  Jihong wants you to include sales highlights from a document she created in the letter to shareholders that you have been working on.

1. **In Word, scroll down if necessary, position the insertion point on the blank line immediately following the text Strategic highlights:, click Insert on the menu bar, then click File**

   The Insert File dialog box opens.

2. **Navigate to the location where you store your Data Files, click N-5.docx, then click Insert**

   The contents of the file, consisting of five lines of text, are inserted at the bottom of the letter, as shown in Figure N-10.

3. **Select the five lines of text you just inserted, click the Home tab if necessary, click the Bulleted List pop-up menu arrow ▤▾ in the Paragraph group, then click the hollow bullet style, as shown in Figure N-11**

   The strategic highlights text is formatted as a bulleted list.

4. **Press [↓], click the Layout tab, click the Break button ▦ in the Page Setup group, then click Page**

   A new page is inserted at the end of the document.

5. **Save your changes to the document**

FIGURE N-10: File inserted in letter

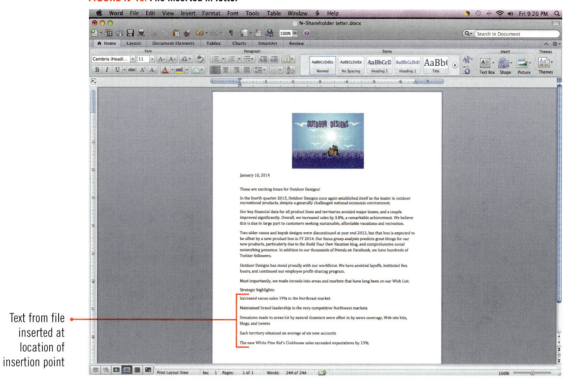

Text from file
inserted at
location of
insertion point

FIGURE N-11: Formatting bulleted text

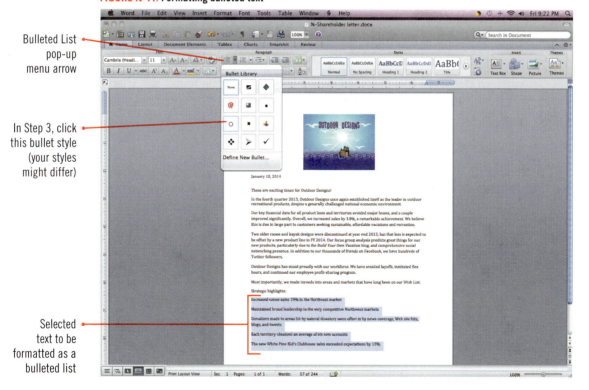

Bulleted List
pop-up
menu arrow

In Step 3, click
this bullet style
(your styles
might differ)

Selected
text to be
formatted as a
bulleted list

Linking an Excel Chart to a Word Document

When you want to keep data updated between two files, you can link the files together. For example, you might have an Excel chart saved in a spreadsheet that you've also pasted into a Word document. If you change the data in the Excel file, and you want the Word document to reflect those changes, you need to link the files. A **link** displays information from a **source** file, which is the original file containing the data, in the **destination** file, the location to which that data is copied or moved. In a Word document, linked data looks just like inserted or embedded data. However, you can edit the linked data in its native program just by double-clicking it. 🎨 Jihong wants to add data from the focus group to the shareholder letter. She is not certain if she wants to include the data, the chart, or both. You decide to link the Excel spreadsheet to the shareholder letter so that if Jihong updates any of the data, the changes will be updated automatically in the letter.

STEPS

QUICK TIP
Using the Keep Source Formatting and Link to Excel option applies the current Excel style and formatting options and permits updating from Word or Excel. This is useful if you want to paste the same data in multiple files and not worry about updating each file individually.

TROUBLE
There is a bug in Word that occurs occasionally when you insert a linked chart. If your chart appears cropped, delete the linked chart, open the Excel file that contains the chart, select the chart, click the Layout tab on the ribbon, click the Size button 🗔, click Page Setup, click the Landscape option button on the Page tab, click OK, save your changes to the Excel file, then repeat Steps 5–8.

1. **Start Excel, open the file N-6.xlsx from the location where you store your Data Files, then save it as N-Focus Group.xlsx**

   The worksheet contains data and a chart.

2. **Click the Sheet1 tab, select the cell range A1:D6, then click the Copy button 🗔 on the Standard toolbar**

   The cells are copied to the operating system Clipboard.

3. **Switch to the Word file, click the Paste button 📋 on the Standard toolbar, click the Paste Options button, as shown in Figure N-12, then click Keep Source Formatting and Link to Excel**

   The cells are pasted in the Word document.

4. **Switch to the Excel file, then click the Focus Group Results tab**

   To link to a chart, the chart has to be the active tab of an Excel file.

5. **Switch to the Word file, press [return], click Insert on the menu bar, then click Object**

   The Object dialog box opens.

6. **Click Microsoft Excel Chart in the Object type list, as shown in Figure N-13, then click the From File button**

   The Insert as Object dialog box opens.

7. **Navigate to the location where you store your Data Files, click the N-Focus Group.xlsx file, then click the Link to File check box in the lower half of the dialog box**

   Inserting the contents of the file as a linked object permits automatic updating from Word or in Excel.

8. **Click Insert**

   The Insert as Object dialog box closes and the Excel chart appears in the Shareholder letter document as a linked worksheet object. When an Excel workbook is linked as a Microsoft Excel Sheet object, only the active sheet in the linked workbook is displayed. The chart is too big to fit neatly on this page. You want to resize it.

9. **Click the chart to select it, click and drag the sizing handle in the lower-left corner until the Help Tag reads "Width: 6.5"," then click a blank area of the document**

   The chart now fits neatly on the page. When resizing the chart using the sizing handles, if you can't get the Width to exactly 6.5 inches, right-click the chart (or [control] click), select Format Object to open the Format Object dialog box, then click the Size tab. In the Width section, change the Absolute value to 6.5".

10. **Save your changes, compare your screen with Figure N-14, then close the N-Shareholder letter document**

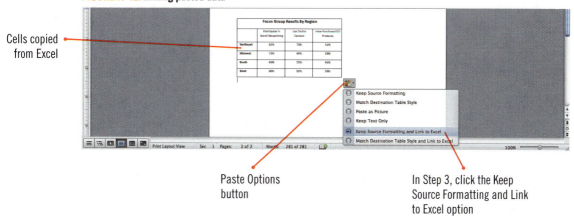

Cells copied from Excel

Paste Options button

In Step 3, click the Keep Source Formatting and Link to Excel option

FIGURE N-13: Object dialog box

Microsoft Excel Chart option

From File button

FIGURE N-14: Excel chart inserted as a linked object in Word

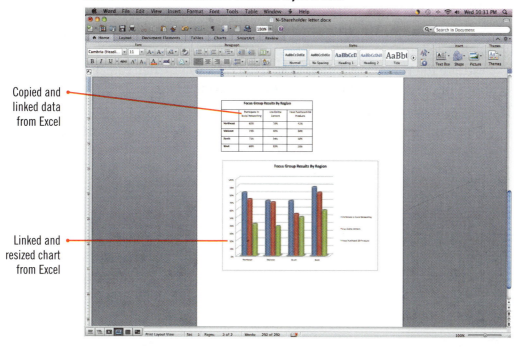

Copied and linked data from Excel

Linked and resized chart from Excel

Understanding the differences between embedding and linking data

When you embed data, such as an Excel chart embedded in a PowerPoint presentation, the data becomes part of the destination document and does not exist as a separate file. If you distribute the file to others, all the embedded data travels within the file. When you link data, however, it's different. To view the linked data, you need access to both the document containing the link and the file containing the data. Sharing a linked document with others, therefore, is a bit more complicated because you have to keep the linked files together. Moving one file can break the link with other documents.

Updating a Linked Excel Chart in a Word Document

The beauty of working with linked files is the ability to update the source file and have every document or file that is linked to the original file be updated automatically. You can also update a linked object manually by selecting the linked object, clicking Edit on the menu bar, clicking Links, selecting the link, and then clicking Update Now.  Jihong just received updates to the focus-group data for the South region. You make the changes in Excel and view the updated results in the linked Word document.

STEPS

1. Switch to Excel, open the N-Focus Group.xlsx file if necessary, then click the Sheet1 tab

2. Edit the data in the N-Focus Group workbook, as shown in the following table:

cell	data
B5	71
C5	54
D5	50

3. Select the cell range A1:D6, click the Home tab if necessary, click the Fill Color button pop-up menu arrow in the Font group, then click the Text 2, Lighter 80% color (fourth column, second row)

   The cells are shaded with a light blue color on the Sheet1 tab.

4. Click the Focus Group Results tab

   The Focus Group Results tab is now active, and the chart sheet is updated in Excel to reflect the new data, as shown in Figure N-15.

5. Switch to the Word file N-Shareholder letter.docx you created earlier, then click Yes in the dialog box prompting you to update the document, as shown in Figure N-16

6. Scroll down to view the updated table

   The table and chart are updated in the Shareholder letter. The table contains the new data and cell shading, and the chart reflects the new data, as shown in Figure N-17.

7. Double-click the linked worksheet object (the chart)

   The N-Focus Group workbook is now the active window.

8. Save your changes to the Excel workbook, then quit Excel

9. Save your changes to the Word document

Integrating Office for Mac 2011 Programs

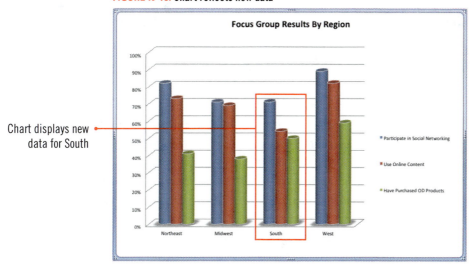

Chart displays new data for South

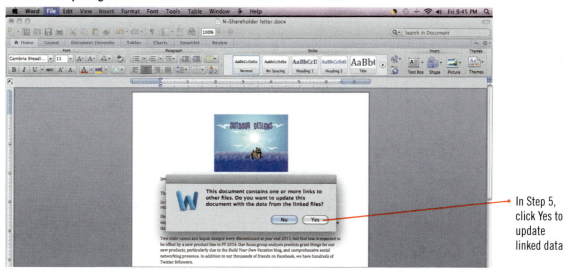

In Step 5, click Yes to update linked data

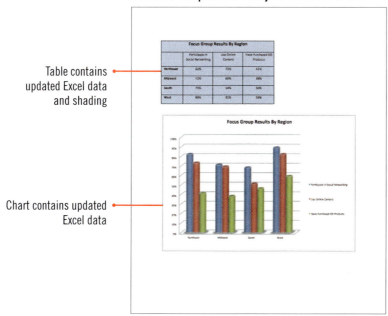

Table contains updated Excel data and shading

Chart contains updated Excel data

Inserting Placeholders in a Word Document

A **form letter** is a document that contains standard body text and a custom heading containing the name and address for one of many recipients. The letter, or **main document**, is usually created in Word; the data for the custom heading, also known as the **data source**, is usually compiled in a table, a worksheet, or a database. From these two files—the main document and the data source—you create a third file, a **merged document**, consisting of multiple "personalized" letters. This process is called **mail merge**. Before performing a mail merge, you add **placeholders**, or fields, to the main document to indicate where the custom information from the data source should appear. Jihong asks you to send the shareholder letter to the company's four principal investors and gives you a file containing their names and addresses.

STEPS

1. **Go to the top of the document, then click the blank line beneath the date**

2. **Click Tools on the menu bar, then click Mail Merge Manager**

   The Mail Merge Manager opens and displays the Select Document Type group, as shown in Figure N-18.

3. **Click the Create New button in the Select Document Type group, then click Form Letters**

   In the Select Document Type group, N-Shareholder letter.docx is now listed as the main document, while the Merge Type is listed as Form Letters.

4. **Click the Get List button in the Select Recipients List group, then click Open Data Source**

   The Choose a File dialog box opens.

5. **If necessary, navigate to the location where you store your Data Files, click N-7.xlsx, click Open, click OK when asked to use the Excel Workbook text converter, verify that Office Address List appears in the Open Document in Workbook field and Entire Worksheet appears in the Cell Range field in the Open Workbook dialog box, then click OK**

   The Open Workbook dialog box closes and the Excel file is designated as the data source (although it is not visible on your screen). You now need to insert the address block placeholders.

6. **In the Mail Merge Manager, drag the Title placeholder from the Insert Placeholders group to the line below the date in the Shareholder letter document, press [spacebar], drag the First_Name placeholder to the document, press [spacebar], drag the Last_Name placeholder to the document, then press [return]**

   The first line of the address block is in place in the document, as shown in Figure N-19.

7. **Drag the Address_Line_1 placeholder to the line below the title and name placeholders, press [return], drag the Address_Line_2 placeholder to the line below the Address_Line_1 placeholder, then press [return]**

8. **Click the down scroll arrow ▼ in the placeholder list three times, drag the City placeholder to the line below the address line 2 placeholder, type , (a comma), press [spacebar], drag the State placeholder to the document, press [spacebar], drag the ZIP_Code placeholder to the document, then press [return]**

   The last line of the address block is in place in the document. Now you will add the greeting.

9. **Press [return] a second time, type Dear, press [spacebar], click the up scroll arrow ▲ in the placeholder list three times, drag the First_Name placeholder to the document, type , (a comma), press [return], compare your screen with Figure N-20, then save your changes to the document**

FIGURE N-18: Selecting a Mail Merge document type

Mail Merge Manager

Create New button

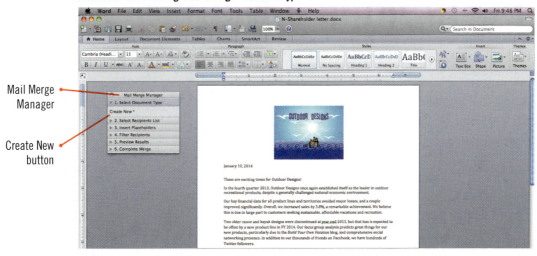

FIGURE N-19: Placeholders inserted into the main document

Get List button

Placeholder options

Title, First Name, and Last Name placeholders inserted into document

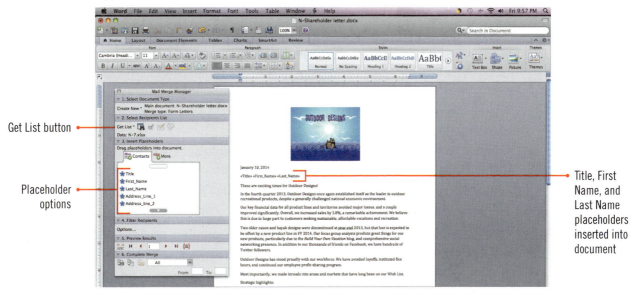

FIGURE N-20: Address block and greeting line inserted in document

Address block and greeting line placeholders

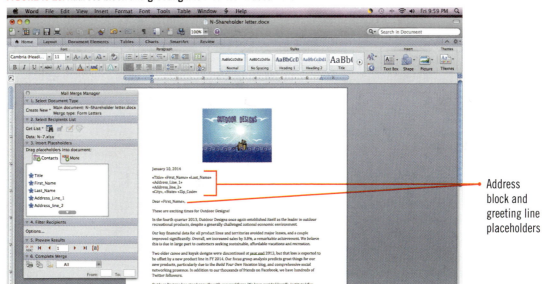

Performing a Mail Merge

After you set up a main document, specify a data source, and insert placeholders, you are ready to **merge**, or combine, the standard text with the custom information to create personalized documents. You can preview the mail merge to ensure that all the information is displayed properly in the final document. Now that the main document, the shareholder letter, has placeholders inserted, you are ready to preview and then merge it with the data source to create the final mail merge letters. You also want to print one of the merged letters for Jihong's review.

QUICK TIP

Use the options in the Filter Recipients group to filter and sort data if you want to send the mail merge letter to specific recipients. You want to include all the recipients in the file, so you don't need to apply any filters.

1. **Click the View all placeholders button {a} in the Preview Results group in the Mail Merge Manager, then compare your screen with Figure N-21**

   The placeholder fields are enclosed by a {MERGEFIELD} tag, making it easy to see where merged data will be inserted in the letter.

2. **Click the View all placeholders button {a} in the Preview Results group to deselect it, then click the View Merged Data button in the Preview Results group**

   The name, address, and salutation for the first recipient in the data source file replace the placeholders in the document. See Figure N-22.

3. **Click the Next Record button ▶ in the Preview Results group three times**

   The data from each record appears in its respective letter. You can use buttons in the Preview Results group to move backward or forward through records, or to find a particular record.

4. **Click the Merge Data Range pop-up menu arrow in the Complete Merge group in the Mail Merge Manager, then click Current Record**

   The current document, containing the text of the main document merged with the data from the fourth record in the data source, is selected in the Complete Merge group.

5. **Click the Merge to Printer button in the Complete Merge group**

   The Print dialog box opens.

6. **In the Print dialog box, click Print if your lab allows printing, or click Cancel**

   The merged document containing the data from the fourth record is printed, as shown in Figure N-23.

7. **Return to the Shareholder letter, click the Merge Data Range pop-up menu arrow in the Complete Merge group, click All, then click the Merge to New Document button in the Complete Merge group**

   A Word document called Form Letters1 opens in a new window. Form Letters1 contains all the merged letters.

QUICK TIP

To add custom text to individual letters, place the insertion point in the appropriate letter in the Form Letters1 document, then type the desired text.

8. **Scroll through the Form Letters1 document and view the different addresses, close the Form Letters1 document, click Don't Save in the Do you want to save dialog box, then close the Mail Merge Manager**

   You want to be certain that the data from the data source is up to date the next time you open this letter, so you do not need to save the merged document.

9. **Save your changes to the Shareholder letter document, then quit Word**

Using Word to create a data source

When you perform a mail merge, you can use an Excel worksheet, the Outlook Address Book, or a FileMaker Pro database as a data source. You can also create a new data source directly in Word. Open the Mail Merge Manager and designate your document as a Form Letter. In the Select Recipients List group, click the Get List button, and then click New Data Source. In the Create Data Source dialog box, remove the field names that you don't want to include in your data source from the Field names in header row box, and then click OK. In the Save Data Source dialog box, choose a location and filename for your data source, and then click Save. In the Data Form dialog box, type the data for your first record, and then click Add New. Continue adding records until all your data has been entered. Click OK when you have finished entering your data. Your new data source is now available to merge with any document.

FIGURE N-21: Viewing all placeholders

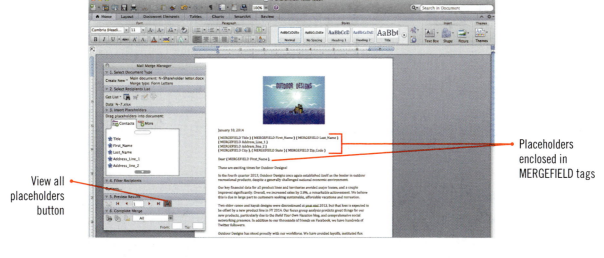

Placeholders enclosed in MERGEFIELD tags

View all placeholders button

FIGURE N-22: Previewing the merged file

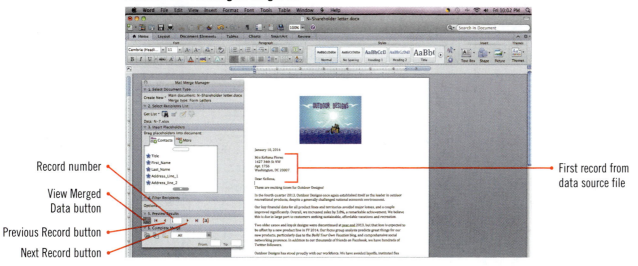

Record number

View Merged Data button

Previous Record button

Next Record button

First record from data source file

FIGURE N-23: Printed merged letter

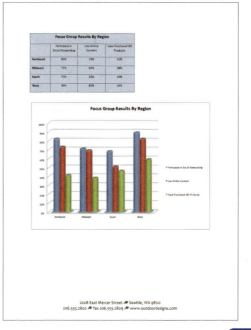

Integration 2011

Practice

Concepts Review

Label the mail merge elements shown in Figure N-24.

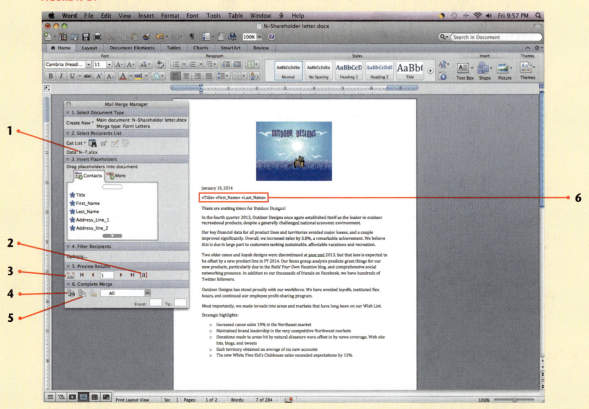

Match each term with the statement that best describes it.

7. Linked object

8. Placeholders

9. Scrapbook

10. Outline view

11. Mail merge

a. Updates data automatically in a destination file when the source file is updated

b. Presents text in a hierarchical structure in Word and automatically formats headings and subheadings

c. The process of combining a main document and a data source file

d. A tab on the Toolbox that makes it easy to share clips among the Office programs

e. Fields that indicate where custom information from a data source should appear

Select the best answer from the list of choices.

12. **Which of the following cannot be produced by performing a mail merge?**

  a. Envelopes

  b. Labels

  c. Form letters

  d. Bookmarks

13. Receiving a prompt to update data in a document indicates that:

   a. The document has been published to the Web.

   b. The document has an embedded object.

   c. The document contains a linked object.

   d. The document is a mail merge document.

14. What does the View all placeholders button do?

   a. Displays the merge fields in a main document

   b. Inserts fields into a main document

   c. Excludes or filters records in a merged document

   d. Verifies the data in a merge file

Skills Review

1. Insert an Excel chart into a PowerPoint slide.

   a. Start PowerPoint, open the file N-8.pptx from the location where you store your Data Files, then save it as **N-Landscape Lightning Sales.pptx**.

   b. Move to Slide 2, then use the content placeholder to insert a 3-D Exploded Pie chart.

   c. In Excel, enter the following data:

cell	data	cell	data
A2	Garden	B1	Sales
A3	Deck	B2	6.7
A4	Path	B3	7.3
A5	Water	B4	8.4
		B5	2.6

   d. Quit Excel.

   e. In PowerPoint, save your changes.

2. Insert PowerPoint slides from a Word document.

   a. Start Word, then open the file N-9.docx from the location where you store your Data Files.

   b. View the document in Outline View.

   c. Save the document as a Rich Text Format (.rtf) file with the same filename, then quit Word.

   d. In PowerPoint, after Slide 2, insert the file N-9.rtf using the Insert Slides from Outline command. Reset the layout of the outline text to match the PowerPoint theme.

   e. Add your name to the slide footer for all slides, then save your changes.

3. Share a clip using the Toolbox.

   a. Open the Toolbox and select the Scrapbook tab.

   b. Add Slide 1 as a clip to the Scrapbook.

   c. Open the file N-10.docx from the location where you store your Data Files, then save it as **N-Landscape Lightning Events.docx**.

   d. Position the insertion point at the top of the document, then paste the slide clip at the insertion point.

   e. Select the clip in the Word document, then apply the Soft Edge Rectangle Style to it.

   f. Change the Height of the clip to 1.3", save your changes to both the Word document and the PowerPoint presentation, then quit PowerPoint. (*Hint*: To make the Height of the clip exactly 1.3", click the clip to select it, click the Format Picture tab, then type 1.3 in the Height spin box.)

4. Insert text from a Word file into an open document.

   a. Switch to Word. Position the insertion point at the beginning of the line that starts "As marketing managers," then insert the file N-11.docx.

   b. Select the three lines of text you just inserted from the file, then format them as a bulleted list using the square black bullet style.

   c. Save your changes.

5. **Link an Excel chart to a Word document.**

   a. Start Excel, open the file N-12.xlsx, save it as **N-Landscape Lightning Event Analysis.xlsx**.

   b. On Sheet1, select and copy the cell range A2:D4.

   c. Switch to Word, press [⌘][end], insert a blank line, then paste the copied cell range, making sure to click Keep Source Formatting and Link to Excel. (*Hint:* You may need to turn off the bullets when you insert the blank line.)

   d. Switch to Excel, click the Event Sales Conversion tab, then save the Excel Workbook.

   e. Switch to Word, position the insertion point below the table, then insert a page break.

   f. At the top of the new page, open the Object dialog box, select Microsoft Excel Chart, click the From File button, click the Link to File check box, then insert the file **N-Landscape Lightning Event Analysis.xlsx**. (*Hint:* If the chart appears cropped, refer to the Trouble Tip on page 334.)

   g. Resize the chart to fit neatly on the page.

   h. Save your changes, close the document, then quit Word.

6. **Update a linked Excel chart in a Word document.**

   a. Switch to the Excel file **N-Landscape Lightning Event Analysis.xlsx**.

   b. On Sheet1, change cell B3 to **86** and cell B4 to **73**, click the Event Sales Conversion tab, save your changes, close the workbook, then quit Excel.

   c. Open the file **N-Landscape Lightning Events.docx** from the location where you store your Data Files. As the file opens, update the document with data from the linked file.

   d. View the updated chart in Word, then save your changes.

7. **Insert placeholders in a Word document.**

   a. Move to the top of the document, then insert two blank lines below the date.

   b. Create a new form letter using the Mail Merge Manager.

   c. Open the file N-13.xlsx as the data source in the Select Recipients List group. (*Hint:* Click OK to use the Excel Workbook text converter.)

   d. Create an address block by dragging the first name, last name, address, city, state, and zip code fields to appropriate locations in the document, then insert two blank lines below the address block.

   e. Create a greeting line that uses just the first name, then insert one blank line below the greeting line.

   f. Save your changes.

8. **Perform a mail merge.**

   a. Use a button on the Mail Merge Manager to view placeholders, then deselect the button.

   b. Preview your results, reviewing each record in the mail merge, add your name to the footer of the document, then compare your screen with Figure N-25.

   c. Select All from the Merge Data Range menu if necessary, then print the merged letters if your lab allows printing.

   d. Save your changes to **N-Landscape Lightning Events.docx**, close the document, then quit Word.

FIGURE N-25

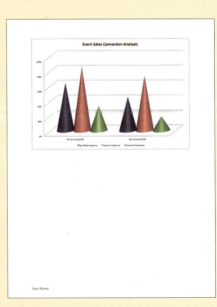

Independent Challenge 1

You are the new intern assigned to Nikkie Kay, the manager of customer service at Luggage xPress. The company delivers lost luggage to airline customers staying at large hotels and also handles luggage pickup for travelers. Luggage xPress is beginning to franchise operations to other cities, and Nikkie needs your help in preparing a PowerPoint presentation. She also needs you to send out a personalized form letter to clients who have lost luggage.

a. Start PowerPoint, open the file N-14.pptx from the location where you store your Data Files, then save it as **N-Luggage xPress Franchise.pptx** in the location where you store your Data Files.

b. In Slide 2, insert a 3-D Pie chart.

c. In Excel, enter the following data, change column widths as necessary so that all newly entered data is visible, select only newly entered data to display in the chart, then quit Excel. (*Hint*: To select only the newly entered data for display, delete the cells containing any remaining sample worksheet data.)

cell	data
B1	Stats
A2	3 Million Bags Lost
B2	3,000,000
A3	Over ½ Million Bags Lost Forever
B3	530,000

d. Start Word, open the file N-15.docx, view the file in Outline view, save the file as **N-15.rtf**, then quit Word.

e. Following Slide 2 in PowerPoint, insert slides from an outline using the file **N-15.rtf**.

f. Add a footer with your name to all slides except the title slide, save your changes, and quit PowerPoint.

g. Start Word, open the file N-16.docx from the location where you store your Data Files, then save it as **N-Luggage xPress Feedback Letter.docx**.

h. Move to the bottom of the page and insert a new page.

i. Open the file N-17.docx from the location where you store your Data Files and add the image in this file as a clip to the Scrapbook, then close this file.

j. At the top of the second page for the **N-Luggage xPress Feedback Letter.docx** file, paste the image clip you just added.

k. Press [return], then close the Toolbox.

l. Start Excel, open the file N-18.xlsx from the location where you store your Data Files, save it as **N-Luggage xPress Feedback Chart.xlsx** in the location where you store your Data Files, then minimize the workbook.

m. Switch to Word, open the Object dialog box, select Microsoft Excel Chart in the Object type list, click From File, verify that the Link to File check box is selected, then insert the **N-Luggage xPress Feedback Chart.xlsx** file.

n. Resize the chart to fit neatly on page 2.

o. Save and close **Luggage xPress Feedback Letter.docx**.

p. Click the icon for the **N-Luggage xPress Feedback Chart.xlsx** on the Dock, click the Sheet1 tab, change the value in cell B3 to **66**, click the Luggage Chart tab, save your changes to the workbook, then quit Excel.

q. Switch to Word, open the file **N-Luggage xPress Feedback Letter.docx**, updating the linked chart as it opens.

r. Add a footer with your name left-aligned.

s. Move to the top of the first page of the document, place the insertion point on the blank line beneath the date, then create a Form Letter mail merge that uses the file N-19.xlsx as the data source file. Add the appropriate fields to create an address block and greeting line. Insert spaces, punctuation, and blank lines as appropriate.

t. Preview your results, then print the third record if your lab allows printing.

u. Save and close any open files, then quit all open programs.

Independent Challenge 2

You and your business partner, chef Melanie Nakano, are planning to start a new restaurant in Ann Arbor, Michigan. You need to apply for a start-up loan to get the business going. Your first task is to write a cover letter that will accompany your loan package you're sending to several banks. You also want to prepare a PowerPoint presentation of a few menu items that potential lenders can view on your Web site.

a. Start Word, then write a letter that you can send to banks along with the loan package. You will add recipient information in a future step; for now, write the body of the letter, including the name and location of your new restaurant, why you are applying for the loan, why the business will be successful, and how much you would like to borrow.

b. Save the letter as **N-Restaurant loan letter.docx** in the location where you store your Data Files.

c. Start Excel, open the file N-20.xlsx from the location where you store your Data Files, then save it as **N-Restaurant sales comparison.xlsx**. This chart shows the success of similar restaurants in a comparable city.

d. Change the chart style, chart layout, or individual chart elements as desired to make the chart readable and attractive, save your changes, close the workbook, then quit Excel.

e. Switch to the Word file **N-Restaurant loan letter.docx**. Position the insertion point at the end of the document, then insert a new page. At the top of the new page, insert a link to the Microsoft Excel chart in the file **N-Restaurant sales comparison.xlsx**. Resize the chart as necessary to fit neatly on the page.

f. Start a mail merge and create a new form letter with a new data source that contains at least four entries. To create the list, use the Mail Merge Manager, click the Get List button in the Select Recipients List group, then click New Data Source. Remove the fields that you do not want in your data source. Save the data source file in the location where you store your Data Files as **N-Restaurant bank loan list.docx**. Enter four names and addresses in the Data Form dialog box, clicking Add New as needed. When the list is complete, click OK.

g. At the top of the Word document, insert the placeholders to create the address block and formal greeting line. Insert spaces, punctuation, and blank lines as appropriate.

h. Insert a footer with your name, left-aligned.

i. Preview the mail merge, print the first record if your lab allows printing, save your changes, close the documents, then quit Word.

j. Start PowerPoint, create a presentation that contains a title slide with the name of your restaurant and a slogan plus four slides that highlight menu items, then save the presentation as **N-Restaurant Menu.pptx** in the location where you store your Data Files.

k. Apply an attractive theme and transitions, insert clip art and photographs that are appropriate for a restaurant, then add your name to the footer on all slides.

l. On the title slide, use a combination of clip art (or photographs) and text to create a logo.

m. Add your logo as a clip to the Scrapbook.

n. Save your changes and quit PowerPoint.

o. Open **N-Restaurant Loan Letter.docx** and paste the logo clip from the Scrapbook into your document at the top of the document. Resize and center it.

p. Save and close any open files, then quit any open programs.

Independent Challenge 3

The Sweet Lake Bass Fishing Challenge is organizing its annual Memorial Day weekend event, which features the region's largest bass fishing contest and a fish-off that benefits local charities. The organization's president, Duane Roberts, has asked you to create a PowerPoint presentation that includes information about bass fishing along with financial information for potential sponsors and participants.

a. Start PowerPoint, create a new, blank presentation using any theme you like, customize it for bass (or a different fish species if you prefer) and change the color scheme if you want, then save it as **N-Fishing Event.pptx** in the location where you store your Data Files.

b. Create at least two slides, including a title slide.

c. Insert the file N-21.rtf after Slide 2 in the presentation.

Independent Challenge 3 (continued)

d. Reset the Layout to Default Settings so the text formatting on the newly added slides matches the text formatting on the preexisting slides. Insert clip art and photographs that are appropriate for a fishing contest.

e. Add your name to the footer on all slides except the title slide.

f. At the end of the presentation, add a new slide titled **We Got Bass**, then insert a chart in the style of your choice that shows the largest fish caught over each of the past five years. (*Hint*: In Excel, enter the years in column A and bass weights in column B. An acceptable weight range for this category is 5–12 pounds.)

g. Save your changes to the presentation.

Advanced Challenge Exercise

- Start Word, then compose an informal confirmation letter for the event. Type the following text in the first line of the document: **Sweet Lake Bass Fishing Challenge Confirmation Form**. Format this text so that it will stand out from the body of the letter. Below the heading you typed, add a line with the current date, write at least two paragraphs for the letter body text, confirming that the recipient is registered for the event. Below the body text, add a line that reads **Entrance fee paid** and a line that reads **Team name: Guppies**. Add your name to the footer.

- For a logo, create a Scrapbook clip from the PowerPoint presentation file **N-Fishing Event.pptx** and paste it at the top of the Word document.

- Save the Word file as **N-Fishing Confirmation ACE.docx** in the location where you store your Data Files.

- Start a mail merge, create a data source in Word that includes first name, last name, one address line, city, state, and zip code, and has at least four records. Save the data source file as **N-Fishing Confirmation List.docx** in the location where you store your Data Files.

- Below the heading at the top of the document, insert placeholders and any necessary punctuation to create an address block and an informal greeting line, preview the mail merge, then print the second letter if your lab allows printing.

h. Close any open files, then quit all programs.

Real Life Independent Challenge

Creating a form letter is a great way to manage your correspondence with efficiency and style. You can use the mail merge features in Word to personalize thank-you notes, e-mail messages, and invitations. Think of an event for which you would like to use personalized form letters to save time yet still include a personal touch. It could be a thank-you note to recipients of a recent party or special event, a party invitation, or perhaps a change-of-address notice. Then create a personalized form letter that you can send to at least four recipients.

a. Start Word, then save a new document as **N-My event.docx** in the location where you store your Data Files.

b. Write a brief letter containing the text of the thank-you, invitation, or other notice. Add clip art or photographs as desired.

c. Include two sentences: one asking the recipient to confirm his or her e-mail address and the other to confirm his or her home phone number.

d. Add your name as the signatory to the document.

e. Open Excel and use it to create a data source that has at least four records and includes first name, last name, street, city, state, zip code, e-mail address, and phone number. Make up the appropriate information to include in the appropriate cells. Save the file as **N-My event list.xlsx** in the location where you store your Data Files.

f. Create a form letter mail merge, select the **N-My event list.xlsx** file as the data source, then at the top of the document, insert placeholders to create an address block and greeting line. Insert spaces, punctuation, and blank lines as needed.

g. After the sentence asking to confirm the e-mail address, insert the e-mail placeholder.

h. After the sentence asking to confirm the phone number, insert the phone number placeholder.

i. Complete the mail merge by merging to a new document. Print the first record if your lab allows printing.

j. Close the Form Letters1 document and do not save it. Save and close all other open files, then quit all programs.

Visual Workshop

Using the skills you learned in this unit, create the PowerPoint slide shown in Figure N-26. To get started, create a new blank presentation using the Austin theme, insert a Title and Content slide, then add your name to the slide footer. Create a Clustered Bar Chart. (*Hint*: Use the following regular fuel mileage values: 1908: **20**; 1998: **23**; Present & beyond: **26**. Use the following hybrid fuel mileage values: 1998: **60**; Present & beyond: **80**.) Delete the title slide and make any other changes or additions to the presentation to match Figure N-26. Save the presentation as **N-Fuel Economy.pptx**, then save the worksheet at **N-Fuel Economy.xlsx** in the location where you store your Data Files. Print the slide if your lab allows printing. Save your changes, close any open files, then exit all programs.

FIGURE N-26

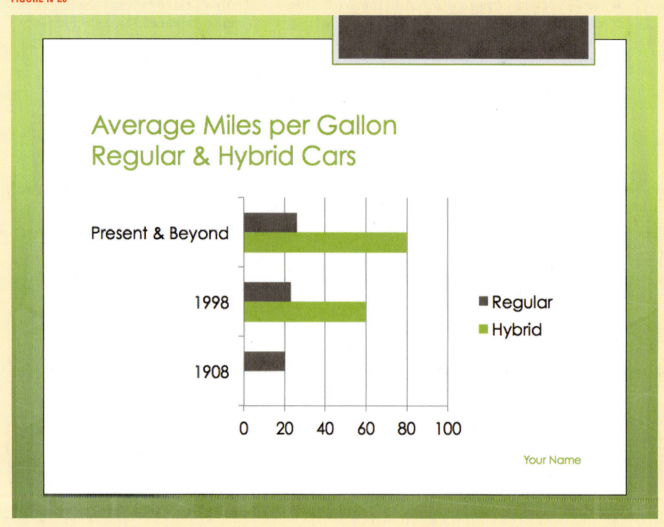

Setting System Preferences

One of the most appealing features of the Mac OS X Snow Leopard operating system is that it is user friendly. You don't need to be a computer expert to change the features and functionality of your Mac or to customize its appearance. When you first turn on a new Mac, the system preferences—such as the desktop background, the Dock location, and the source for the system date and time—have been preset by the manufacturer (Apple). These are called **default settings**, or simply defaults. Over time, most people change the system preferences in one way or another to better fit their needs. This appendix explains how to change the settings for the Snow Leopard operating system, such as the desktop background image, screen saver, Dock, screen resolution, sleep settings, and system date and time. You also learn how to use the Time Machine to back up your computer, how to update your software, and how to modify your system's sound options.

OBJECTIVES

Change the desktop background and screen saver

Change the Dock

Change the screen resolution

Change the sleep settings

Change the date and time

Use Time Machine

Update your software

Change sound options

Changing the Desktop Background and Screen Saver

When you start your Mac, Snow Leopard displays the Aurora image as the background image on the desktop by default. You can select a different image to appear as the background, either one of several built-in background images provided with the operating system or an image of your own. You can change the desktop background image using the Desktop & Screen Saver dialog box. Another setting you can change in this dialog box is the **screen saver**, which appears when you leave your computer idle for several minutes; it is an image that moves around the screen to prevent damage to your monitor. Without the screen saver, the crystals in an LCD monitor can be damaged and will continue to display an image faintly even after the on-screen image has changed. This is known as **image persistence**. You can select from several different screen saver options provided with Snow Leopard. You decide to change the desktop background and screen saver to give your Mac a more personalized look and to protect your screen from damage.

STEPS

QUICK TIP

You can also open the System Preferences dialog box by clicking the Apple icon on the menu bar, then clicking System Preferences.

1. **Click the System Preferences icon on the Dock**

   As shown in Figure A-1, the System Preferences dialog box opens. It is divided into four or five categories: Personal, Hardware, Internet & Wireless, System, and Other. Depending on how your Mac is configured, your screen might differ. Certain buttons and the Other category might not appear in your dialog box.

2. **In the Personal category, click the Desktop & Screen Saver button**

   The Desktop & Screen Saver dialog box opens with the Desktop tab selected, as shown in Figure A-2. At the top of the Desktop tab, a preview of the current background image appears (Aurora). On the left side of the tab is a list of folders containing images that can be used as the background image. You can access the standard Apple choices or use an image stored in your Pictures folder. When a folder is selected on the left, the sample box on the right displays thumbnails of the images available in the selected folder.

3. **In the list of image folders, click a folder of your choice, then click any image in the sample box**

   The desktop background changes to the image you selected. The preview at the top of the Desktop tab now shows the selected image.

4. **Click the Screen Saver tab**

   The options on the Screen Saver tab become available, as shown in Figure A-3. On the left side of the Screen Saver tab is the Screen Savers list, which includes several built-in Apple choices as well as stock pictures. You can even select an image or photo you created if it's stored in the Pictures folder in your home folder. When you select a static image, the screen saver changes the screen display over time by increasing and decreasing the dimensions of the photo; the movement is what protects the crystals on your screen. On the right side of the Screen Saver tab is a Preview box, which shows how the currently selected screen saver appears when activated.

QUICK TIP

To return to the System Preferences dialog box from the Desktop & Screen Saver dialog box, click the Show All button or the Back button in the upper-left corner of the dialog box.

5. **Click a screen saver option in the Screen Savers list, watch the preview in the Preview box, then continue clicking screen saver options in the Screen Savers list until you select the screen saver you would like to use**

   The Preview box displays the selected screen saver.

6. **Drag the Start screen saver slider to 15**

   The slider below the Preview box lets you select when the screen saver will activate. With the slider set at 15, the screen saver will start after 15 minutes of no activity on your screen.

7. **Click the Desktop tab, then close the Desktop & Screen Saver dialog box**

   The desktop background image and screen saver options you just selected are now active.

FIGURE A-1: System Preferences dialog box

Desktop & Screen Saver button

Categories (you might not have the "Other" category)

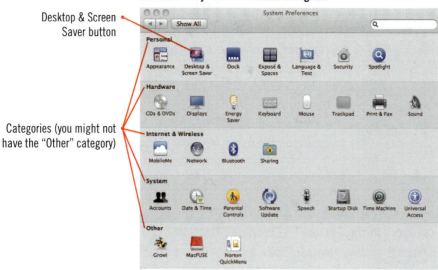

FIGURE A-2: Desktop tab in Desktop & Screen Saver dialog box

Desktop tab

Current background image

Background image folders

Background image thumbnails

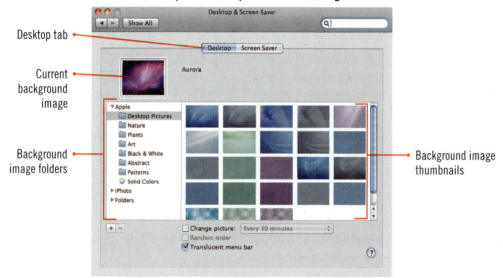

FIGURE A-3: Screen Saver tab in Desktop & Screen Saver dialog box

Close button

Screen Saver tab

Screen saver image options

Preview of Shell screen saver

Start screen saver slider

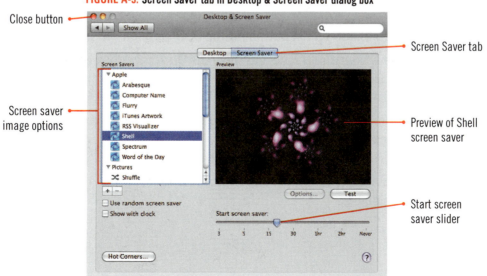

Changing the Dock

By default, the Dock is displayed across the bottom of your screen, and when you point to an item on the Dock, a Help Tag with the name of the item appears above its icon. Using the Dock dialog box, you can change the location and size of the Dock and how the Dock icons appear when you point to them. For instance, you might prefer for the Dock to be hidden until you need it, or you might want to position it vertically along the left or right edge of the screen. You decide to explore the Dock options to determine where you want the Dock to appear on the screen and how you want the icons to appear when you point to them.

STEPS

QUICK TIP

You can also open the Dock dialog box by clicking the Apple icon 🍎 on the menu bar, pointing to Dock, then clicking Dock Preferences.

1. **Click the System Preferences icon 🖼 on the Dock, then click the Dock button ⚟ in the Personal category in the System Preferences dialog box**

   The Dock dialog box opens, as shown in Figure A-4. At the top of the dialog box is the Size slider, which you use to control the size of the Dock and its elements. The Magnification check box (below the Size slider), when checked, increases the size of the Dock icons when you point to them. Use the Position on screen option buttons to change the position of the Dock to the left, bottom, or right of the screen. The Minimize windows using options allow you to choose the effect used to animate items as they are minimized to the Dock.

2. **Click and drag the Size slider toward the Small end of the slider bar, then click and drag the Size slider toward the Large end of the slider bar**

   As you move the slider toward Small, the size of the Dock decreases, and as you move the slider toward Large, the size of the Dock increases. The effect of the Size slider depends on the size of your computer screen because the Dock size is proportional to your screen size. The larger your screen, the more of an effect the Size slider will have.

3. **Position the Size slider so that the Dock is the size you prefer**

QUICK TIP

You can also turn Magnification on or off by clicking 🍎 on the menu bar, pointing to Dock, then clicking Turn Magnification On or Turn Magnification Off.

4. **Click to select the Magnification check box, drag the Magnification slider to Max if necessary, then point to any icon on the Dock**

   The Dock icons around the icon to which you point grow larger; the icon to which you point directly to is the largest.

5. **Drag the Magnification slider to the location on the slider bar that magnifies the Dock icons the amount that you prefer**

QUICK TIP

You can also reposition the Dock by clicking 🍎 on the menu bar, pointing to Dock, then clicking Position on Left, Position on Bottom, or Position on Right.

6. **Click to deselect the Magnification check box, then click the Left option button to the right of Position on screen**

   The Dock moves to the left side of the screen in a vertical position, as shown in Figure A-5. If you click the Right option button, the Dock appears vertically on the right edge of your screen.

7. **Click the position option button for the Dock position you prefer**

8. **Click the Automatically hide and show the Dock check box to select it**

   As shown in Figure A-6, the Dock is hidden, maximizing the space of the work area on your desktop. If you prefer to have the Dock open and visible at all times, make sure to deselect this check box.

QUICK TIP

You can also show or hide the Dock by clicking 🍎 on the menu bar, pointing to Dock, then clicking Turn Hiding On or Turn Hiding Off.

9. **Move the on-screen pointer to the edge of the computer screen where the Dock was last positioned**

   The Dock slides into view and is available for use.

10. **Click the Automatically hide and show the Dock check box to deselect it, then close the Dock dialog box**

FIGURE A-4: Dock dialog box

Magnification check box

Minimize windows using options

Automatically hide and show the Dock check box

Size slider

Magnification slider

Dock position options

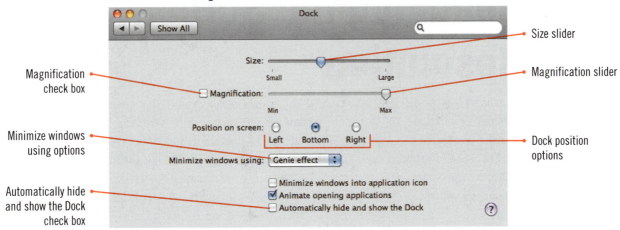

FIGURE A-5: Left Dock position

FIGURE A-6: Screen with the Dock hidden

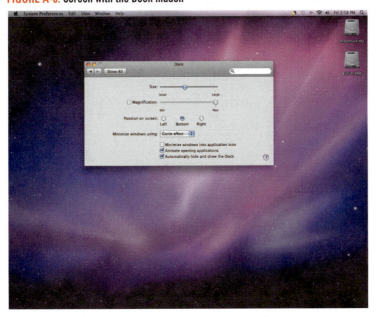

Changing the Screen Resolution

Your Mac has many different options to choose from that allow you to change the size and quality of your monitor's screen image. Your monitor's **screen resolution** is the number of pixels, or dots, used to display the computer screen image. In a screen resolution setting such as 800 x 600, the first number (800) is the number of horizontal pixels in the image, and the second number (600) is the number of vertical pixels in the image. The higher your screen resolution, the better the quality of the screen image and the smaller the components within the image (such as icons) appear. To adjust the screen resolution for your computer, you use the Display tab of the iMac (SyncMaster, Color LCD, or Apple Studio Display) dialog box. You can also use the Display tab to change the brightness of your screen to an appropriate level based on the amount of ambient lighting in the room where your Mac is located.  You decide to investigate the display options for your screen to determine the resolution and brightness you prefer as you work.

STEPS

1. **Click the System Preferences icon 🔘 on the Dock, then click the Displays button 🖥 in the Hardware category in the System Preferences dialog box**

   The iMac dialog box (yours might be the SyncMaster, Color LCD, or Apple Studio Display dialog box depending on which Mac model you are working with) opens with the Display tab selected, as shown in Figure A-7. On the left side of the Display tab is the Resolutions list, containing several resolution options. In Figure A-7, the current resolution setting is 1280 × 1024, but the resolution setting of your computer might differ.

   > **TROUBLE**
   > If the 1024 × 768 resolution setting is not available, click the setting that is closest to 1024 × 768.

2. **Click 1024 × 768 in the Resolutions list**

   If your computer was previously at a lower resolution setting than 1024 × 768, more of the background image is now visible and the dialog box appears smaller. If your computer was previously at a higher resolution setting than 1024 × 768, less of the background image is now visible and the dialog box appears larger. See Figure A-8.

3. **Click 800 × 600 in the Resolutions list**

   Your computer screen displays a larger dialog box and less of the background image than at the 1024 × 768 resolution setting. Your Dock icons might appear less clear when you use this resolution.

4. **Click the setting in the Resolutions list that you prefer**

5. **Under the Resolutions list, drag the Brightness or Contrast slider to the left and right**

   As you drag the slider to the left, the brightness of your screen decreases. As you drag the slider to the right, the brightness of your computer screen increases. Depending on the Mac computer you are using, you might not have a Brightness or Contrast slider.

6. **Move the Brightness or Contrast slider to the location you prefer**

7. **Close the iMac (or SyncMaster, Color LCD, or Apple Studio Display) dialog box**

FIGURE A-7: Display tab in iMac dialog box

Resolution options

Brightness (or Contrast) slider

Current resolution (yours might differ)

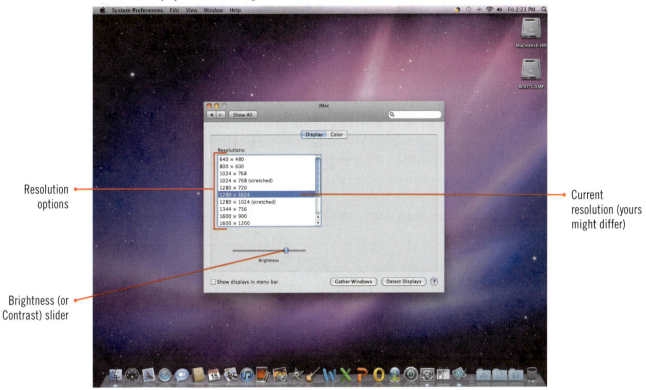

FIGURE A-8: 1024 × 768 screen resolution

Size of dialog box changes

Size of Dock might change

Amount of background that is visible changes

Changing the Sleep Settings

After you haven't used your computer for a period of time, it "goes to sleep," which means that it goes into a low-power mode but does not shut off. There are separate sleep settings for your monitor display and for your computer. When your display is about to go to sleep, it dims. When the display or the computer is asleep, the screen is black and the Mac appears to be turned off. To "wake up" your Mac, you press any key on the keyboard or move the on-screen pointer in any direction. When asleep, your Mac uses much less energy to keep running. In addition, once you are ready to use your Mac again, it takes less time to wake your Mac up from sleep than it does to start it up after being shut down. You can work more efficiently and optimize the energy needed to power your computer by adjusting the sleep settings for your Mac. The sleep settings are located in the Energy Saver dialog box. You'd like to conserve energy that your Mac uses and plan to adjust the sleep settings so that your computer goes to sleep after it is inactive for a brief time.

STEPS

TROUBLE
Depending on the Mac model you are working with, you might need to click Show details to expand the Energy Saver dialog box to see all the settings.

1. **Click the System Preferences icon on the Dock, then click the Energy Saver button in the Hardware category in the System Preferences dialog box**

   The Energy Saver dialog box opens, as shown in Figure A-9 (your dialog box and settings might differ). This dialog box contains two sliders: one to put your computer to sleep and one to put your display to sleep. The two sliders can have the same or different times selected. Putting the display to sleep before the computer can be beneficial if you use a program that requires a long time to process data. Putting the display to sleep earlier reduces power to the display but keeps full power to the computer, enabling active programs to continue running. On a laptop, the Energy Saver dialog box contains two tabs, Battery and Power Adapter, so that you can adjust the power settings for each power source.

2. **Click and drag the Computer sleep slider to the 15 min mark on the slider bar**

   After 15 minutes of inactivity, all components of your Mac will go to sleep and the computer will use less energy.

QUICK TIP
As you drag either slider, the number of minutes currently selected appears above the right end of the slider bar.

3. **Click and drag the Display sleep slider to the tick mark to the left of the 15 min mark on the slider bar**

   After 10 minutes of inactivity, only your display will go to sleep and draw less power. Note that the settings for when your screen saver is activated and when your display goes to sleep can differ. Both prevent image persistence, but sleep draws less power than a screen saver. A warning may appear in the dialog box stating that the display will go to sleep before your screen saver activates. To change the screen saver settings, you click the Desktop & Screen Saver button from the System Preferences dialog box.

4. **Close the Energy Saver dialog box**

FIGURE A-9: Energy Saver dialog box

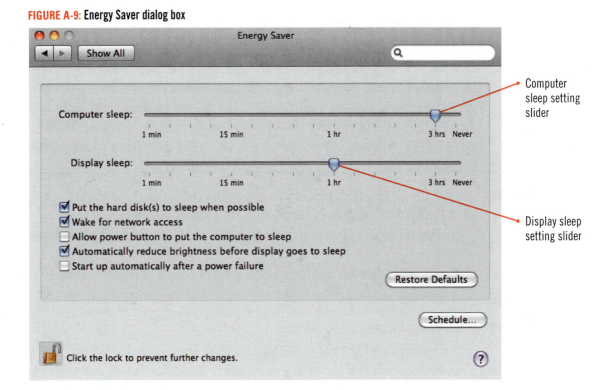

Changing the Date and Time

There may be times you'll need to change the system date and time displayed by your computer. It's important to make sure your computer displays the accurate date and time because all the date references for files, such as when they are saved, modified, or last opened, are determined by the system clock. You can adjust the date and time settings manually using the Date & Time dialog box. 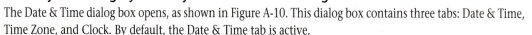 You want to explore how to change the system date and time in case you need to correct it manually in the future.

STEPS

QUICK TIP

You can also open the Date & Time dialog box by clicking the day and time on the right end of the menu bar, then clicking Date & Time Preferences.

1. **Click the System Preferences icon 🔲 on the Dock, then click the Date & Time button 🕐 in the System category in the System Preferences dialog box**

   The Date & Time dialog box opens, as shown in Figure A-10. This dialog box contains three tabs: Date & Time, Time Zone, and Clock. By default, the Date & Time tab is active.

2. **Click the Set date & time automatically check box to deselect it, if necessary**

   When this check box is checked, your computer displays the current time automatically based on the information it receives from Apple's time Web site. When the check box is unchecked, you can change the date on the calendar and the time on the clock manually.

3. **If necessary, click the date spin box, click the number of the month, type a new month number (or use the up and down arrows to select a different month), repeat these operations to select a different day and year, then click the time spin box, type a new hour, minute, and second (or use the up and down arrows) to select a different time**

   The date and time shown on the calendar and clock in the dialog box reflect your changes. You can also change the date by clicking a date in the calendar; click the arrows in the upper-left corner of the calendar to move between months. You can also change the time by dragging the hands on the clock to new locations; click AM or PM in the spin box, and then click the up or down arrows to switch to PM or AM.

QUICK TIP

To set the date and time automatically from Apple's Asia or Europe time Web sites, click the pop-up menu arrow next to Apple Americas/U.S., then click Apple Asia or Apple Europe.

4. **Click the Set date & time automatically check box to select it**

   The date and time displayed on the calendar and clock return to the current date and time, updated automatically from Apple's time Web site.

5. **Click the Time Zone tab**

   Options for changing the time zone appear in the dialog box, as shown in Figure A-11. Click the Closest City pop-up menu arrow to see a list of major cities in your time zone. You can also click a section of the map to locate a major city near your home and change the time zone if necessary. Once you have selected a major city in your time zone, the date and time on the Date & Time tab are updated accordingly.

6. **Click the Clock tab**

   The Clock tab displays options for changing the appearance of the clock on your menu bar, as shown in Figure A-12. You can change how the date and time are displayed on the menu bar, and you can choose to have the computer announce the time out loud by clicking the Announce the time check box and choosing the timing of the announcement. By default, the date and time are displayed digitally on the right end of the menu bar.

7. **Click the Analog option button to the right of Time options**

   The digital clock on the menu bar changes to an analog clock.

8. **Click the Show date and time in menu bar check box to deselect it**

   The menu bar no longer displays the clock icon.

9. **Click the Show date and time in menu bar check box to select it, then click the Digital option button to the right of Time options**

   The menu bar displays the date and time in digital format on the menu bar again. Additional check boxes under the Digital and Analog option buttons enable you to further adjust the display of the date and time.

10. **Click the Date & Time tab, then close the Date & Time dialog box**

FIGURE A-10: Date & Time tab in Date & Time dialog box

Date & Time tab

Set date and time automatically check box

Date spin box

Time spin box

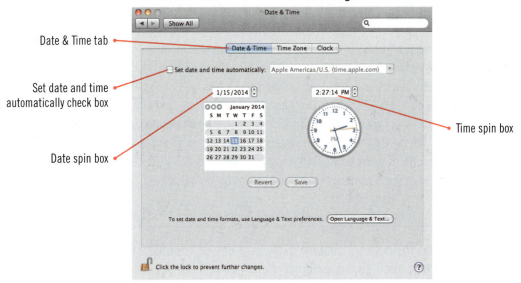

FIGURE A-11: Time Zone tab in Date & Time dialog box

Time Zone tab

Selected time zone

Closest City pop-up menu arrow

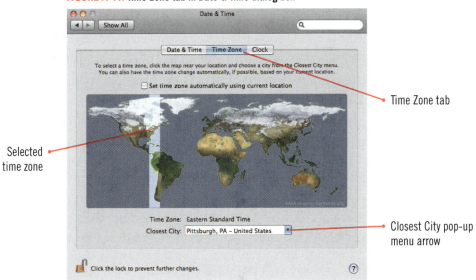

FIGURE A-12: Clock tab in Date & Time dialog box

Show date and time in menu bar check box

Announce the time check box

Digital clock on menu bar

Clock tab

Time options

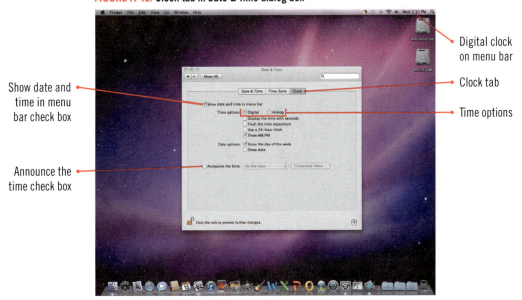

Using Time Machine

Time Machine is a feature in Snow Leopard that helps you maintain your files, folders, and programs by backing up everything on your computer or external storage device on a regular basis. The first time you use Time Machine, it backs up not only all of the files, folders, and programs on your computer, but also your system files, accounts, and preferences. After the initial backup, Time Machine subsequently backs up only those items that have changed. Time Machine has options for keeping hourly backups for the past 24 hours, daily backups for the past month, and weekly backups. Backups are cataloged by date, so you can restore your entire system from any backup, or you can recover individual files or folders. You want to back up the contents of your computer to prevent the loss of data if something were to go wrong, so you set up Time Machine for your computer.

STEPS

The following instructions require a storage device capable of storing the entire contents of your computer, such as an external hard drive. This device should be dedicated for Time Machine use only.

1. **Connect your storage device to the appropriate port**

   Depending on the make and model of your storage device, it may connect to a USB port or to a FireWire port. Please read the manufacturer's instructions for setup of the storage device before proceeding.

2. **Click the System Preferences icon on the Dock, then click the Time Machine button in the System category in the System Preferences dialog box**

   The Time Machine dialog box opens, as shown in Figure A-13.

3. **Click and drag the Time Machine Off/On switch to the On position**

   This activates Time Machine and opens a window listing the drives available for making your backups, as shown in Figure A-14. After you set up Time Machine to make automatic backups, you can turn off Time Machine at any time by clicking and dragging the On switch to the Off position. Backups will no longer be made.

4. **Select the storage device you want to use as backup, then click Use for Backup**

   If the storage device is not blank, you may receive a message that the device needs to be erased to continue. Click OK to continue. The backup starts. This process may take several minutes the first time you run it. While the files are being copied, you will see progress bars. When complete, the dialog box will change to that shown in Figure A-15. For Time Machine to make periodic backups automatically, the storage device must remain attached to your computer. Should you need to restore a file, folder, or program from the Time Machine device, click the Time Machine icon on the Dock to access the cataloged backups.

5. **Close the Time Machine dialog box**

FIGURE A-13: Time Machine dialog box

Time Machine
Off/On switch

FIGURE A-14: List of backup storage devices

Available storage devices that
can be used for backup
purposes (yours will differ)

FIGURE A-15: Backup complete

Backup storage
device on
desktop

Time Machine
icon on Dock

Updating Your Software

To ensure that your computer runs efficiently, you should keep your system and application software up to date. The software manufacturer provides software updates as improvements are made and bugs are corrected. You can use the Software Update dialog box to set your Mac to search for and download Apple software updates on a daily, weekly, or monthly basis. You can also click the Check Now button in the Software Update dialog box to activate a search for updates yourself. You want to ensure that the software on your Mac is kept up to date, so you set up your computer to search for updates and alert you when they are ready to be installed.

STEPS

An Internet connection is required to successfully complete the following steps.

1. Click the **System Preferences icon** 🖼 on the Dock, then click the **Software Update button** 🔘 in the System category in the System Preferences dialog box

   The Software Update dialog box opens with the Scheduled Check tab selected, as shown in Figure A-16.

QUICK TIP

You can also check for software updates by clicking 🍎, then clicking Software Update.

---

2. Click to select the **Check for updates check box**, if necessary

   When this check box is selected, your Mac will check for software updates on a regular basis. Depending on the settings for the Mac you are using, this check box might already be selected.

3. Click the **pop-up menu arrows** to the right of Check for updates, then select **Weekly** if necessary

   The options for how frequently your computer will search for software updates are Daily, Weekly, and Monthly. Your Mac will notify you when updates are available for software on your computer.

TROUBLE

The option Download updates automatically is only available if the Check for updates check box has been selected.

---

4. Click the **Download updates automatically check box** to select it, if necessary

   When this check box is checked, your Mac will automatically download critical software updates as soon as they are available and will alert you when they are ready to be installed.

5. Click the **Check Now button**

   A new dialog box opens and a progress bar appears as your Mac checks for updates, as shown in Figure A-17. If there are any available updates, you will see this message "Software updates are available for your computer. Do you want to download and install them?" If your Mac is up to date, you'll receive a message notifying you that your software is up to date.

6. If any updates are available for your home computer, click **Continue** (for your home computer) or **Not Now** (for your school's computer)

   For a lab computer, always check with your instructor before downloading any updates.

7. Close the Software Update dialog box

FIGURE A-16: Software Update dialog box

Scheduled Check tab

Check for updates check box

Download updates automatically check box

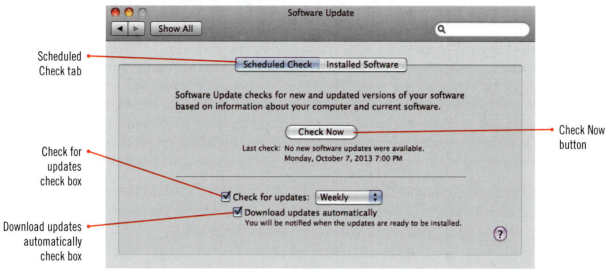

Check Now button

FIGURE A-17: Checking for updates

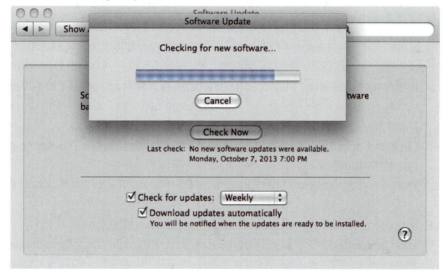

Changing Sound Options

Your Mac comes equipped with built-in sound effects to help you become an effective Mac user. The **alert sound** feature provides a sound effect when you try to perform an action or command that is not available or when an alert dialog box appears. The alert sound is also played as **feedback** when you adjust the system volume to let you hear the volume at its new setting. You can change the alert sound using the Sound dialog box. You also use the Sound dialog box to adjust the system volume and select whether or not you can change the system volume using an icon on the menu bar.  You want to change the alert sound played by your Mac and explore the other sound and volume options available for your system.

STEPS

1. **Click the System Preferences icon** 🔘 **on the Dock, then click the Sound button** 🔊 **in the Hardware category in the System Preferences dialog box**

   The Sound dialog box opens. The dialog box contains three tabs: Sound Effects, Output, and Input. The Output tab allows you to select which speakers to use (internal or external) if you have external speakers connected to your computer. The Internal tab allows you to select the built-in (or internal) microphone or an external microphone (if one is connected to your computer) to record sounds.

2. **If necessary, click the Sound Effects tab**

   The Sound Effects tab, as shown in Figure A-18, displays a list of options for the alert sound and several check boxes for turning sound options on and off. By default, Funk is selected as the alert sound.

3. **In the Choose an alert sound list, scroll up, then click Basso**

   The Basso alert sound is played.

4. **Click additional alert sound options to listen to them, then click the alert sound that you prefer**

5. **Drag the Alert volume slider to select a volume level for the alert sound that you prefer**

6. **If necessary, click the Play user interface sound effects check box**

   Selecting this check box ensures that you will hear **user interface sound effects**, which are the sounds you hear when you perform Finder actions such as dragging a file to the Trash and emptying the Trash.

7. **If necessary, click the Play feedback when volume is changed check box**

   Selecting this check box ensures that you will hear an alert sound at the new volume setting when the system volume is changed.

8. **Click and drag the Output volume slider to the location you prefer to adjust the system volume**

   When you drag the slider to a new location and then release the pointer button, the alert sound plays at the new volume setting.

9. **If necessary, click the Show volume in menu bar check box**

   Selecting this check box places the speaker icon 🔊 near the right end of the menu bar, which gives you quick access to it without opening a dialog box. You can click the speaker icon on the menu bar to access the vertical slider to adjust the volume up or down.

10. **Close the Sound dialog box**

    All options selected are saved when the dialog box closes.

FIGURE A-18: Sound dialog box

Sound Effects tab

Alert sound options

Play user interface sound effects check box

Play feedback when volume is changed check box

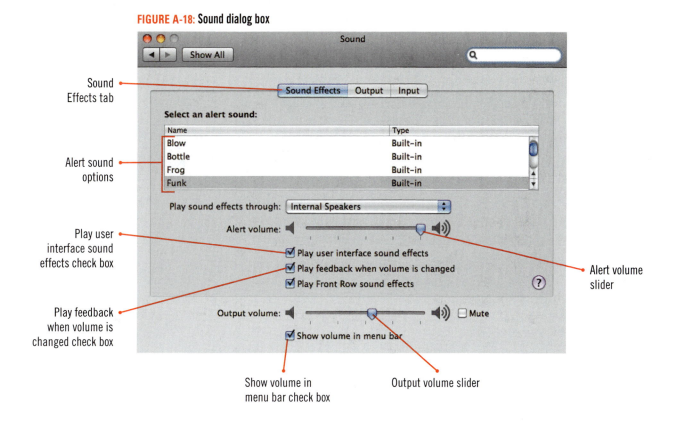

Alert volume slider

Show volume in menu bar check box

Output volume slider

Working with SkyDrive and Office Web Apps

Files You Will Need:

WEB-1.pptx
WEB-2.xlsx
WEB-3.docx

If the computer you are using has an active Internet connection, you can take advantage of the Microsoft Windows Live service to access a wide variety of services and Web applications. For example, you can check your e-mail through Windows Live, network with your friends and coworkers, and use SkyDrive to store and share files. From SkyDrive, you can also use Office Web Apps to create and edit Microsoft Word, PowerPoint, and Excel files, even when you are using a computer that does not have the Microsoft Office suite installed.  You work in the Vancouver branch of Quest Specialty Travel. Your supervisor, Mary Lou Jacobs, asks you to explore Windows Live and learn how she can use SkyDrive and Office Web Apps to work with her files online.

(*Note:* SkyDrive and Office Web Apps are dynamic Web pages, and as such, might change over time, including the way they are organized and how commands are performed. The steps and figures in this appendix were accurate at the time this book was published.)

OBJECTIVES

Explore how to work online

Obtain an ID and sign in

Upload files to SkyDrive

Work with the PowerPoint Web App

Create folders and organize files on SkyDrive

Add people to your network and share files

Work with the Excel Web App

Work with the Word Web App

Microsoft Office Web Apps Quick Reference

Exploring How to Work Online

When data, applications, and even resources are stored on servers accessed over the Internet rather than on users' computers, you are said to be using "cloud computing." Many individuals and companies are moving toward "the cloud" for at least some of their needs. Google Docs and Microsoft Web Apps provide both free and paid versions of various applications that you access by logging in to their Web sites. For now, these applications are not as robust as the programs you install on your own machine, but that is likely to change in the future. From any computer connected to the Internet, you can use Safari or any Web browser to upload your files to Google Docs or Windows Live/SkyDrive. With SkyDrive, you can work on the files from right in your browser using Office Web Apps, and you can share your files with people in your Windows Live network. You review the concepts and services related to working online from Windows Live.

DETAILS

- ### What is Windows Live?

  Microsoft created **Windows Live** as a collection of services and Web applications that you can use to help you be more productive both personally and professionally. For example, you can use Windows Live to send and receive e-mail, to chat with friends via instant messaging, to share photos, to create a blog, and to store and edit files using SkyDrive. Windows Live is a free service that you sign up for. When you register, you receive a Windows Live ID, which you use to sign in to Windows Live. When you work with files on Windows Live, you are using cloud computing.

- ### What is SkyDrive?

  SkyDrive is an online storage and file-sharing service. With a Windows Live account, you receive access to your own SkyDrive, which is a personal storage area on the Internet. On your SkyDrive, you are given space to store up to 25 GB of data. Each file can be a maximum size of 50 MB. You can also use SkyDrive to access the online Office Web Apps, which you use to create and edit files created in Word, PowerPoint, and Excel in your Web browser.

- ### Why use SkyDrive?

  SkyDrive gives you access to additional storage for your files. You don't have to worry about backing up your files to a memory stick or other storage device that could be lost or damaged. Another advantage of storing your files on SkyDrive is that you can access your files from any computer that has an active Internet connection. Figure B-1 shows a user's SkyDrive Web page that appears when signed in to a Windows Live account. From SkyDrive, you can also access Office Web Apps.

- ### What are Office Web Apps?

  Office Web Apps are versions of Word, Excel, and PowerPoint that you can access online from your Windows Live account. The current Office Web Apps do not include all of the features and functions included with the full Office versions of each application. However, you can use Office Web Apps from any computer that is connected to the Internet, even if the Microsoft Office suite is not installed on that computer.

- ### How do SkyDrive and Office Web Apps work together?

  You first create a file in Word, Excel, or PowerPoint 2011 and then upload the file to your SkyDrive. You can then open the Office file saved to SkyDrive and edit it using your Web browser and the corresponding Office Web App. Figure B-2 shows a PowerPoint presentation open in the PowerPoint Web App. You can also use an Office Web App to create a new file, which is saved automatically to SkyDrive while you work. In addition, you can download a file created with an Office Web App and continue to work with the file in the full version of the corresponding Office program. Finally, you can create a SkyDrive network that consists of the people you want to be able to view your folders and files on your SkyDrive. You can give people permission to view and edit your files using any computer with an active Internet connection and a Web browser.

FIGURE B-1: SkyDrive on Windows Live

Safari (browser) window

The name of the person who signed in to Windows Live appears here

By default, one folder is available on SkyDrive; you can create additional folders

Monitors the amount of space still available on your SkyDrive

FIGURE B-2: PowerPoint presentation open in the PowerPoint Web App

Name of PowerPoint presentation open in the PowerPoint Web App

Ribbon available in PowerPoint Web App

Presentation in PowerPoint Web App maintains the same look and feel as the same presentation in the desktop version of PowerPoint

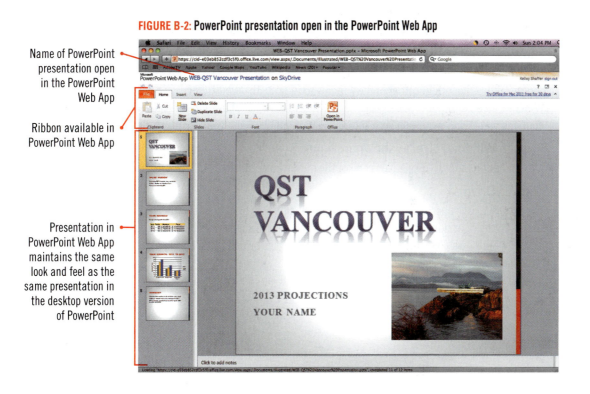

Obtaining an ID and Signing In

To work with your files online using SkyDrive and Office Web Apps, you need a Windows Live ID. You obtain a Windows Live ID by going to the Windows Live Web site and creating a new account. Once you have a Windows Live ID, you can access SkyDrive and then use it to store your files, create new files, and share your files with friends and coworkers. Mary Lou Jacobs, your supervisor at QST Vancouver, asks you to obtain a Windows Live ID so that you can work on documents with your coworkers. You go to the Windows Live Web site, create a Windows Live ID, and then sign in to your SkyDrive.

STEPS

QUICK TIP

If you already have a Windows Live ID, sign in as directed using your account and go to Step 6.

1. **Open Safari, type home.live.com in the Address bar, then press [return]**

   The Windows Live home page opens. From this page, you can create a Windows Live account and receive your Windows Live ID.

2. **Click the Sign up button** (*Note: You may see a Sign up link instead of a button*)

   The Create your Windows Live ID page opens.

3. **Click the Or use your own e-mail address link under the Check availability button, or if you are already using Hotmail, Messenger, or Xbox LIVE, click the Sign in now link in the Information statement near the top of the page**

   If you want, you can sign up for a Windows Live e-mail address such as yourname@live.com so that you can also access the Windows Live e-mail service.

4. **Enter the required information, as shown in Figure B-3**

TROUBLE

The code can be difficult to read. If you receive an error message, enter the new code that appears.

5. **Enter the code shown at the bottom of your screen, then click the I accept button**

   The Windows Live home page opens. The name you entered when you signed up for your Windows Live ID appears in the upper-right corner of the window to indicate that you are signed in to Windows Live. From the Windows Live home page, you can access all the services and applications offered by Windows Live. See the Verifying your Windows Live ID box for information on finalizing your account setup.

TROUBLE

You may need to verify your Windows Live ID before your computer screen resembles Figure B-4.

6. **Point to Windows Live, as shown in Figure B-4**

   A list of options appears. SkyDrive is one of the options you can access directly from Windows Live.

TROUBLE

Click I accept if you are asked to review and accept the Windows Live Service Agreement and Privacy Statement.

7. **Click SkyDrive**

   The SkyDrive page opens. Your name appears in the upper-right corner, and the amount of space available is shown on the right side of the SkyDrive page. The amount of space available is monitored, as indicated by the gauge that fills with color as space is used. Using SkyDrive, you can add files to the existing folder and you can create new folders.

FIGURE B-3: Creating a Windows Live ID

Click to sign in using a Hotmail, Messenger, or Xbox LIVE account

Once your registration is complete, you will be asked to verify your ID

A different code will appear on your screen

Type your e-mail address

You can choose to get a Windows Live e-mail address

Enter the information requested

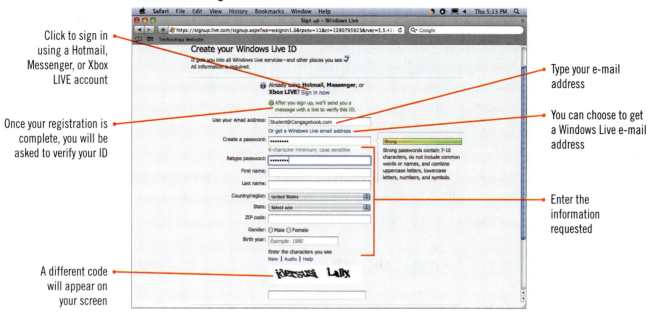

FIGURE B-4: Selecting SkyDrive

Windows Live

SkyDrive in the list of Windows Live options

Your name appears here

An advertisement appears here

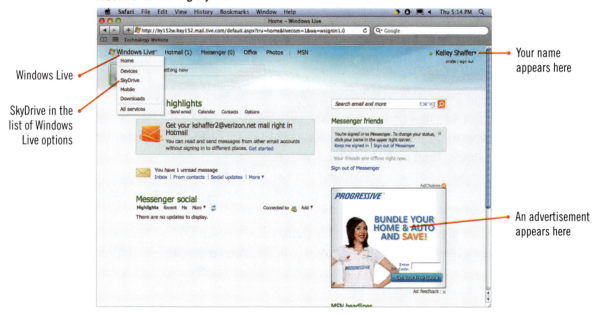

Verifying your ID

As soon as you accept the Windows Live terms, an e-mail is sent to the e-mail address you supplied when you created your Windows Live ID. Open your e-mail program, and then open the e-mail from Microsoft with the Subject line: Confirm your e-mail address for Windows Live. Follow the simple, step-by-step instructions in the e-mail to confirm your Windows Live ID. When the confirmation is complete, you will be asked to sign in to Windows Live, using your e-mail address and password. Once signed in, you will see your Windows Live home page.

Uploading Files to SkyDrive

Once you have created your Windows Live ID, you can sign in to Windows Live directly from Word, Excel, or PowerPoint and start saving and uploading files. You upload files to your SkyDrive so you can share the files with other people, access the files from another computer, or use SkyDrive's additional storage. 🎨 You open a PowerPoint presentation in PowerPoint 2011, access your Windows Live account, and save a file to SkyDrive. You also create a new folder on SkyDrive called Cengage and add a file to it.

STEPS

1. **Start PowerPoint, open the file WEB-1.pptx from the location where you store your Data Files, then save it as WEB-QST Vancouver Presentation.pptx**

2. **Click File on the menu bar, point to Share, then click Save to SkyDrive**

    As shown in Figure B-5, you'll be asked to sign in to your Windows Live account.

3. **Type your Windows Live ID, press [tab], type your Password, then click Sign In**

    The My Documents folder appears in the SkyDrive Save As dialog box, as shown in Figure B-6.

4. **Click Save**

    The Progress Indicator indicates that the file is being uploaded to SkyDrive. When the 🌀 disappears, the file is saved to your My Documents folder on the SkyDrive that is associated with your Windows Live account.

5. **Quit PowerPoint**

6. **Switch to Safari, then click My Documents on the SkyDrive Web page**

    Your My Documents folder opens and displays its contents, as shown in Figure B-7. The PowerPoint file WEB-QST Vancouver Presentation.pptx is displayed under the heading Today. Next, you will create a new folder and upload files directly to SkyDrive from the location where you store your Data Files.

7. **Click New on the menu bar, click Folder, type Cengage in the Name text box, then click Create folder**

    The Cengage folder is created in your My Documents folder and is open.

TROUBLE

When you click Add files on the menu bar, your screen might differ. You might need to click and drag files into the designated area to upload files to SkyDrive.

8. **Click Add files on the menu bar, click the first Choose File button, navigate to the location where you store your Data Files, click WEB-QST Vancouver Presentation.pptx, click Choose, then click the Upload button**

    The PowerPoint file WEB-QST Vancouver Presentation.pptx is now displayed in the Cengage folder. You have successfully added this file twice to your SkyDrive: in your My Documents folder and in the Cengage folder. You want to delete the file in the My Documents folder.

9. **Click My Documents in the file path, point to WEB-QST Vancouver Presentation.pptx, click the Delete button ✕, then click OK when prompted to confirm the deletion**

    The PowerPoint file WEB-QST Vancouver Presentation.pptx is successfully deleted from your My Documents folder. The file remains in your Cengage folder.

FIGURE B-5: Signing in to Windows Live from PowerPoint

Windows Live Sign In dialog box opens when you choose Save to SkyDrive

Enter your Windows Live ID and password

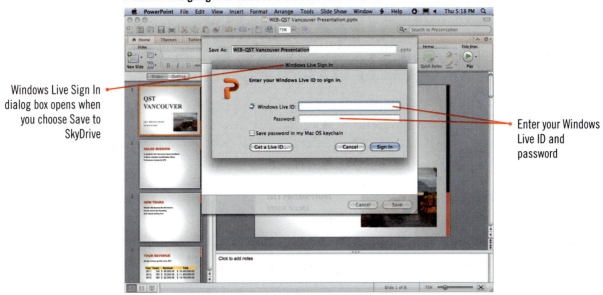

FIGURE B-6: Save to SkyDrive dialog box

Filename

My Documents folder on SkyDrive (you might see additional folders)

Save button

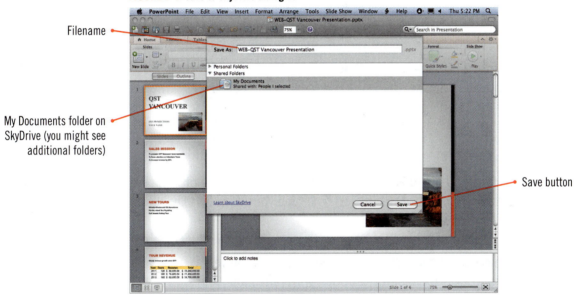

FIGURE B-7: PowerPoint file uploaded to SkyDrive

File path

New button

Add files button

Uploaded file

Menu bar

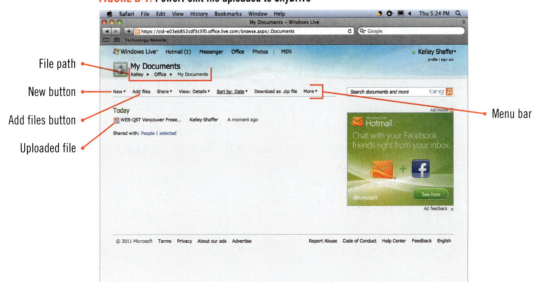

Working with the PowerPoint Web App

Once you have uploaded a file to SkyDrive, you can work on it using its corresponding Office Web App. Office Web Apps provide you with the tools you need to view documents online and to edit them right in your browser. You do not need to have Office programs installed on the computer you use to access SkyDrive and Office Web Apps. From SkyDrive, you can also open the document directly in the full Office program (for example, PowerPoint) if the program is installed on the computer you are using. You use the PowerPoint Web App to make some edits to the PowerPoint presentation. You then open the presentation in PowerPoint and use the full version to make additional edits.

STEPS

QUICK TIP

If you receive an alert message about Microsoft Silverlight, you can ignore it. Silverlight is a Microsoft product that enhances the quality of videos for Windows browsers.

1. **Click the Cengage folder, then click WEB-QST Vancouver Presentation**

   The presentation opens in your browser window. A toolbar is available, which includes the options you have for working with the file.

2. **Click the Edit in Browser button**

   In a few moments, the PowerPoint presentation opens in the PowerPoint Web App, as shown in Figure B-8. Table B-1 lists the commands you can perform using the PowerPoint Web App.

3. **Replace YOUR NAME on Slide 1 with your name, click Slide 3 (New Tours) in the Slides and Outline pane, then click the Delete Slide button 🗑 in the Slides group**

   The slide is removed from the presentation. You decide to open the file in the full version of PowerPoint on your computer so you can apply Text Effects to the slide title. You work with the file in the full version of PowerPoint when you want to use features, such as Text Effects, that are not available in the PowerPoint Web App.

TROUBLE

If you try to open the file in PowerPoint and you receive an error message that the "file is locked and read-only," or "locked for editing," click Cancel and try again.

4. **Click the Open in PowerPoint button 📧 in the Office group, click Open in the "Do you want to open the file?" dialog box, type your Windows Live ID and password if requested, then click Sign In**

   In a few moments, the revised version of the PowerPoint slide opens in PowerPoint on your computer.

5. **Select QST Vancouver on the title slide, click the Text Effects button A ▾ in the Font group, click the Blue-Gray option with reflection (fourth row, fifth option), then click a blank area outside the slide**

   The text effect is applied to the presentation title. Next, you save the revised version of the file to SkyDrive.

TROUBLE

If you get an error stating the upload failed, reconnect to SkyDrive, then try again.

6. **Click Save 💾 on the Standard toolbar**

   The file is saved to your SkyDrive.

QUICK TIP

If you receive the message "Windows Live couldn't sign you out," your browser may be set to block cookies. To prevent seeing this message in the future, change your browser settings to allow cookies. If you see this message and do not want to change your browser setting, just quit your browser.

7. **Click the Safari icon on the Dock to access your SkyDrive page, then click Office next to your first name in the SkyDrive file path to view a list of recent documents, as shown in Figure B-9**

   The WEB-QST Vancouver Presentation file is displayed under the heading Today on SkyDrive.

8. **Click the sign out link under your name in the upper-right corner of SkyDrive, quit Safari, then quit PowerPoint**

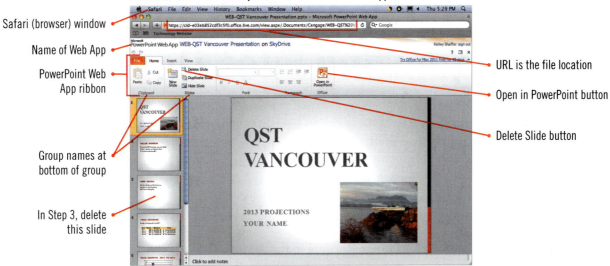

FIGURE B-8: Presentation opened in the PowerPoint Web App

Safari (browser) window
Name of Web App
PowerPoint Web App ribbon
Group names at bottom of group
In Step 3, delete this slide

URL is the file location
Open in PowerPoint button
Delete Slide button

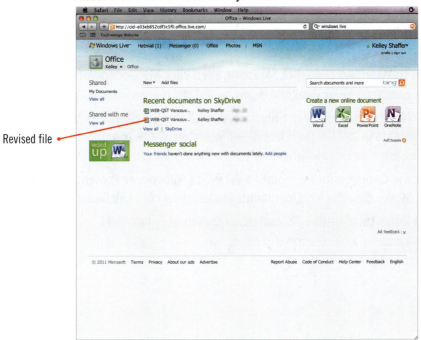

FIGURE B-9: Recent documents on SkyDrive list

Revised file

TABLE B-1: Commands on the PowerPoint Web App

tab	commands available
File	• Open in PowerPoint: Select to open the file in PowerPoint on your computer • Where's the Save Button?: When you click this option, the following message appears, "In PowerPoint Web App, there is no save button because your presentation is being saved automatically." • Print • Share • Properties • Give Feedback • Privacy • Terms of Use • Close
Home	• Clipboard group: Cut, Copy, Paste • Slides group: New Slide, Delete Slide, Duplicate Slide, and Hide Slide • Font group: Work with text – change the font, style, color, and size of selected text • Paragraph group: Work with paragraphs – add bullets and numbers, indent text, align text • Theme group: Change the theme of the PowerPoint presentation • Office group: Open the file in PowerPoint on your computer
Insert	• Insert group: Insert a picture, clip art, or SmartArt diagram • Links group: Insert a link such as to another file on SkyDrive or to a Web page
View	• Presentation Views group: Editing View (the default), Reading View, Slide Show view • Show group: Notes button turns the Notes pane on and off

Creating Folders and Organizing Files On SkyDrive

As you have learned, you can sign in to SkyDrive directly from the Office programs PowerPoint, Excel, and Word, or you can access SkyDrive directly through your browser. This option is useful when you are away from the computer on which you normally work or when you are using a computer that does not have Office programs installed. You can go to SkyDrive, create and organize folders, and then create or open files to work on with Office Web Apps. You access SkyDrive from your Web browser and create a new folder called Illustrated.

STEPS

QUICK TIP
Go to Step 3 if you are already signed in.

1. **Open Safari, type home.live.com in the Address field, then press [return]**

   The Windows Live home page opens. From here you can sign in to your Windows Live account and then access SkyDrive.

QUICK TIP
Type your Windows Live ID and password, then click Sign In if prompted to do so.

2. **Sign in to Windows Live as directed**

   You are signed in to your Windows Live page. From this page, you can take advantage of the many applications available on Windows Live, including SkyDrive.

3. **Point to Windows Live, click SkyDrive, then click My Documents**

   The contents of your My Documents folder on SkyDrive is displayed, as shown in Figure B-10.

4. **Click New, click Folder, type Illustrated, click the Create folder button, then click My Documents in the file path beneath Illustrated at the top of the window**

   You return to your list of folders, where you see the new Illustrated folder.

5. **Click the Cengage folder, point to WEB-QST Vancouver Presentation.pptx, click More, click Move, click the My Documents folder, then click the Illustrated folder**

6. **Click Move this file into Illustrated, as shown in Figure B-11**

   The file is moved to the Illustrated folder.

Exploring Office Web Apps

Another Office Web App is OneNote. OneNote is a Windows program from Microsoft Office 2010 that lets you collect and organize notes, photos, videos, and Web links—for any project you are working on. You can use OneNote online and share it with Windows users. To familiarize yourself with the commands available in an Office Web App, open the file and then review the commands on each tab on the ribbon. If you want to perform a task that is not available in the Office Web App, open the file in the full version of the program.

In addition to working with uploaded files, you can create new files on SkyDrive. Simply sign in to SkyDrive and open a folder. With a folder open, click New and then select the Web App you want to use to create the new file.

FIGURE B-10: Folders on your SkyDrive

Current location

Folders currently available

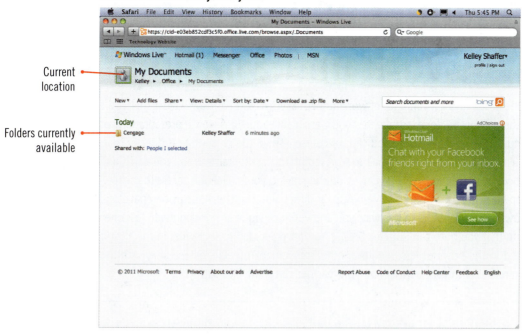

FIGURE B-11: Moving a file to the Illustrated folder

Click to move file to this location

Name of file to be moved

Be sure to rename a file before moving it if you are moving it to a location where another copy of the same file exists

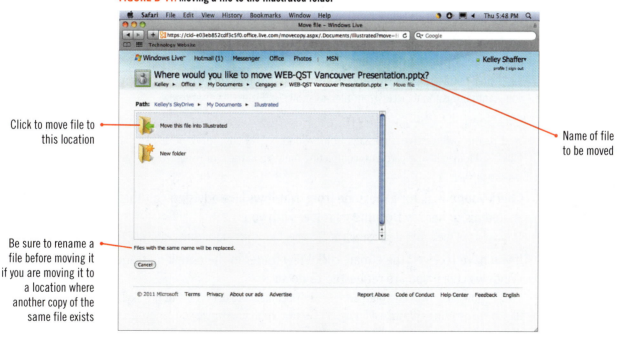

Adding People to your Network and Sharing Files

One of the great advantages of working with SkyDrive on Windows Live is that you can share your files with others. Suppose, for example, that you want a colleague to review a presentation you created in PowerPoint and then add a new slide. You can, of course, e-mail the presentation directly to your colleague, who can then make changes and e-mail the presentation back. Alternatively, you can save time by uploading the PowerPoint file directly to SkyDrive and then giving your colleague access to the file. Your colleague can edit the file using the PowerPoint Web App, and then you can check the updated file on SkyDrive, also using the PowerPoint Web App. In this way, you and your colleague are working with just one version of the presentation that you both can update. 🎨 You have decided to share files in the Illustrated folder that you created in the previous lesson with another individual. You start by working with a partner so that you can share files with your partner and your partner can share files with you.

1. **Identify a partner with whom you can work, and obtain his or her e-mail address; you can choose someone in your class or someone on your e-mail list, but it should be someone who will be completing these steps with you**

2. **Click My Documents, click Share, then click Edit permissions**
   The Edit permissions for My Documents page opens. On this page, you can select the individual with whom you would like to share the contents of the Illustrated folder.

3. **Click in the Enter a name or an e-mail address text box, type the e-mail address of your partner, then press [return]**
   You can define the level of access that you want to give your partner.

4. **Click the Can view files menu arrow shown in Figure B-12, click Can add, edit details, and delete files option if necessary, then click Save**
   The Send a notification Web page opens giving you the option to send a notification to each individual when you grant permission to access your files, as shown in Figure B-13.

5. **Click Send**
   Your partner will receive a message from Windows Live advising him or her that you have shared your Illustrated folder. If your partner is completing the steps at the same time, you will also receive an e-mail from your partner.

6. **Check your e-mail for a message from Windows Live advising you that your partner has shared his or her My Documents folder with you**
   The subject of the e-mail message will be "[Name] has shared documents with you."

7. **If you have received the e-mail, click View folder in the e-mail message, then sign in to Windows Live if you are requested to do so**
   You are now able to access your partner's My Documents folder on his or her SkyDrive. You can download files in your partner's Illustrated folder to your own computer where you can work on them and then upload them again to your partner's Illustrated shared folder.

8. **Sign out of SkyDrive, then quit Safari**

FIGURE B-12: Editing folder permissions

Permissions must be changed in the My Documents folder

Click to select network permission options

Person whose permission status will change

Click to select person from list of contacts

Permission options

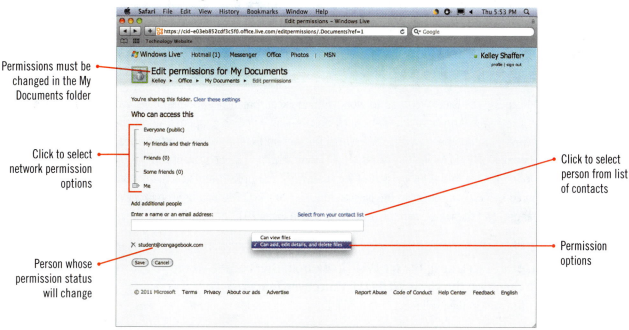

FIGURE B-13: Sending a notification message

Notification recipient's e-mail address

Send button

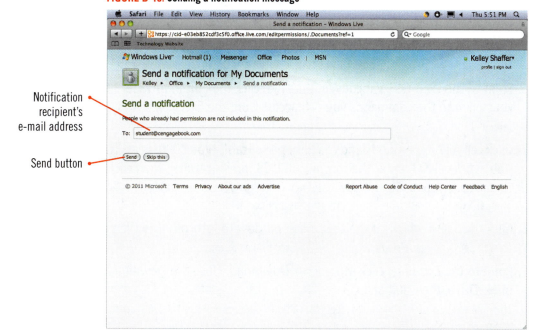

Working with the Excel Web App

You can use the Excel Web App to work with an Excel spreadsheet on SkyDrive. Workbooks opened using the Excel Web App have the same look and feel as workbooks opened using the full version of Excel. However, just like the PowerPoint Web App, the current Excel Web App has fewer features available than the full version of Excel. When you want to use a command that is not available on the Excel Web App, you need to open the file in the full version of Excel. You upload an Excel file containing a list of the tours offered by QST Vancouver to the Illustrated folder on SkyDrive. You use the Excel Web App to make some changes, and then you open the revised version in Excel 2011 on your computer.

STEPS

1. **Start Excel, open the file WEB-2.xlsx from the location where you store your Data Files, then save the file as WEB-QST Vancouver Tours.xlsx**
   The data in the Excel file is formatted using the Excel table function.

QUICK TIP
You can also add this file directly to SkyDrive by using the Add files option on the SkyDrive Web page.

2. **Click File on the menu bar, point to Share, click Save to SkyDrive, sign in to Windows Live, select My Documents folder if necessary, click Save, wait a few moments, then quit Excel**
   After a few moments, the file WEB-QST Vancouver Tours is saved in your My Documents folder.

3. **Open Safari, go to home.live.com, sign in, then navigate to the WEB-QST Vancouver Tours.xlsx file in your My Documents folder on SkyDrive**
   Windows Live opens to your My Documents folder on SkyDrive, where the Excel file WEB-QST Vancouver Tours is displayed. You want to move this file into the Illustrated folder.

4. **Point to the WEB-QST Vancouver Tours file, click More, then click Move**
   The Web page "Where would you like to move WEB-QST Vancouver Tours.xlsx?" will open.

5. **Click My Documents, click the Illustrated folder, then click Move this file into Illustrated**
   The Excel file WEB-QST Vancouver Tours is now located in the Illustrated folder and this folder is selected.

6. **Point to the WEB-QST Vancouver Tours file, click the Edit in browser link, then familiarize yourself with the commands you can access from the Excel Web App**
   Table B-2 summarizes the commands that are available.

7. **Click cell A12, type Gulf Islands Sailing, press [tab], type 3000, press [tab], type 10, press [tab], click cell D3, enter the formula =B3*C3, press [return], then click cell A1**
   The formula is copied automatically to the remaining rows, as shown in Figure B-14, because the data in the original Excel file was created and formatted as an Excel table.

8. **Click the SkyDrive link at the top of the window to return to the Web page**
   The changes you made to the Excel spreadsheet are saved automatically.

9. **Point to the Excel file, click More, click Download, close the Downloads window, sign out of SkyDrive, then quit Safari**
   The updated version of the spreadsheet is saved on your computer in the Downloads folder and on SkyDrive. You want to move the file to the location where you store your Data Files.

10. **Open a Finder window, open the Downloads folder, click and drag the WEB-QST Vancouver Tours file to the location where you store your Data Files, then click Replace when prompted if you want to replace the existing file**
    The file is moved or copied to the location where you store your Data Files.

11. **Delete the file from the Downloads folder on your computer, if necessary**

FIGURE B-14: Updated table in the Excel Web App

Click to return to Illustrated folder

New entry

Totals calculated based on formula in cell D3

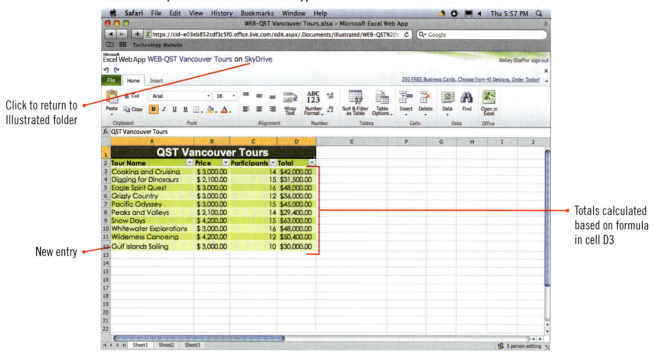

TABLE B-2: Commands on the Excel Web App

tab	commands available
File	• Open in Excel: Select to open the file in Excel on your computer • Where's the Save Button?: When you click this option, a message appears telling you that you do not need to save your spreadsheet when you are working in it with Excel Web App; the spreadsheet is saved automatically as you work • Save As • Share • Download a Copy: The file can be opened and edited in the full version of Excel • Properties • Give Feedback • Privacy Statement • Terms of Use • Close
Home	• Clipboard group: Cut, Copy, Paste • Font group: Change the font, style, color, and size of selected labels and values, as well as border styles and fill colors • Alignment group: Change vertical and horizontal alignment and turn on the Wrap Text feature • Number group: Change the number format and increase or decrease decimal places • Tables: Sort and filter data in a table and modify Table Options • Cells: Insert and delete cells • Data: Refresh data, refresh connections, recalculate workbook, and find labels or values • Office: Open the file in Excel on your computer
Insert	• Insert a function • Insert a table • Insert charts • Insert a hyperlink to a Web page
View	• Document views: Editing View and Reading View

Working with the Word Web App

You can use the Word Web App to work with a Word document on SkyDrive. Documents opened using the Word Web App have the same look and feel as documents opened using the full version of Word. However, just like the PowerPoint and Excel Web Apps, the Word Web App has fewer features available than the full version of Word. When you want to use a command that is not available on the Word Web App, you need to open the file in the full version of Word. You upload a Word file containing a proposal for a new tour for QST Vancouver to your My Documents folder on SkyDrive. You use the Word Web App to make some changes, and then you open the revised version in Word 2011 on your computer.

STEPS

1. **Start Word, open the file WEB-3.docx from the location where you store your Data Files, then save the file as WEB-QST Tour Proposal.docx**

QUICK TIP
You can also add this file directly to SkyDrive by using the Add files option on the SkyDrive Web page.

2. **Click File on the menu bar, point to Share, click Save to SkyDrive, sign in to Windows Live, select My Documents folder if necessary, click Save, wait a few moments, then quit Word**

   After a few moments, the file WEB-QST Tour Proposal is saved in your My Documents folder.

3. **Open Safari, type home.live.com in the Address field, press [return], sign in to Windows Live, point to Windows Live, click SkyDrive, then click My Documents**

   Windows Live opens to your My Documents folder on SkyDrive, where the Word file WEB-QST Tour Proposal is displayed in addition to the Cengage and Illustrated folders. You want to add some formatting to the Word file using the Word Web App.

4. **Point to the WEB-QST Tour Proposal file, then click Edit in browser**

   The WEB-QST Tour Proposal.docx opens in the Word Web App, as shown in Figure B-15.

5. **Review the ribbon and its tabs to familiarize yourself with the commands you can access from the Word Web App**

   Table B-3 summarizes the commands that are available.

6. **Select the title of the document QST Vancouver Tours, click the Bold button B in the Font group, click the Font Size pop-up menu arrow, click 16, then click the Center button ≡ in the Paragraph group**

   The document title is now larger, bold, and centered between the left and right margins.

7. **Select San Juan Islands (7 days), click B, select the price $1,300, then click B**

   The tour name and price are now bold. You now want to add a footer. To add a footer, you need to open this document in the full version of Word on your computer.

8. **Click the Open in Word button W in the Office group, click Save when prompted if you would like to save those changes, click Open when prompted "Do you want to open the file?," then enter your Windows Live ID and password, if necessary**

   The tour proposal document opens in Word on your computer, as shown in Figure B-16.

9. **Click View on the menu bar, click Header and Footer, click the Header and Footer tab, click the Go to Footer button ⊡, type Your Name at the left margin in the footer, then click the Close button Close ⊗**

10. **Click the Save button ⊞ on the Standard toolbar, then quit Word**

    WEB-QST Tour Proposal.docx is saved to your My Documents folder on your SkyDrive.

11. **Sign out of Windows Live, then quit Safari**

FIGURE B-15: Word document opened in the Word Web App

Word Web App open

Filename of open document

Open in Word button

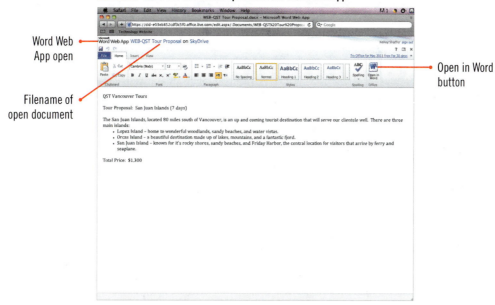

FIGURE B-16: Word document opened in the full version of Word

Save button saves changes to SkyDrive

Revisions made in the Word Web App

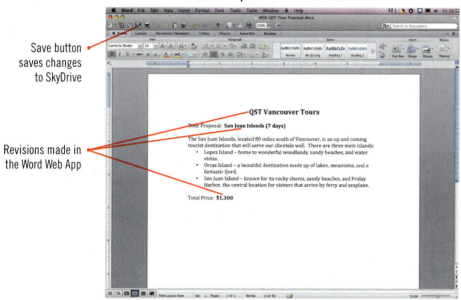

TABLE B-3: Commands on the Word Web App

tab	commands available
File	• Open in Word: Select to open the file in Word on your computer • Save • Print • Share • Properties • Give Feedback • Privacy • Terms of Use • Close
Home	• Clipboard group: Cut, Copy, Paste • Font group: Change the font, font size, clear formatting, style, and color of selected text • Paragraph group: Create a bulleted or number list; decrease or increase an indent; left-, center-, or right-align a paragraph; or change your text direction • Styles group: Change the style of selected text • Spelling group: Check the spelling of a document • Office group: Open the file in Word on your computer
Insert	• Table group: Insert a table • Pictures group: Insert a picture from file or clip art • Insert a hyperlink to a Web page
View	• Change view to Editing View or Reading View

Microsoft Office Web Apps Quick Reference

to do this	go here
Sign in to Windows Live	From Safari, type *home.live.com*, then click Sign In
Access SkyDrive on Windows Live	From the Windows Live home page, point to Windows Live, then click SkyDrive
Save to Windows Live from Word, Excel, or PowerPoint	Click File on the menu bar, point to Share, then click Save to SkyDrive
Create a new folder on SkyDrive	From SkyDrive, click My Documents, click New, click Folder, type the name of the new folder, then click Create folder
Edit a file with a Web App	From SkyDrive, click the file, then click the Edit in Browser button, or From SkyDrive, point to the file, then click the Edit in Browser link
Open a file in the full version of the program from a Web App: Word, Excel, PowerPoint	Click the Open in [Application Name] button in the Office group in each Office Web App, or From SkyDrive, point to the file, then click the Open in [Application Name] link
Share files on Windows Live	From SkyDrive, click My Documents, click Share, click Edit permissions, enter the e-mail address of the person to share files with, click Save, then click Send if you'd like to notify the person that he or she has access to your SkyDrive files

Glossary

Absolute cell reference In Excel, a cell reference that does not change when the formula is copied and pasted to a new location; for example, the formula "=$B$5*$C$5" in cell D5 does not change to "=$B$6*$C$6" when copied to cell D6. *See also* Relative cell reference.

Action button A button on the Finder toolbar that provides access to file management commands such as creating a new folder, opening a file, or copying a file or folder.

Active cell In an Excel worksheet, the current location of the cell pointer.

Active window The window that is currently in use.

Add a bookmark button A button found on the Safari toolbar that enables users to name a bookmark and add it to the bookmarks bar or to the Bookmarks menu.

Address field A text field on the Safari toolbar that displays the address of the Web page that is open in the active tab.

Adware Software installed with another program that generates advertising revenue for the program's creator by displaying targeted ads to the program's user.

Alert sound A sound that occurs when you try to perform an action or command that is not available, when an alert dialog box appears, or when you change the system volume.

Alias A link that provides quick access to a file, folder, or program located on the hard disk; for example, each icon on the dock is an alias for a program, folder, or file stored elsewhere on the computer.

Alignment In Word, the position of text in a document relative to the margins; in Excel, the position of text in a cell relative to the cell edges, such as left, center, or right.

American Standard Code for Information Interchange *See* ASCII.

Analog signal A continuous wave signal (sound wave) that can traverse ordinary phone lines.

Animation In PowerPoint, a special effect that determines how an individual slide element moves or changes. Types of animation include Entrance Effects, Emphasis Effects, and Exit Effects.

Anti spyware software Software that detects and removes spyware.

Antivirus software Software that searches executable files for the sequences of characters that may cause harm and disinfects the files by erasing or disabling those commands. Also called virus protection software.

Application Software used to perform a specific task, such as creating a document, analyzing data, or creating a presentation. Also called a program.

Architecture The design and construction of a computer. Also called configuration.

Area chart A chart that shows the relative importance of values over a period of time.

Argument A value, cell reference, or text used in an Excel function. Commas or a colon separate arguments and parentheses enclose them; for example, AVERAGE(A1,10,5) or SUM(A1:A5).

ASCII (American Standard Code for Information Interchange) The number system that personal computers use to represent character data.

Attributes Styling characteristics such as bold, italic, and underline that users can apply to change the way text and numbers look in a document.

AutoCorrect A feature that automatically detects and corrects typing errors, minor spelling errors, and capitalization, and inserts certain typographical symbols as a user types.

AutoFit A feature that automatically adjusts the width of a column or the height of a row to accommodate its widest or tallest entry.

AVERAGE function In Excel, a function that calculates the average value of the arguments in a function.

Axis titles Labels in a chart that identify the information represented by each axis.

Back button A button commonly found at the top of a window that, when clicked, displays the previous Web page, file, folder, or drive in the window.

Backup A copy of a file stored in another location.

Bar chart A chart that compares values among individual items, with minimal emphasis on time.

BD-R A Blu-ray disc on which you can record data once.

BD-RE A Blu-ray disc on which you can record data as on a BD-R, and then delete or rerecord data on it as needed.

Bibliography A detailed list of citations from works referenced in a document that is usually placed at the end of the document.

Binary digit (bit) The representation of data as a 1 or 0.

BIOS (Basic Input/Output System) Instructions that initialize the motherboard, recognize peripheral devices, and start the boot process.

Bit *See* Binary digit.

Bits per second (bps) The unit of measurement for the speed of data transmission.

Bluetooth A wireless technology standard that allows electronic devices to use short range radio waves to communicate with one another or connect to the Internet; the radio waves can be transmitted around corners and through walls.

Blu-ray A disc used for storing high-definition video that stores 25 GB of data per layer.

Bold A font style that makes text appear in darker type; used to emphasize text in a document, spreadsheet, or presentation.

Bold command On a menu, a command or operation that can be executed.

Bookmark To add a favorite Web page to the bookmarks bar or Bookmarks menu, where the page can be easily accessed in the future by clicking instead of entering the Web address in the address field.

Bookmarks bar A feature of Safari that contains buttons users can click to go directly to bookmarked Web pages, to the bookmarks library, to a page showing Top Sites, or to several popular Web sites whose bookmarks are built in to the bookmarks bar.

Bookmarks menu In Safari, a list of bookmark collections that can be used to view, organize, add, and delete bookmarks and bookmark folders.

Boot process The set of events that occurs between the moment the computer is turned on and the moment you begin to use the computer.

Boot up The act of turning on the computer.

Booting The process that Snow Leopard steps through to get the computer up and running.

Broadband connection A high-speed connection to the Internet.

Browser A software program, such as Safari, used to access the Internet and display Web pages.

Browser window The rectangular area on the computer screen where the current Web page appears.

Built-in graphics card See Graphics processor.

Bullet A small graphic symbol used to identify items in a list.

Byte One character of storage space on disk or in RAM; composed of a series of 8 bits.

Cable Plastic-enclosed wires that attach a peripheral device to a computer port.

Cache memory Special high-speed memory chips on the motherboard or CPU that store frequently accessed and recently accessed data and commands. Also called RAM cache or CPU cache.

Card A removable circuit board that is inserted into a slot in the motherboard to expand the capabilities of the motherboard.

Category axis See Horizontal axis.

CD (compact disc) An optical storage device that can store approximately 700 MB of data.

CD-R (compact disc recordable) A CD on which users can record data with a laser that changes the reflectivity of a dye layer on the blank disc, creating dark spots on the disc's surface that represent the data; once the data is recorded, it cannot be erased or modified.

CD-ROM (compact disc read-only memory) A CD that contains software or music when you purchase it, but you cannot record additional data on it.

CD-RW (compact disc rewritable) A CD on which you can record data as on a CD-R, and then delete or rerecord data on it as needed.

Cell The intersection of a row and a column in an Excel worksheet or a Word table.

Cell address In Excel, a column letter followed by a row number that specifies the location of a cell.

Cell pointer In Excel, the blue border that surrounds the active cell or cells.

Cell range In Excel, a group of cells that shares boundaries and is selected.

Cell reference The address of a cell in an Excel worksheet that defines its location in the worksheet by column letter and row number (for example, A1), and that can be used in formulas and functions.

Central processing unit (CPU) See Microprocessor.

Channel The medium, such as a telephone line or coaxial cable, over which a message is sent in data communications.

Chart A visual representation of selected worksheet data.

Chart area The entire chart and all the chart elements.

Chart layout A predefined arrangement of chart elements, such as the placement of the legend and the chart title.

Chart object An individual component of a chart, such as the chart background or legend that can be moved or resized independently.

Chart sheet A worksheet in an Excel workbook that contains a chart.

Chart style A predefined set of chart colors and fills that can be applied to any chart.

Check box A box that turns an option on when checked or off when unchecked.

Check mark When displayed, indicates a command is currently selected or active.

Chip An integrated circuit embedded in semiconductor material.

Circuit A path along which an electric current travels.

Circuit board A rigid piece of insulating material with circuits on it that control specific functions.

Citation A reference to a source that usually includes the author's name and page number of the referenced material.

Citations A tab on the Word Toolbox that enables users to insert citations and build a bibliography. (Office Toolbox)

Click To quickly press and release the left button on a pointing device. Also called single-click.

Client A computer connected to a network that is dependent on a server.

Client/server network A network with a server and computers dependent on the server.

Clip A media object or file, such as a graphic, photograph, sound, movie, or animation, that has been added to the Scrapbook and can be inserted into an Office document.

Clip art Simple art objects that are included as collections with many software packages.

Clip Gallery A library of clip art, animations, videos, and photographs that all Office programs share.

Clipboard A temporary storage area in the computer's memory containing an item that was cut or copied from a file and is available for pasting. *See also* System Clipboard.

Clock speed The pulse of the processor measured in megahertz or gigahertz.

Cloud computing When data, applications, and resources are stored on servers accessed over the Internet or a company's internal network rather than on user's computers.

CMOS *See* Complementary metal-oxide semiconductor memory.

Collapse button A button that shrinks a portion of a dialog box to hide some settings.

Color scales Shading patterns that use two or three colors to show the relative values of a range of cells.

Column chart A chart that compares values across categories over time.

Column headings In Excel, the boxes containing letters that appear above every column.

Column sparkline In Excel, a tiny column chart that includes a column for each cell in a specified range.

Columns view A view of items in a window that displays the contents of a device or folder in a multicolumn format.

Command An instruction to perform a task.

Command button A button that completes or cancels an operation.

Compact disc *See* CD.

Compact disc read-only memory *See* CD-ROM.

Compact disc recordable *See* CD-R.

Compact disk rewritable *See* CD-RW.

Compatibility Report A tab on the Office Toolbox that enables users to check for compatibility issues with earlier versions of the Office suite, including both Windows and Mac versions.

Complementary metal-oxide semiconductor (CMOS) memory A chip installed on the motherboard powered by a battery whose content changes every time you add or remove hardware on your computer system and that is activated during the boot process so it can identify where essential software is stored. Also called semipermanent memory.

Complex formula A formula in Excel that contains more than one mathematical operator (for example, +, –, *, or /) and performs more than one calculation at a time.

Computer An electronic device that accepts input, processes data, displays output, and stores data for retrieval later.

Computer network The hardware and software that make it possible for two or more computers to share information and resources.

Computer system A computer, its peripheral devices, and software.

Conditional formatting In Excel, formatting that is applied to cells in a spreadsheet when specified criteria are met.

Configuration *See* Architecture.

Context-sensitive Help On-screen guidance tools that display topics and instructions geared to the specific task the user is performing.

Contextual tab A tab that only appears on the ribbon when text or an object is selected that can use the tools on this tab.

[control]-click To press and hold [control] while clicking the mouse button once; functions as a right-click for a single-button pointing device.

Controller card A card that plugs into a slot on the motherboard and connects to a port to provide an electrical connection to a peripheral device. Also called expansion card or interface card.

Copy To create a duplicate of a file in a new location, while the original file stays in its current location.

Copy-and-paste operation The feature in document production software that allows you to duplicate selected words and objects somewhere else in the document.

Cover Flow A view of items in a window that provides a preview of the first page of the files and a detailed list of the files in the currently selected location.

CPU *See* Microprocessor.

CPU cache *See* Cache memory.

Create a new tab button A button at the right side of the tab bar in Safari that, when clicked, opens a new Web page tab in the browser window.

Criteria In Excel, conditions or qualifications that determine whether data is chosen for a filter.

Cut To remove data from a file and place it on the Clipboard, usually to be pasted into another location or file.

Data The words, numbers, figures, sounds, and graphics that describe people, events, things, and ideas.

Data bars In Excel, colored bars that make it easy to identify the large and small values in a selected range of cells and also highlight the relative value of cells to each other.

Data bus The path between the microprocessor, RAM, and the peripherals along which communication travels.

Data communications The transmission of data from one computer to another or to a peripheral device via a channel using a protocol.

Data file A file created by a user, usually with software, such as a report written with a word processing program.

Data label Text in a chart that describes or names a data series value, a data series, or a category.

Data marker A bar, area, dot, slice, or other symbol in a chart that represents a single data point or value that originates from a worksheet cell.

Data series In a chart, a sequence of related numbers that shows a trend, such as sales amounts of various months, quarters, or years.

Data source The file that stores the custom information for a form letter or other mail merge document.

Data table A grid in a chart that contains the chart's underlying worksheet data and that is usually placed below the x-axis.

Database A collection of information stored on one or more computers organized in a uniform format of records and fields.

Database management software Software used to collect and manage data.

Default setting A setting preset by the manufacturer of an operating system or program.

Desktop The graphical user interface (GUI) displayed on screen after you start your computer that you use to interact with the operating system and other software on your computer.

Desktop computer A personal computer designed to sit compactly on a desk.

Destination file When linking and embedding data between documents, the location to which the data is copied or moved to.

Device *See* Storage device.

Device driver System software that handles the transmission protocol between a computer and its peripheral devices. Also called a driver.

Devices group A group on the sidebar in the Finder window that provides quick access to all of the storage devices available to your Mac, such as the hard disk and any external drives.

Dialog box A window that opens to enable users to select options or provide the information needed to complete an operation.

Digital signal A stop-start signal that your computer outputs.

Digital subscriber line *See* DSL.

Dimmed command On a menu, a command or operation that is not currently available.

Disclosure triangle A small triangle that indicates a command or group has additional options or categories available.

DNS server A computer responsible for directing Internet traffic.

Dock A glossy ribbon at the bottom of the computer screen that contains icons for frequently used programs, folders and files, and the Trash.

Document An electronic file that you create using a program such as Word.

Document production software Software, such as word processing software, desktop publishing software, e-mail editors, and Web authoring software, that assists users in writing and formatting documents, including changing the font and checking the spelling.

Document window The main work area within the program window that displays all or part of an open document.

Documents folder A folder generated by the operating system, located in your Home folder, that is the default location where most of your files will be saved.

Domain name The name of a Web site that appears after *www* in a Web address; for example, in *www.apple.com*, *apple* is the domain name.

Dot matrix printer A printer that transfers ink to paper by striking a ribbon with pins.

Dot pitch (dp) The distance between pixels on a monitor.

Double-click To press and release the left mouse button twice quickly, opening a window or program.

dp *See* Dot pitch.

Draft view In Word, a view that lets you create and edit text in a simplified layout.

Drag To point to an object, press and hold the left button on the pointing device, move the object to a new location, and then release the left button.

Drag and drop The action of moving or copying an entire file or selected text in a document by dragging it with the mouse and placing it at a new location.

Driver *See* Device driver.

DSL (digital subscriber line) A high-speed connection over phone lines.

Dual-core processor A CPU that has two processors on the chip.

DVD An optical storage device that can store up to 15.9 GB of data; was originally an acronym for digital video disc and later digital versatile disc.

DVD+R, DVD-R A DVD on which you can record data once.

DVD+RW, DVD-RW A DVD on which you can record data as on a DVD-R, and then delete or rerecord data on it as needed.

DVI (digital video interface) port A port that digitally transmits video.

Edit To change the content or format of an existing file.

Ellipsis (...) On a menu, indicates that the command opens a dialog box containing additional options.

Embed To insert a separate copy of a file in a different program that can be edited using the tools of the program in which it was created. The data becomes part of the new file.

Emphasis effects In PowerPoint, an animation group that adds an effect to an object already visible on a slide.

End-of-cell mark In a Word table, the formatting mark in each cell that appears to the right of typed text.

End-of-row mark In a Word table, the formatting mark that appears to the right of each row.

Endnote A note or citation that corresponds to a number or symbol in a document and appears at the end of the document. *See also* Footnote.

Enter To type information in a document or dialog box.

Entrance effects In PowerPoint, a group of animation effects that specifies the way text or objects move onto a slide.

Ergonomic Designed to fit the natural placement of the body to reduce the risk of repetitive-motion injuries.

Ethernet port A port used to connect computers in a LAN or sometimes directly to the Internet; it allows for high-speed data transmission.

Executable file A file that contains the instructions that tell a computer how to perform a specific task, such as the files that are used during the boot process.

Exit effects In PowerPoint, an animation group that specifies the way text or an object leaves the slide.

Expand button A button that expands a dialog box to display additional settings.

Expansion card *See* Controller card.

Expansion port The interface between a cable and a controller card. Also called port.

Expansion slot An electrical connector on the motherboard into which a card is plugged. Also called a slot.

Exposé A Mac feature that allows you to easily manage open windows by displaying thumbnail images of all open windows.

Feedback The playing of an alert sound when the system volume is adjusted.

Field One piece of information in a database record.

File A collection of stored electronic data, such as text, a picture, video, or music, that has a unique name, distinguishing it from other files.

File extension Additional characters assigned by a program to the end of a filename to identify the type of file.

File hierarchy A logical structure for folders and files that mimics how you would organize files and folders in a filing cabinet.

File management A strategy for organizing files and folders so you can find your data quickly and easily.

Filename A unique, descriptive name for a file that identifies the file's content.

Fill handle In Excel, a small square that appears on the lower-right corner of the cell pointer that users can drag to the left, right, up, or down to copy the cell's contents into adjacent cells or to fill out a pattern or series.

Filter A command that displays only the data that you want to see in an Excel worksheet based on criteria you set.

Find command A search option in Office 2011 that helps you quickly and easily find a word or phrase in a document. (Office)

Find command Search option available on the Finder File menu that performs the same operation as Finder's Search field. (Snow Leopard)

Finder Part of the Mac operating system (Snow Leopard) that provides access to files and programs and controls the desktop.

Firewall Hardware or software that prevents other computers on the Internet from accessing a computer or prevents a program on a computer from accessing the Internet.

FireWire A standard for transferring information between digital devices developed by Apple Inc. and the Institute of Electrical and Electronics Engineers (IEEE); was standardized as IEEE 1394 interface.

First line indent In Word, a paragraph indent in which the first line of a paragraph is indented more than subsequent lines.

Flash drive *See* USB flash storage device.

Flash memory Memory that is similar to ROM except that it can be written to more than once.

Flash memory card A small, portable card encased in hard plastic to which data can be written and rewritten.

Flash storage device *See* USB flash storage device.

Flat panel monitor A lightweight monitor that takes up very little room on the desktop and uses LCD technology to create the image on the screen.

Floating image A graphic to which text wrapping has been applied, making the graphic independent of text and able to be moved anywhere on a page.

Folder A container for a group of related files.

Folder name A unique, descriptive name for a folder that identifies what you store in that folder.

Font The design of a set of characters; for example, Arial or Times New Roman.

Font effects Special enhancements to fonts, such as small caps, shadow, and superscript, that you can apply to selected text in a document, spreadsheet, or presentation.

Font size The size of text characters, measured in units called points (pts); a point is equal to 1/72 inch.

Font style Attribute that changes the appearance of text when applied; bold, italic, and underline are common font styles.

Footer Information, such as text, a page number, or a graphic, that appears in the bottom margin of a page in a document.

Footnote A note or citation that corresponds to a number or symbol in a document and that is placed at the bottom of the document page.

Form letter A mail merge document that contains standard body text and a custom heading for each recipient.

Format To enhance the appearance of text in a document, spreadsheet, or presentation without changing the content.

Format Painter A feature used to copy the format settings applied to selected text to other text you want to format the same way.

Formula An equation that calculates a new value from existing values. Formulas can contain numbers, mathematical operators, cell references, and built-in equations called functions.

Formula AutoComplete In Excel, a feature that helps you enter a formula in a cell by suggesting a listing of functions as you type letters and providing syntax information to help you write the formula correctly.

Formula bar In Excel, the band below the ribbon in which users enter, edit, or display a formula or data in the selected cell.

Formula Builder A tab on the Excel Toolbox that helps users create mathematical calculations.

Forward button A button commonly found at the top of a window that, when clicked, displays the next Web page, file, or folder.

Full Screen view A view in Word that maximizes the space while working in a reading or authoring mode, allowing users to concentrate on the document content.

Function A prewritten formula you can use instead of typing a formula from scratch. Each function includes the function name, a set of parentheses, and function arguments separated by commas and enclosed in parentheses. *See also* Formula.

GB *See* Gigabyte.

GHz *See* Gigahertz.

Gigabyte (G or GB) 1,073,741,824 bytes, or about one billion bytes.

Gigahertz (GHz) One billion cycles per second.

Graphic Interchange Format (GIF) File format for graphics that is often used for line art and clip art images.

Graphical user interface (GUI) A computer environment in which the user manipulates graphics, icons, and dialog boxes to execute commands.

Graphics card The card installed on the motherboard that controls the signals the computer sends to the monitor. Also called a video display adapter or video card.

Graphics display A monitor that is capable of displaying graphics by dividing the screen into a matrix of pixels.

Graphics processor A processor that controls the signals the computer sends to the monitor. Also called built-in graphics card.

Graphics software Software that allows you to create illustrations, diagrams, graphs, and charts.

Gridlines Horizontal and vertical lines connected to the x-axis and y-axis in a chart that make it easier to identify the value of each data series.

Group A collection of related commands in a tab on the ribbon or Toolbox.

GUI *See* Graphical user interface.

Handheld computer A small computer designed to fit in the palm of your hand and that generally has fewer capabilities than personal computers.

Handouts In PowerPoint, hard copies of a presentation that are printed for distribution to an audience, showing one or more slides per page.

Hanging indent In Word, a paragraph indent in which the second and subsequent lines of text in a paragraph are indented further than the first line by a set amount of space.

Hard copy A printed, paper copy of computer output.

Hard disk A magnetic storage device that contains several magnetic oxide-covered metal platters that are usually sealed in a case inside the computer, providing built-in, high-capacity, high-speed storage for all the software, folders, and files on a computer. Also called a hard drive.

Hard drive *See* Hard disk.

Hardware The physical components of a computer system.

HDMI (high-definition multimedia interface) port A port that digitally transmits video and audio.

Header Information, such as text, a page number, or a graphic, that appears in the top margin of a page in a document.

Header row A row at the top of an Excel table that contains column headings.

Help Tag A label that appears on screen when you point to an item, providing the name of the item and sometimes a brief description.

Hits The items in a list of search results that include your keyword(s) or that meet the search criteria. *See also* Search results.

Home folder A folder provided by Snow Leopard for each user that contains several subfolders in which you can save your files on the hard disk.

Home page The first Web page that opens every time you start Safari; also, the main page of a Web site.

Home tab A tab that is displayed on the ribbon in all Office programs that contains commands for performing the most frequently used features of the active Office program.

Horizontal axis The line at the base of a chart that shows categories. Also known at the x-axis or category axis.

Horizontal ruler An on-screen ruler at the top of the document window in Word that helps you place objects in a precise location.

Horizontal scroll bar *See* Scroll bar.

Hyperlink Words, phrases, or graphics that, when clicked, open a new location on the current document or page, open a file or a new Web page, or play audio or video. Also called a link.

I-beam The pointer symbol that identifies where you can type, select, insert, or edit text.

I/O *See* Input and output.

Icon A small image on the desktop or in a window that represents a program, tool, folder, or file.

Icon view A view of items in a window that displays the contents of a selected device or folder as icons.

IEEE 1394 interface *See* FireWire.

Image A nontextual piece of information, such as a picture, piece of clip art, drawn object, or graph.

Image persistence Damage to the crystals in an LCD computer monitor that occurs when an image stays too long on screen without changing; the crystals continue to display the image faintly even after the on-screen image has changed.

Inactive window An open window you are not currently using.

Indent A set amount of space between the edge of a paragraph and the right or left margin.

Information management software Software that keeps track of schedules, appointments, contacts, and "to-do" lists.

Infrared technology A wireless technology in which devices communicate with one another using infrared light waves; the devices must be positioned so that the infrared ports are pointed directly at one another.

Inkjet printer A printer that sprays ink onto paper and produces output whose quality is comparable with that of a laser printer.

Inline graphic A graphic that is part of a line of text.

Input The data or instructions you type into the computer.

Input and output (I/O) The flow of data from the microprocessor to memory to peripherals and back again.

Input device An instrument, such as a keyboard or a mouse, that you use to enter data and issue commands to the computer.

Insertion point A flashing vertical line that indicates where the next character will appear when the user types.

Integration The act of inserting and linking information among applications. *See also* Object Linking and Embedding.

Interface card *See* Controller card.

Internet A network of connected computers and computer networks located around the world.

Intranet A private computer network with restricted access, such as computers in a company office.

Italic Formatting applied to text to make the characters slant to the right.

Joint Photographic Experts Group (JPEG) File format that is often used for photographs because it uses and compresses color so well.

Justified text Text aligned equally between the right and left margins.

K *See* Kilobyte.

KB *See* Kilobyte.

Keyboard An input device that consists of three major parts: the main keyboard, the numeric keypad, and the function keys.

Keyboard shortcut A combination of keyboard keys that you press to perform a command.

Keyword A descriptive word or phrase you enter to obtain a list of results that includes that word or phrase.

Kilobyte (KB or K) 1,024 bytes, or approximately one thousand bytes.

Label Descriptive text used to identify worksheet data in Excel.

LAN *See* Local area network.

Landscape orientation A layout orientation for a document that specifies to print the page so it is wider than it is tall.

Laptop computer *See* Notebook computer.

Laser printer A printer that produces high-quality output quickly and efficiently by transferring a temporary laser image onto paper with toner.

Launch To open or start a program on your computer.

Layout *See* Slide layout.

Layout tab A tab on the ribbon containing commands for changing the layout of your document on the printed page.

LCD (liquid crystal display) A display technology that creates images by manipulating light within a layer of liquid crystal.

LED (light-emitting diode) monitor A flat panel monitor that uses LEDs to provide backlight.

Left indent In Word, a set amount of space between the left margin and the left edge of an entire paragraph.

Legend Area in a chart that explains what the labels, colors, and patterns of the chart represent.

Line chart A graph of data mapped by a series of lines. Because line charts show changes in data or categories of data over time, they are often used to document trends.

Line spacing The amount of space between lines of text.

Line sparkline In Excel, a miniature line chart that is displayed in a single cell that is ideal for showing a trend over a period of time.

Link *See* Hyperlink. (Internet)

Link A connection created between a source file and a destination file. When an object created in a source file is linked to a destination file, any changes made to the object in the source file also appear in the object contained in the destination file. (Office)

Liquid crystal display *See* LCD.

List view A view of items in the Finder window that displays the contents of the selected storage device or folder as an alphabetic list with additional details about each file and folder such as Name, Date Modified, Size, and Kind.

Local area network (LAN) A network in which the computers and peripheral devices are located relatively close to each other, generally in the same building, and are usually connected with cables.

Log in/log on To sign in with a user name and password before being able to use a computer.

Log Out An option for ending a Snow Leopard session in which all open files and programs are closed, all drives are disengaged and memory is cleared, and then the current user's session ends but the Mac continues running so the next user can log in and begin using the computer immediately, without waiting for the computer to boot up.

Mac OS X v10.6 Mac operating system, version 10.6. Also known as Snow Leopard.

Macintosh HD icon The only icon that appears on the Snow Leopard desktop by default; provides quick access to all items stored on the computer.

Magnetic storage device A storage device that stores data as magnetized particles on mylar, a plastic, which is then coated on both sides with magnetic oxide.

Mail merge The process of combining a Word document that contains placeholders with data from a data source to create a third document that contains multiple personalized letters or labels.

Main document A document that stores the standard body text for a form letter or other mail merge document.

Mainframe computer A computer used by larger business and government agencies that provides centralized storage, processing, and management for large amounts of data.

Malware A broad term that describes any program that is intended to cause harm or convey information to others without the owner's permission; short for malicious software.

Margin In a document, the amount of space between the edge of the page and the text in your document.

MAX function In Excel, a function that calculates the largest value in the list of arguments.

MB *See* Megabyte.

Media Browser A feature in Office 2011 that provides a series of tabs that gives you quick, easy access to media elements that can be inserted in an Office document or file.

Megabyte (MB) 1,048,576 bytes, or about one million bytes.

Megahertz (MHz) One million cycles per second.

Memory A set of storage locations on the main circuit board that stores instructions and data.

Memory capacity The amount of data that a device can handle at any given time. Also called storage capacity.

Menu A list of commands in a program (for example, the File menu) that you can use to accomplish a task.

Menu bar A bar at the top of the desktop that provides access to most of a program's features through categories of related commands.

Merge To combine information from a data source, such as an Excel spreadsheet, with standard text contained in a Word document to create personalized form letters or other mail merge documents. *See also* Mail merge.

Merged document A file or printout that contains all the personalized letters or labels in a mail merge document.

MHz *See* Megahertz.

Microprocessor A silicon chip, located on the motherboard, that is responsible for executing instructions to process data; also called processor or central processing unit (CPU).

Microsoft Excel A spreadsheet program created by Microsoft Corporation that you can use to manipulate, analyze, and chart quantitative data as well as to calculate financial information.

Microsoft Office Web Apps A set of scaled-down versions of Microsoft Office applications that run over the Internet.

Microsoft Outlook An e-mail program and information manager created by Microsoft Corporation that you can use to send and receive e-mail; schedule appointments; maintain to-do lists; and store names, addresses, and other contact information.

Microsoft PowerPoint A presentation graphics program created by Microsoft Corporation that you can use to develop materials for presentations, including electronic slide shows, computer-based presentations, speaker notes, and audience handouts.

Microsoft Word A word processing program created by Microsoft Corporation that you can use to create text-based documents such as letters, memos, newsletters, and reports.

MIN function In Excel, a function that calculates the smallest value in a list of arguments.

Mini notebook *See* Subnotebook computer.

Minimized window A window that has collapsed to an icon on the right side of the Dock.

Modem Stands for *modulate-dem*odulate; a device that converts the digital signals from your computer into analog signals that can traverse ordinary phone lines, and then converts analog signals back into digital signals at the receiving computer.

Modifier key A keyboard key that is used in conjunction with another keyboard key to execute a keyboard shortcut.

Monitor The TV-like peripheral device that displays the output from the computer.

Motherboard The main circuit board of the computer on which processing tasks occur.

Mouse A pointing device that contains buttons for clicking commands; you control the movement of the pointer by moving the entire mouse around on your desk.

.mov *See* QuickTime Movie.

Move To change the location of a file or a selection in a document by physically placing it in another location different from its original location.

MP3 player A handheld computer that is used primarily to play and store music, but that can also be used to watch digital movies and television shows.

Multimedia authoring software Software that allows you to record digital sound files, video files, and animations that can be included in presentations and other documents.

Multitasking Working with more than one window or program at a time.

Name box In Excel, displays the name or address of the currently selected cell in the worksheet.

Netbook A type of subnotebook computer that is primarily designed to allow users to access the Internet and check e-mail.

Network Two or more computers connected to each other and to peripheral devices enabling the user to share data and resources.

Network interface card (NIC) The card in a computer on a network that creates a communications channel between the computer and the network.

Network software Software that establishes the communications protocols that will be observed on the network and controls the "traffic flow" as data travels throughout the network.

NIC *See* Network interface card.

Node Any device connected to a network.

Nonvolatile memory *See* Read-only memory.

Normal view In PowerPoint, a three-pane layout that displays the Slides and Outline pane, the Slide pane, and the Notes pane. In Excel, the default view that displays the worksheet data in a simplified format.

Notebook computer A small, lightweight computer designed for portability. Also called a laptop computer.

Notebook Layout view A view option in Word that displays the contents of a document as if they were typed on a lined sheet of paper, allowing users to take notes, flag items, and record audio notes.

Notes Page view In PowerPoint, the view available from the View menu that displays the slide and associated speaker notes.

Notes pages Hard copy of a PowerPoint presentation that contains a miniature version of each slide plus the text added in the Notes pane.

Notes pane In PowerPoint, the area in Normal view located below the slide that is used to input text relevant to the current slide; can be used as an audience handout or reference notes during a presentation.

Object A graphic or other item or set of items that can be moved and resized as a single unit. In Word, any item that is embedded or linked to the document is called an object. In Excel, the components of a chart are called objects. In PowerPoint, each graphic or text element is an object.

Object Linking and Embedding (OLE) The ability to use data created in one application in a document created by another application. Linking creates a "live" connection between an object in a source file and a linked version in a destination file; embedding places an unconnected copy in the destination file.

Office Web Apps *See* Microsoft Office Web Apps.

OLE *See* Object Linking and Embedding.

Operating environment An operating system that provides a graphical user interface that acts as a liaison between the user and all of the computer's hardware and software, such as Microsoft Windows and Mac OS.

Operating system A computer program that manages the complete operation of your computer and keeps all the hardware and software working together properly. The operating system allocates system resources, manages storage space, maintains security, detects equipment failure, and controls basic input and output. Examples of

the operating system for Mac are Mac OS X Snow Leopard, Mac OS X Leopard, and Mac OS X Tiger.

Optical storage device A polycarbonate disc coated with a reflective metal on which data is recorded using laser technology as a trail of tiny pits or dark spots in the surface of the disc; the data that these pits or spots represent can then be "read" with a beam of laser light.

Option button A small circle in a dialog box to select only one of two or more related options.

Order of operations The order in which Excel calculates a formula; the order of precedence is exponents, multiplication and division, addition and subtraction. Calculations in parentheses are evaluated first.

Order of precedence for arithmetic operations *See* Order of operations.

Orientation *See* Page orientation.

Outline tab In PowerPoint, the section in Normal view that displays your presentation text in the form of an outline, without graphics.

Outline view In Word, a view that shows the headings of a document organized as an outline.

Output The result of the computer processing input.

Output device Any peripheral device that receives and/or displays output from a computer.

Page orientation Printing or viewing a page of data in either a portrait (8.5 inches wide by 11 inches tall) or landscape (11 inches wide by 8.5 inches tall) direction.

PAN *See* Personal area network.

Paragraph In Word, any text that ends with a hard return.

Password A string of characters used to verify the identity of the user.

Paste To insert items stored on the Clipboard or Scrapbook into a document at the insertion point.

PDF Portable Document Format.

Peer-to-peer network A network in which all the computers are considered equal, and programs and data are distributed among them.

Peripheral device The components of a computer that accomplish its input, output, and storage functions.

Permanent memory *See* Read-only memory.

Personal area network (PAN) A network that allows two or more devices located close to each other to communicate or to connect a device to the Internet.

Personal computer A computer typically used by a single user in the home or office for general computing tasks, such as word processing, working with photographs or graphics, e-mail, and Internet access.

Pharm To break into a DNS server and redirect any attempts to access a particular Web site to a spoofed site.

Phish To send e-mails to customers or potential customers of a legitimate Web site asking them to click a link in the e-mail and then verify their personal information, which may then be used for illegal purposes; the link leads to a spoofed site.

Photo-editing software Software that allows you to manipulate digital photos.

Picture A digital photograph, or a piece of line art or clip art that is created in another program and can be inserted into an Office program.

Pie chart A chart that describes the relationship of parts to the whole.

Pixel One of the small dots in a matrix into which a graphics display is divided.

Placeholder A container for text or graphics on a slide used to reserve space for text or graphics the user will insert in its place. (PowerPoint)

Placeholder A field name from a specified data source that is inserted in a main document to indicate where the custom information from the data source should appear. (Word)

Places group A group on the sidebar in the Finder window that provides quick access to the user's Desktop folder, Applications folder, home folder, and Documents folder.

Plot area The part of a chart contained within the horizontal and vertical axes.

Point A unit of measurement for font size; a point equals 1/72 of an inch.

Pointer A small arrow or other symbol on the screen controlled by a pointing device.

Pointing Positioning the pointer over an item and hovering on it.

Pointing device A device, such as a mouse or trackpad, that controls the on-screen pointer.

Pop-up On the Internet, windows that open on your computer screen when you visit Web sites, generally to advertise products that you may or may not want.

Pop-up menu A menu that opens when you click a set of pop-up menu arrows, displaying a list of options from which you can choose.

Pop-up menu arrows Arrows that, when clicked, display a pop-up menu of options from which you can choose.

Port The interface between a cable and a controller card.

Portable Network Graphics (PNG) A graphics file format used primarily by Macs and the default file type created when the Preview program generates an image, originally developed for image use on the Internet.

Portrait orientation A print setting that positions the document on the page so the page is taller than it is wide.

Poster frame In PowerPoint, an image stored on your computer or an image from a movie frame that serves as the movie's cover or preview image on the slide.

Presentation graphics program Software designed to develop materials for presentations, including slide shows, computer-based presentations, speaker notes, and audience handouts.

Presentation software A software program used to create illustrations, diagrams, graphs, and charts that can be projected before a group, printed out for quick reference, or transmitted to remote computers.

Presenter view A PowerPoint view available from the View menu that helps the presenter practice the presentation by providing a timer, speaker notes, and a preview of the next slide on screen.

Print Layout view A view in Word that displays layout, graphics, and footnotes exactly as they will appear when printed.

Printer The peripheral device that produces a hard copy of the text or graphics processed by the computer.

Process To modify data in a computer.

Processor *See* Microprocessor.

Program Software you can use to perform a task, such as create a document, analyze data, or create a presentation. Also called an application.

Programming language A language used to write computer instructions that are translated into electrical signals that the computer can manipulate and process.

Protocol The set of rules that establishes the orderly transfer of data between the sender and the receiver in data communications.

Publishing Layout view In Word, a view that enables users to work with the contents of a document as a desktop publishing document.

Quad-core processor A CPU with four processors on the chip.

Quick Look A tool in Finder that displays the contents of a selected file as a large preview without actually opening the file.

QuickTime Movie The default video file type used in PowerPoint for Mac.

Radar chart A chart type that shows changes in data or data frequency relative to a center point.

RAM *See* Random access memory

RAM cache *See* Cache memory.

Random access memory (RAM) A temporary storage place for data and instructions (software) while being used by the CPU.

Range A selected area of adjacent cells in an Excel worksheet.

Read-only memory (ROM) A chip on the motherboard that is prerecorded with and permanently stores the set of instructions that the computer uses when you turn it on; also called nonvolatile memory or permanent memory.

Receiver The computer or peripheral at the message's destination in data communications.

Record A collection of related fields that contains all information for an entry in a database such as a customer, item, or business.

Reference mark The mark next to a word in a document that indicates a footnote or endnote is associated with the word or phrase.

Reference Tools A tab on the Office Toolbox that contains dictionary, bilingual dictionary, thesaurus, translation tools, and Web search (Bing).

Relative cell reference In Excel, a cell reference that changes when copied to refer to cells relative to the new location. For example, the formula "=B5*C5" in cell D5 changes to "=B6*C6" when you copy the formula to cell D6. *See also* Absolute cell reference.

Repaginate To renumber the pages in a document; Office programs automatically repaginate files as necessary when you add or delete information.

Replace command A command in the Office programs that enables users to search for a word or phrase in a document, spreadsheet, or presentation and substitute a new word or phrase in its place.

Resolution The number of pixels used to display the screen image on a computer monitor. Also called screen resolution.

Restart To shut down your computer, and then start it again.

Restore To move a file from the Trash to a new location on the computer.

Ribbon A new feature in Office 2011 that provides quick access to the tools you use as you work with an Office program. It is a band that stretches across the top of each Office window that contains tabs with commands from which you can choose to complete tasks.

Right-click To press and release the right mouse button once, opening a shortcut menu on the screen.

Right indent In Word, a paragraph indent in which the right edge of a paragraph is moved in from the right margin by a set amount of space.

ROM *See* Read-only memory.

Router A device that controls traffic between network components and usually has a built-in firewall.

Row headings In Excel, the boxes containing numbers that appear to the left of each row.

Safari A popular browser made by Apple that comes installed on the Mac.

Save To store a file permanently on a disk or to overwrite the copy of a file that is stored on a disk with the changes made to the file.

Save As A command used to save a file for the first time or to create a new file with a different filename or location, leaving the original file intact.

Scale To increase or decrease the size of data on the printed page.

Scanner A device that transfers the content on a piece of paper into memory; you place a piece of paper on the glass, a beam of light moves across the glass, similar to a photocopier, and stores the image or words on the piece of paper as digital information.

Scrapbook A tab on the Office Toolbox that enables users to copy and paste multiple items to and from Office documents.

Screen resolution *See* Resolution.

Screen saver A moving image that appears on the computer screen after the computer is idle for several minutes; prevents image persistence.

Screen size The diagonal measurement from one corner of the computer screen to the other.

Scroll bar A bar on the right edge (vertical scroll bar) or bottom edge (horizontal scroll bar) of a document window that allows you to move around in a document that is too large to fit on the screen all at once.

Scroll wheel A wheel on a mouse that you roll to scroll vertically on the page.

Scroller A rounded rectangle located within the vertical and horizontal scroll bars that indicates your relative position in a file and that you can drag to view other parts of the document or page in the window.

SDRAM *See* Synchronous dynamic RAM.

Search box A text box accessible from the Help menu where you type keywords to search the built-in Help files.

Search command *See* Find command.

Search engine A special Web site that searches the Internet for Web sites based on words or phrases that you enter.

Search field A text box on the Finder toolbar that the user can use to search for files by filename or file content. (Snow Leopard)

Search field A text box on the Safari toolbar that uses the Google search engine to help users search the Internet for Web sites about a particular topic. (Safari)

Search For group A group on the sidebar in the Finder window that helps locate a file quickly by viewing files used recently or by viewing only a certain type of file.

Search results A list of items or links produced by entering keywords or specific criteria in a Search field.

Security The steps a computer owner takes to prevent unauthorized use of or damage to the computer.

Select To highlight an item in order to perform some action on it.

Selection box A dashed border that appears around a text object or placeholder, indicating that it is ready to accept text.

Semipermanent memory *See* Complementary metal-oxide semiconductor memory.

Sender The computer that originates the message in data communications.

Serial value A number used in an Excel worksheet that represents a date or time used in calculations; a date that is formatted in General format will appear as a serial value.

Server A computer on a network that acts as the central storage location for programs and provides mass storage for most of the data used on the network.

Shared group A group on the sidebar in the Finder window that is shown only when your Mac is connected to a network; lists all shared computers and servers that the user has access to.

Shortcut menu A menu that appears when you right-click an object, listing common commands for the object.

Shut down An option for ending a Snow Leopard session in which all open files and programs are closed, all drives are disengaged and memory is cleared, and then the Mac safely turns itself off.

Sidebar A new feature in Word that opens on the left side of the Word window containing tabs for the Thumbnails pane, Reviewing pane, and Find and Replace. (Office)

Sidebar The left section of a window (such as the Finder window) or a dialog box (such as the Open or Save As dialog boxes) that provides quick access to many frequently used resources. (Snow Leopard)

Single-click *See* Click.

Single-core processor A CPU with one processor on the chip.

Size control The lower-right corner of a window that enables the user to resize the window by clicking and dragging.

Sizing handles Small squares or circles that appear when an object is selected that you can drag to change the size of the object.

SkyDrive A large storage space on the Internet that you and others can access from any location. To establish SkyDrive, you must set up your own ID on Windows Live, which is a free online service from Microsoft.

Slate computer A thin computer primarily used to read electronic books, view video, and access the Internet, and that does not have an external keyboard or a mouse; instead users touch the screen or use a stylus to accomplish tasks.

Sleep A partial shut-down option that puts the Mac in a low power state to conserve energy while not in use.

Slide On-screen page for use in a PowerPoint slide show.

Slide layout In PowerPoint, an arrangement of placeholders and formatting configured to support a particular type of content.

Slide Master A feature of PowerPoint that contains the layouts, design elements, and other formatting attributes for a presentation; enables users to make design changes to multiple slides at once.

Slide pane In PowerPoint, the largest section of Normal view that displays the full layout of the current slide.

Slide Show A view in PowerPoint that displays presentation slides full screen as the audience will see them.

Slide Show toolbar The toolbar that appears in PowerPoint Slide Show that lets you navigate to different slides or change the pointer to a pen or arrow to identify key slide points.

Slide Sorter view A view in PowerPoint that displays a thumbnail of all slides in the order in which they appear in your presentation; used to rearrange and delete slides.

Slide timing *See* Timing.

Slide transition *See* Transition.

Slides tab In Normal view in PowerPoint, the area to the left of the Slide pane that displays thumbnails of every slide in a presentation.

Slot *See* Expansion slot.

SmartArt A feature for creating professional quality diagrams, such as organizational charts, process diagrams, and timelines.

SmartArt style A preset combination of formatting options that follows the design theme that you can apply to a SmartArt graphic.

Smartphone A handheld computer used to make and receive phone calls, maintain an address book and electronic appointment book, use a calculator and notepad, send e-mail, connect to the Internet, play music, take photos or video, and perform some of the same functions as a PC, such as word processing.

Snow Leopard The Mac OS X v10.6 operating system.

Software The intangible components of a computer system, particularly the programs or instructions that the computer needs to perform a specific task.

Solid state storage *See* Flash memory.

Sort A command that organizes columns in an Excel spreadsheet or a Word table numerically or alphabetically, and in ascending or descending order.

Source The file from which data is copied or linked into another file.

Source file When linking and embedding data between documents, the file from which information is copied or used. An Excel file inserted into a Word report is a source file. *See also* Destination file.

Sparklines In Excel, tiny charts that fit in one cell and illustrate trends in selected cells.

Speaker notes In PowerPoint, notes that accompany slides; used to help the speaker remember important information that should not appear on the slides themselves.

Specifications The technical details about a hardware component.

Spell check The feature in document production software that helps you avoid typographical and grammatical errors.

Spin box A text box with up and down arrows; you can type a setting in the text box or click the arrows to increase or decrease a setting.

Spoofed site A Web site set up to look exactly like another Web site, such as a bank's Web site, but which does not actually belong to the organization portrayed in the site.

Spotlight search field A search option accessible in all programs by clicking the magnifying glass on the right side of the menu bar.

Spreadsheet Another word for a workbook or worksheet.

Spreadsheet program *See* Spreadsheet software.

Spreadsheet software Software that you can use to manipulate, analyze, and chart quantitative data as well as to calculate financial information.

Spring-loaded folder A folder in the Finder window that springs open when a file is dragged on top of it, displaying its contents in the right pane of the Finder window and enabling the user to drag and drop files between different locations without having to open additional Finder windows.

Spyware Programs that track a computer user's Internet usage and send this data back to the company or person who created it, most often without the computer user's permission or knowledge.

Stack A method of displaying the contents of a folder on the Dock; when the user clicks a folder on the Dock, the folder springs open in an arc or a grid to reveal its contents.

Standalone computer A personal computer that is not connected to a network.

Standard colors A group of 10 colors that appears below the Theme Colors in any Office color palette and that contains basic hues such as red, orange, green, and blue.

Standard toolbar A bar below the title bar in all Office program windows that contains buttons to perform the most common tasks in a program.

Status bar In Snow Leopard, the bar at the bottom of the Finder window that lists the number of items in the selected device or folder and the available space on a device. In Office, the bar at the bottom of an Office program window that displays information such as the current page and word count. In Safari, the bar at the bottom of the Safari window that displays information about the Web page that is loading and that displays the Web address of a link when you point to it.

Storage capacity The amount of data a device can handle at any given time.

Storage device A physical location for storing files.

Strong password A string of at least eight characters of upper- and lowercase letters and numbers.

Style A setting that controls how text and paragraphs are formatted using predefined formatting attributes.

Subfolder A folder within another folder for organizing sets of related files into smaller groups.

Subnotebook computers Notebook computers that are smaller and lighter than ordinary notebooks. Also called ultraportable computer and mini notebook.

Suite A collection of programs that shares a common user interface and is distributed together. Microsoft Office for Mac 2011 is a software suite.

SUM function In Excel, the function used to calculate the total of the arguments.

Supercomputer The largest and fastest type of computer used by large corporations and government agencies for processing a tremendous volume of data.

Synchronous dynamic RAM (SDRAM) RAM that is synchronized with the CPU to allow faster access to its contents.

System Clipboard A clipboard that stores only the last item cut or copied from a document. *See also* Clipboard.

System resource Any part of the computer system, including memory, storage devices, and the microprocessor, that can be used by a computer program.

System software A collection of programs and data that helps the computer carry out its basic operating tasks.

Tab A clickable item near the top of the ribbon, Toolbox, or dialog box that switches to a different set of options or tools.

Tab A horizontal position where text is aligned. (Word)

Tab bar A bar at the top of the Safari window that contains the name of the Web pages currently open in tabs in the Web browser.

Tab indicator In Word, a tool that enables users to align text differently where tab stops are set.

Tab stop A location on the horizontal ruler to which the insertion point moves when [tab] is pressed.

Tabbed browsing Web browsing that enables you to open more than one Web page at a time on individual tabs in a browser window.

Table In Word, a grid made up of rows and columns of cells that you can fill with text and graphics. In Excel, a range of cells containing fields and records that you can analyze, sort, and filter separately from other cells in a worksheet.

Table style A predefined set of formatting attributes such as shading, fonts, and border color that specifies how a table looks.

Tablet PC A computer designed for portability that includes the capability of recognizing ordinary handwriting on the screen.

TB *See* Terabyte.

Telecommunications The transmission of data over a comparatively long distance using a phone line or some other conduit.

Template A special file that contains predesigned formatting, text, and other tools for creating common business documents such as letters, invoices, and business presentations.

Template Gallery A series of galleries in Office 2011 that contains templates for each Office program. It is made up of the Word Document Gallery, the Excel Workbook Gallery, and the PowerPoint Presentation Gallery.

Temporary memory *See* Random access memory.

Terabyte (TB) 1,024 GB, or approximately one trillion bytes.

Text box A box in which you type text.

Theme A coordinated set of styles, colors, fonts, and effects that can be applied to any Office 2011 document.

Themes Gallery Thumbnail images of the themes available in any Office program.

Thumbnails A miniature version of an image or slide.

Time Machine A feature that enables users to maintain files, folders, and programs by backing up everything on the computer to an external storage device on a regular basis.

Timing The number of seconds a PowerPoint slide remains on the screen before advancing to the next slide.

Title bar The area across the top of a window that displays the program name, document name, or the name of the currently selected file, folder, or device.

Title slide The first slide in a PowerPoint presentation.

Toner A powdery substance used by laser printers to transfer a laser image onto paper.

Toolbar A customizable set of buttons that allows you to activate commands using one click.

Toolbar control A feature in the Finder window that hides or unhides the toolbar and sidebar when clicked.

Toolbox A feature of Office for Mac 2011 that provides quick access to several tabs of tools you can use as you work within an Office program.

Top-level domain The part of a Web site address that identifies the type of site you are visiting; examples of top-level domains are com (for commercial site), edu (for educational institutions), and org (for organizations).

Top Sites A feature of Safari that displays your most frequently visited Web sites as thumbnail images on a page in the browser window.

Total row An extra row at the bottom of an Excel table that Excel inserts to add the values in each column.

Touchscreen A display that shows you output and allows you to touch it with your finger or a stylus to input commands.

Trackball A pointing device with a rolling ball on the top side and buttons for clicking commands; you control the movement of the on-screen pointer by moving the ball.

Trackpad A touch-sensitive device used to control the on-screen pointer by dragging your finger across the device, swiping the device, or pressing to click.

Transition In PowerPoint, a special effect that determines how a slide appears as it enters or leaves the screen in Slide Show.

Trash A storage area on your computer's hard disk for deleted files, which remain in the Trash until you empty it.

Triple-click To press and release the left mouse button three times quickly. In some programs, including Word, this action causes an entire paragraph to be selected.

Ultraportable computer *See* subnotebook computer.

Uniform Resource Locator (URL) The address of a Web page.

Universal Serial Bus port *See* USB port.

URL (Uniform Resource Locator) The address of a Web page.

USB connector A small, rectangular plug attached to a peripheral device and that you connect to a USB port.

USB drive *See* USB flash storage device.

USB flash storage device A popular, removable storage device for folders and files that provides ease of use and portability. Also called a USB drive or flash drive.

USB (Universal Serial Bus) port A high-speed port to which you can connect a device with a USB connector to have the computer recognize the device and allow you to use it immediately.

User interface The collection of buttons and tools you use to interact with a software program.

User interface sound effect A sound effect that occurs when you perform certain Finder actions such as dragging a file to the Trash.

Utility A type of system software that augments the operating system by taking over some of its responsibility for allocating hardware resources.

Value In Excel, numeric data entered in a cell.

Value axis *See* Vertical axis.

Vertical axis The vertical line that defines the left edge of a chart and usually measures values. Also called the y-axis, or value axis.

Vertical scroll bar *See* Scroll bar.

VGA (video graphics array) port A port that transmits analog video.

Video card *See* Graphics card.

Video display adapter *See* Graphics card.

Video-editing software Software that allows you to edit video by clipping it, adding captions or a sound track, or rearranging clips.

View A preset configuration that determines which elements of a file are visible on screen in an Office program; does not affect the actual content of the document. (Office)

View A way of displaying files and folders in the Finder window. (Snow Leopard)

View buttons Buttons that change the arrangement and view of the contents of a window.

Virtual memory Space on the computer's storage devices that simulates additional RAM.

Virus A harmful program that instructs a computer to perform destructive activities, such as erasing a disk drive.

Virus protection software *See* Antivirus software.

Volatile memory *See* Random access memory.

WAN *See* Wide area network.

Web *See* World Wide Web.

Web browser *See* Browser.

Web page A document located on another computer that you can view over the Internet and that often contains words, phrases, and graphics that link to other documents.

Web site A group of Web pages focused on a particular subject.

Web site creation and management software Software that allows you to create and manage Web sites and to see what the Web pages will look like as you create them.

Wi-Fi *See* Wireless fidelity.

Wide area network (WAN) A network that covers a large geographic area and usually connects one or more LANs.

WiMAX (Worldwide Interoperability for Microwave Access) A standard of wireless communication defined by the IEEE that allows computers to communicate wirelessly over many miles; signals are transmitted from WiMAX towers to a WiMAX receiver in a device.

Window A rectangular work area on a screen that can contain a program, the contents of a file, and/or other usable data.

Window control buttons Buttons located in the upper-left corner of most windows and some dialog boxes that allow you to close, minimize, or increase the size of the window or dialog box.

Windows Live A collection of services and Web applications that are available online that can help you be more productive. Some of these services include e-mail, chat, photo sharing, blogging, and storing and editing files using SkyDrive.

Win/loss sparkline In Excel, a tiny bar chart that shows only two types of bars: one for gains and one for losses.

Wireless fidelity The term created by the nonprofit Wi-Fi Alliance to describe networks connected using a standard radio frequency established by the Institute of Electrical and Electronics Engineers (IEEE); frequently referred to as *Wi-Fi*.

Wireless local area network (WLAN) A LAN connected using high frequency radio waves rather than cables.

WLAN *See* Wireless local area network.

Word processing program A program used to create and manipulate text-based documents, such as memos, newsletters, and reports.

Word size The number of bits that are processed at one time.

Word wrap In Word, a feature that automatically pushes text to the next line when the insertion point meets the right margin.

Workbook A collection of related worksheets saved in a single Excel file.

Worksheet An Excel spreadsheet composed of rows and columns of information that is used for performing numeric calculations, displaying business data, presenting information on the Web, and other purposes.

Workstation A computer that is connected to the network.

World Wide Web The part of the Internet that contains Web pages that are linked together. *See also* Internet.

Worldwide Interoperability for Microwave Access *See* WiMAX.

Wrap *See* Word wrap.

Wrapping style The setting for how text flows in relation to a graphic.

WWW *See* World Wide Web.

X-axis *See* Horizontal axis.

XY (Scatter) chart A chart that shows the relationship between two kinds of data.

Y-axis *See* Vertical axis.

Zoom To change the magnification level of the screen.

Zoom slider Located at the right end of the Office status bar, this tool allows you to adjust the magnification level of the document on screen.

Index